ORESAMA TEACHER

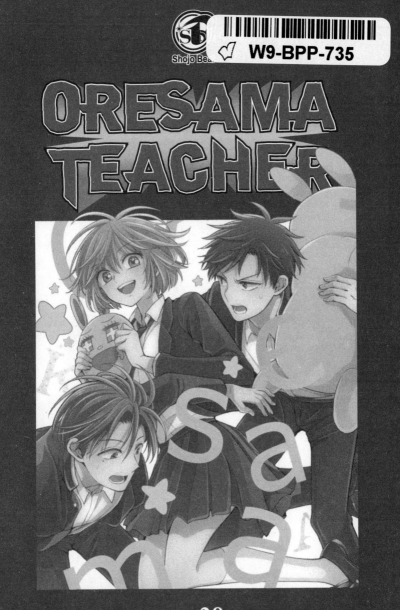

Vol. 29

Story & Art by

Izumi Tsubaki

ORESAMA TEACHER

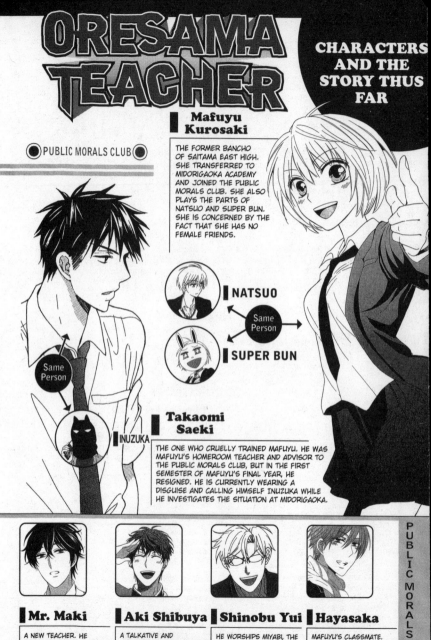

CHARACTERS AND THE STORY THUS FAR

PUBLIC MORALS CLUB

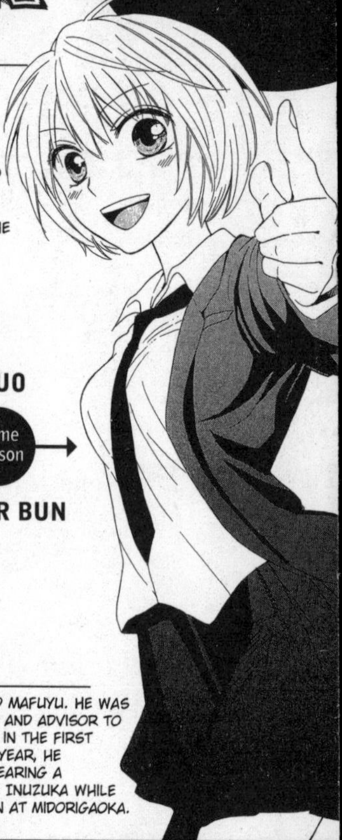

Mafuyu Kurosaki

THE FORMER BANCHO OF SAITAMA EAST HIGH. SHE TRANSFERRED TO MIDORIGAOKA ACADEMY AND JOINED THE PUBLIC MORALS CLUB. SHE ALSO PLAYS THE PARTS OF NATSUO AND SUPER BUN. SHE IS CONCERNED BY THE FACT THAT SHE HAS NO FEMALE FRIENDS.

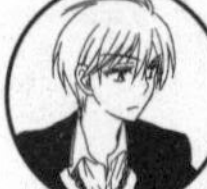

NATSUO

Same Person

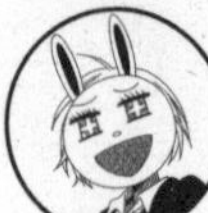

SUPER BUN

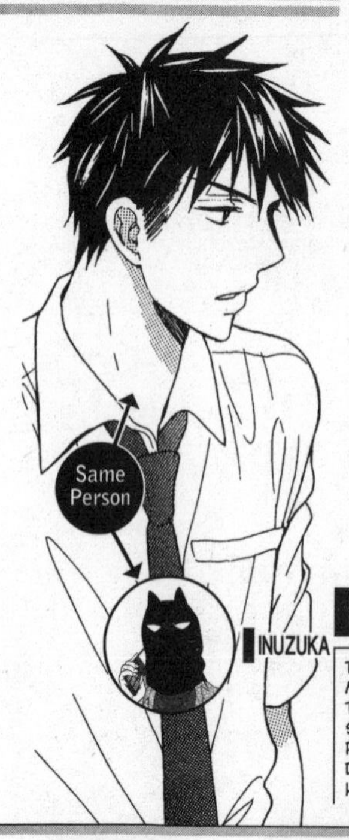

Same Person

INUZUKA

Takaomi Saeki

THE ONE WHO CRUELLY TRAINED MAFUYU. HE WAS MAFUYU'S HOMEROOM TEACHER AND ADVISOR TO THE PUBLIC MORALS CLUB, BUT IN THE FIRST SEMESTER OF MAFUYU'S FINAL YEAR, HE RESIGNED. HE IS CURRENTLY WEARING A DISGUISE AND CALLING HIMSELF INUZUKA WHILE HE INVESTIGATES THE SITUATION AT MIDORIGAOKA.

PUBLIC MORALS CLUB

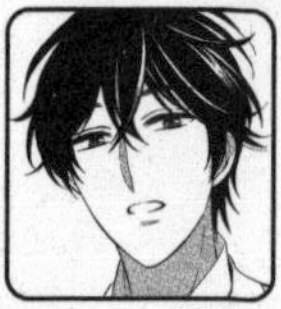

Mr. Maki

A NEW TEACHER. HE REPLACED TAKAOMI AS THE PUBLIC MORALS CLUB ADVISOR.

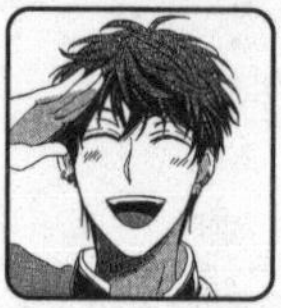

Aki Shibuya

A TALKATIVE AND WOMANIZING UNDERCLASSMAN. HIS NICKNAME IS AKKI. HE'S NOT GOOD AT FIGHTING.

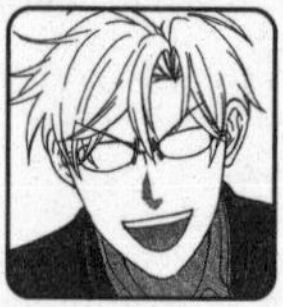

Shinobu Yui

HE WORSHIPS MIYABI, THE FORMER STUDENT COUNCIL PRESIDENT, BUT REJOINED THE PUBLIC MORALS CLUB. HE IS A SELF-PROCLAIMED NINJA.

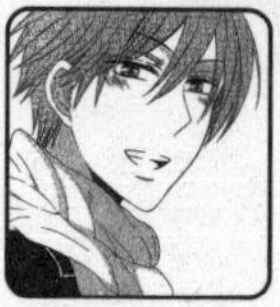

Hayasaka

MAFUYU'S CLASSMATE. HE APPEARS TO BE A PLAIN AND SIMPLE DELINQUENT, BUT HE'S ACTUALLY QUITE DILIGENT.

MIDORIGAOKA

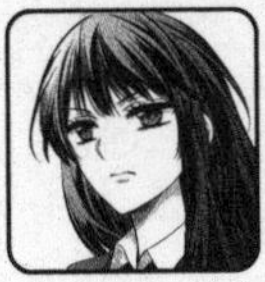

Toko Hanabusa

SHE HAS A STOIC ATTITUDE AND WATCHES OVER HANABUSA, AND SHE HAS FEELINGS FOR YUI. SHE'S THE NEW STUDENT COUNCIL PRESIDENT.

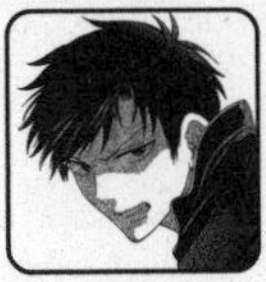

Reito Ayabe

HE LOVES CLEANING. HE GETS STRONGER IN DIRTY PLACES. HE IS A STUDENT COUNCIL OFFICER, BUT HE'S FRIENDS WITH MAFUYU.

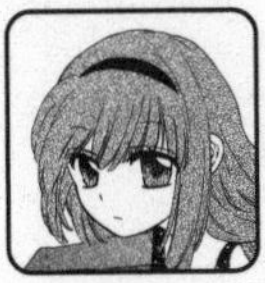

Komari Yukioka

USING HER CUTE LOOKS, SHE CONTROLS THOSE AROUND HER WITHOUT SAYING A WORD. INSIDE, SHE'S LIKE A DIRTY OLD MAN.

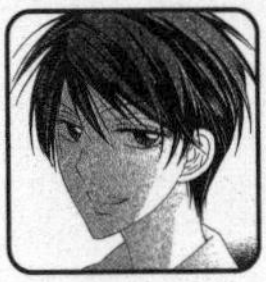

Miyabi Hanabusa

THE SCHOOL DIRECTOR'S SON AND THE FORMER PRESIDENT OF THE STUDENT COUNCIL. HE CAN CHARM OTHERS WITH HIS GAZE. HE IS ATTENDING COLLEGE IN TOKYO.

THE GRADUATES

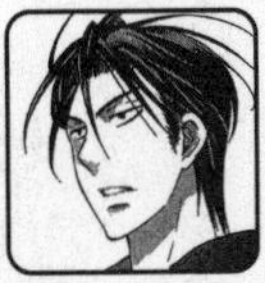

Kyotaro Okegawa

THE FORMER BANCHO OF EAST HIGH. HE IS ATTENDING A LOCAL COLLEGE. HE AND MAFUYU ARE ANONYMOUS PEN PALS.

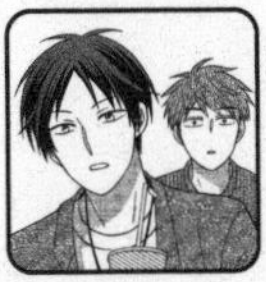

Kawauchi & Goto

OKEGAWA'S FOLLOWERS. KAWAUCHI RESPECTS OKEGAWA, BUT IS MEAN TO HIM. GOTO IS VERY LUCKY.

EAST HIGH STUDENTS

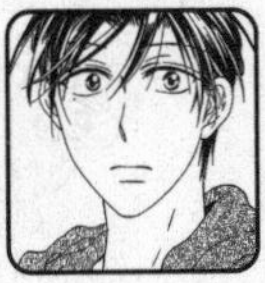

Kohei Kangawa

ONE YEAR YOUNGER THAN MAFUYU. HE IS THE CURRENT BANCHO OF EAST HIGH AND DEEPLY ADMIRES HIS PREDECESSOR, MAFUYU. HE CAN BE CHILDISH.

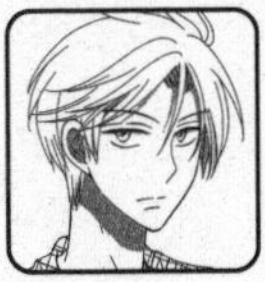

Yuto Maizono

ONE YEAR OLDER THAN MAFUYU AND FORMERLY THE NUMBER TWO AT EAST HIGH. HE CALLS HIMSELF "THE ONE WHO LURES YOU INTO THE WORLD OF MASOCHISM."

story

★ MAFUYU KUROSAKI WAS A BANCHO FROM EAST HIGH WHO CONTROLLED ALL OF SAITAMA, BUT ONCE SHE TRANSFERRED TO MIDORIGAOKA ACADEMY, SHE COMPLETELY CHANGED AND BECAME A SPIRITED HIGH SCHOOL GIRL...OR AT LEAST SHE WAS SUPPOSED TO. TAKAOMI SAEKI, HER CHILDHOOD FRIEND AND HOMEROOM TEACHER, FORCED HER TO JOIN THE PUBLIC MORALS CLUB, AND SHE HAS TO CONTINUE TO LIVE A LIFE THAT IS FAR FROM AVERAGE.

★ MAFUYU AND HER FRIENDS ARE FINALLY THIRD-YEAR STUDENTS. MIYABI'S YOUNGER SISTER, TOKO, HAS ENROLLED AS A FIRST-YEAR STUDENT. BUT AS SOON AS SHE ENTERS THE PICTURE, TAKAOMI RESIGNS AND DISAPPEARS. MEANWHILE, MAFUYU AND HER FRIENDS LEARN THAT THEIR NEW TEACHER, MR. MAKI, WAS FORMERLY THE #2 DELINQUENT AT WEST HIGH AND IS TRYING TO GET HIS REVENGE ON TAKAOMI.

★ MEANWHILE, THE SECOND DAY OF THE MIDORIGAOKA SCHOOL FESTIVAL BEGINS, BUT TOKO'S INTENTIONS REMAIN UNCLEAR. MAFUYU AND HER FRIENDS ARE WELL ON THEIR WAY TO BEATING THE SCARY DUDES WHO HAVE OCCUPIED THE GYM, BUT THINGS GET COMPLICATED WHEN MR. MAKI SHOWS UP. TAKAOMI ENDS UP RUSHING TO THE SCENE AND SETTLING THINGS WITH MR. MAKI, AND ON THE SURFACE THE FESTIVAL CLOSING CEREMONY PROCEEDS WITHOUT A HITCH. BUT TOKO USES HER STAGE TIME TO TRY TO DECLARE THE END OF MIDORIGAOKA ACADEMY. HOWEVER, WITH MIYABI'S HELP, MAFUYU CLEVERLY FOILS TOKO'S PLAN BY TURNING HER REMARKS INTO THE OPENING MONOLOGUE OF A SPECIAL PERFORMANCE OF THE CANCELED PLAY!

ORESAMA TEACHER

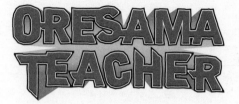

Volume 29
CONTENTS

Chapter 165

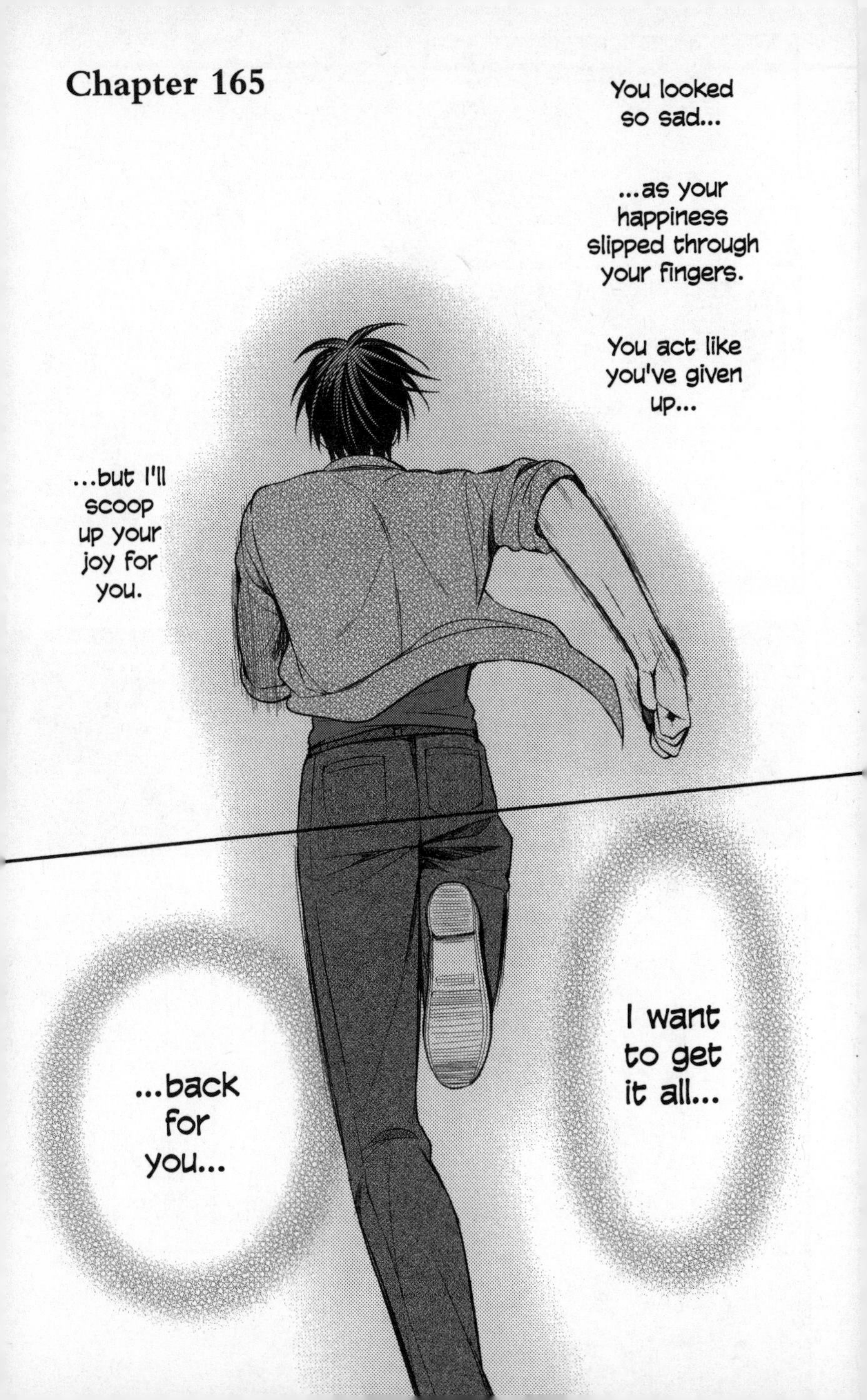

You looked so sad...
...as your happiness slipped through your fingers.
You act like you've given up...
...but I'll scoop up your joy for you.
I want to get it all...
...back for you...

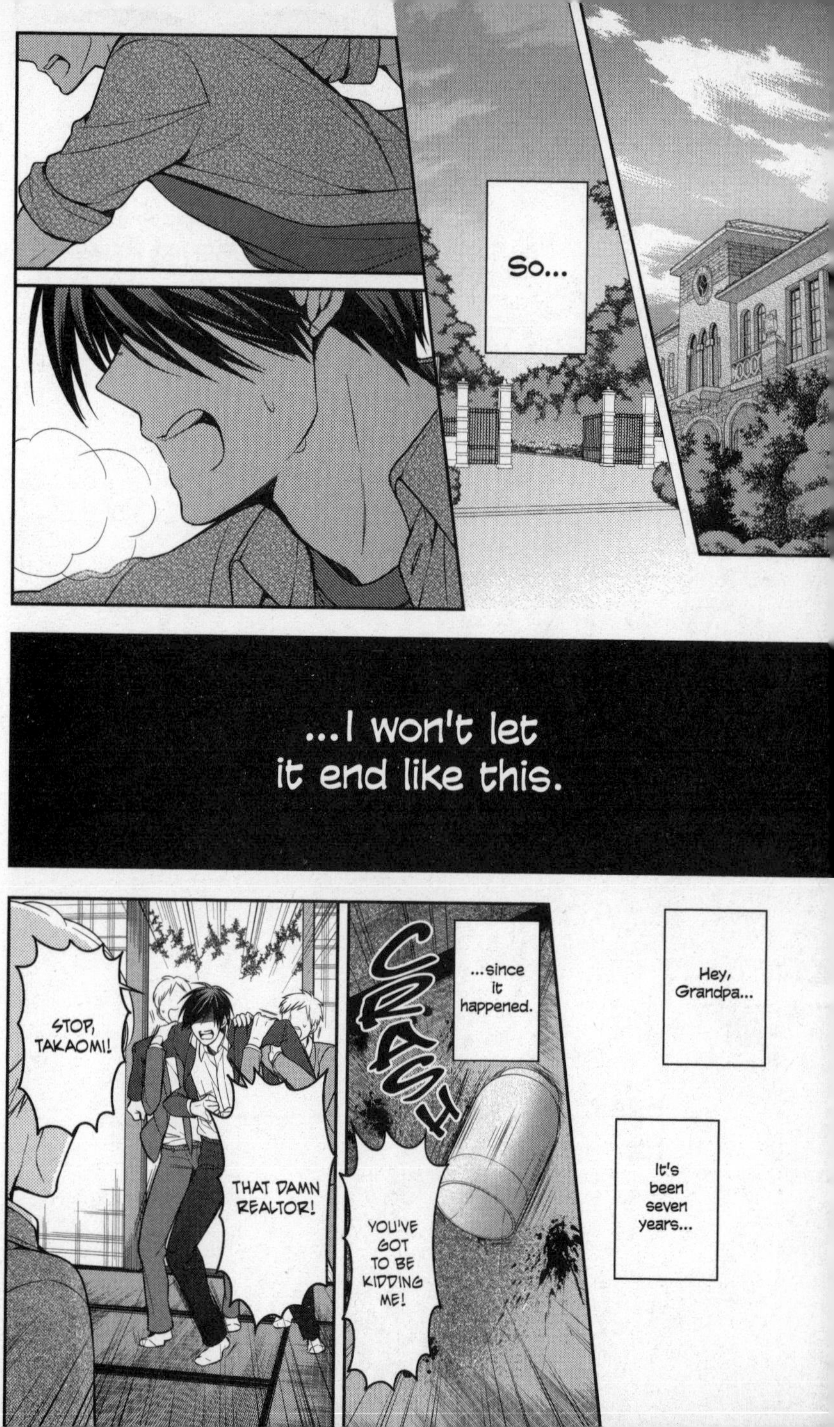
So...
...I won't let it end like this.
Hey, Grandpa...
It's been seven years...
...since it happened.
CRASH
YOU'VE GOT TO BE KIDDING ME!
THAT DAMN REALTOR!
STOP, TAKAOMI!

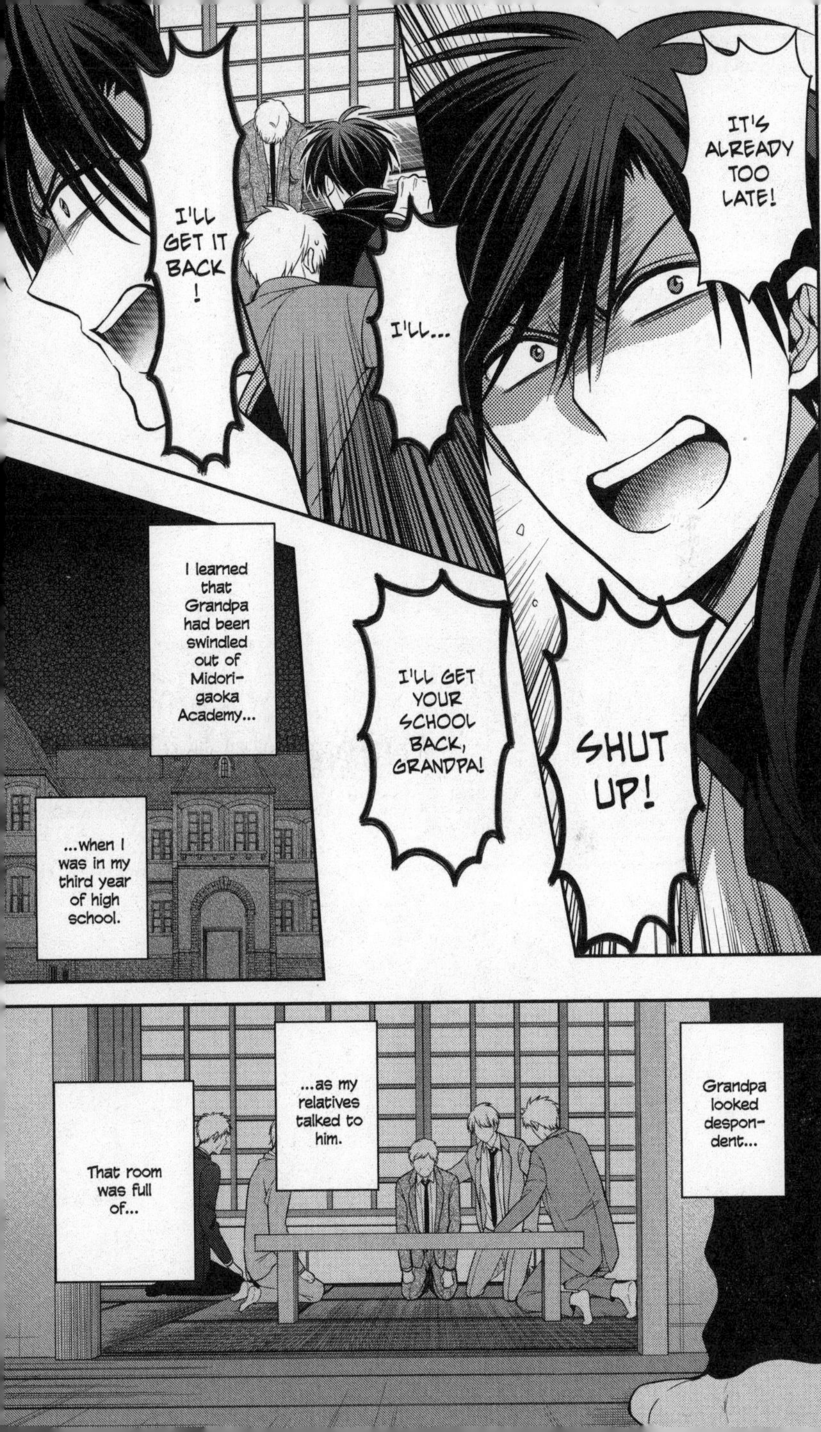
IT'S ALREADY TOO LATE!
SHUT UP!
I'LL GET YOUR SCHOOL BACK, GRANDPA!
I'LL...
I'LL GET IT BACK!
I learned that Grandpa had been swindled out of Midori-gaoka Academy...
...when I was in my third year of high school.
Grandpa looked despon-dent...
...as my relatives talked to him.
That room was full of...

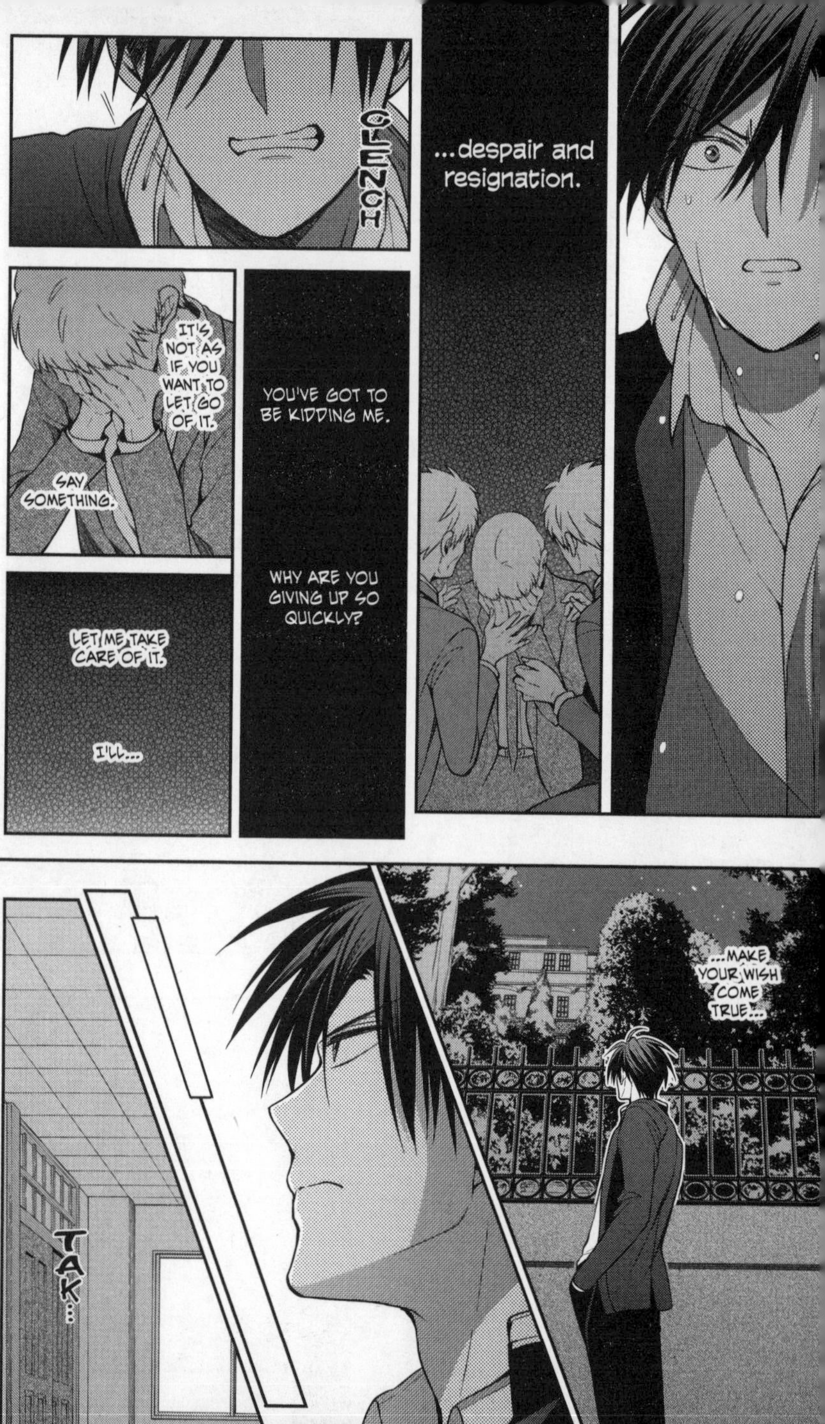
...despair and resignation.
CLENCH
YOU'VE GOT TO BE KIDDING ME.
WHY ARE YOU GIVING UP SO QUICKLY?
IT'S NOT AS IF YOU WANT TO LET GO OF IT.
SAY SOMETHING.
LET ME TAKE CARE OF IT.
I'LL...
...MAKE YOUR WISH COME TRUE...
TAK...

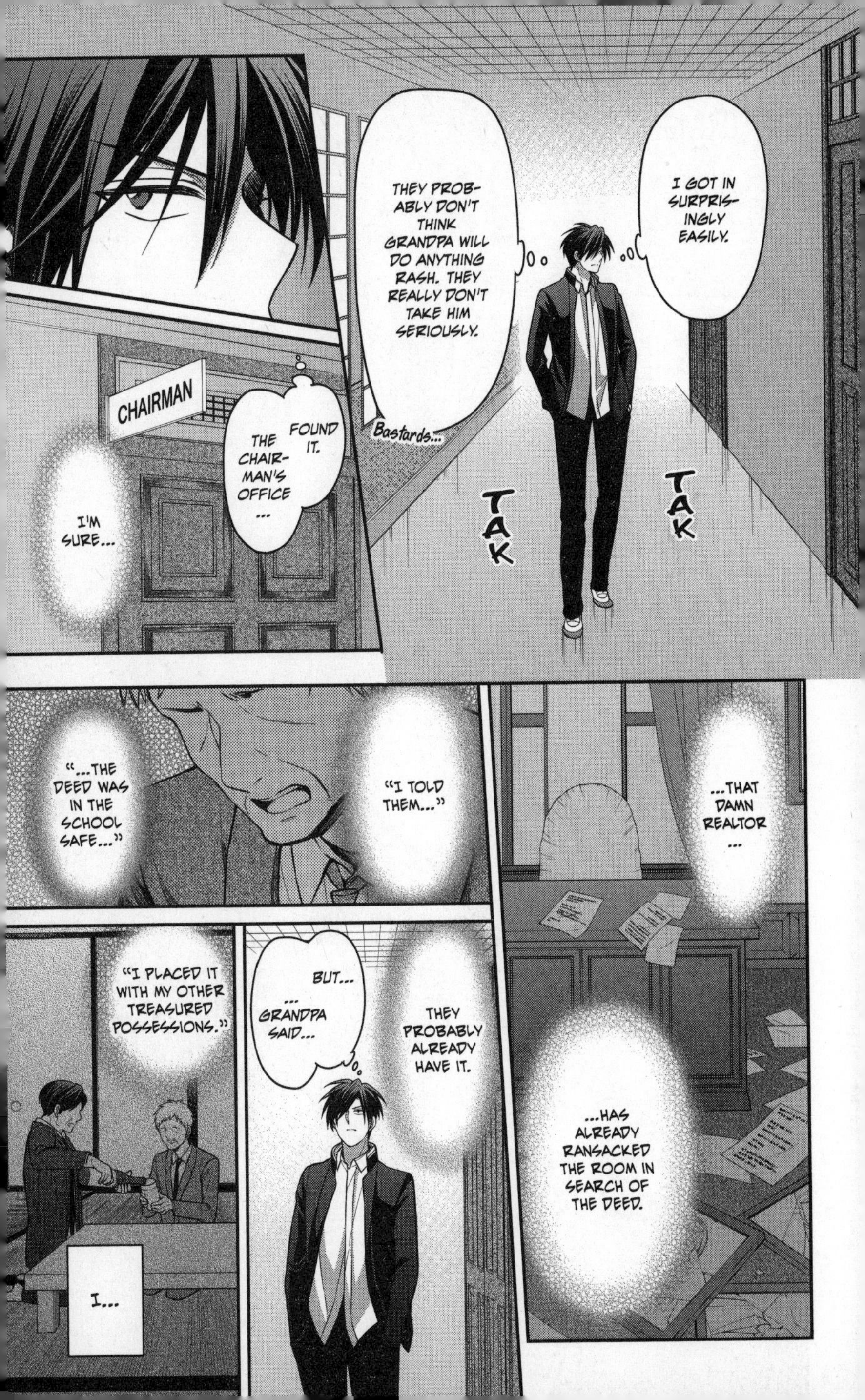
I GOT IN SURPRISINGLY EASILY.
THEY PROBABLY DON'T THINK GRANDPA WILL DO ANYTHING RASH. THEY REALLY DON'T TAKE HIM SERIOUSLY.
Bastards...
TAK
TAK
FOUND IT.
THE CHAIRMAN'S OFFICE...
CHAIRMAN
I'M SURE...
...THAT DAMN REALTOR...
...HAS ALREADY RANSACKED THE ROOM IN SEARCH OF THE DEED.
"I TOLD THEM..."
"...THE DEED WAS IN THE SCHOOL SAFE..."
THEY PROBABLY ALREADY HAVE IT.
BUT...
...GRANDPA SAID...
"I PLACED IT WITH MY OTHER TREASURED POSSESSIONS."
I...

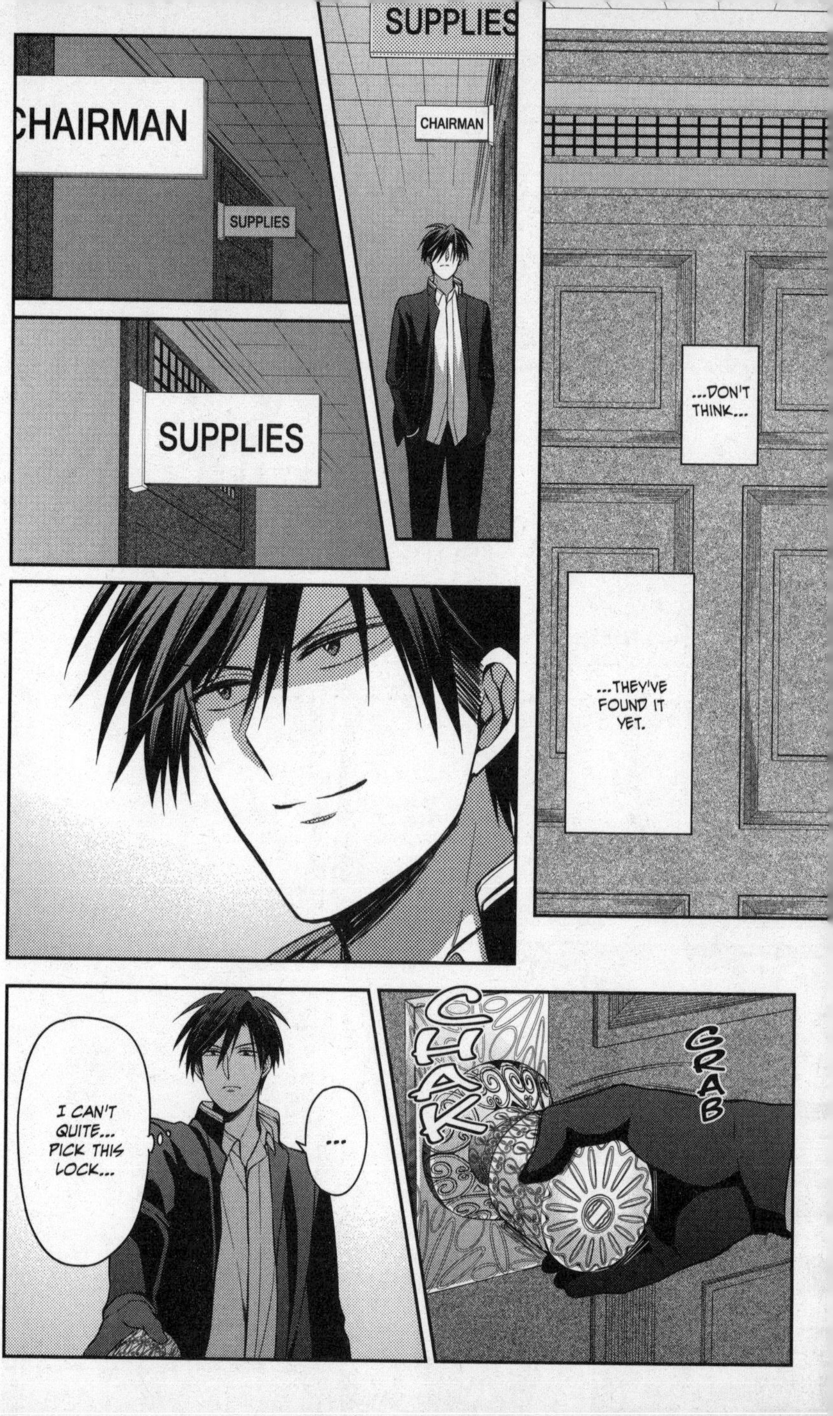
...DON'T THINK...
...THEY'VE FOUND IT YET.
SUPPLIES
CHAIRMAN
CHAIRMAN
SUPPLIES
SUPPLIES
GRAB
CHAK
...
I CAN'T QUITE... PICK THIS LOCK...

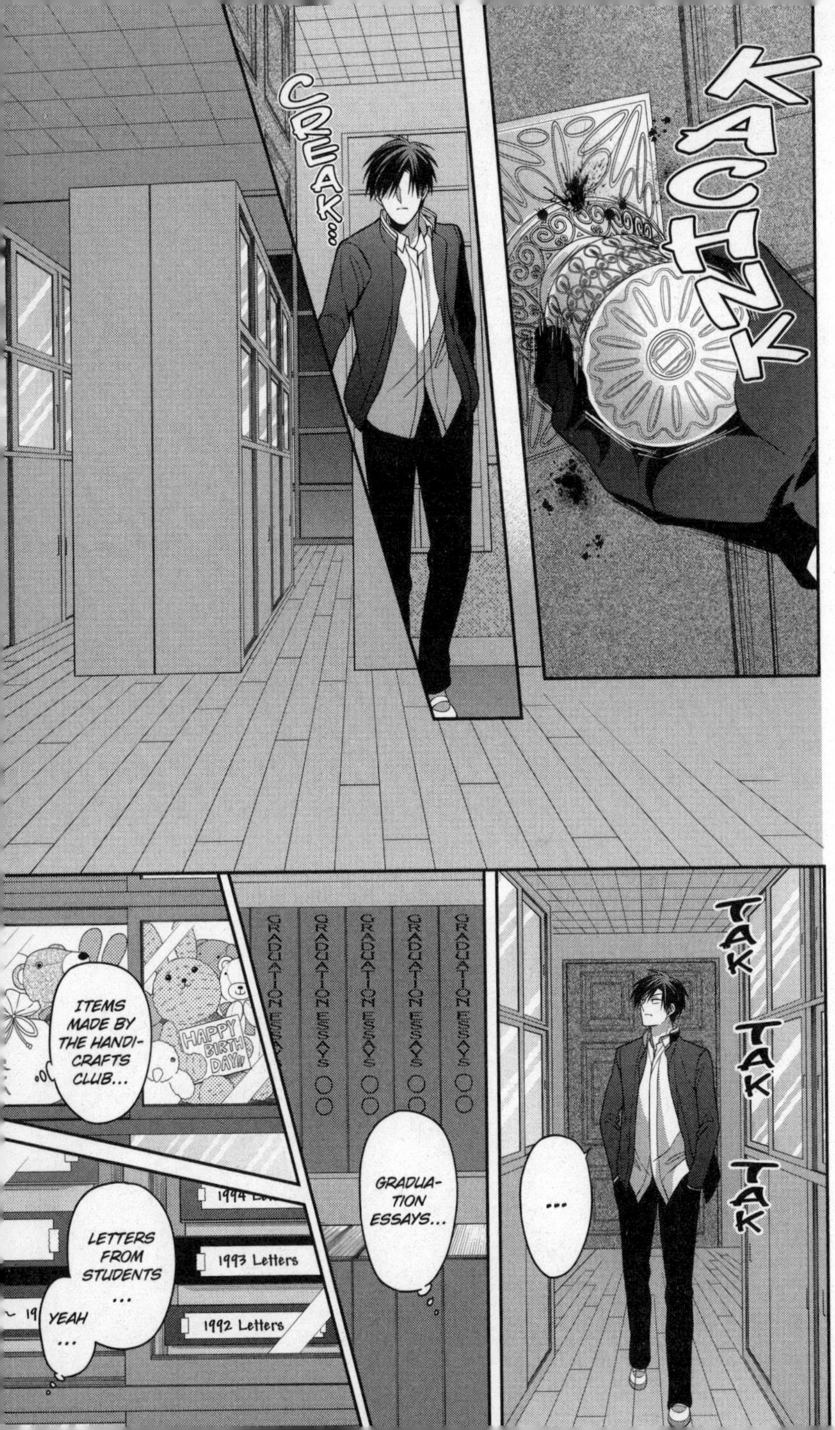
KACHINK
CREAK...
TAK TAK TAK
...
GRADUATION ESSAYS
GRADUATION ESSAYS
GRADUATION ESSAYS
GRADUATION ESSAYS
GRADUATION ESSAYS
GRADUATION ESSAYS...
HAPPY BIRTHDAY!!
ITEMS MADE BY THE HANDICRAFTS CLUB...
1994 Le
1993 Letters
1992 Letters
LETTERS FROM STUDENTS...
YEAH...

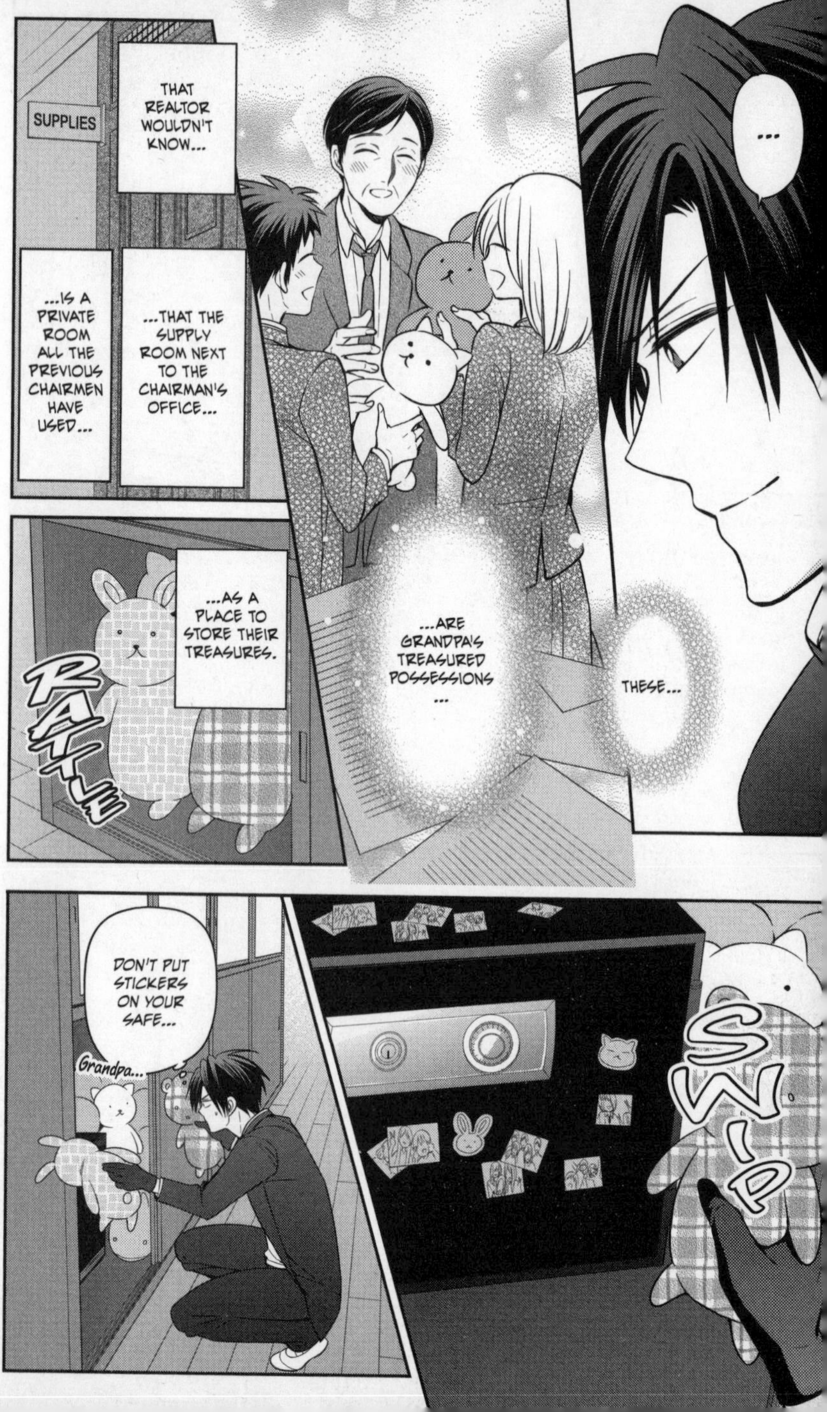
...
THESE...
...ARE GRANDPA'S TREASURED POSSESSIONS ...
THAT REALTOR WOULDN'T KNOW...
SUPPLIES
...THAT THE SUPPLY ROOM NEXT TO THE CHAIRMAN'S OFFICE...
...IS A PRIVATE ROOM ALL THE PREVIOUS CHAIRMEN HAVE USED...
...AS A PLACE TO STORE THEIR TREASURES.
RATTLE
SWIP
DON'T PUT STICKERS ON YOUR SAFE...
Grandpa...

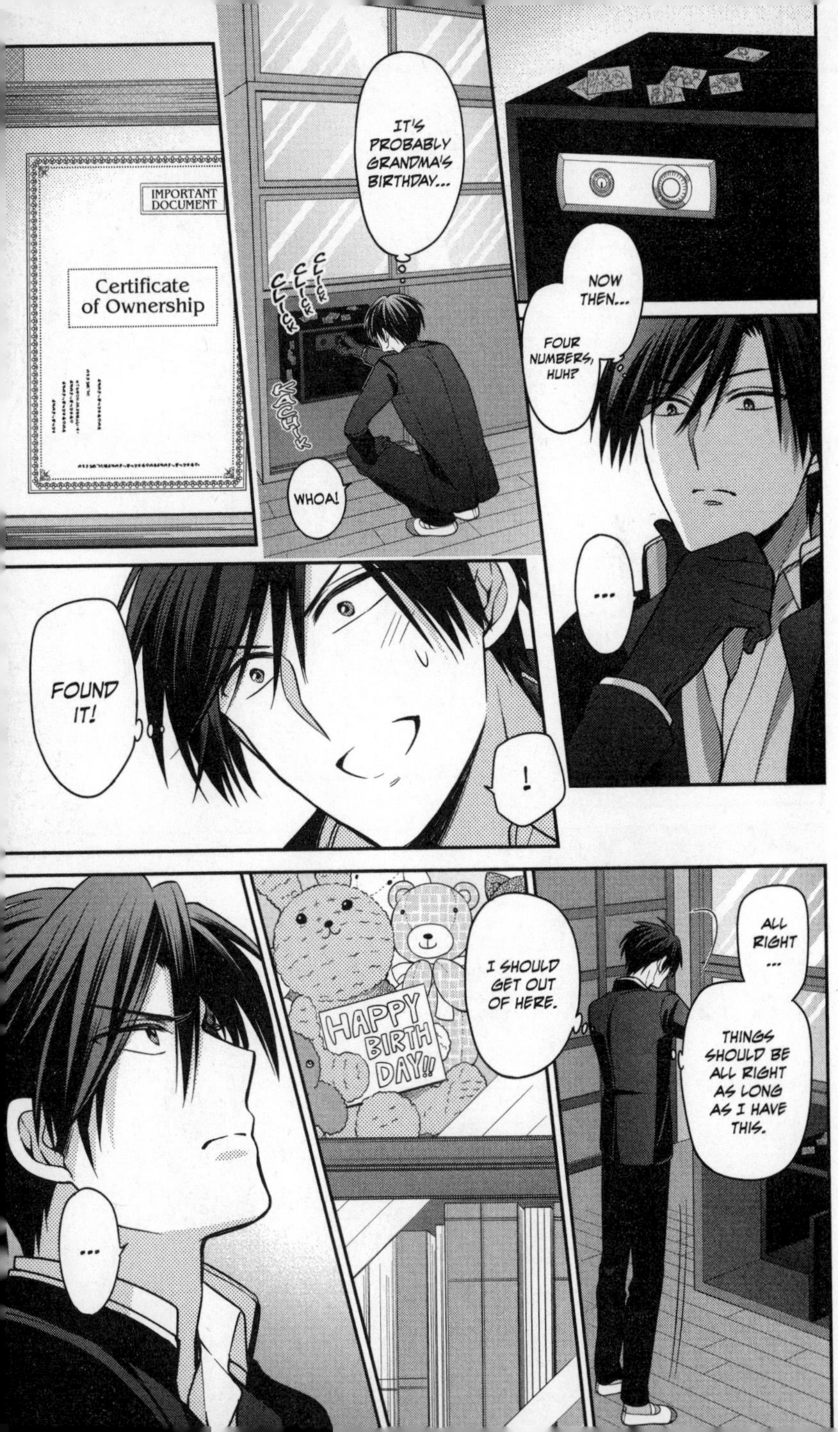
NOW THEN...
FOUR NUMBERS, HUH?
...
IT'S PROBABLY GRANDMA'S BIRTHDAY...
CLICK
CLICK
CLICK
KACHUNK
WHOA!
IMPORTANT DOCUMENT
Certificate of Ownership
!
FOUND IT!
ALL RIGHT...
THINGS SHOULD BE ALL RIGHT AS LONG AS I HAVE THIS.
I SHOULD GET OUT OF HERE.
HAPPY BIRTHDAY!!
...

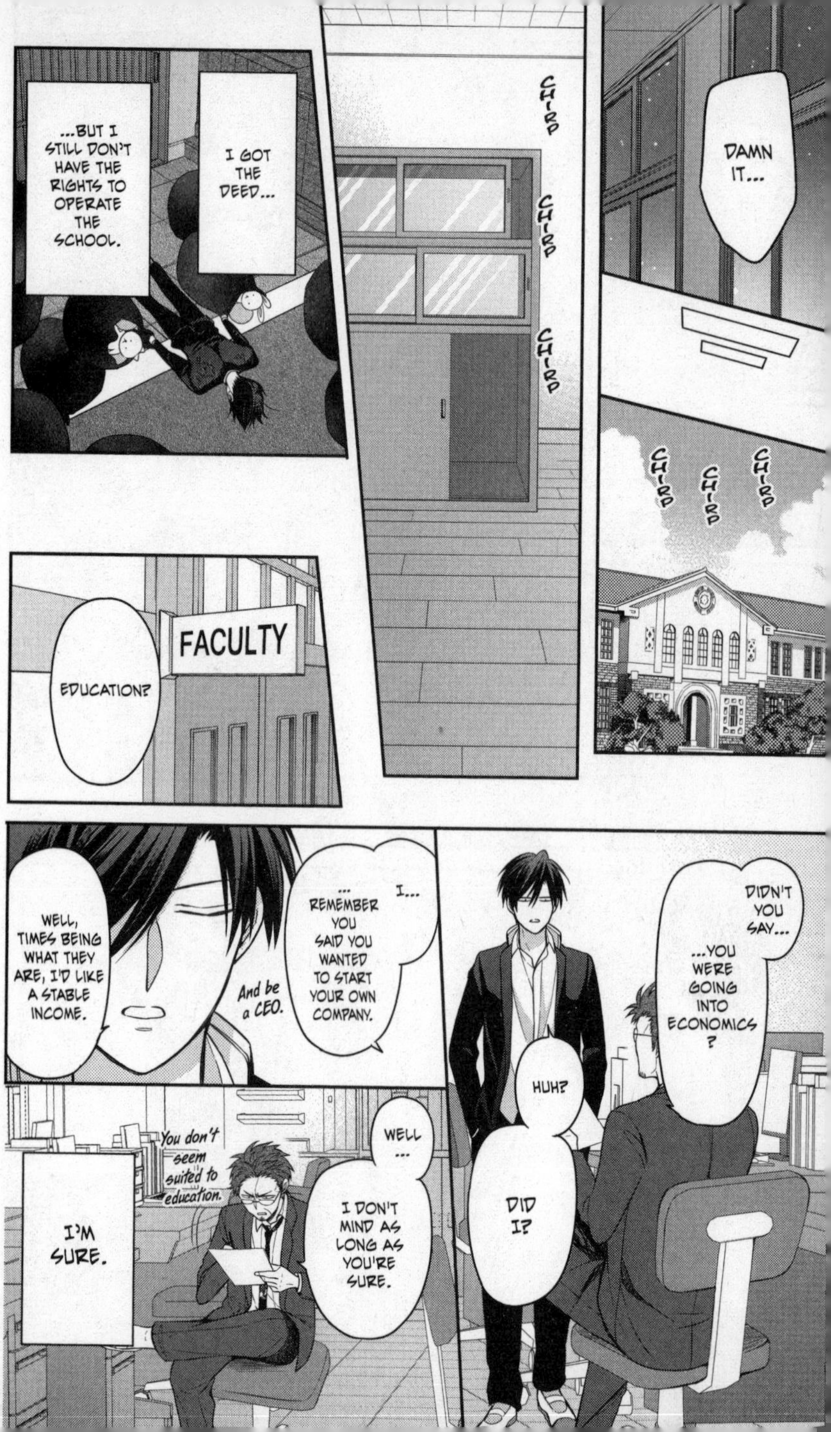
DAMN IT...
CHIRP
CHIRP
CHIRP
CHIRP
CHIRP
CHIRP
I GOT THE DEED...
...BUT I STILL DON'T HAVE THE RIGHTS TO OPERATE THE SCHOOL.
FACULTY
EDUCATION?
DIDN'T YOU SAY...
...YOU WERE GOING INTO ECONOMICS?
HUH?
DID I?
I...
...REMEMBER YOU SAID YOU WANTED TO START YOUR OWN COMPANY.
And be a CEO.
WELL, TIMES BEING WHAT THEY ARE, I'D LIKE A STABLE INCOME.
WELL...
I DON'T MIND AS LONG AS YOU'RE SURE.
You don't seem suited to education.
I'M SURE.

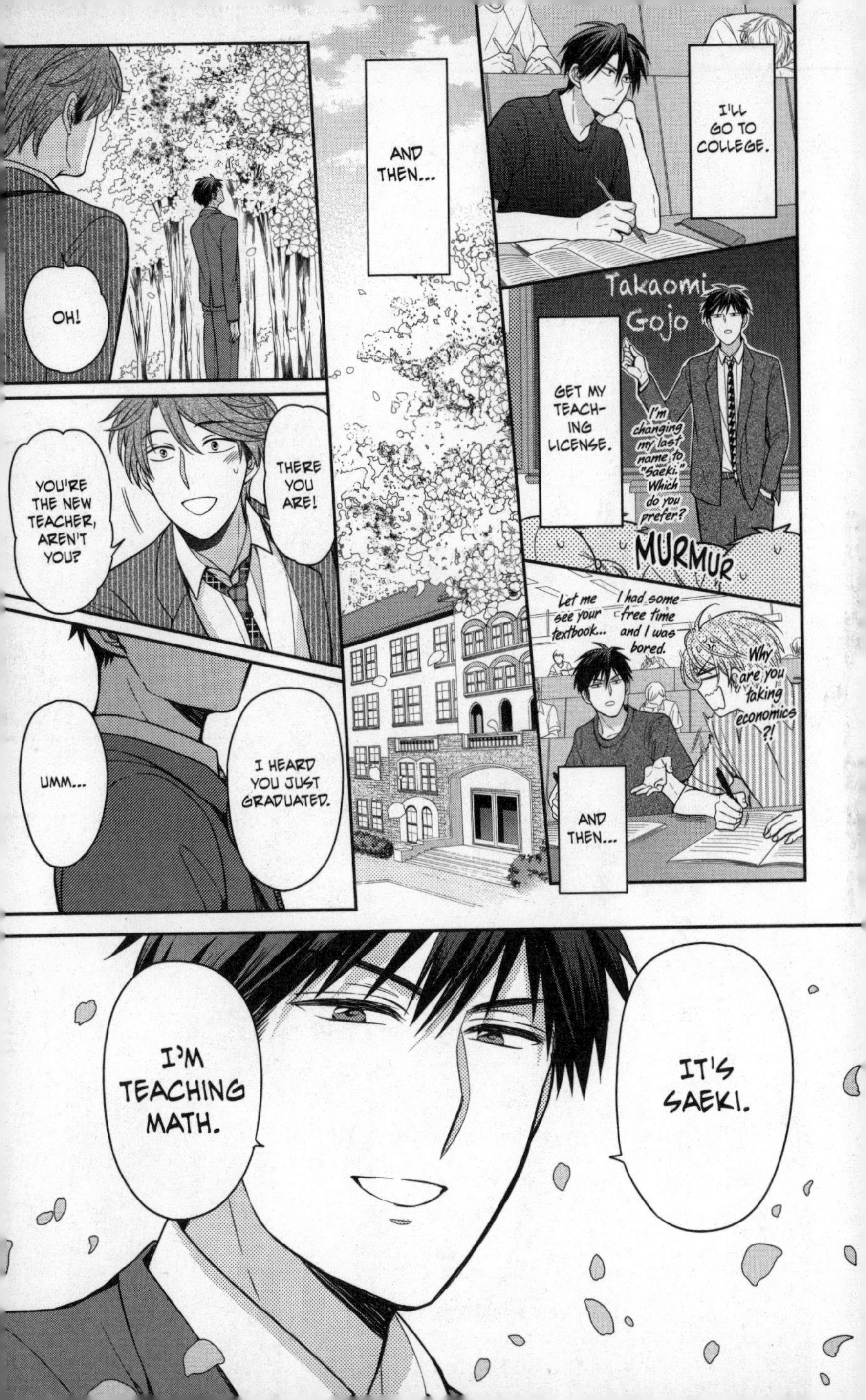
I'LL GO TO COLLEGE.
Takaomi Gojo
GET MY TEACHING LICENSE.
I'm changing my last name to "Saeki." Which do you prefer?
MURMUR
Why are you taking economics?!
I had some free time and I was bored.
Let me see your textbook...
AND THEN...
AND THEN...
OH!
THERE YOU ARE!
YOU'RE THE NEW TEACHER, AREN'T YOU?
I HEARD YOU JUST GRADUATED.
UMM...
IT'S SAEKI.
I'M TEACHING MATH.

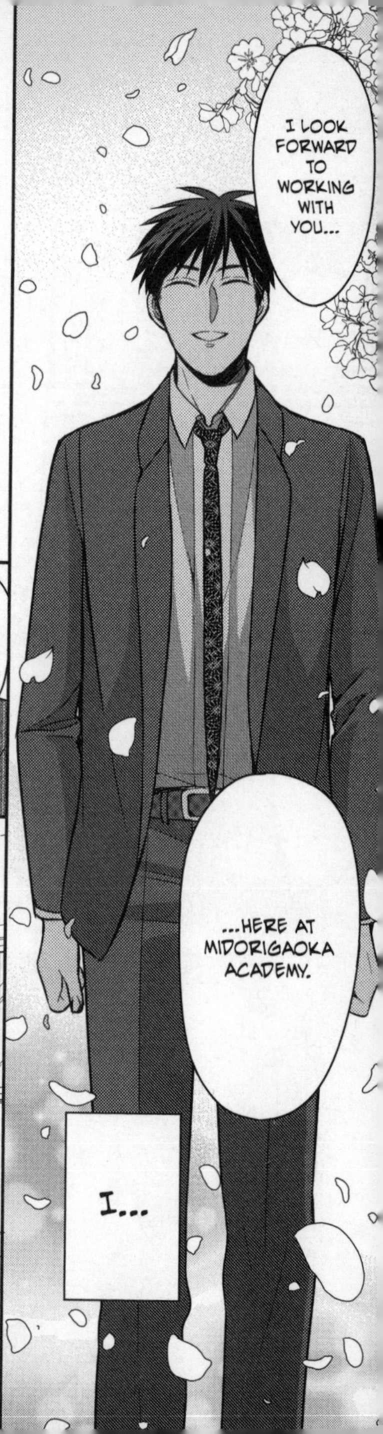
I LOOK FORWARD TO WORKING WITH YOU...
...HERE AT MIDORIGAOKA ACADEMY.
I...
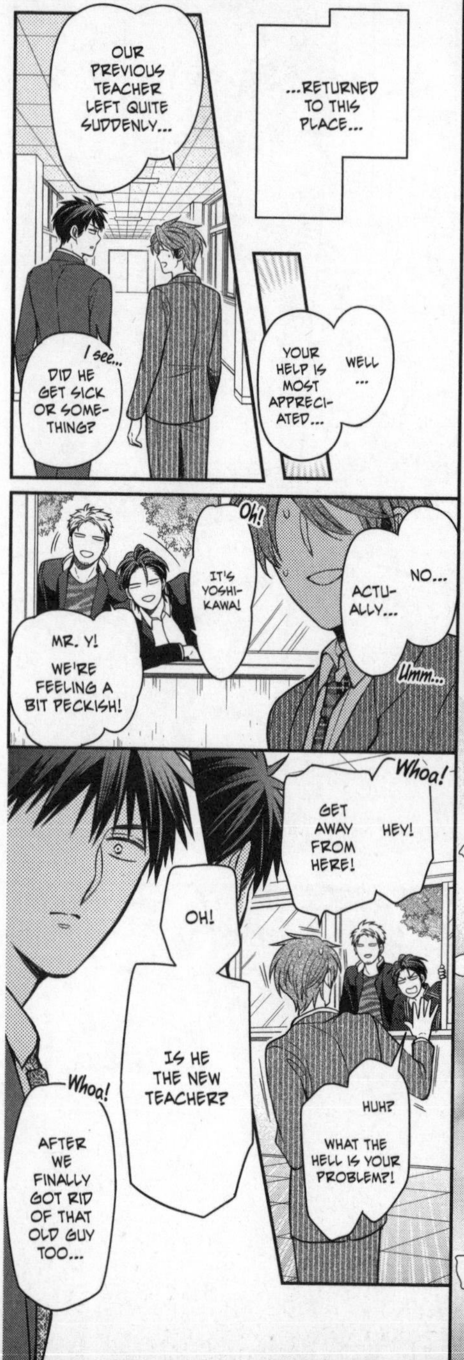
...RETURNED TO THIS PLACE...
OUR PREVIOUS TEACHER LEFT QUITE SUDDENLY...
WELL...
YOUR HELP IS MOST APPRECIATED...
I see...
DID HE GET SICK OR SOMETHING?
NO...
ACTUALLY...
Umm...
Oh!
IT'S YOSHIKAWA!
MR. Y!
WE'RE FEELING A BIT PECKISH!
Whoa!
HEY!
GET AWAY FROM HERE!
OH!
IS HE THE NEW TEACHER?
HUH?
WHAT THE HELL IS YOUR PROBLEM?!
Whoa!
AFTER WE FINALLY GOT RID OF THAT OLD GUY TOO...

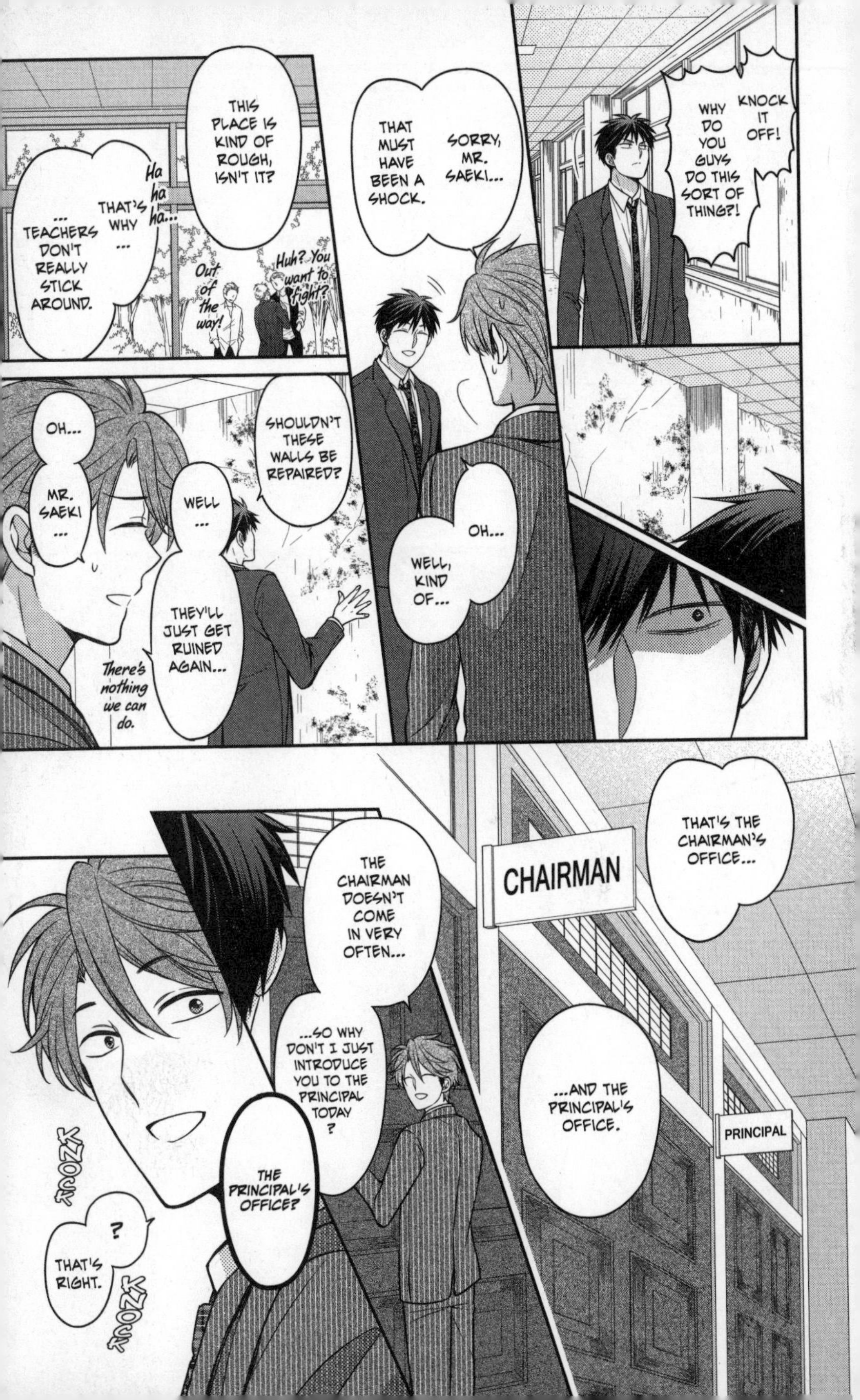
KNOCK IT OFF!
WHY DO YOU GUYS DO THIS SORT OF THING?!
SORRY, MR. SAEKI...
THAT MUST HAVE BEEN A SHOCK.
OH...
WELL, KIND OF...
THIS PLACE IS KIND OF ROUGH, ISN'T IT?
Ha ha ha...
THAT'S WHY...
...TEACHERS DON'T REALLY STICK AROUND.
Huh? You want to fight?
Out of the way!
SHOULDN'T THESE WALLS BE REPAIRED?
WELL...
THEY'LL JUST GET RUINED AGAIN...
There's nothing we can do.
OH...
MR. SAEKI...
THAT'S THE CHAIRMAN'S OFFICE...
CHAIRMAN
...AND THE PRINCIPAL'S OFFICE.
PRINCIPAL
THE CHAIRMAN DOESN'T COME IN VERY OFTEN...
...SO WHY DON'T I JUST INTRODUCE YOU TO THE PRINCIPAL TODAY?
THE PRINCIPAL'S OFFICE?
?
THAT'S RIGHT.
KNOCK
KNOCK

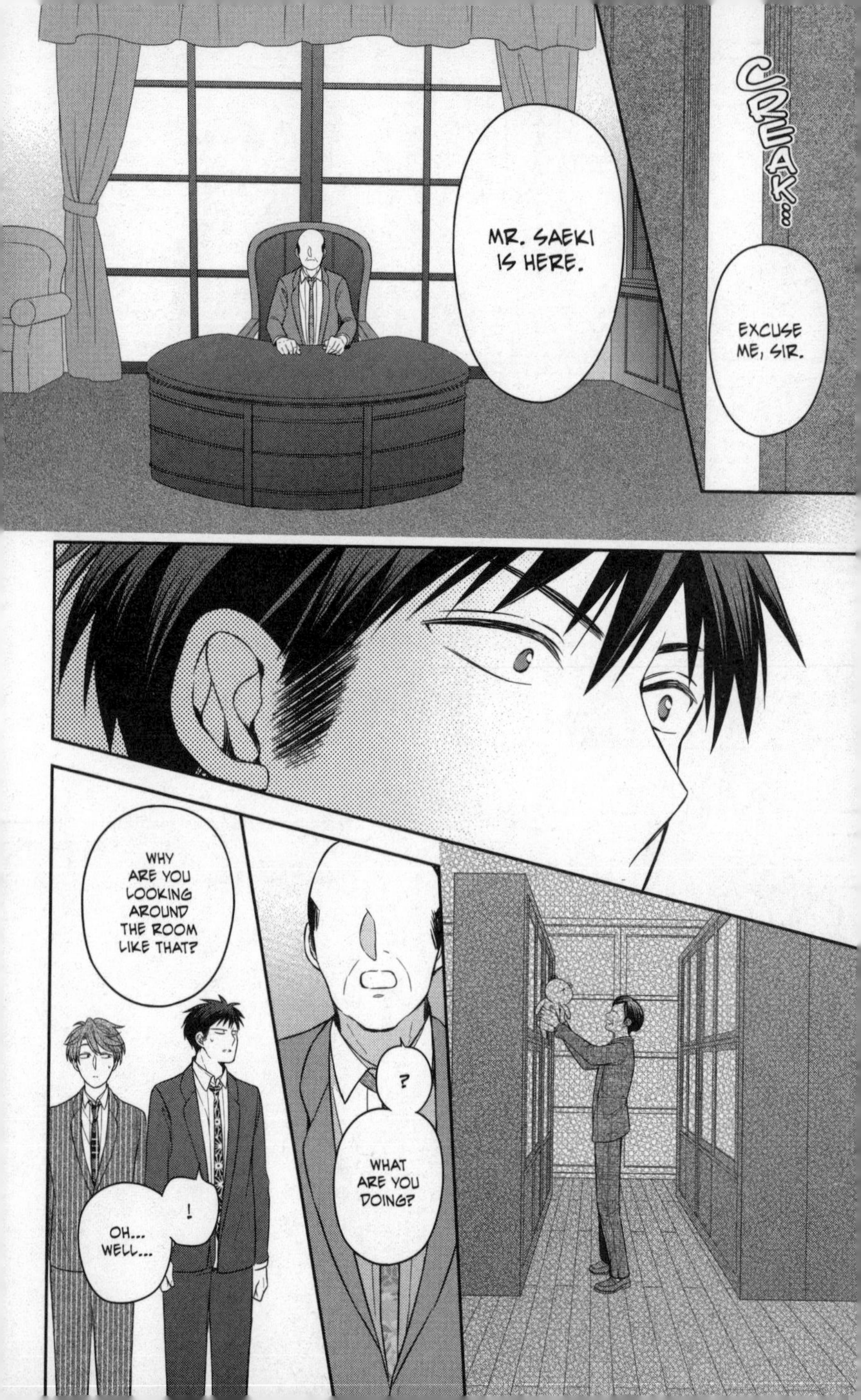
CREAK...
EXCUSE ME, SIR.
MR. SAEKI IS HERE.
?
WHAT ARE YOU DOING?
WHY ARE YOU LOOKING AROUND THE ROOM LIKE THAT?
!
OH... WELL...

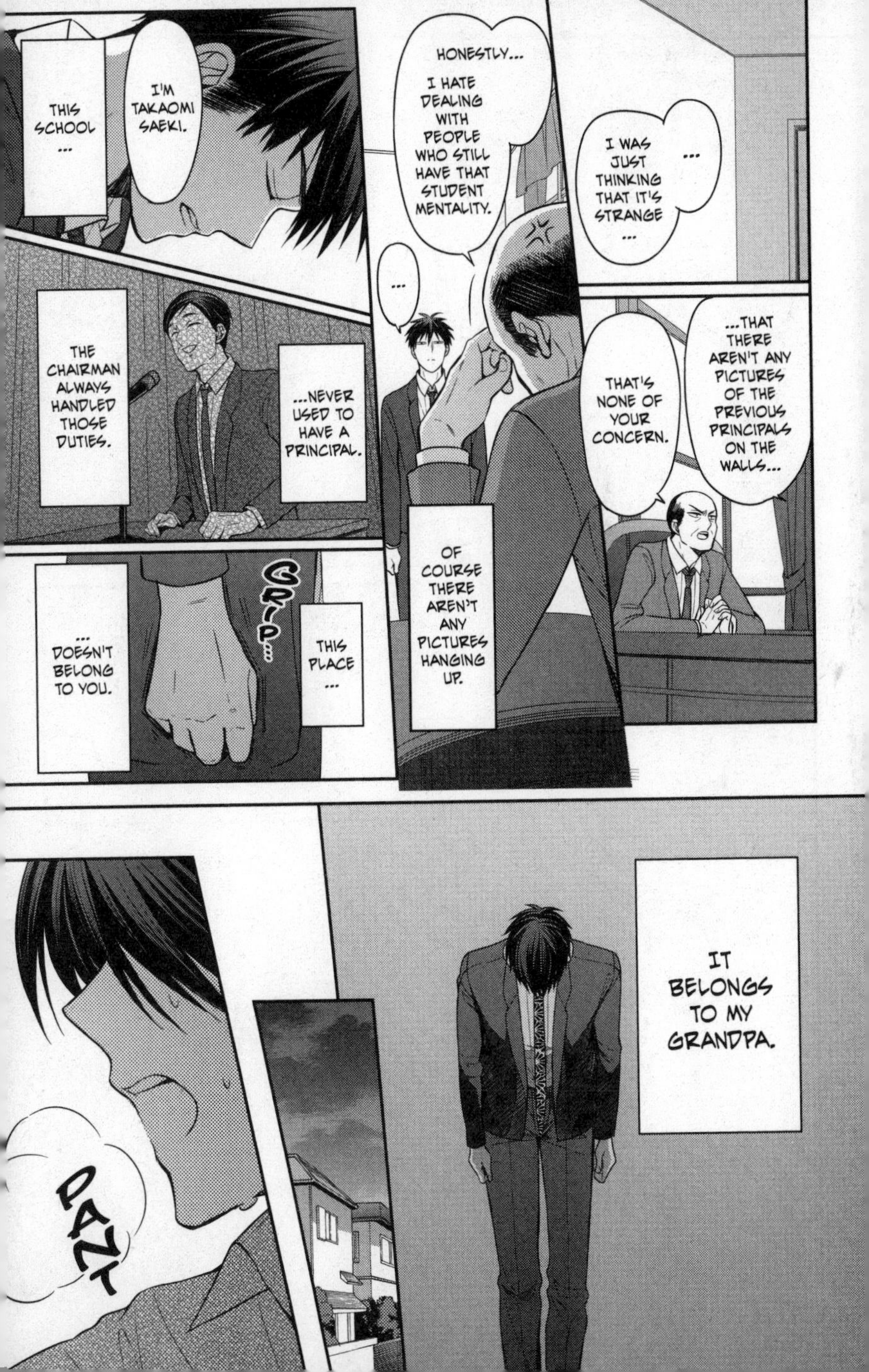
I WAS JUST THINKING THAT IT'S STRANGE ...
...
...THAT THERE AREN'T ANY PICTURES OF THE PREVIOUS PRINCIPALS ON THE WALLS...
THAT'S NONE OF YOUR CONCERN.
HONESTLY... I HATE DEALING WITH PEOPLE WHO STILL HAVE THAT STUDENT MENTALITY.
...
OF COURSE THERE AREN'T ANY PICTURES HANGING UP.
I'M TAKAOMI SAEKI.
THIS SCHOOL ...
...NEVER USED TO HAVE A PRINCIPAL.
THE CHAIRMAN ALWAYS HANDLED THOSE DUTIES.
THIS PLACE ...
GRIP...
... DOESN'T BELONG TO YOU.
IT BELONGS TO MY GRANDPA.
PANT

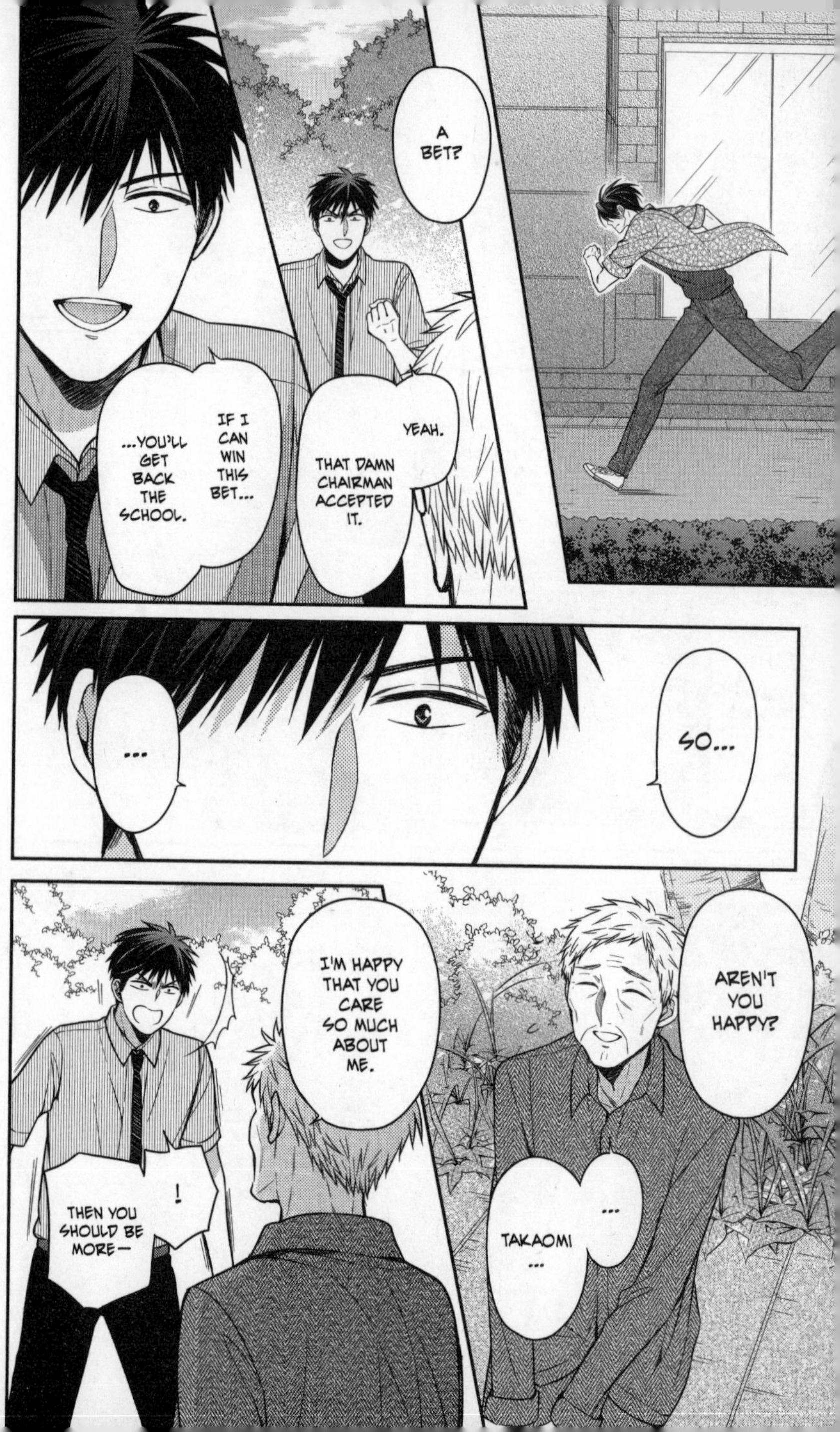
A BET?
YEAH.
THAT DAMN CHAIRMAN ACCEPTED IT.
IF I CAN WIN THIS BET...
...YOU'LL GET BACK THE SCHOOL.
SO...
...
AREN'T YOU HAPPY?
I'M HAPPY THAT YOU CARE SO MUCH ABOUT ME.
!
THEN YOU SHOULD BE MORE—
...
TAKAOMI ...

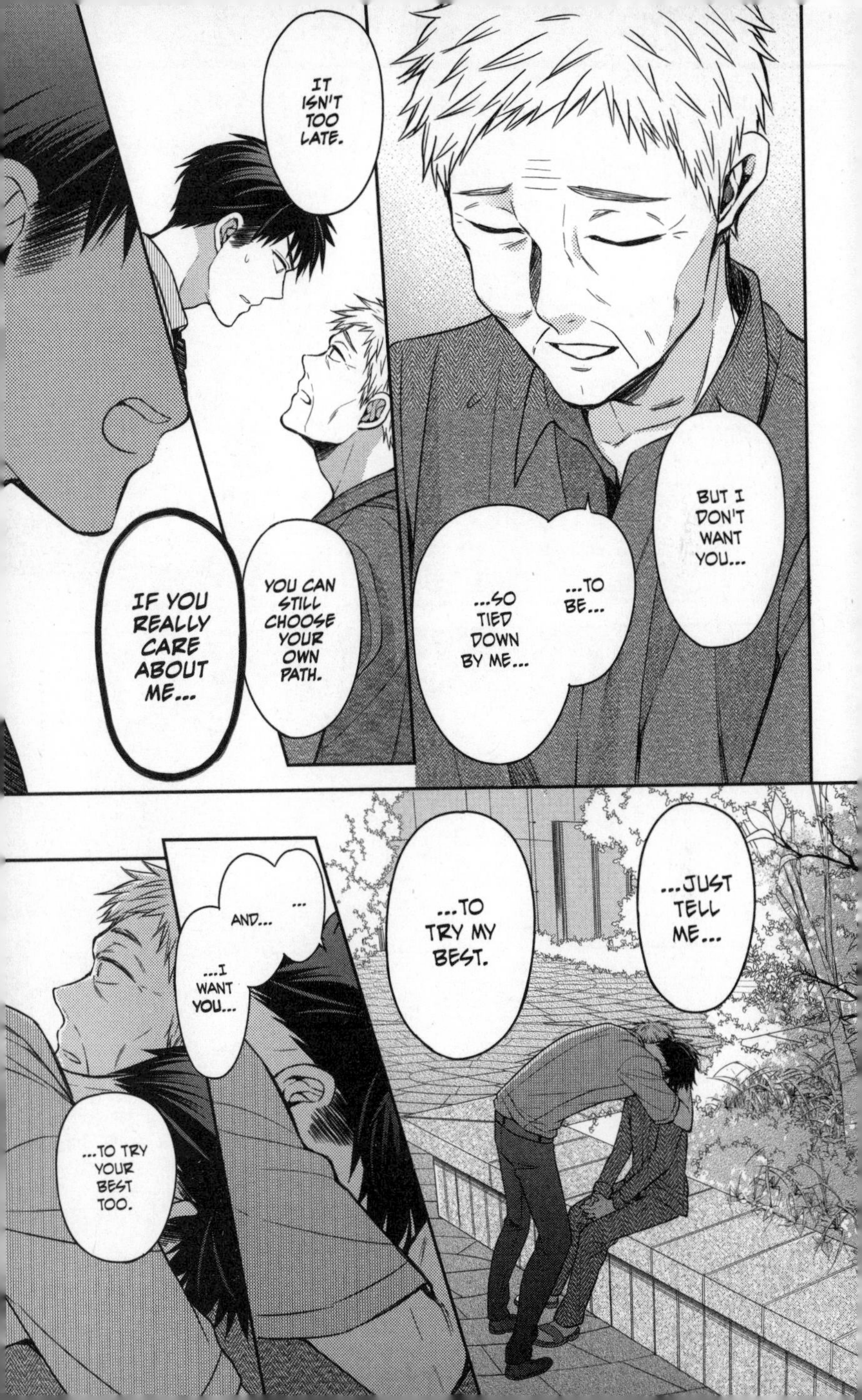
BUT I DON'T WANT YOU...
...TO BE...
...SO TIED DOWN BY ME...
IT ISN'T TOO LATE.
YOU CAN STILL CHOOSE YOUR OWN PATH.
IF YOU REALLY CARE ABOUT ME...
...JUST TELL ME...
...TO TRY MY BEST.
...
AND...
...I WANT YOU...
...TO TRY YOUR BEST TOO.

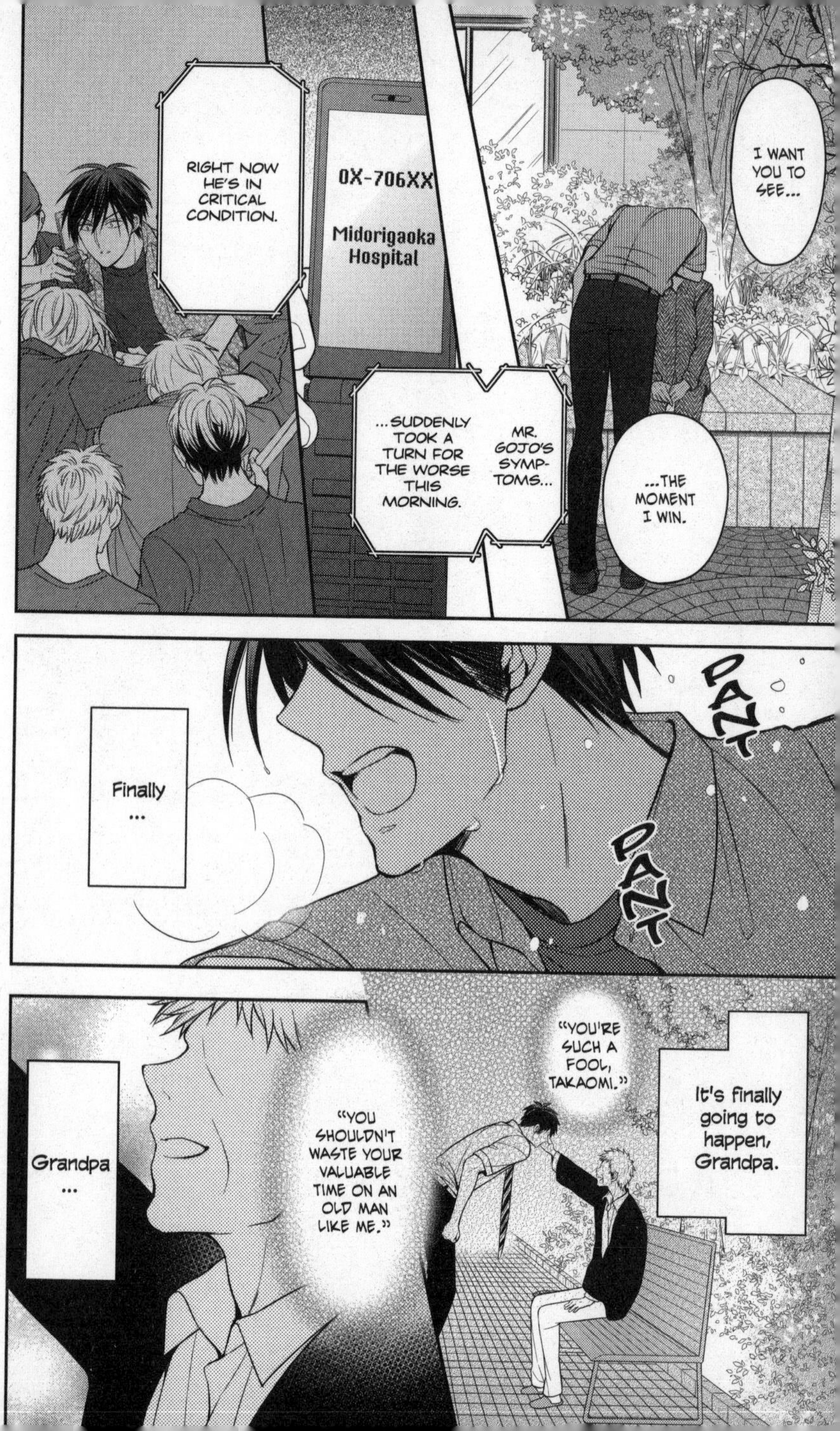
I WANT YOU TO SEE...
...THE MOMENT I WIN.
0X-706XX
Midorigaoka Hospital
MR. GOJO'S SYMPTOMS...
...SUDDENLY TOOK A TURN FOR THE WORSE THIS MORNING.
RIGHT NOW HE'S IN CRITICAL CONDITION.
PANT
PANT
Finally...
It's finally going to happen, Grandpa.
"YOU'RE SUCH A FOOL, TAKAOMI."
"YOU SHOULDN'T WASTE YOUR VALUABLE TIME ON AN OLD MAN LIKE ME."
Grandpa...

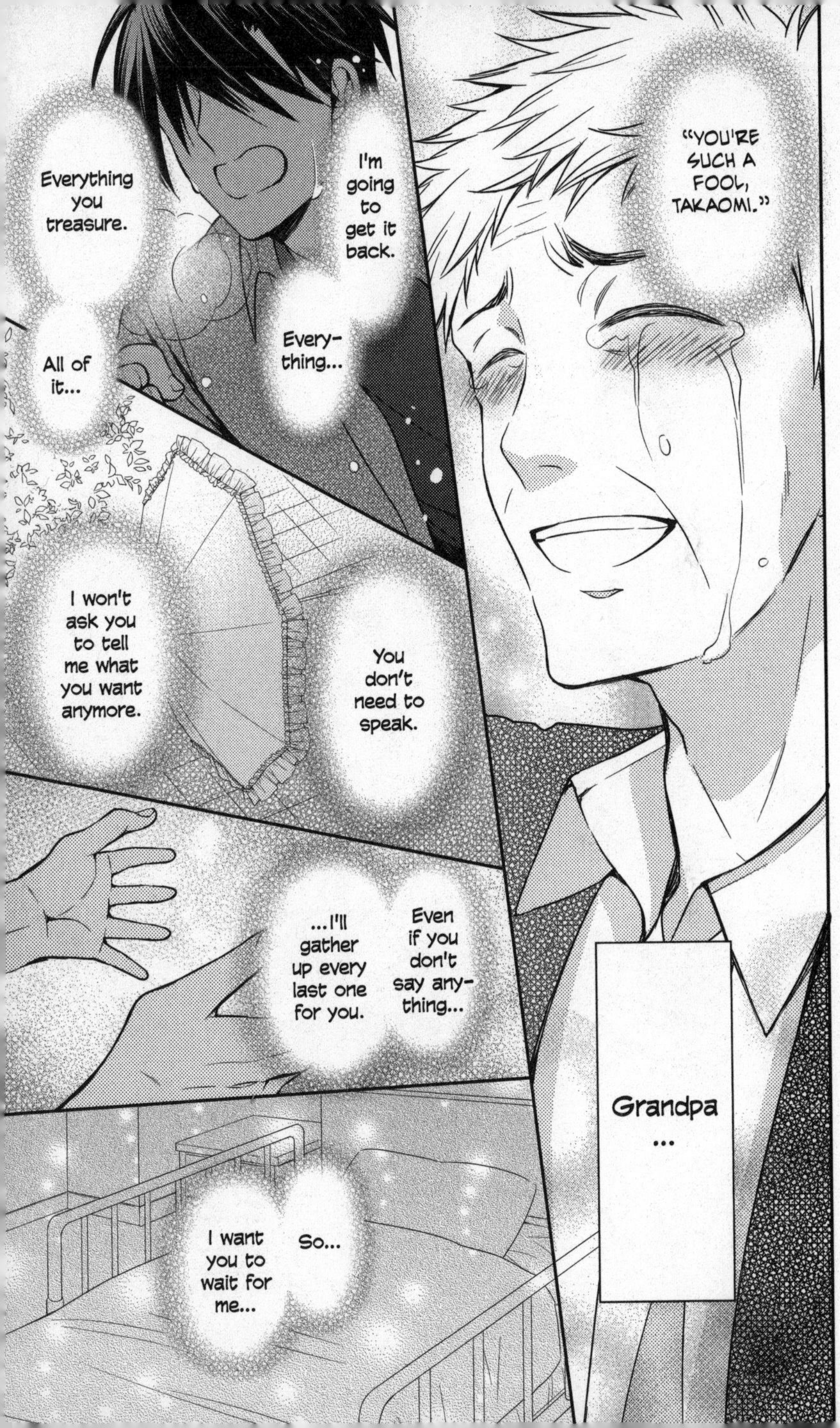

"YOU'RE SUCH A FOOL, TAKAOMI."
Grandpa ...
I'm going to get it back.
Everything you treasure.
Every-thing...
All of it...
You don't need to speak.
I won't ask you to tell me what you want anymore.
Even if you don't say any-thing...
...I'll gather up every last one for you.
So...
I want you to wait for me...

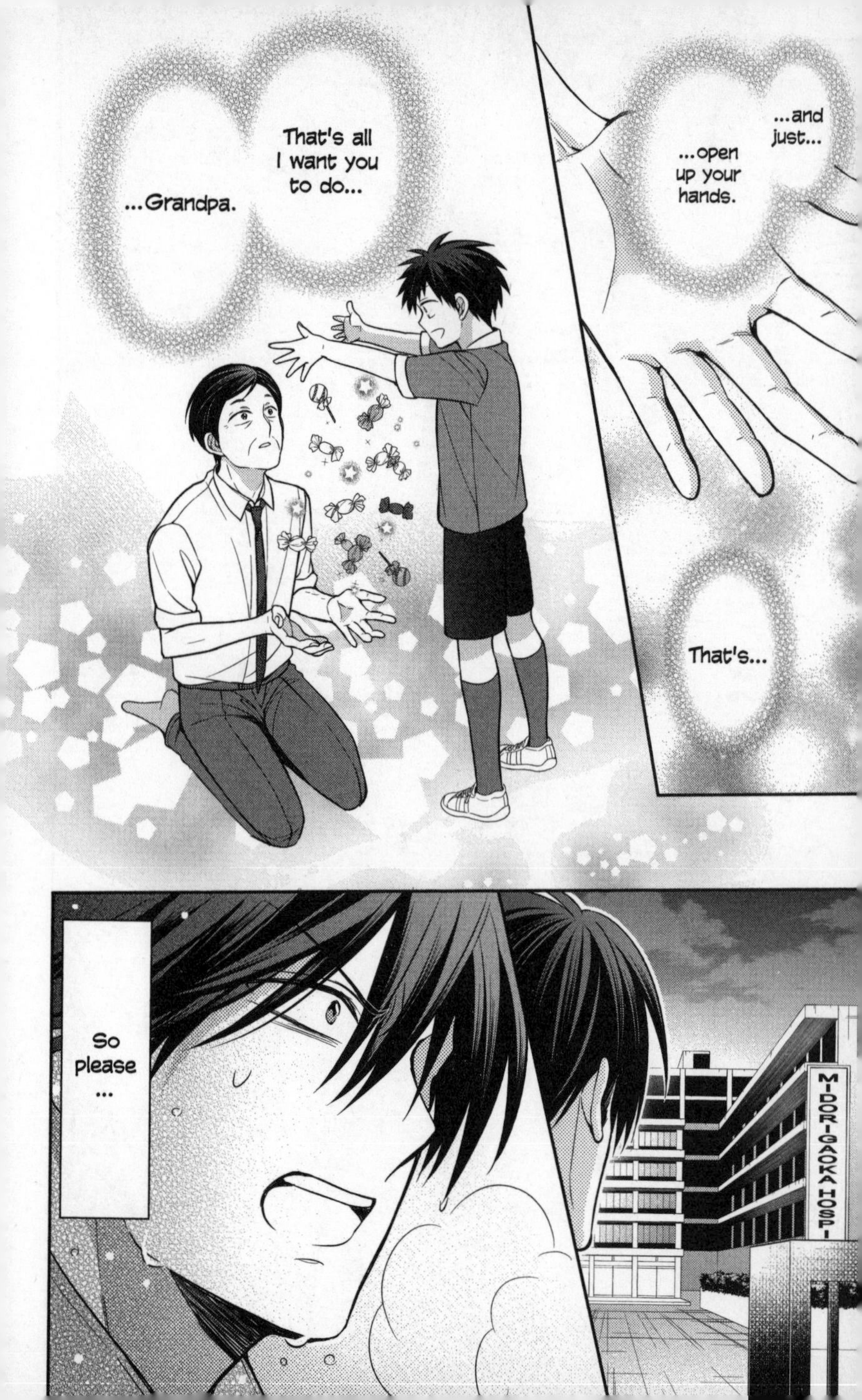
...and just...
...open up your hands.
That's...
That's all I want you to do...
...Grandpa.
MIDORIGAOKA HOSPI
So please ...

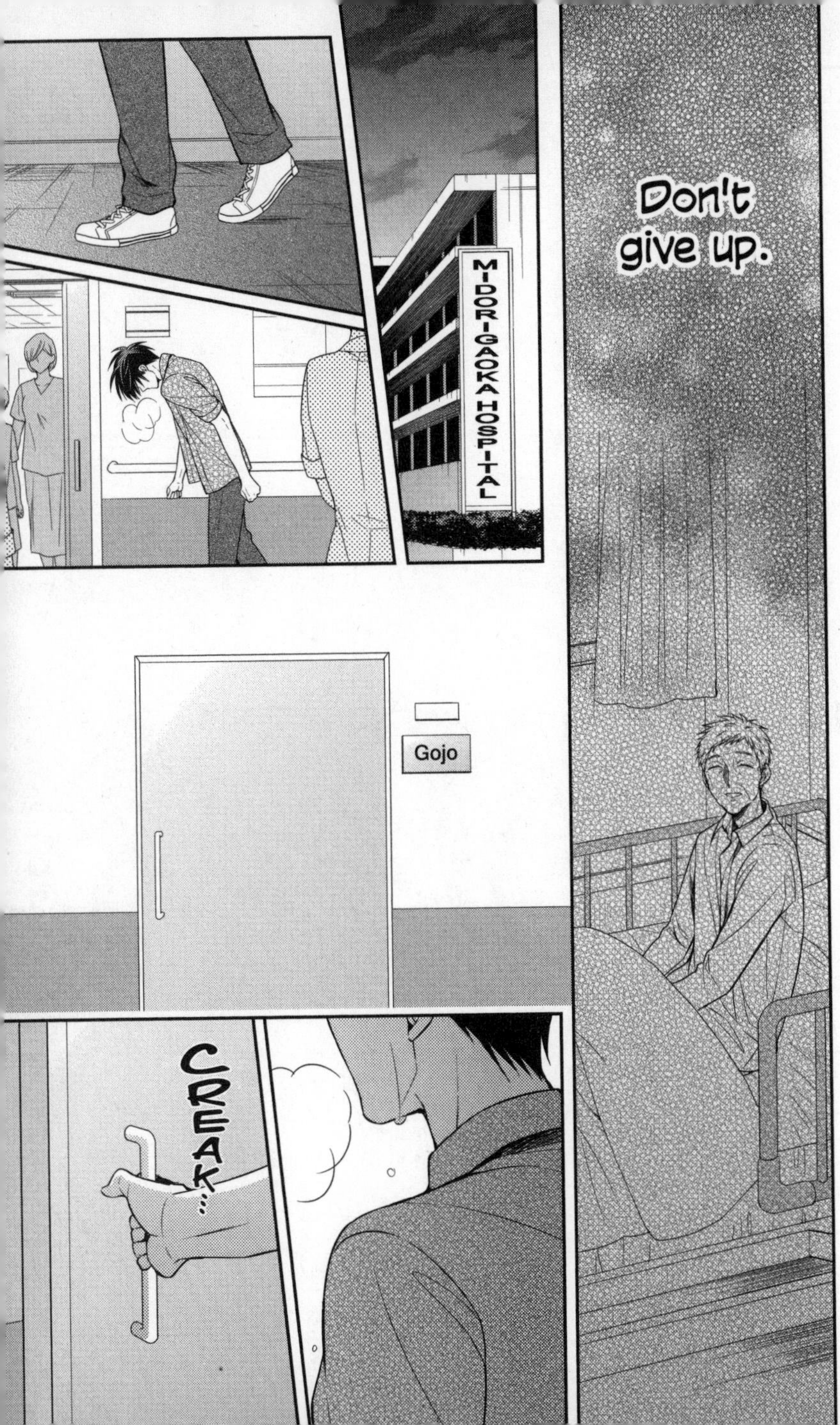
Don't give up.
MIDORIGAOKA HOSPITAL
Gojo
CREAK...

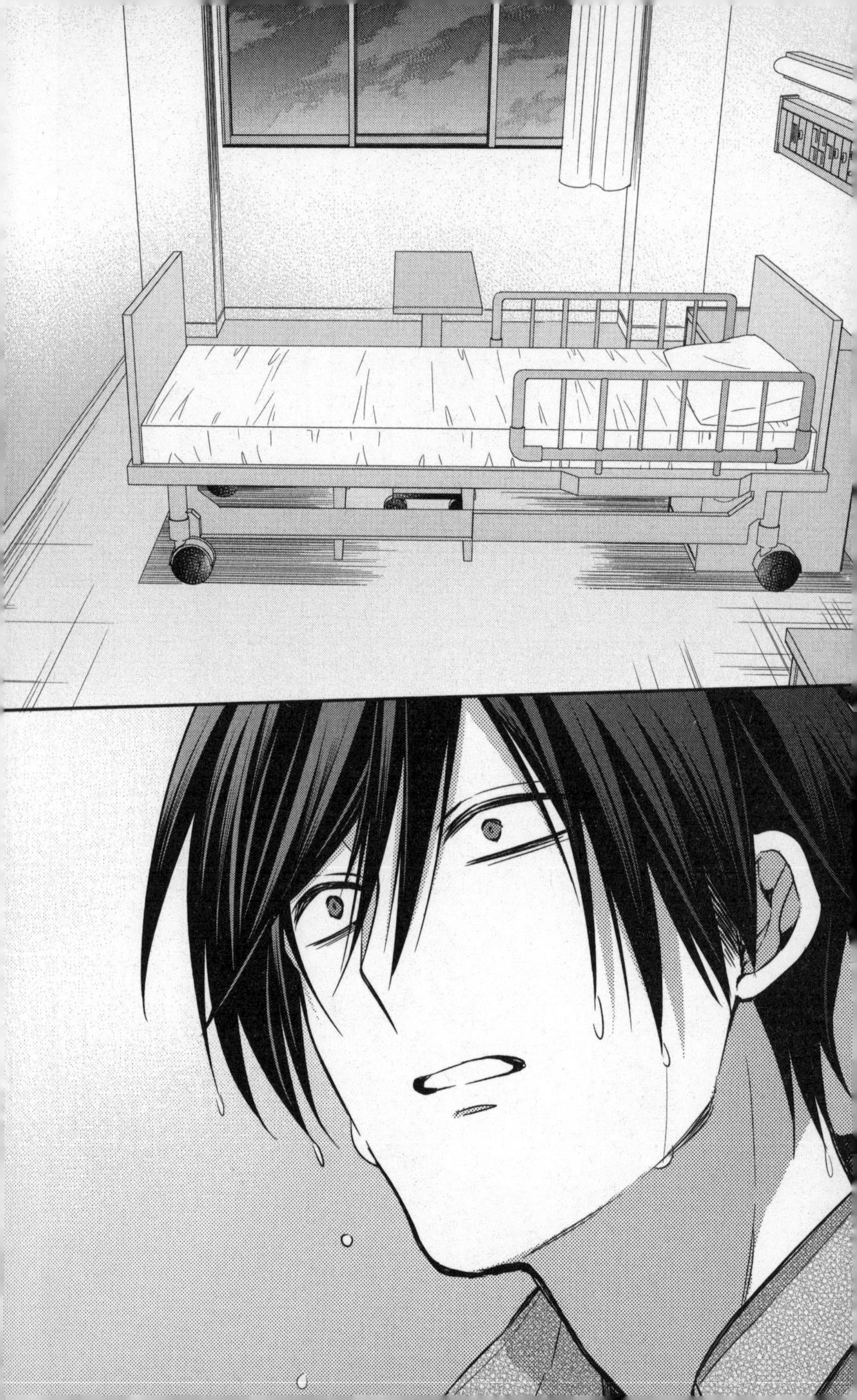

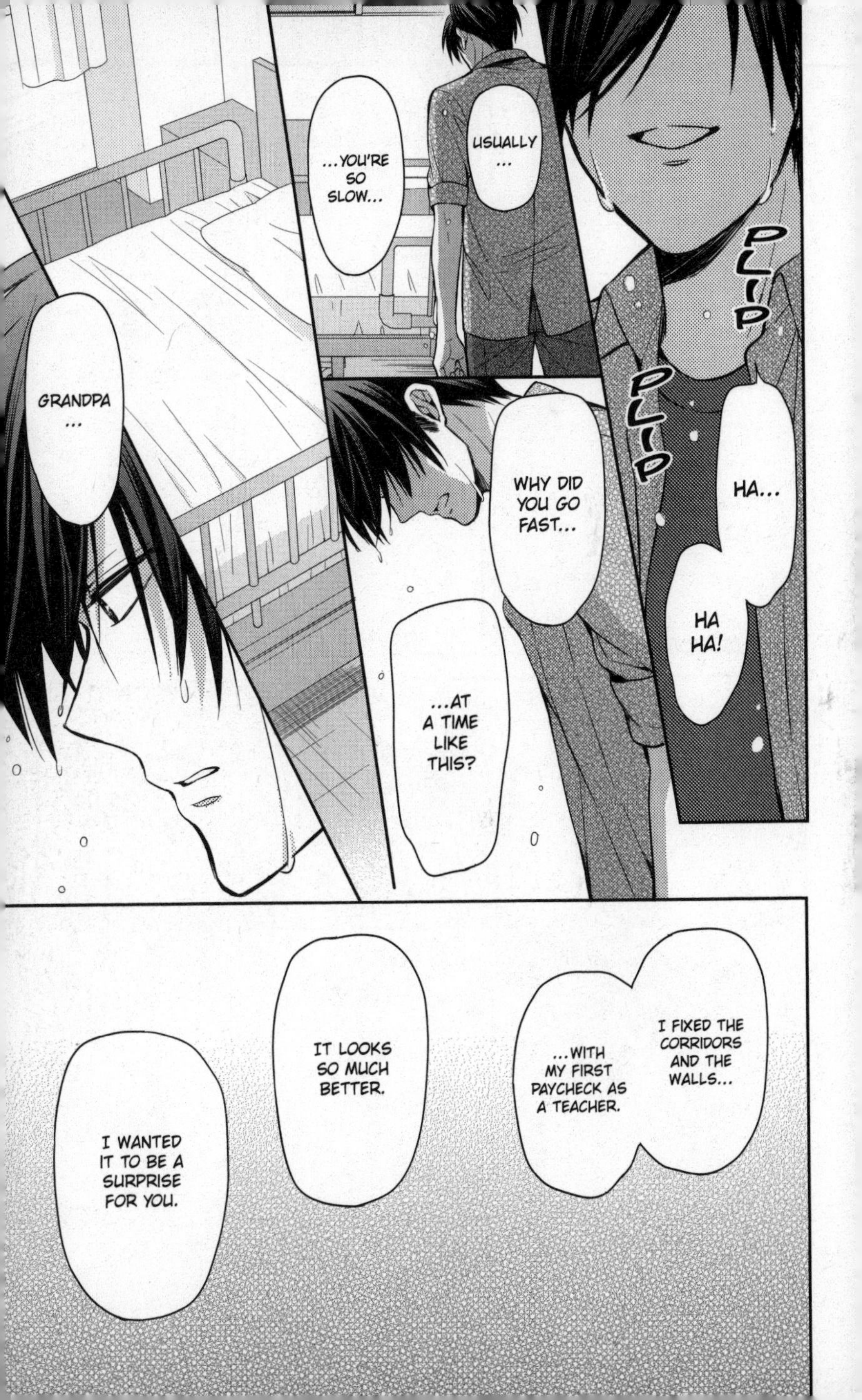
PLIP
PLIP
PLIP
HA...
HA HA!
USUALLY...
...YOU'RE SO SLOW...
WHY DID YOU GO FAST...
...AT A TIME LIKE THIS?
GRANDPA...
I FIXED THE CORRIDORS AND THE WALLS...
...WITH MY FIRST PAYCHECK AS A TEACHER.
IT LOOKS SO MUCH BETTER.
I WANTED IT TO BE A SURPRISE FOR YOU.

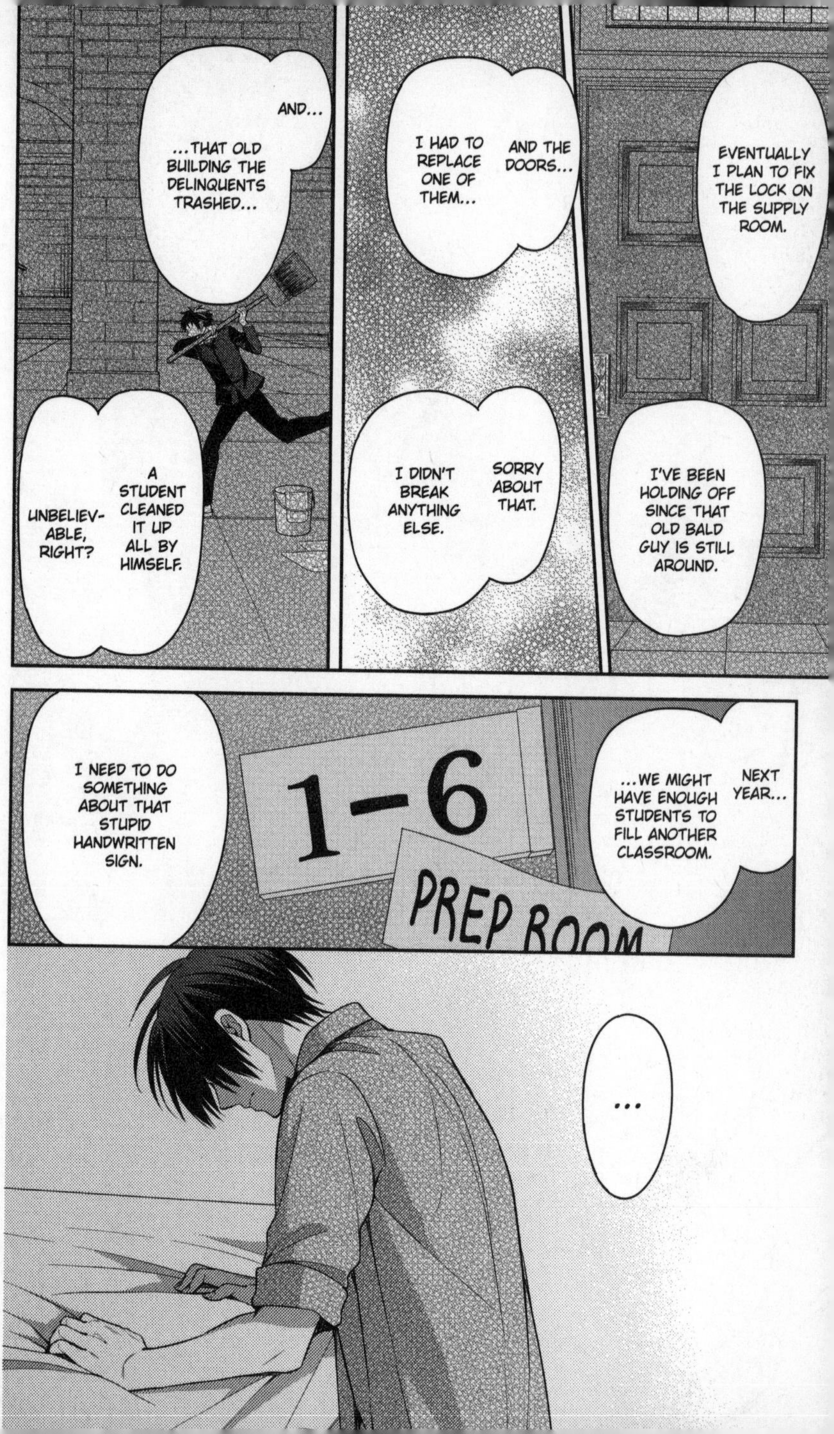
EVENTUALLY I PLAN TO FIX THE LOCK ON THE SUPPLY ROOM.
I'VE BEEN HOLDING OFF SINCE THAT OLD BALD GUY IS STILL AROUND.
AND THE DOORS...
I HAD TO REPLACE ONE OF THEM...
SORRY ABOUT THAT.
I DIDN'T BREAK ANYTHING ELSE.
AND...
...THAT OLD BUILDING THE DELINQUENTS TRASHED...
A STUDENT CLEANED IT UP ALL BY HIMSELF.
UNBELIEV-ABLE, RIGHT?
NEXT YEAR...
...WE MIGHT HAVE ENOUGH STUDENTS TO FILL ANOTHER CLASSROOM.
1-6
PREP ROOM
I NEED TO DO SOMETHING ABOUT THAT STUPID HANDWRITTEN SIGN.
...

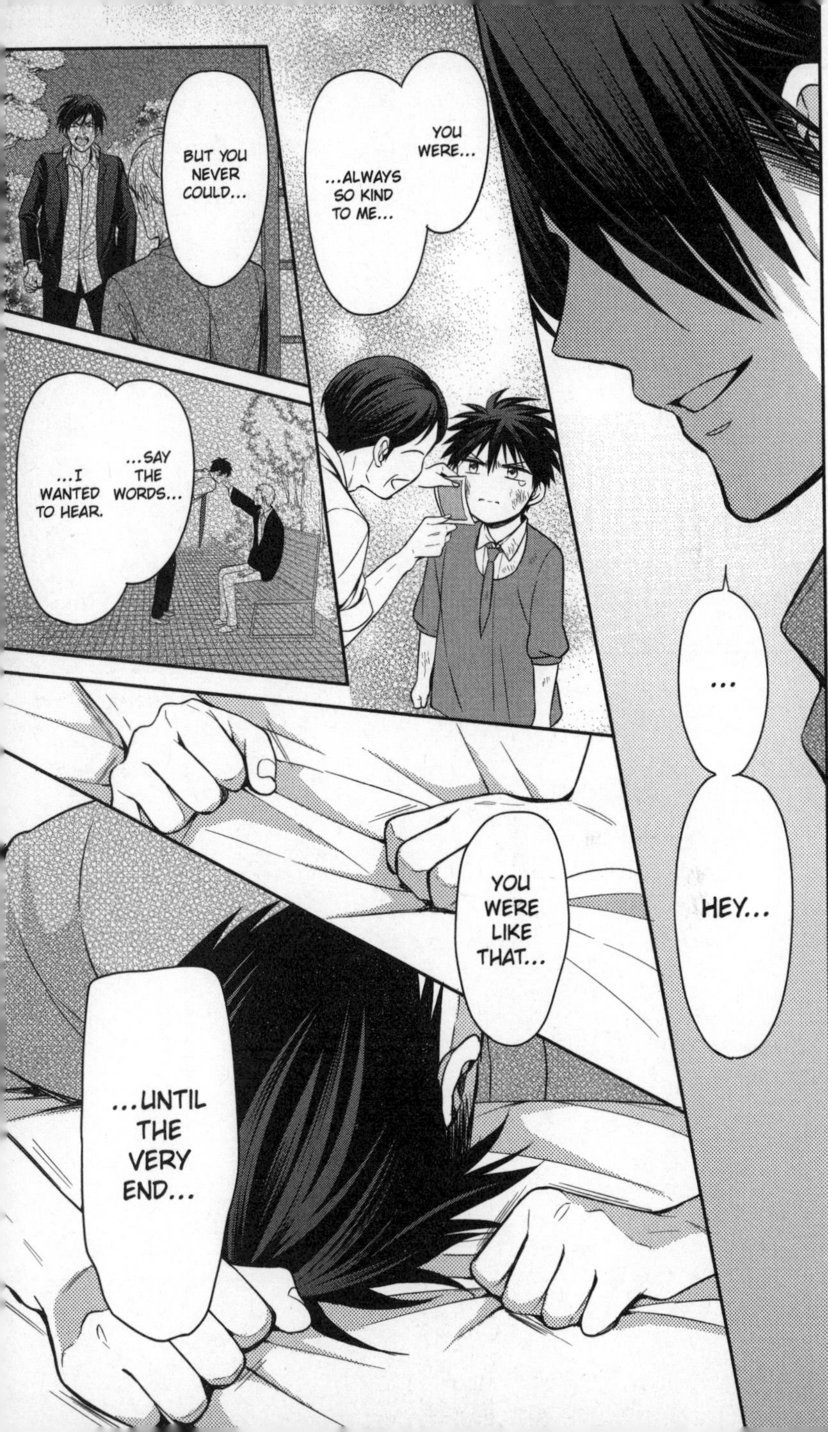
...
HEY...
YOU WERE...
...ALWAYS SO KIND TO ME...
BUT YOU NEVER COULD...
...SAY THE WORDS...
...I WANTED TO HEAR.
YOU WERE LIKE THAT...
...UNTIL THE VERY END...

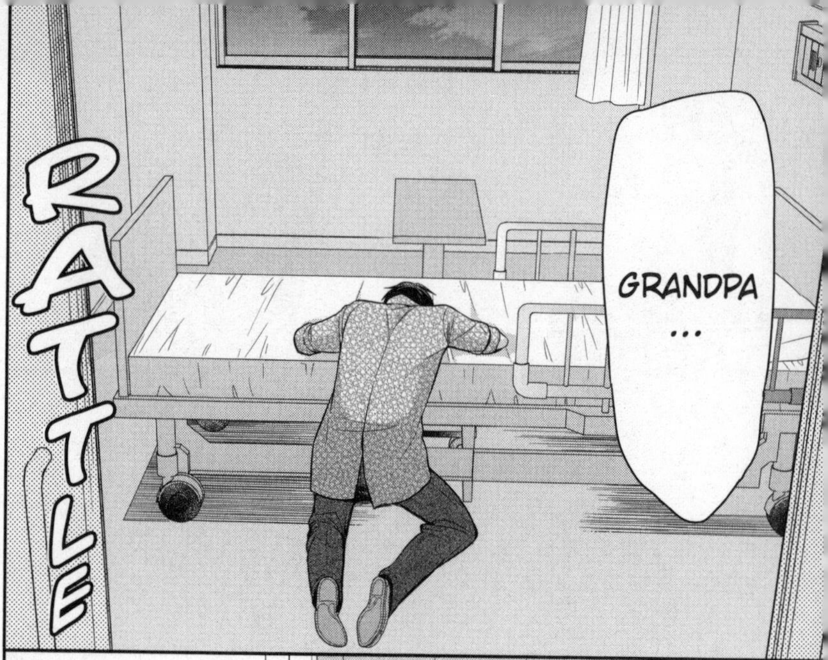
GRANDPA ...
RATTLE
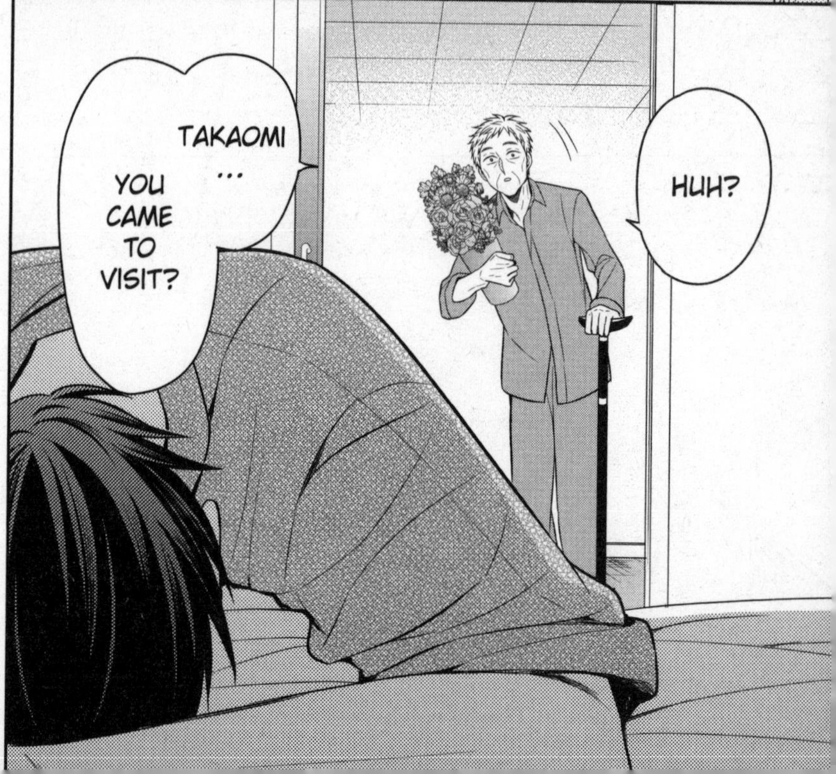
HUH?
TAKAOMI ...
YOU CAME TO VISIT?

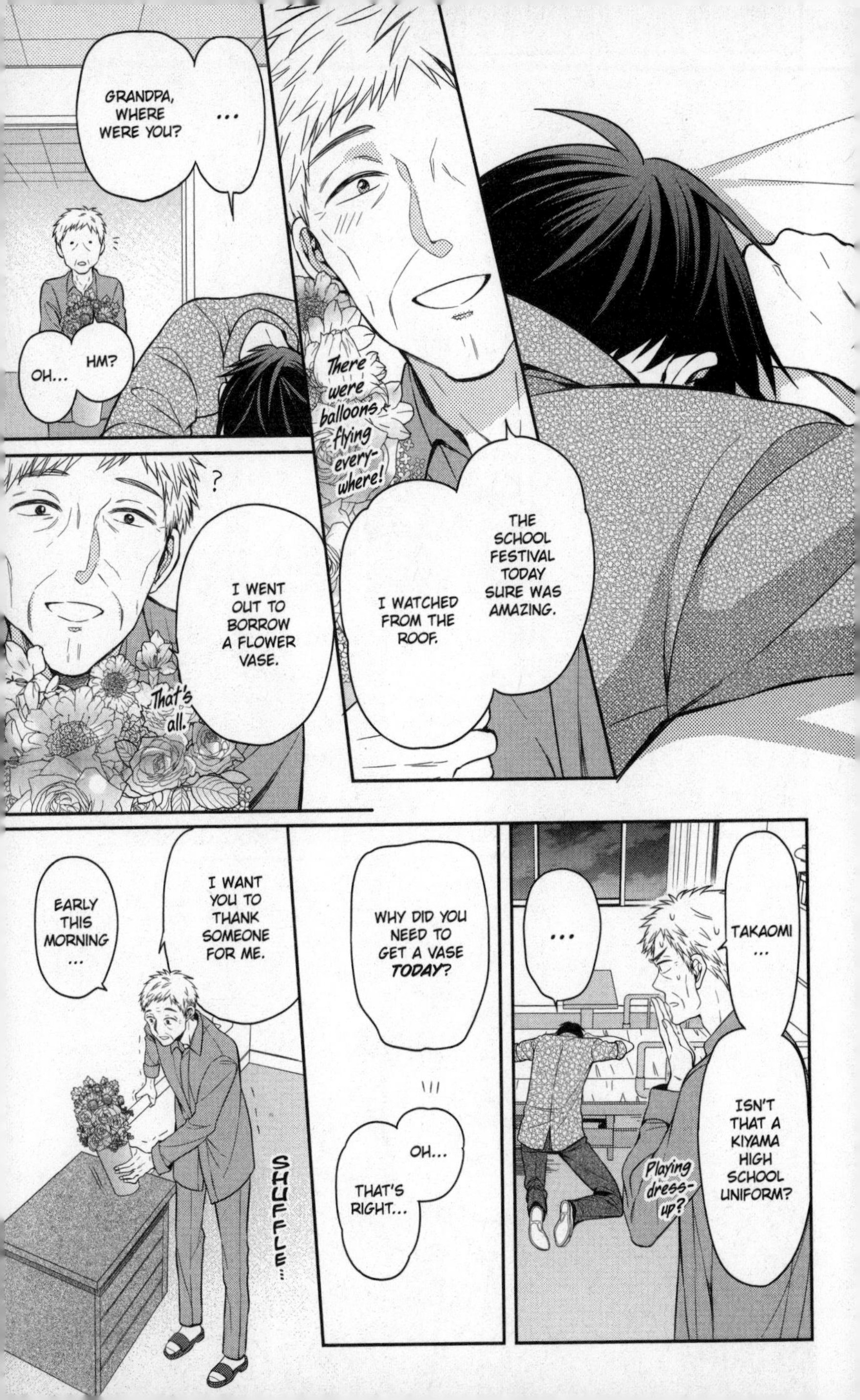
THE SCHOOL FESTIVAL TODAY SURE WAS AMAZING.
I WATCHED FROM THE ROOF.
There were balloons flying every-where!
GRANDPA, WHERE WERE YOU?
...
HM?
OH...
?
I WENT OUT TO BORROW A FLOWER VASE.
That's all.
TAKAOMI ...
...
ISN'T THAT A KIYAMA HIGH SCHOOL UNIFORM?
Playing dress-up?
WHY DID YOU NEED TO GET A VASE TODAY?
OH...
THAT'S RIGHT...
I WANT YOU TO THANK SOMEONE FOR ME.
EARLY THIS MORNING ...
SHUFFLE...

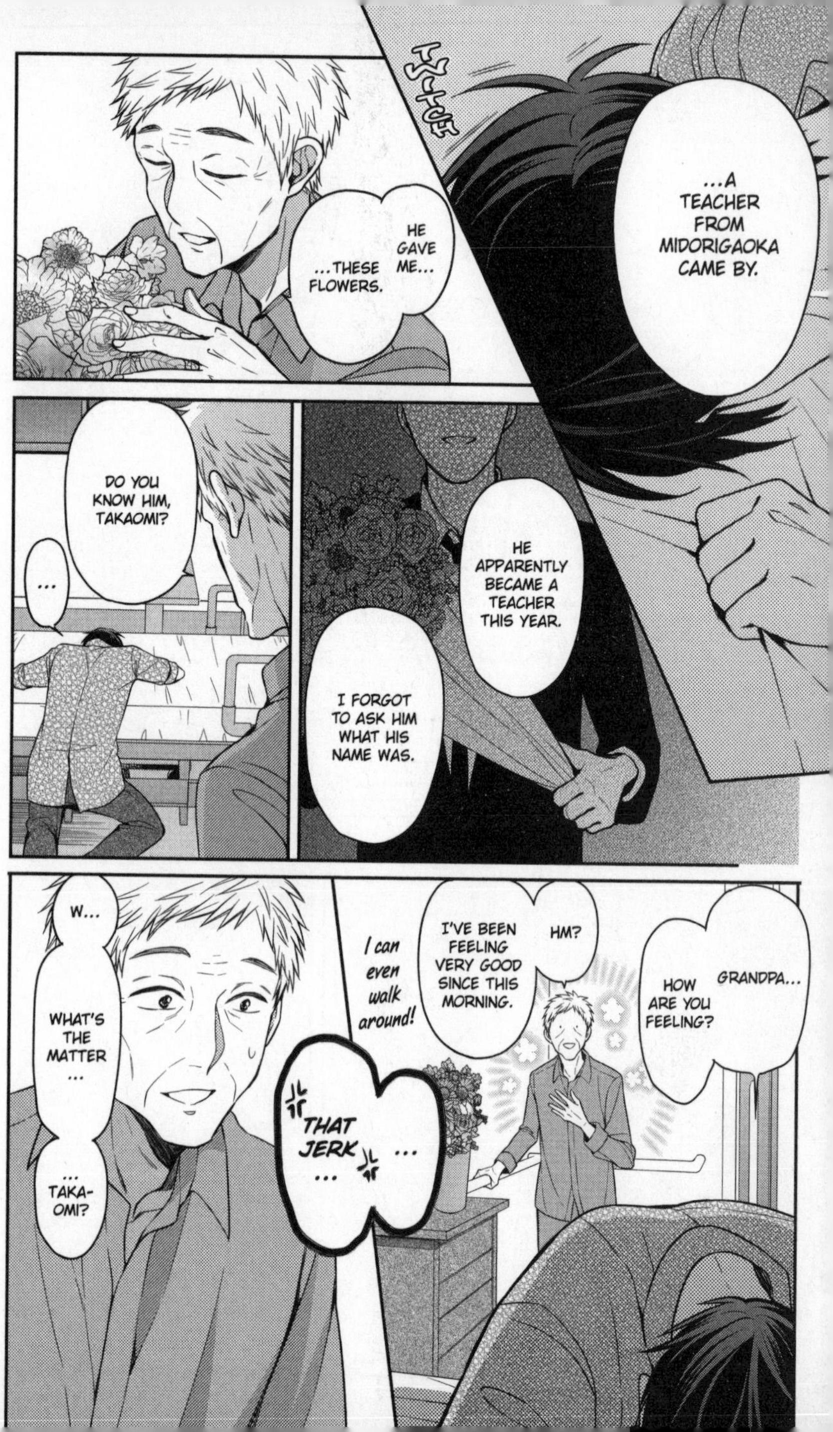
...A TEACHER FROM MIDORIGAOKA CAME BY.
HE GAVE ME...
...THESE FLOWERS.
HE APPARENTLY BECAME A TEACHER THIS YEAR.
I FORGOT TO ASK HIM WHAT HIS NAME WAS.
DO YOU KNOW HIM, TAKAOMI?
...
GRANDPA...
HOW ARE YOU FEELING?
HM?
I'VE BEEN FEELING VERY GOOD SINCE THIS MORNING.
I can even walk around!
THAT JERK... ...
W...
WHAT'S THE MATTER...
...TAKA-OMI?

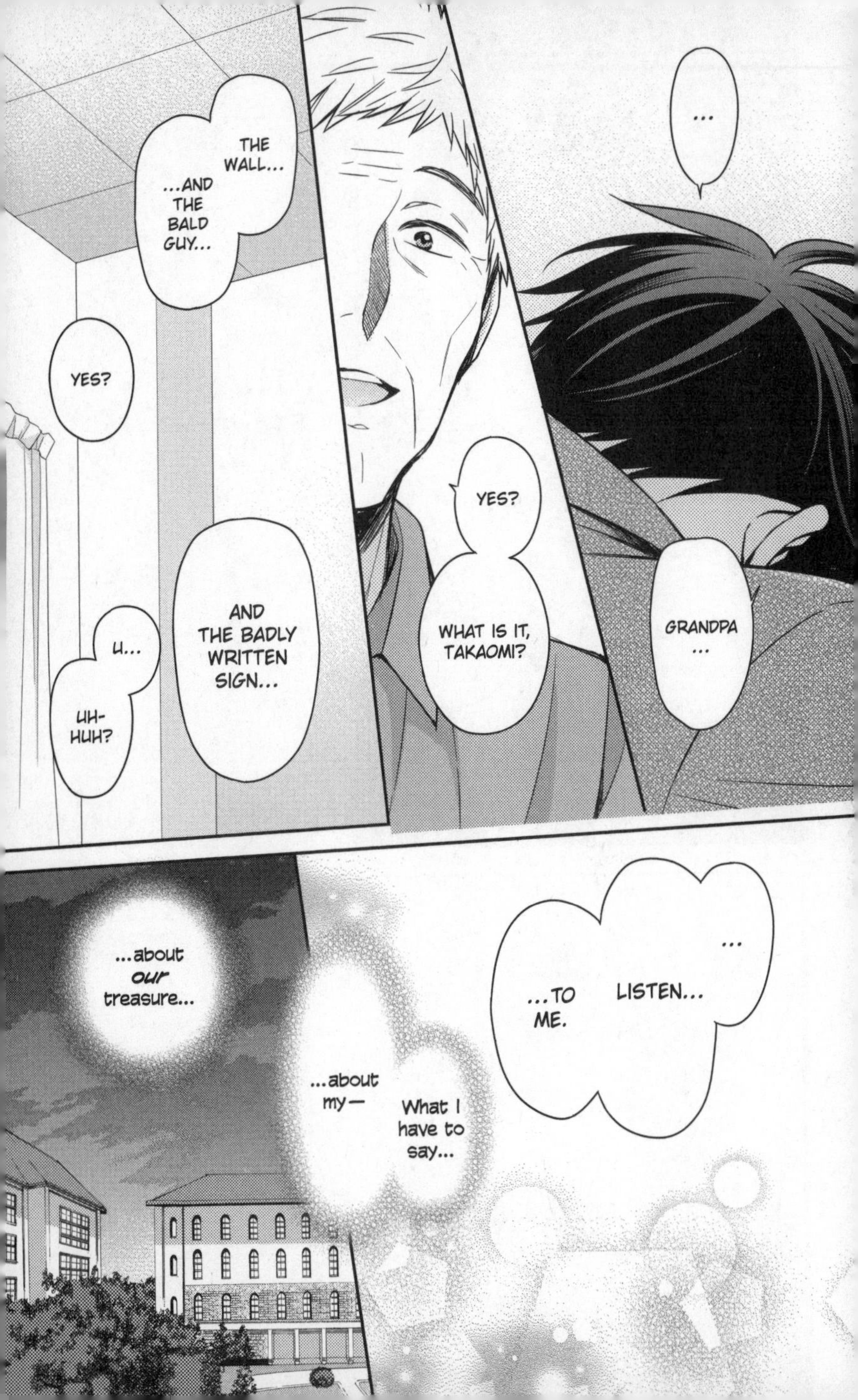
...
GRANDPA...
YES?
WHAT IS IT, TAKAOMI?
THE WALL... ...AND THE BALD GUY...
YES?
AND THE BADLY WRITTEN SIGN...
U... UH-HUH?
... LISTEN... ...TO ME.
What I have to say...
...about my—
...about *our* treasure...

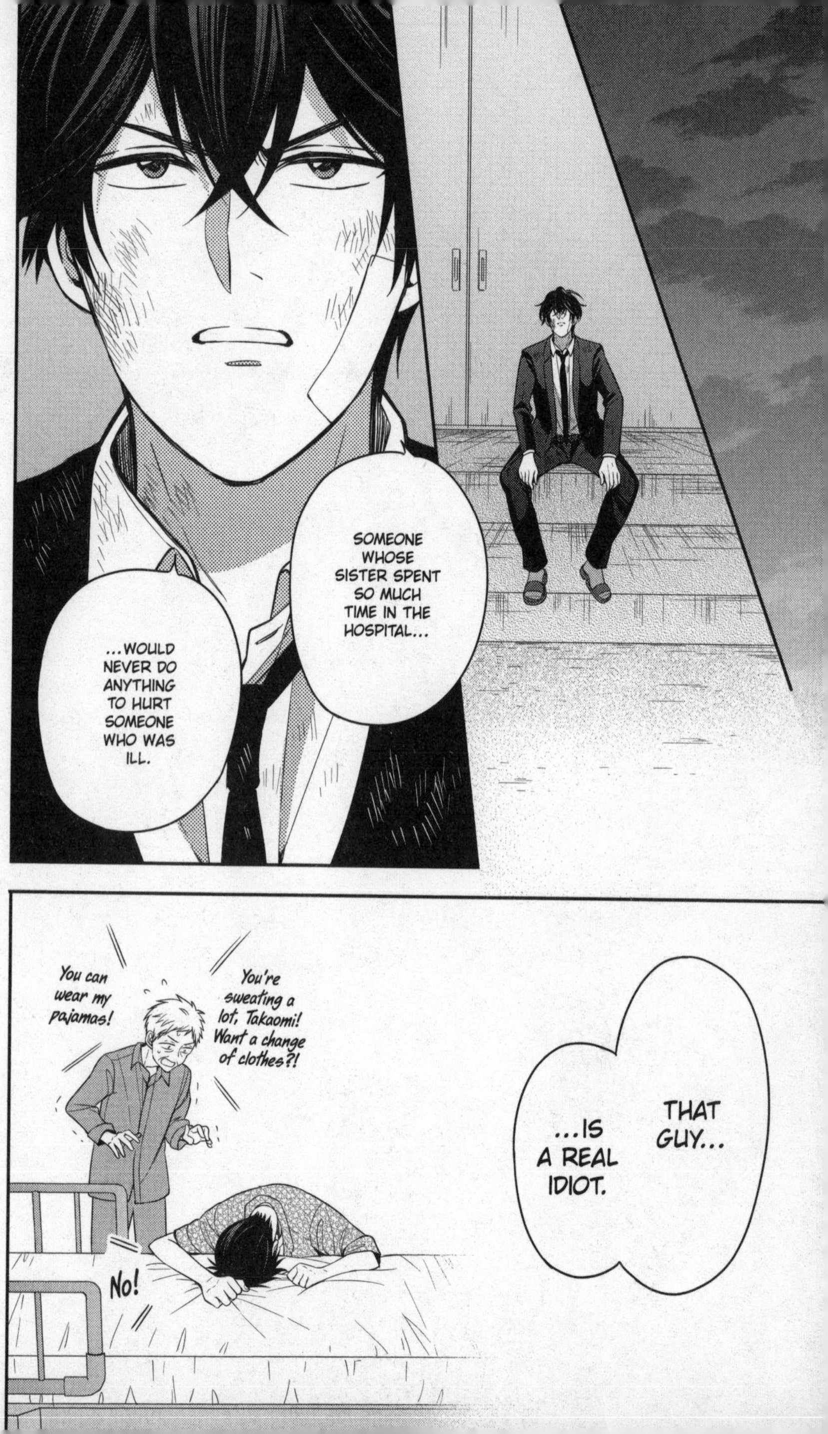
SOMEONE WHOSE SISTER SPENT SO MUCH TIME IN THE HOSPITAL...
...WOULD NEVER DO ANYTHING TO HURT SOMEONE WHO WAS ILL.
THAT GUY...
...IS A REAL IDIOT.
You're sweating a lot, Takaomi! Want a change of clothes?!
You can wear my pajamas!
No!

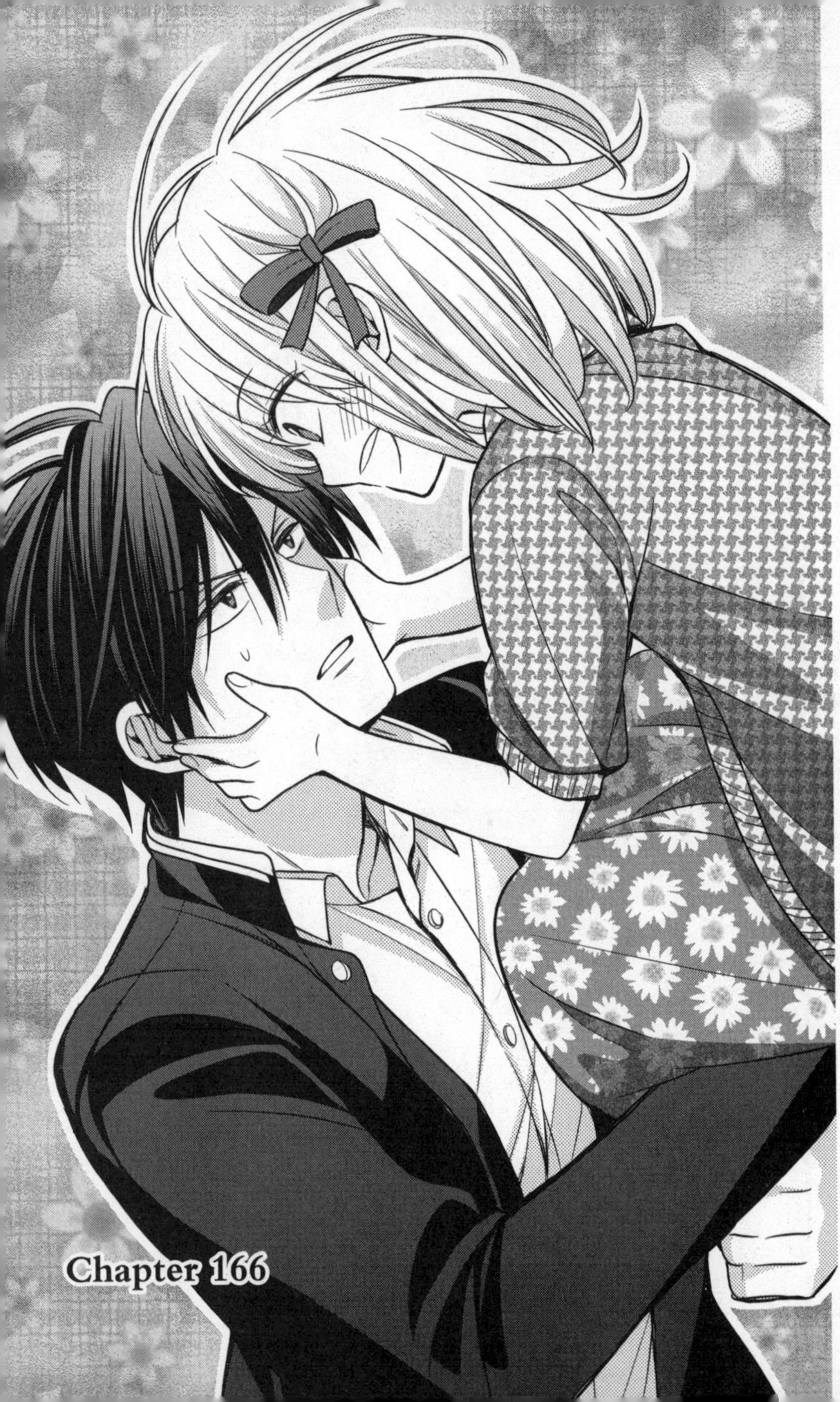
Chapter 166

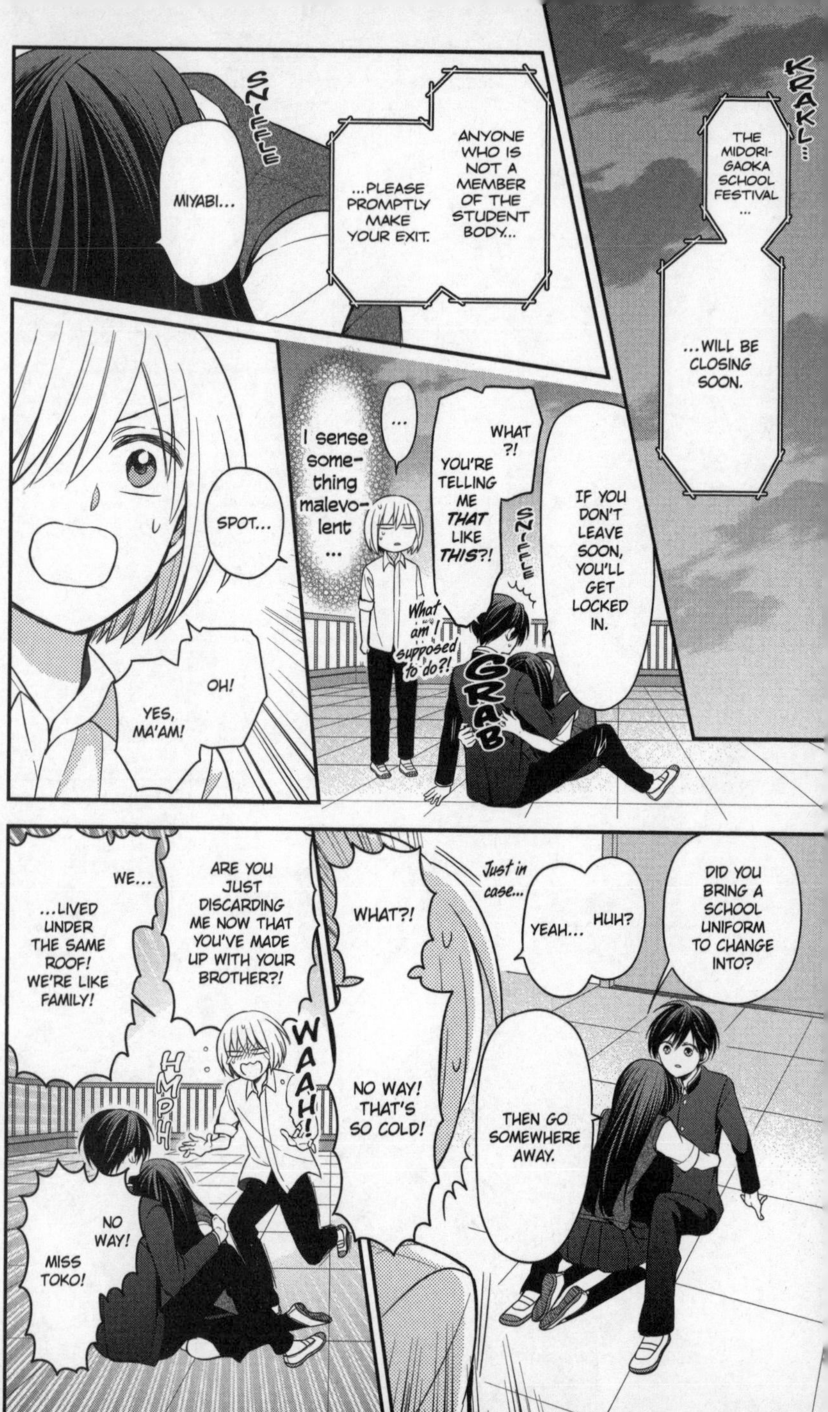
KRAKL...
THE MIDORI-GAOKA SCHOOL FESTIVAL...
...WILL BE CLOSING SOON.
ANYONE WHO IS NOT A MEMBER OF THE STUDENT BODY...
...PLEASE PROMPTLY MAKE YOUR EXIT.
SNIFFLE
MIYABI...
IF YOU DON'T LEAVE SOON, YOU'LL GET LOCKED IN.
SNIFFLE
WHAT?!
YOU'RE TELLING ME THAT LIKE THIS?!
What am I supposed to do?!
GRAB
...
I sense something malevolent...
SPOT...
OH!
YES, MA'AM!
DID YOU BRING A SCHOOL UNIFORM TO CHANGE INTO?
HUH?
YEAH...
Just in case...
THEN GO SOMEWHERE AWAY.
WHAT?!
NO WAY! THAT'S SO COLD!
ARE YOU JUST DISCARDING ME NOW THAT YOU'VE MADE UP WITH YOUR BROTHER?!
WAAAH!
WE...
...LIVED UNDER THE SAME ROOF! WE'RE LIKE FAMILY!
HMPH
NO WAY!
MISS TOKO!

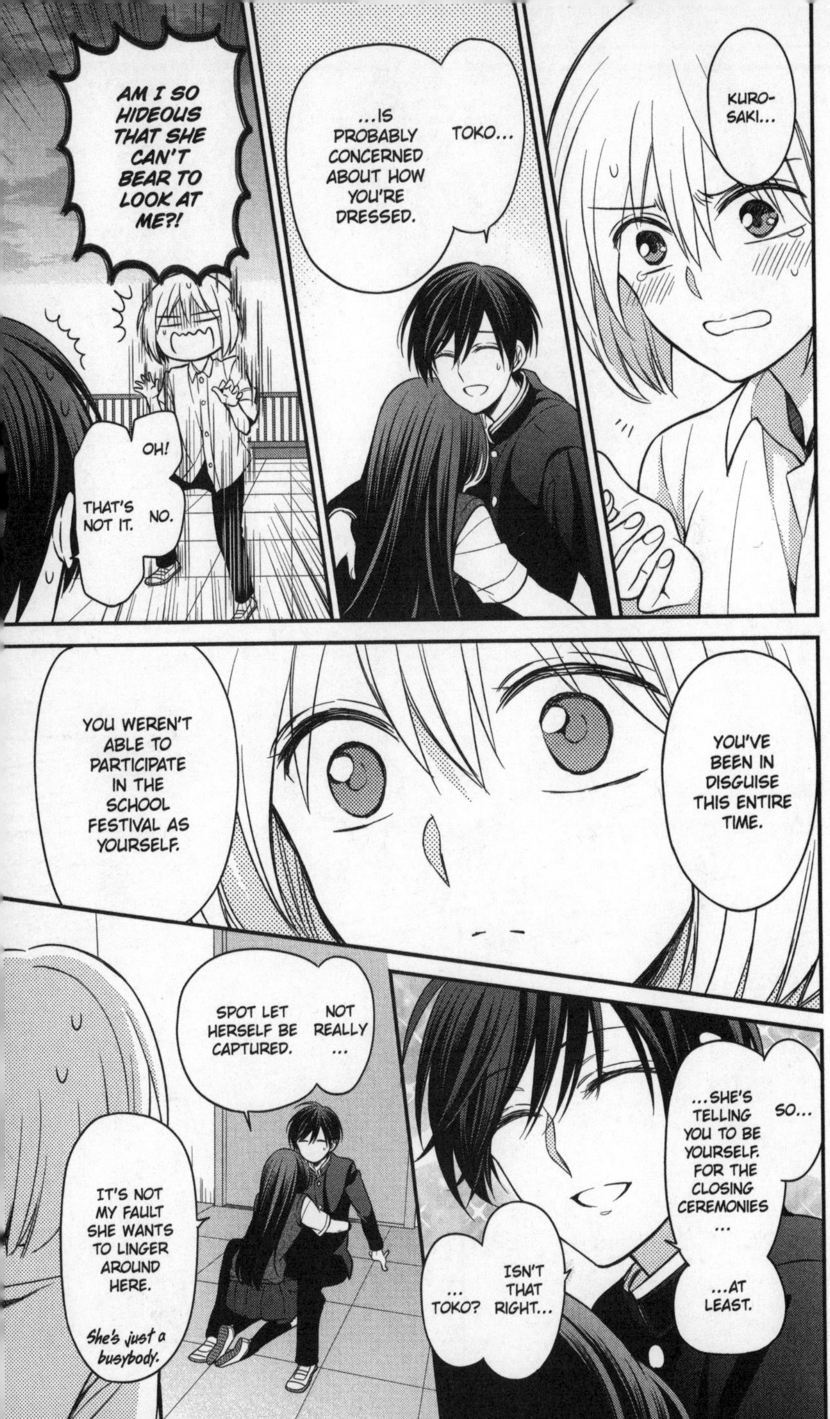
KURO-SAKI...
TOKO...
...IS PROBABLY CONCERNED ABOUT HOW YOU'RE DRESSED.
AM I SO HIDEOUS THAT SHE CAN'T BEAR TO LOOK AT ME?!
OH!
NO.
THAT'S NOT IT.
YOU'VE BEEN IN DISGUISE THIS ENTIRE TIME.
YOU WEREN'T ABLE TO PARTICIPATE IN THE SCHOOL FESTIVAL AS YOURSELF.
SO...
...SHE'S TELLING YOU TO BE YOURSELF. FOR THE CLOSING CEREMONIES...
...AT LEAST.
ISN'T THAT RIGHT...
...TOKO?
NOT REALLY...
SPOT LET HERSELF BE CAPTURED.
IT'S NOT MY FAULT SHE WANTS TO LINGER AROUND HERE.
She's just a busybody.

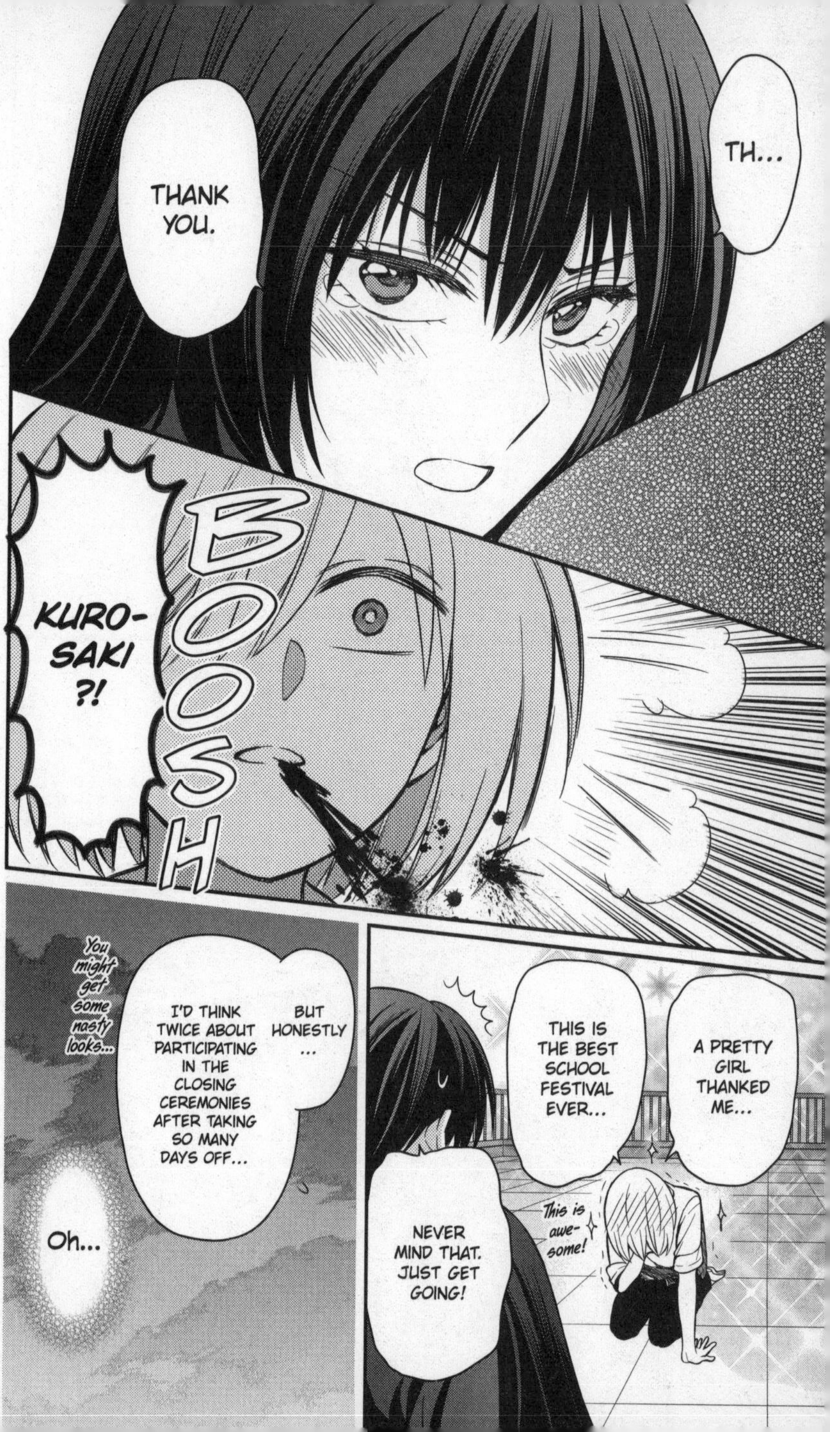
TH...
THANK YOU.
KURO-SAKI?!
BOOSH
A PRETTY GIRL THANKED ME...
THIS IS THE BEST SCHOOL FESTIVAL EVER...
This is awe-some!
NEVER MIND THAT. JUST GET GOING!
BUT HONESTLY...
I'D THINK TWICE ABOUT PARTICIPATING IN THE CLOSING CEREMONIES AFTER TAKING SO MANY DAYS OFF...
You might get some nasty looks...
Oh...

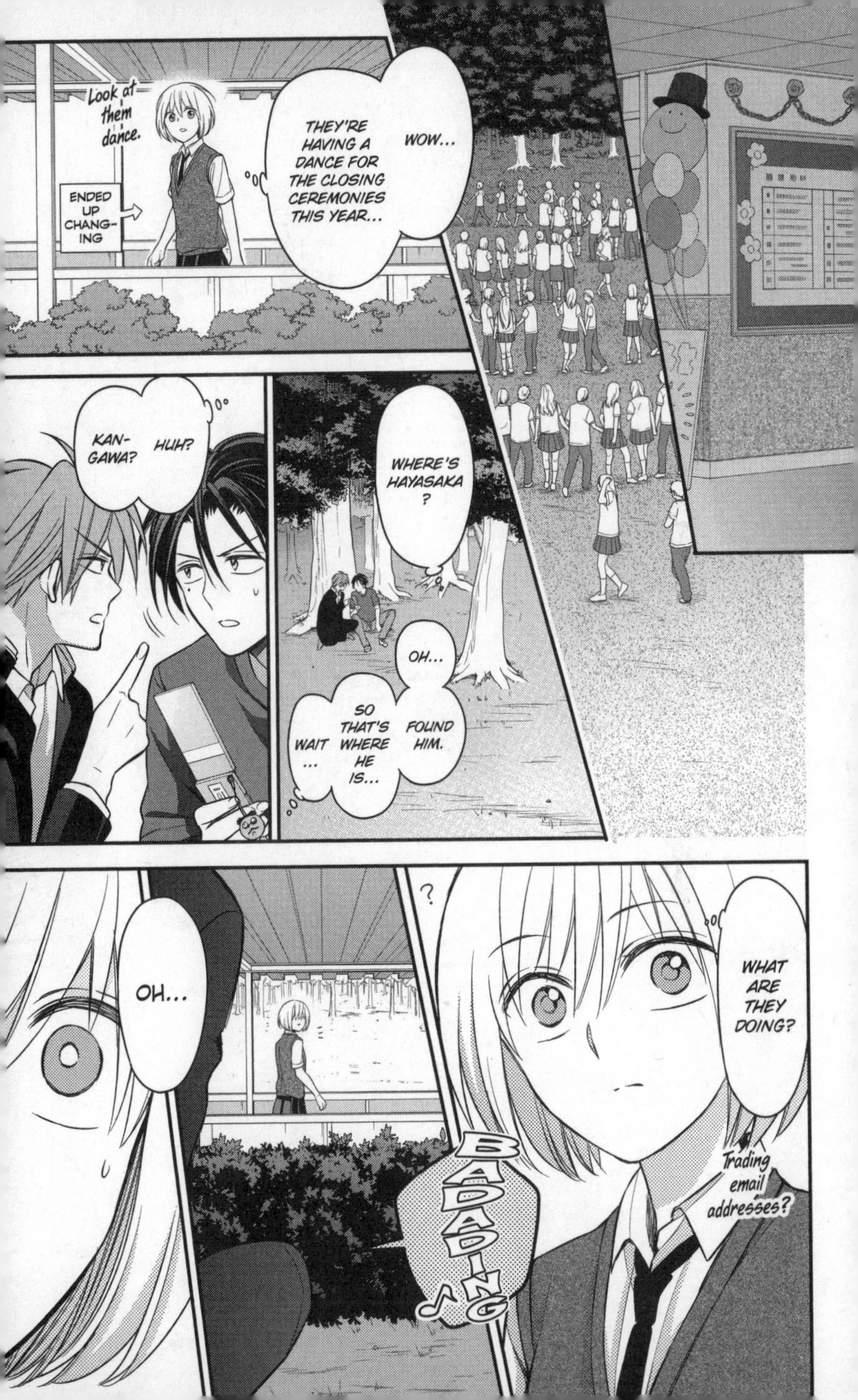
WOW... THEY'RE HAVING A DANCE FOR THE CLOSING CEREMONIES THIS YEAR...
Look at them dance.
ENDED UP CHANGING
WHERE'S HAYASAKA?
OH... FOUND HIM.
SO THAT'S WHERE HE IS... WAIT...
HUH? KANGAWA?
?
WHAT ARE THEY DOING?
Trading email addresses?
BADADING♪
OH...

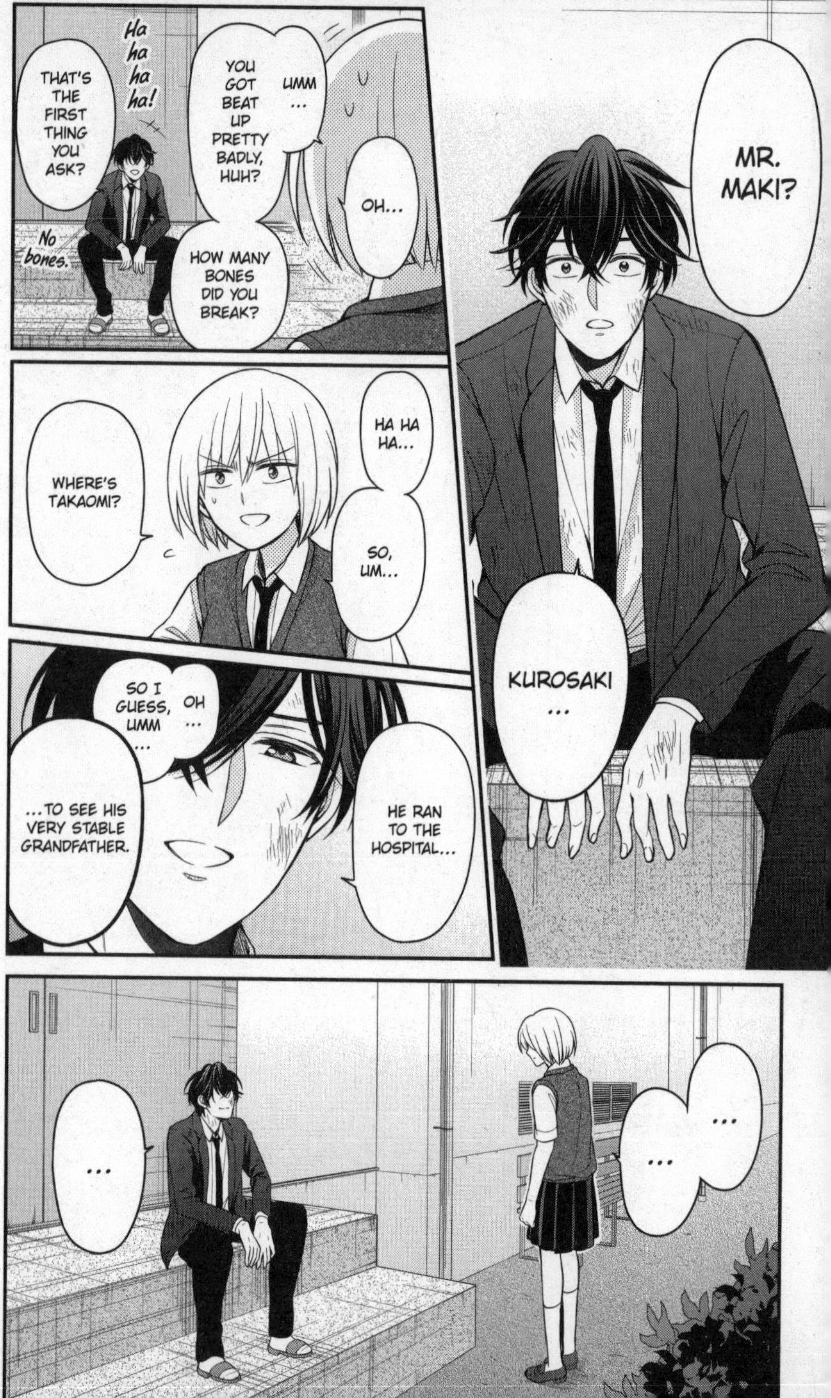
MR. MAKI?
KUROSAKI ...
UMM ...
OH...
YOU GOT BEAT UP PRETTY BADLY, HUH?
HOW MANY BONES DID YOU BREAK?
Ha ha ha ha!
THAT'S THE FIRST THING YOU ASK?
No bones.
HA HA HA...
SO, UM...
WHERE'S TAKAOMI?
OH ...
SO I GUESS, UMM ...
HE RAN TO THE HOSPITAL...
...TO SEE HIS VERY STABLE GRANDFATHER.
... ...
...

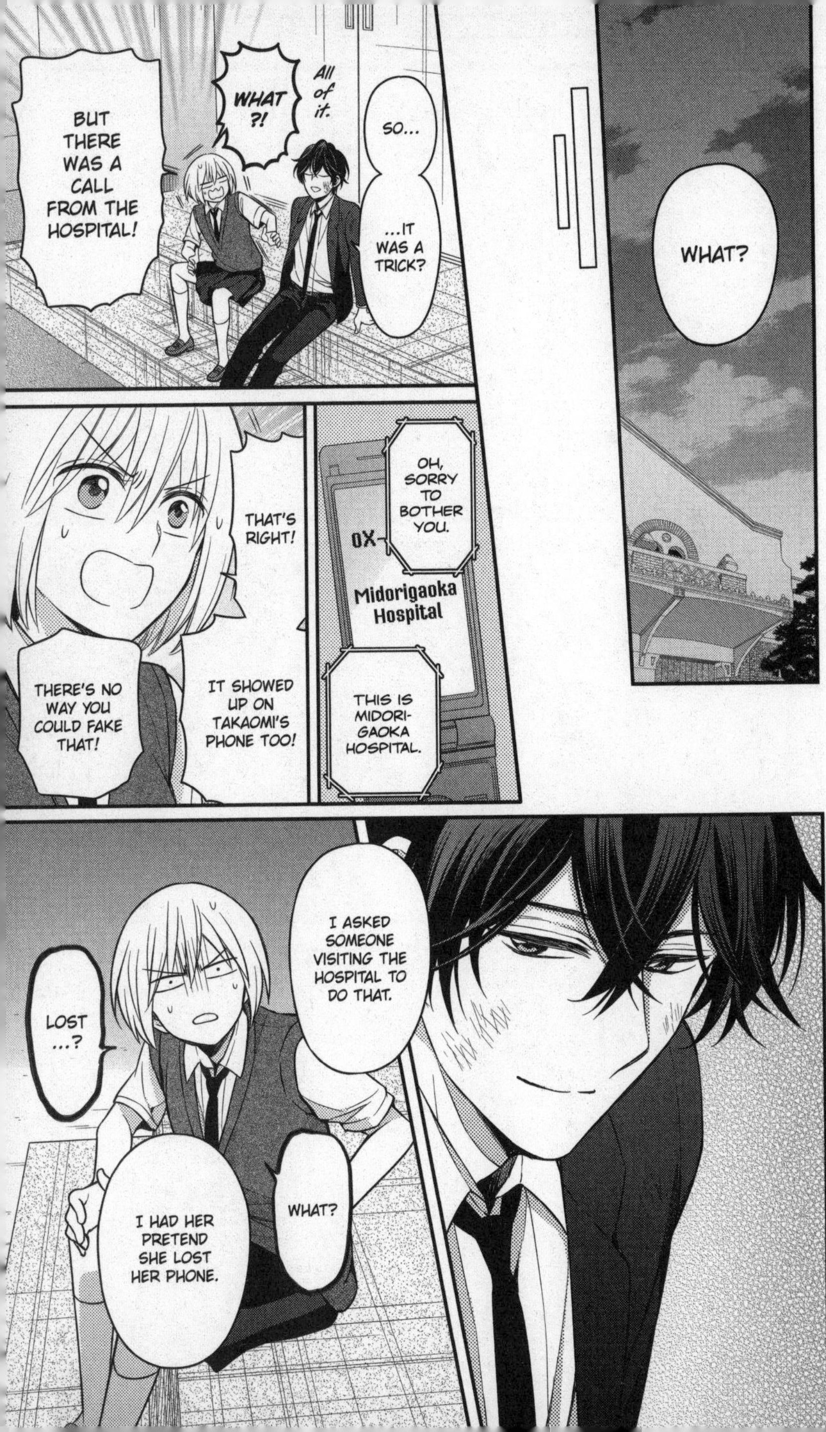
WHAT?
SO...
...IT WAS A TRICK?
All of it.
WHAT ?!
BUT THERE WAS A CALL FROM THE HOSPITAL!
OH, SORRY TO BOTHER YOU.
0X-
Midorigaoka Hospital
THIS IS MIDORI-GAOKA HOSPITAL.
THAT'S RIGHT!
IT SHOWED UP ON TAKAOMI'S PHONE TOO!
THERE'S NO WAY YOU COULD FAKE THAT!
I ASKED SOMEONE VISITING THE HOSPITAL TO DO THAT.
WHAT?
I HAD HER PRETEND SHE LOST HER PHONE.
LOST ...?

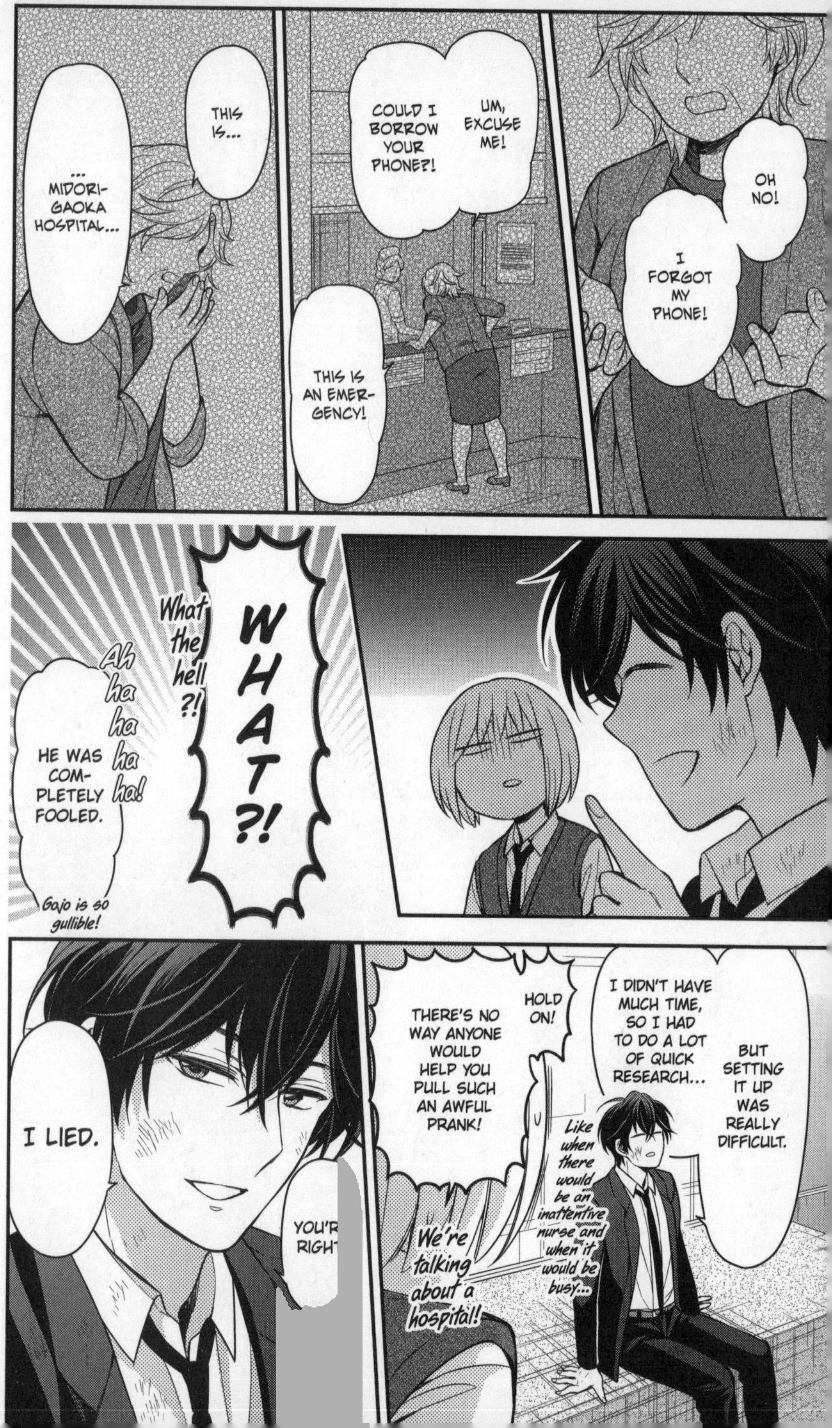
OH NO!
I FORGOT MY PHONE!
UM, EXCUSE ME!
COULD I BORROW YOUR PHONE?!
THIS IS AN EMERGENCY!
THIS IS...
...MIDORI-GAOKA HOSPITAL...
WHAT?!
What the hell?!
Ah ha ha ha ha ha!
HE WAS COMPLETELY FOOLED.
Gojo is so gullible!
I DIDN'T HAVE MUCH TIME, SO I HAD TO DO A LOT OF QUICK RESEARCH...
BUT SETTING IT UP WAS REALLY DIFFICULT.
Like when there would be an inattentive nurse and when it would be busy...
HOLD ON!
THERE'S NO WAY ANYONE WOULD HELP YOU PULL SUCH AN AWFUL PRANK!
We're talking about a hospital!
YOU'R RIGHT
I LIED.

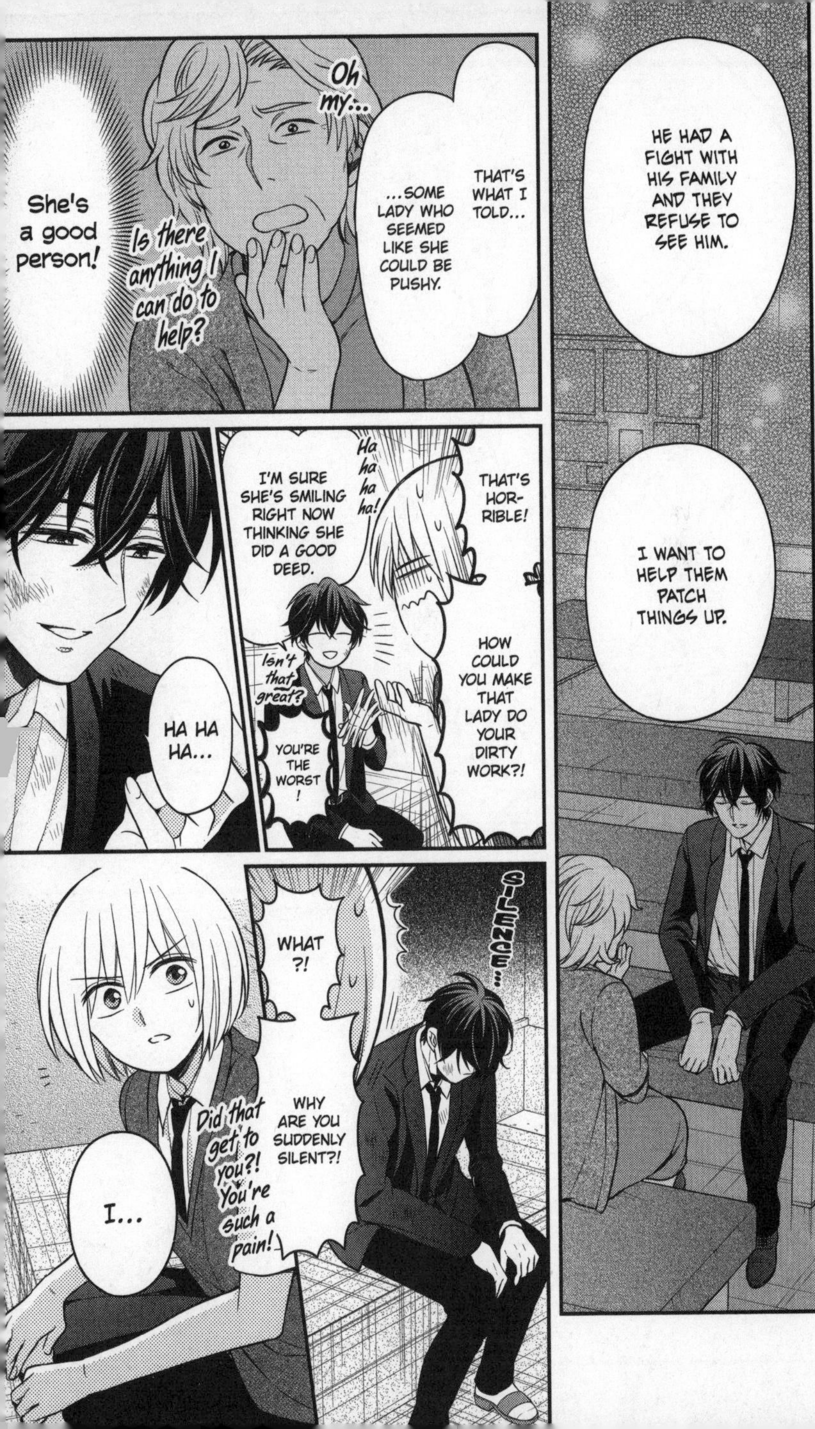
HE HAD A FIGHT WITH HIS FAMILY AND THEY REFUSE TO SEE HIM.
I WANT TO HELP THEM PATCH THINGS UP.
Oh my...
THAT'S WHAT I TOLD...
...SOME LADY WHO SEEMED LIKE SHE COULD BE PUSHY.
Is there anything I can do to help?
She's a good person!
THAT'S HOR-RIBLE!
Ha ha ha ha!
I'M SURE SHE'S SMILING RIGHT NOW THINKING SHE DID A GOOD DEED.
HOW COULD YOU MAKE THAT LADY DO YOUR DIRTY WORK?!
Isn't that great?
YOU'RE THE WORST!
HA HA HA...
SILENCE...
WHAT?!
WHY ARE YOU SUDDENLY SILENT?!
Did that get to you?! You're such a pain!
I...

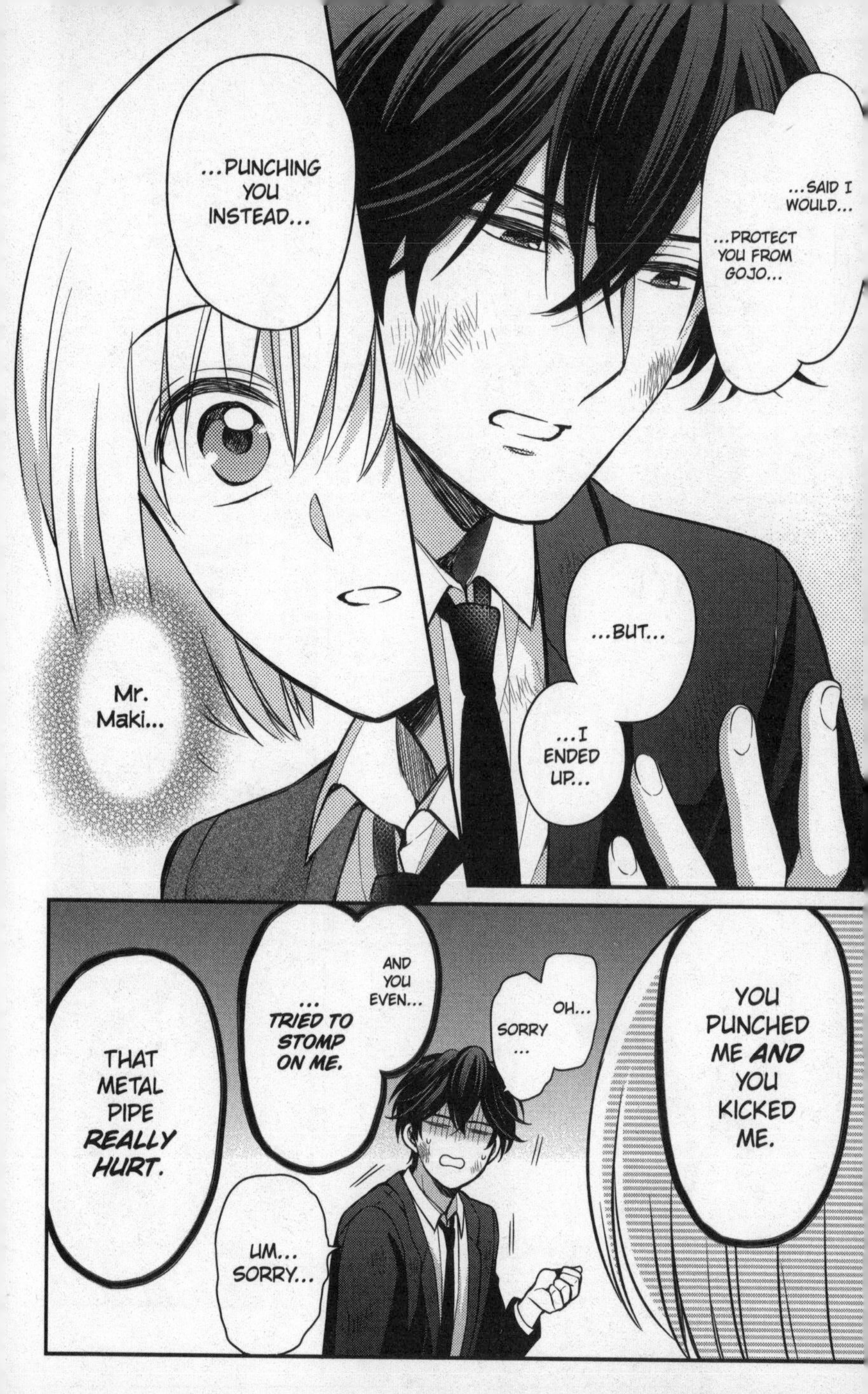
...SAID I WOULD...
...PROTECT YOU FROM GOJO...
...BUT...
...I ENDED UP...
...PUNCHING YOU INSTEAD...
Mr. Maki...
YOU PUNCHED ME AND YOU KICKED ME.
OH... SORRY...
AND YOU EVEN... ...TRIED TO STOMP ON ME.
THAT METAL PIPE REALLY HURT.
UM... SORRY...

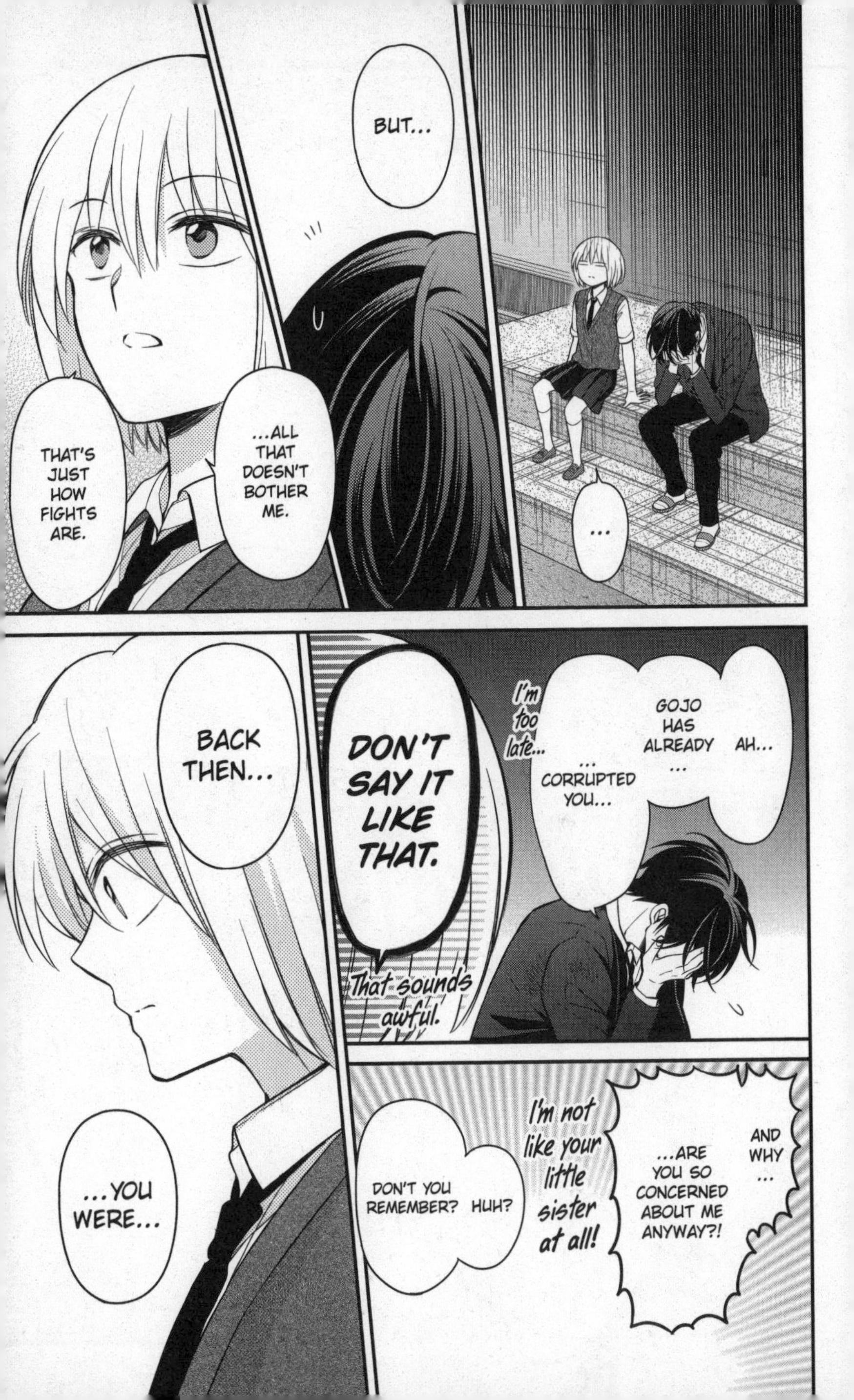
...
BUT...
...ALL THAT DOESN'T BOTHER ME.
THAT'S JUST HOW FIGHTS ARE.
AH...
GOJO HAS ALREADY ... ... CORRUPTED YOU...
I'm too late...
DON'T SAY IT LIKE THAT.
That sounds awful.
AND WHY ...
...ARE YOU SO CONCERNED ABOUT ME ANYWAY?!
I'm not like your little sister at all!
DON'T YOU REMEMBER? HUH?
BACK THEN...
...YOU WERE...

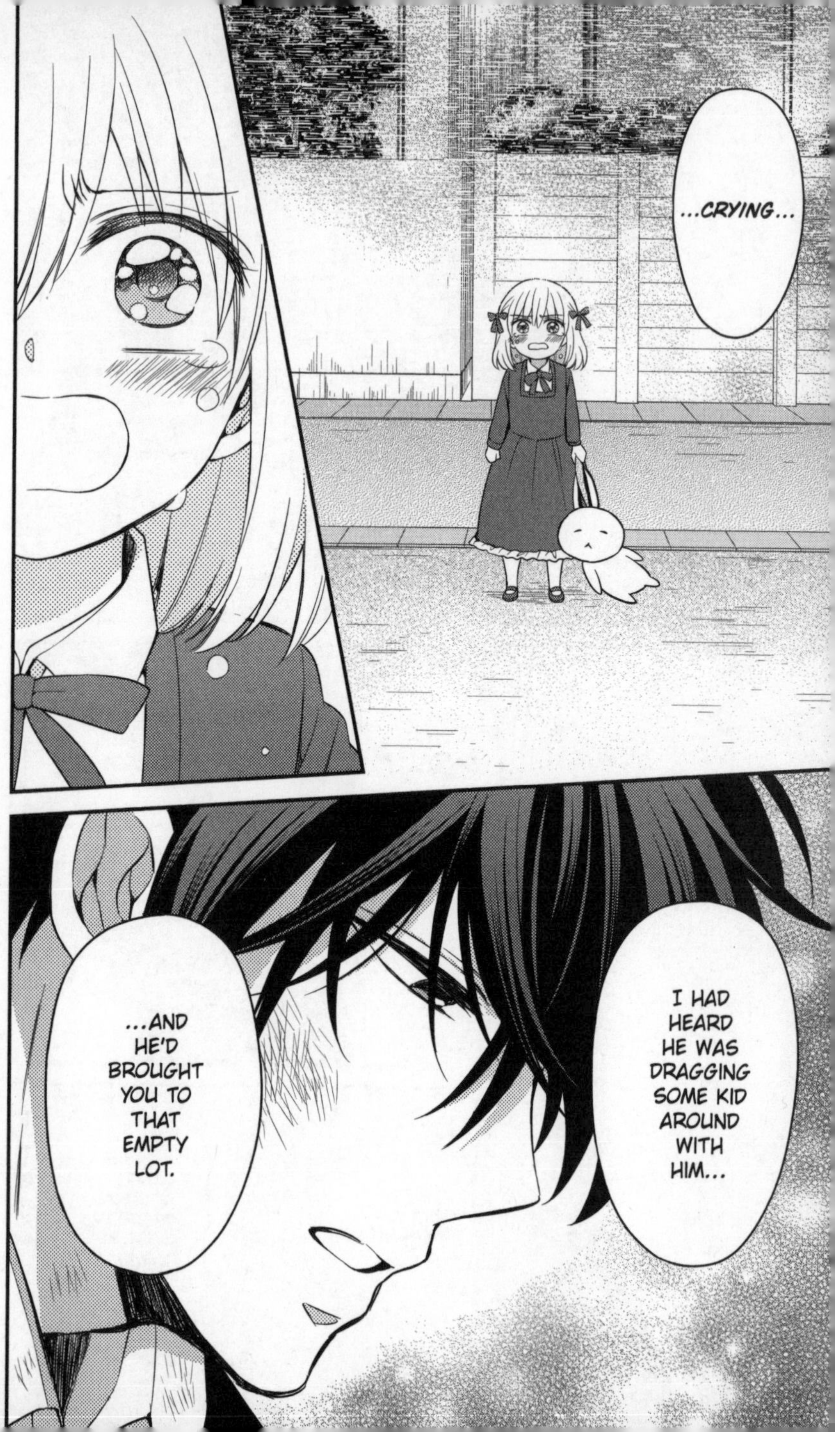
...CRYING...
I HAD HEARD HE WAS DRAGGING SOME KID AROUND WITH HIM...
...AND HE'D BROUGHT YOU TO THAT EMPTY LOT.

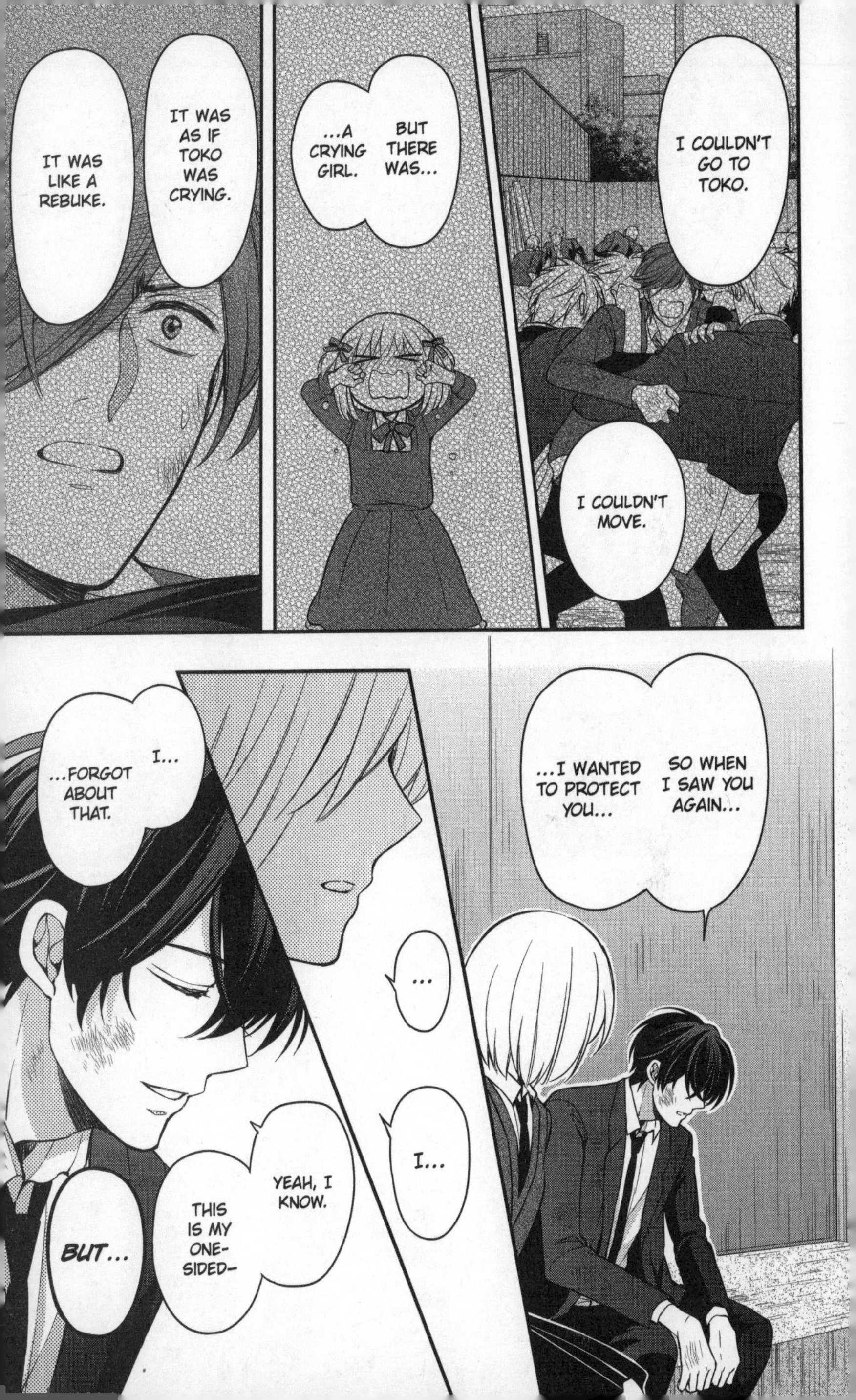
I COULDN'T GO TO TOKO.
I COULDN'T MOVE.
BUT THERE WAS...
...A CRYING GIRL.
IT WAS AS IF TOKO WAS CRYING.
IT WAS LIKE A REBUKE.
SO WHEN I SAW YOU AGAIN...
...I WANTED TO PROTECT YOU...
...
I...
I...
...FORGOT ABOUT THAT.
YEAH, I KNOW.
THIS IS MY ONE-SIDED-
BUT...

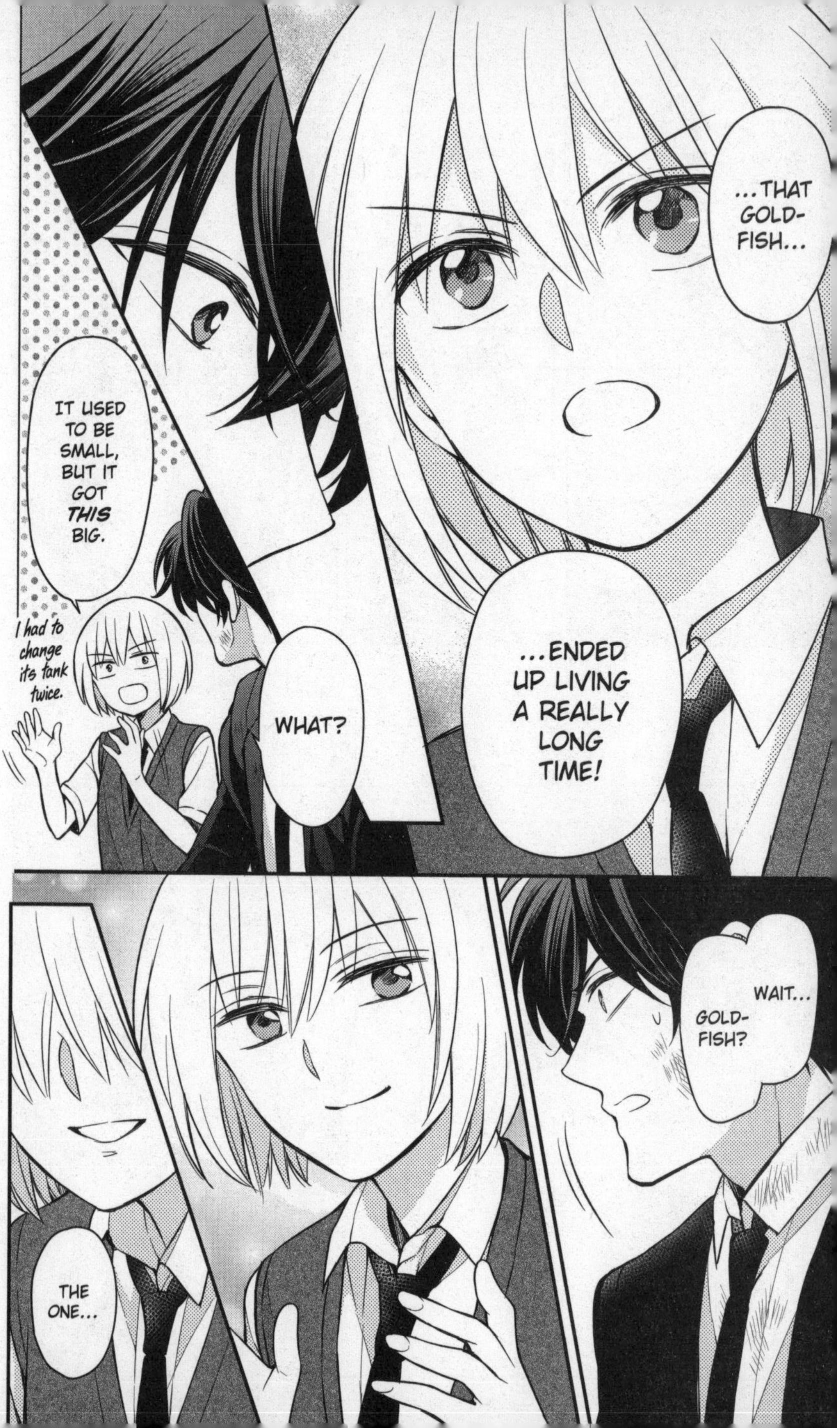
...THAT GOLDFISH...
...ENDED UP LIVING A REALLY LONG TIME!
WHAT?
IT USED TO BE SMALL, BUT IT GOT **THIS** BIG.
I had to change its tank twice.
WAIT... GOLDFISH?
THE ONE...

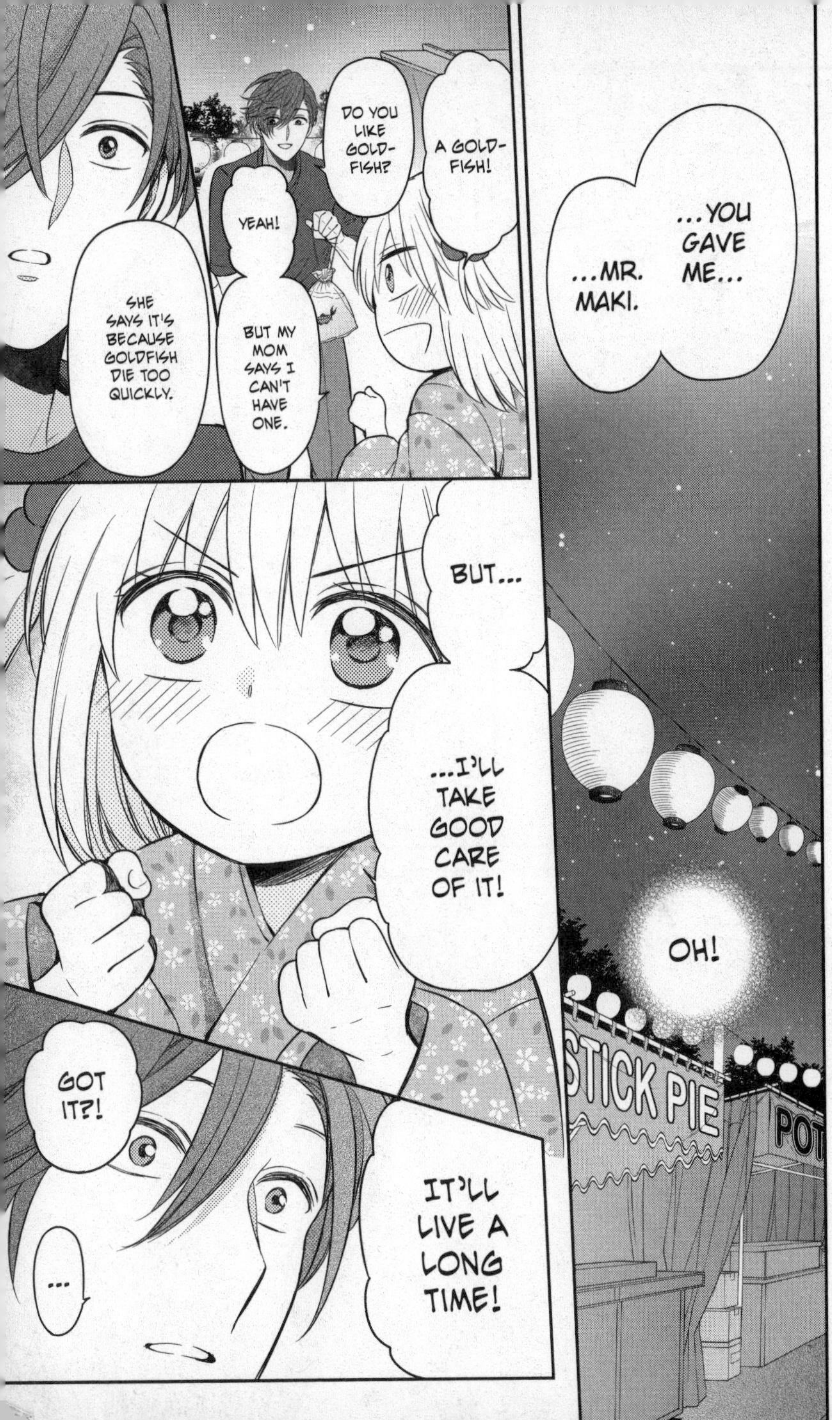
...YOU GAVE ME...
...MR. MAKI.
OH!
STICK PIE
POT
A GOLD-FISH!
DO YOU LIKE GOLD-FISH?
YEAH!
BUT MY MOM SAYS I CAN'T HAVE ONE.
SHE SAYS IT'S BECAUSE GOLDFISH DIE TOO QUICKLY.
BUT...
...I'LL TAKE GOOD CARE OF IT!
IT'LL LIVE A LONG TIME!
GOT IT?!
...

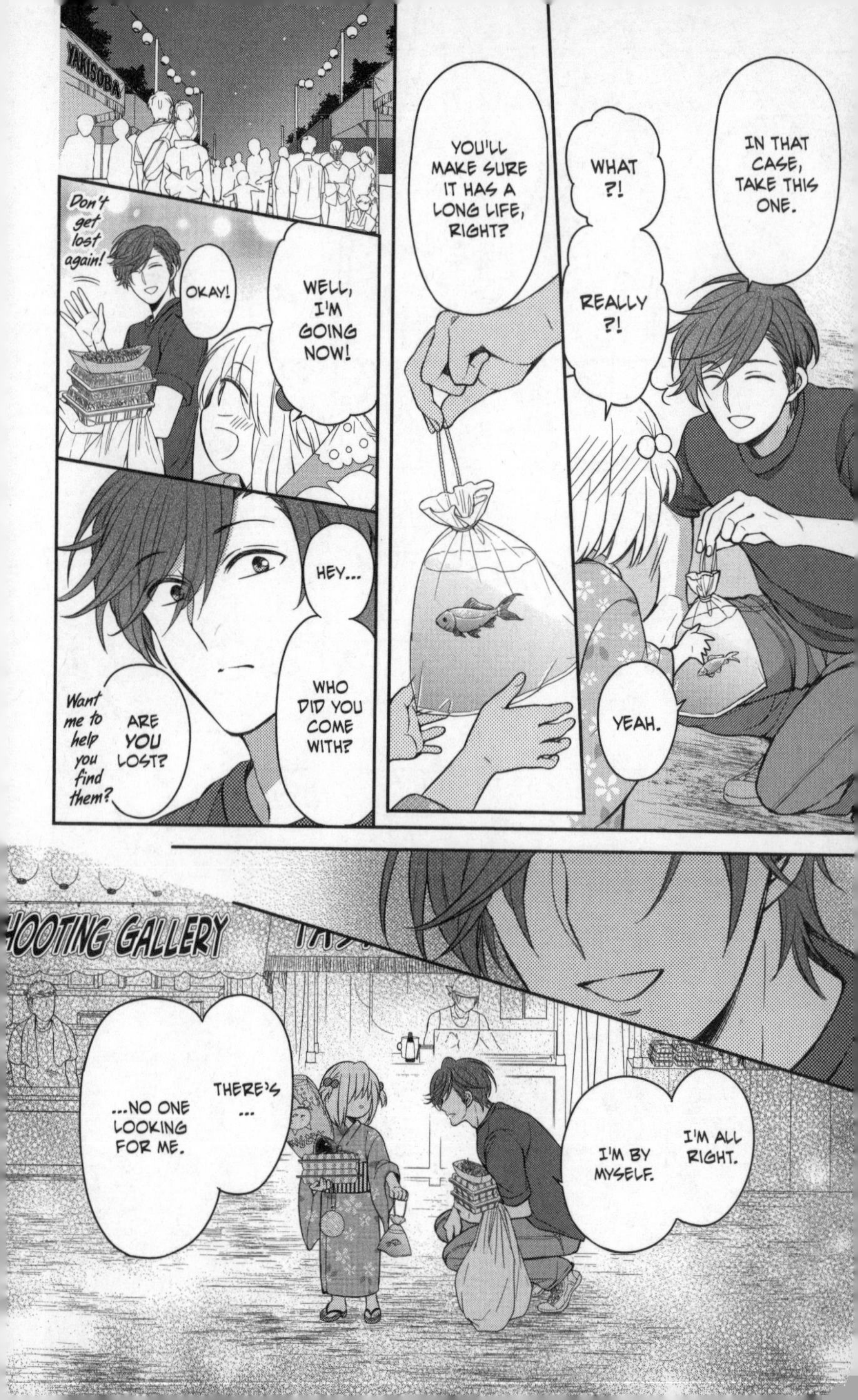
IN THAT CASE, TAKE THIS ONE.
WHAT?!
REALLY?!
YEAH.
YOU'LL MAKE SURE IT HAS A LONG LIFE, RIGHT?
YAKISOBA
WELL, I'M GOING NOW!
OKAY!
Don't get lost again!
HEY...
WHO DID YOU COME WITH?
ARE YOU LOST?
Want me to help you find them?
I'M ALL RIGHT.
I'M BY MYSELF.
HOOTING GALLERY
THERE'S...
...NO ONE LOOKING FOR ME.

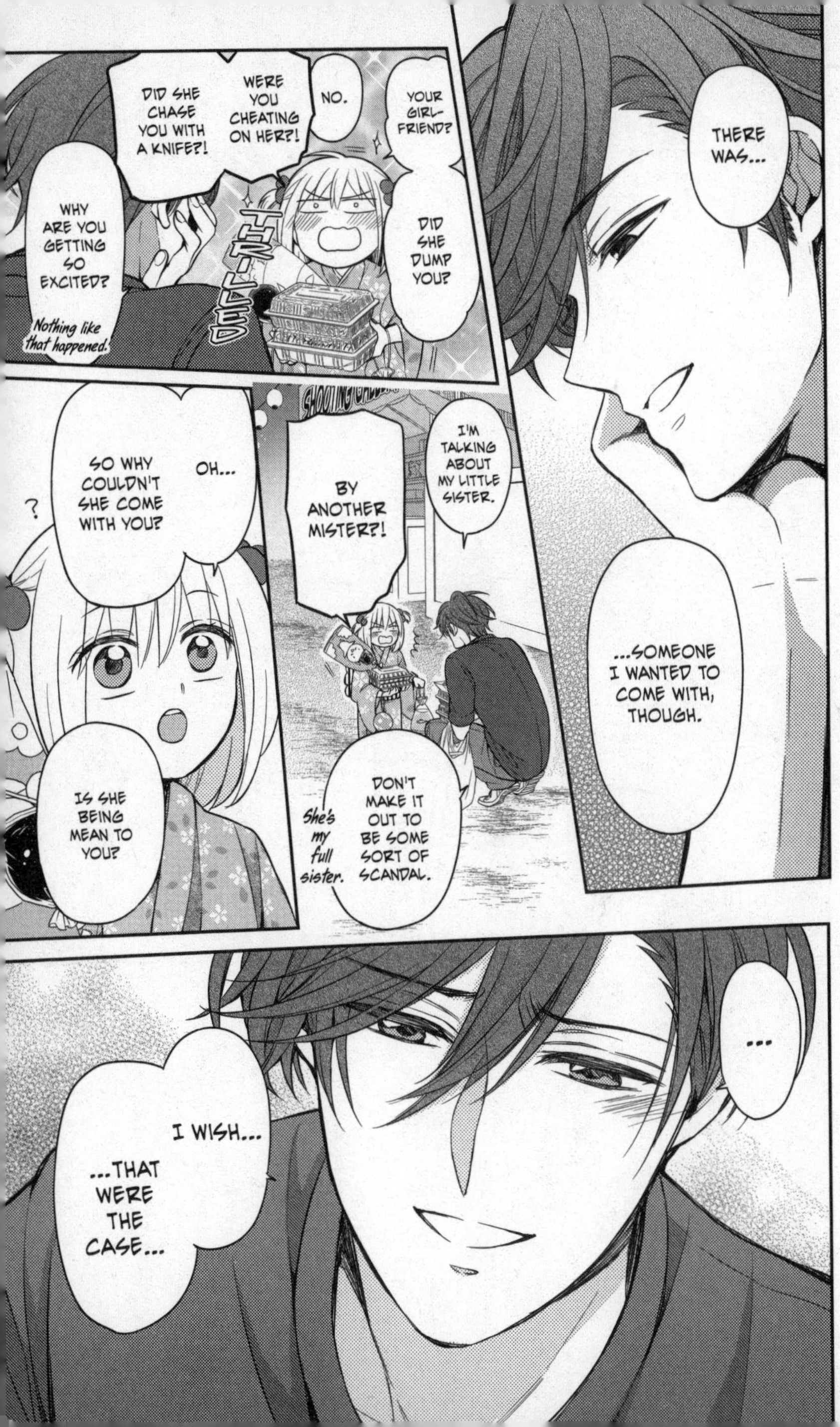
THERE WAS...
...SOMEONE I WANTED TO COME WITH, THOUGH.
YOUR GIRLFRIEND?
NO.
WERE YOU CHEATING ON HER?!
DID SHE CHASE YOU WITH A KNIFE?!
DID SHE DUMP YOU?
THRILLED
WHY ARE YOU GETTING SO EXCITED?
Nothing like that happened!
I'M TALKING ABOUT MY LITTLE SISTER.
BY ANOTHER MISTER?!
DON'T MAKE IT OUT TO BE SOME SORT OF SCANDAL.
She's my full sister.
OH...
SO WHY COULDN'T SHE COME WITH YOU?
?
IS SHE BEING MEAN TO YOU?
...
I WISH...
...THAT WERE THE CASE...

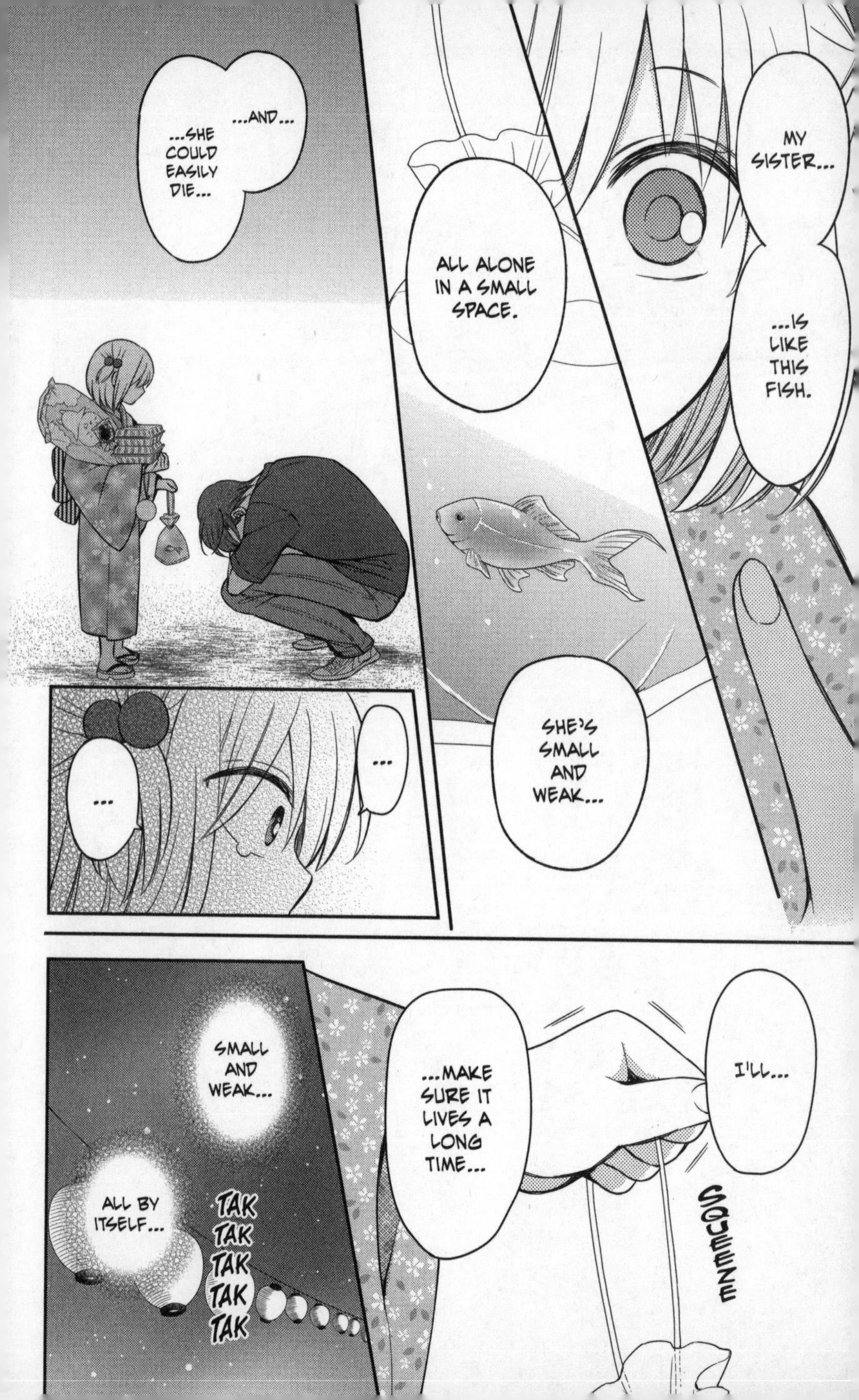
MY SISTER...
...IS LIKE THIS FISH.
ALL ALONE IN A SMALL SPACE.
SHE'S SMALL AND WEAK...
...AND...
...SHE COULD EASILY DIE...
...
...
I'LL...
...MAKE SURE IT LIVES A LONG TIME...
SQUEEZE
SMALL AND WEAK...
ALL BY ITSELF...
TAK TAK TAK TAK TAK

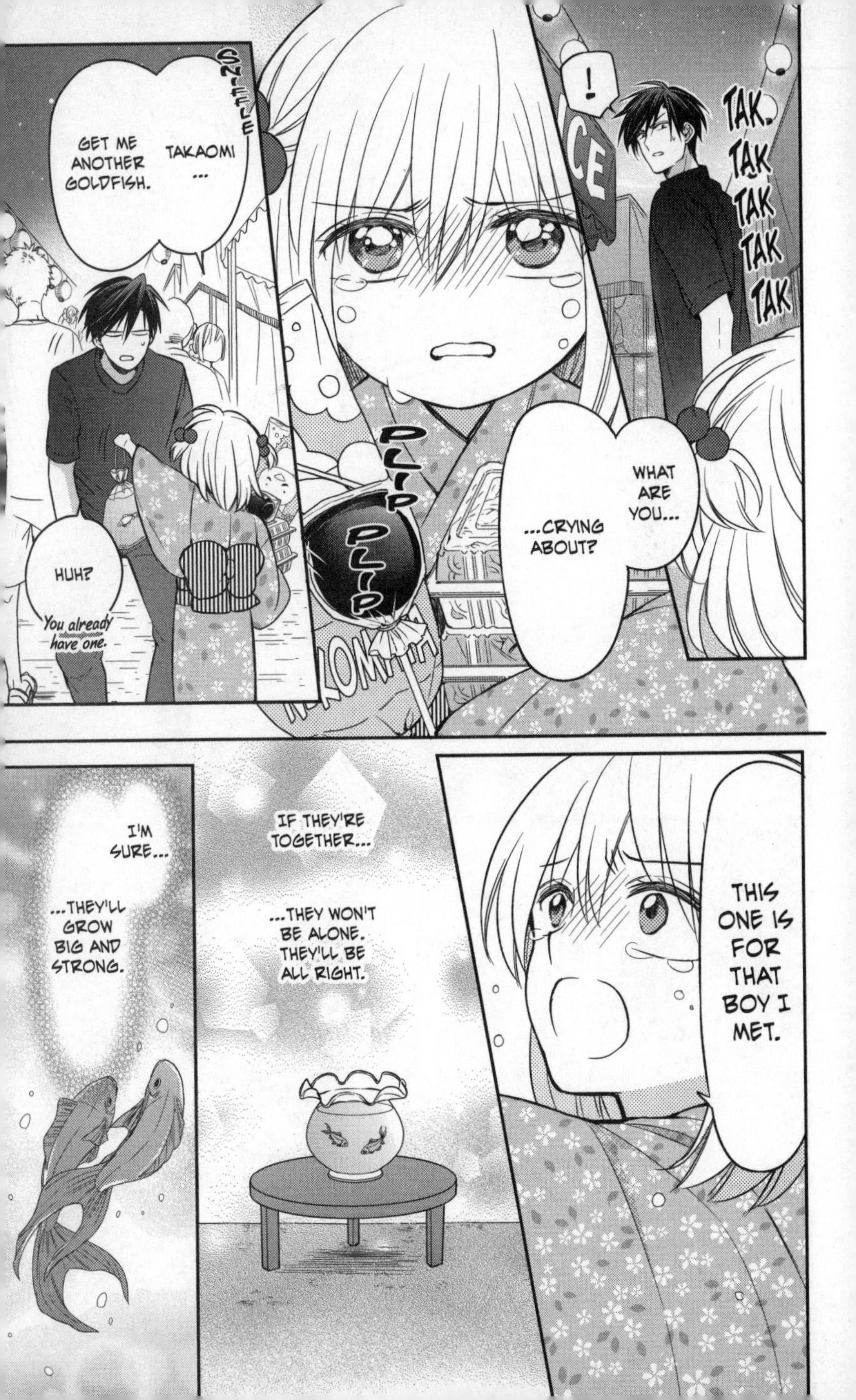
!
ICE
TAK. TAK TAK TAK TAK
WHAT ARE YOU...
...CRYING ABOUT?
SNIFFLE
PLIP PLIP PLIP
TAKAOMI ...
GET ME ANOTHER GOLDFISH.
HUH?
You already have one.
THIS ONE IS FOR THAT BOY I MET.
IF THEY'RE TOGETHER...
...THEY WON'T BE ALONE. THEY'LL BE ALL RIGHT.
I'M SURE...
...THEY'LL GROW BIG AND STRONG.

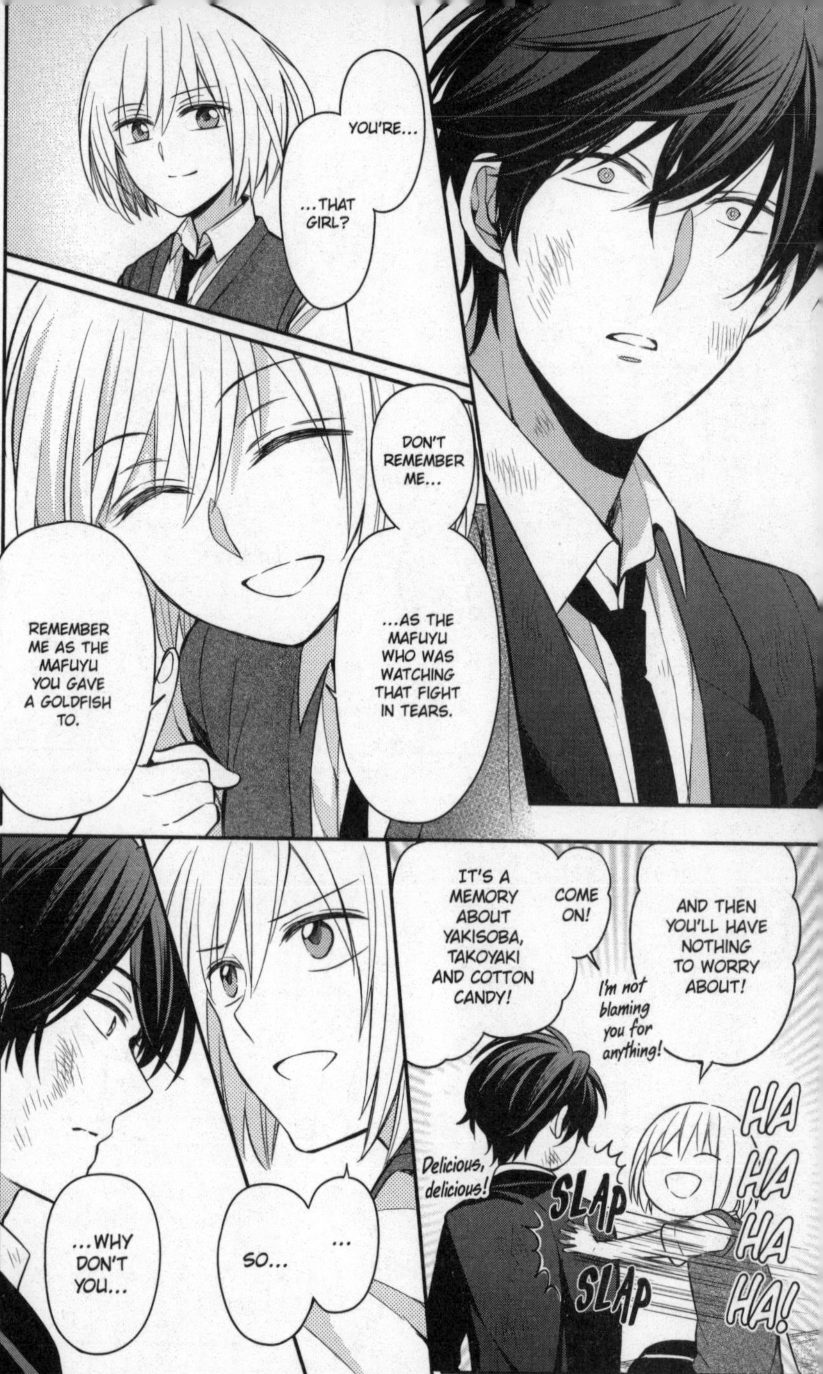
YOU'RE...
...THAT GIRL?
DON'T REMEMBER ME...
...AS THE MAFUYU WHO WAS WATCHING THAT FIGHT IN TEARS.
REMEMBER ME AS THE MAFUYU YOU GAVE A GOLDFISH TO.
AND THEN YOU'LL HAVE NOTHING TO WORRY ABOUT!
I'm not blaming you for anything!
COME ON!
IT'S A MEMORY ABOUT YAKISOBA, TAKOYAKI AND COTTON CANDY!
HA HA HA HA!
SLAP
SLAP
Delicious, delicious!
...
SO...
...WHY DON'T YOU...

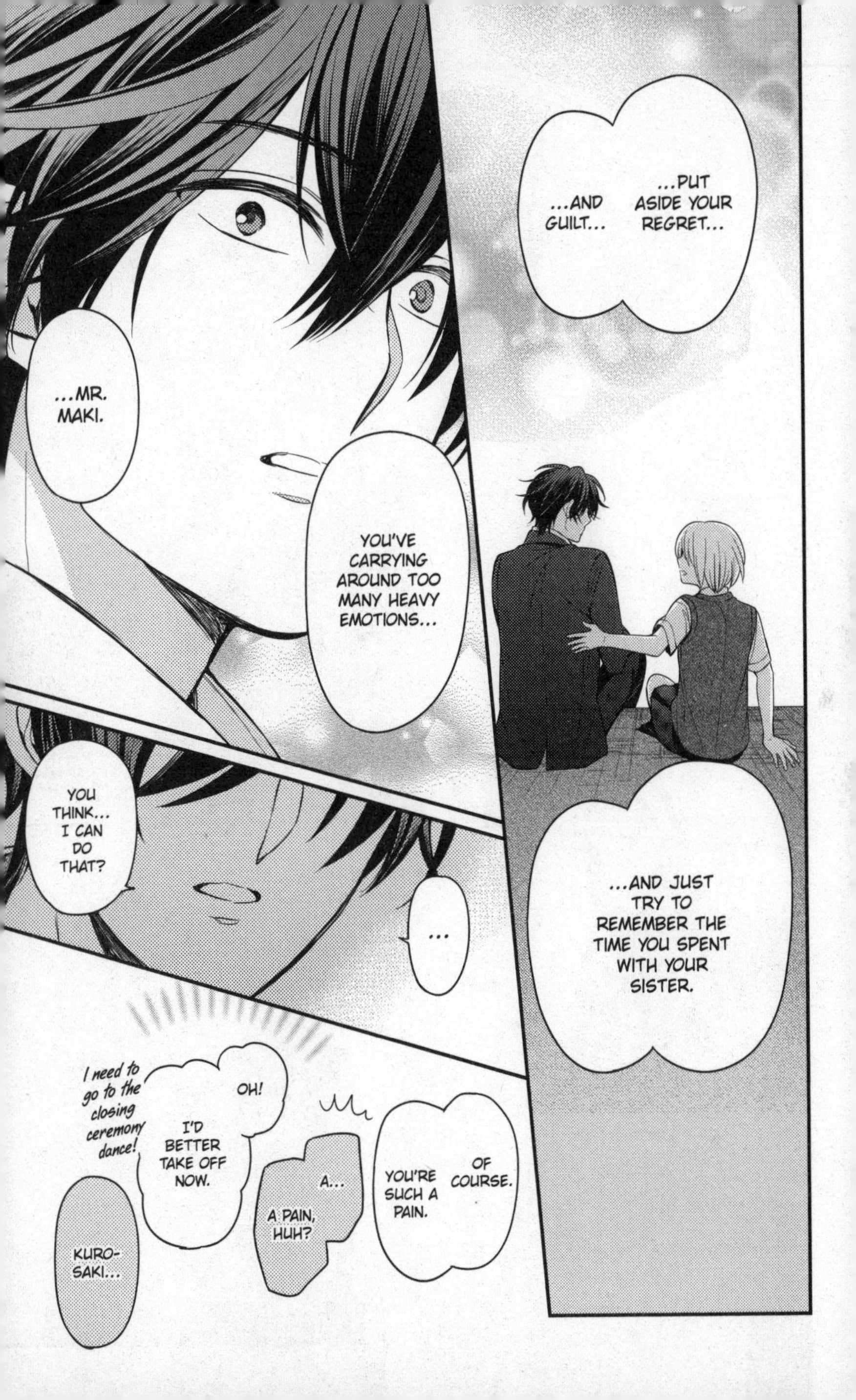
...PUT ASIDE YOUR REGRET...
...AND GUILT...
...AND JUST TRY TO REMEMBER THE TIME YOU SPENT WITH YOUR SISTER.
...MR. MAKI.
YOU'VE CARRYING AROUND TOO MANY HEAVY EMOTIONS...
YOU THINK... I CAN DO THAT?
...
OF COURSE.
YOU'RE SUCH A PAIN.
A...
A PAIN, HUH?
OH!
I'D BETTER TAKE OFF NOW.
I need to go to the closing ceremony dance!
KURO-SAKI...

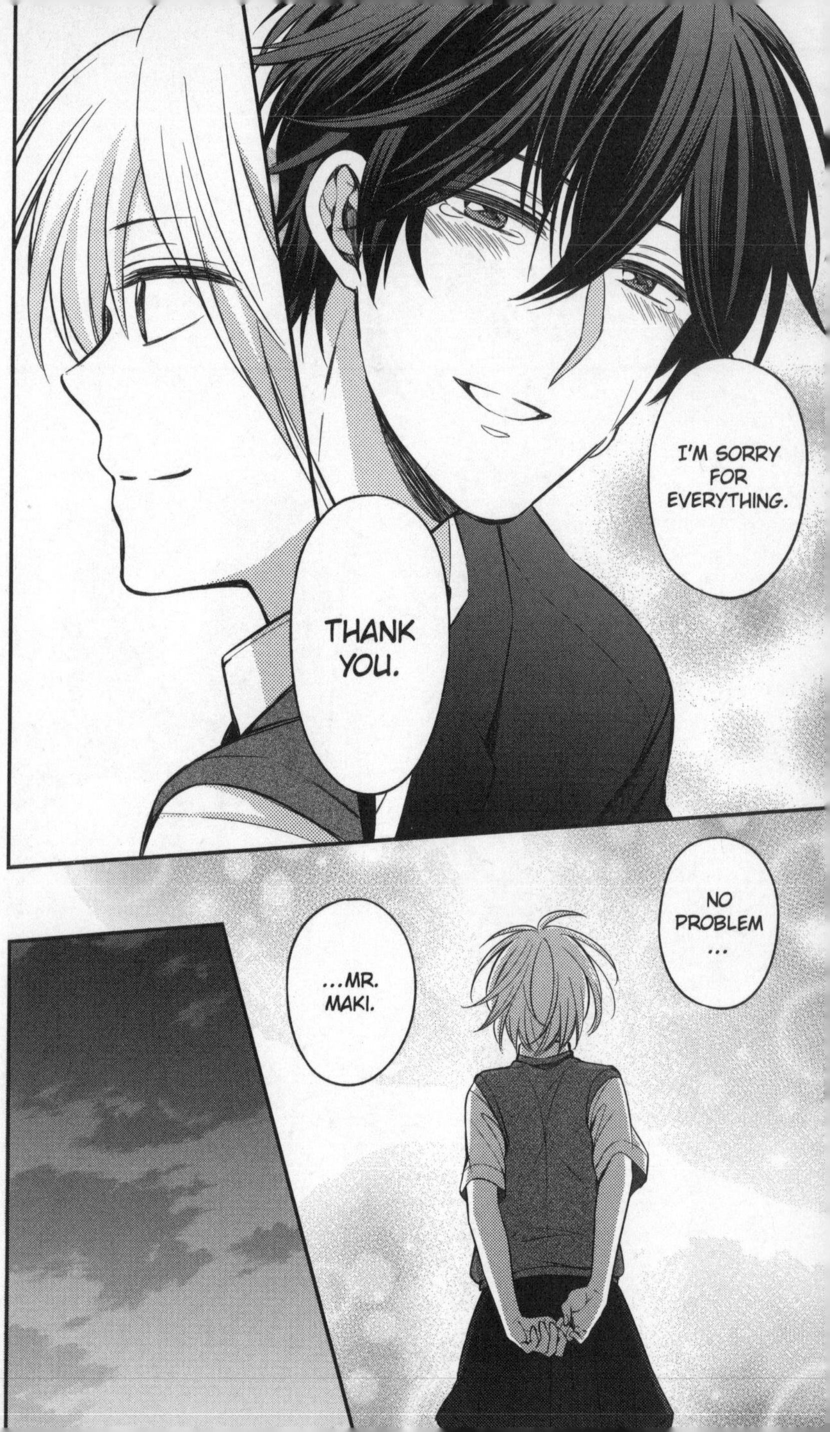
I'M SORRY FOR EVERYTHING.
THANK YOU.
NO PROBLEM ...
...MR. MAKI.

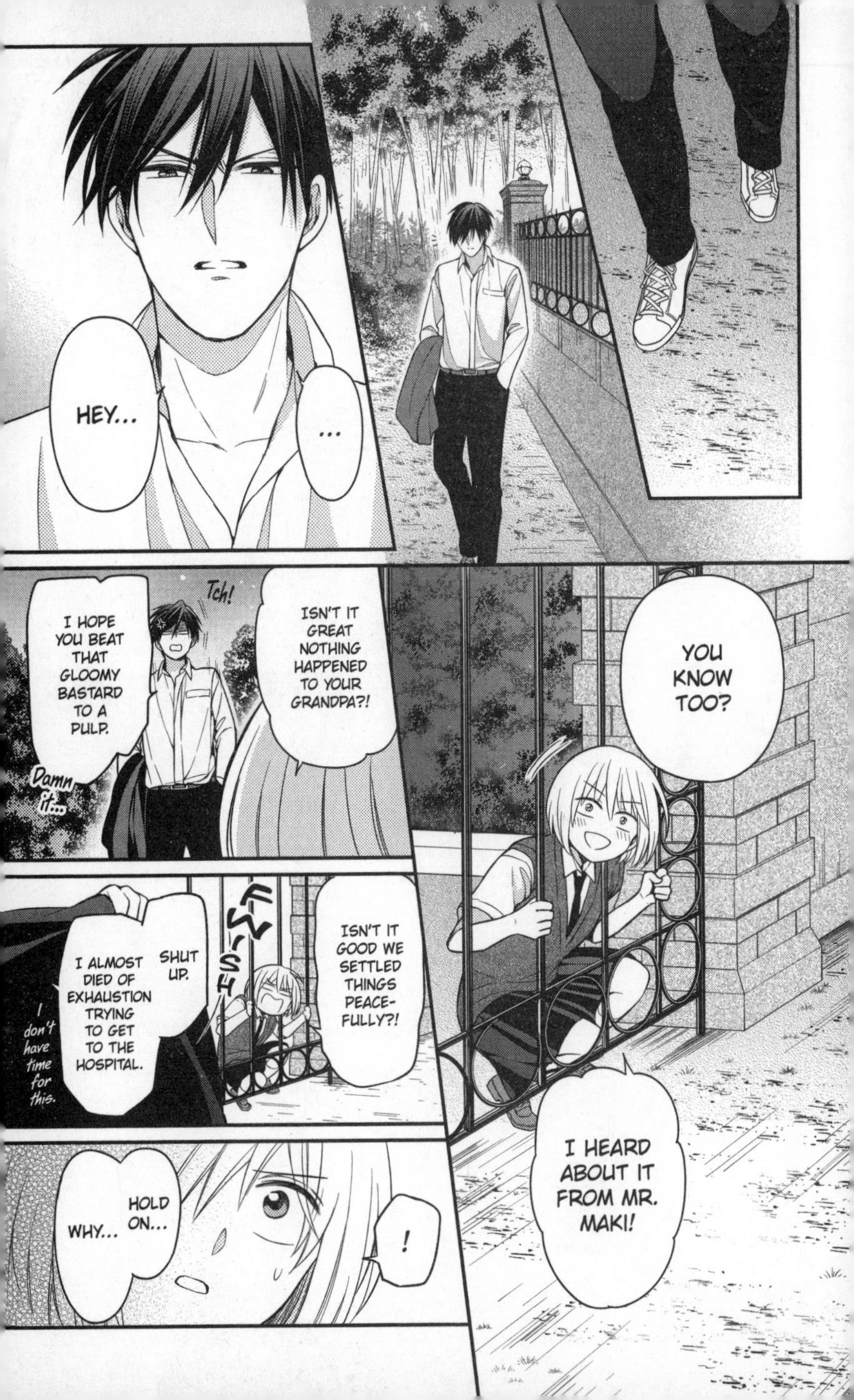
...
HEY...
YOU KNOW TOO?
I HEARD ABOUT IT FROM MR. MAKI!
ISN'T IT GREAT NOTHING HAPPENED TO YOUR GRANDPA?!
Tch!
I HOPE YOU BEAT THAT GLOOMY BASTARD TO A PULP.
Damn it...
ISN'T IT GOOD WE SETTLED THINGS PEACE-FULLY?!
FWISH
SHUT UP.
I ALMOST DIED OF EXHAUSTION TRYING TO GET TO THE HOSPITAL.
I don't have time for this.
!
HOLD ON...
WHY...

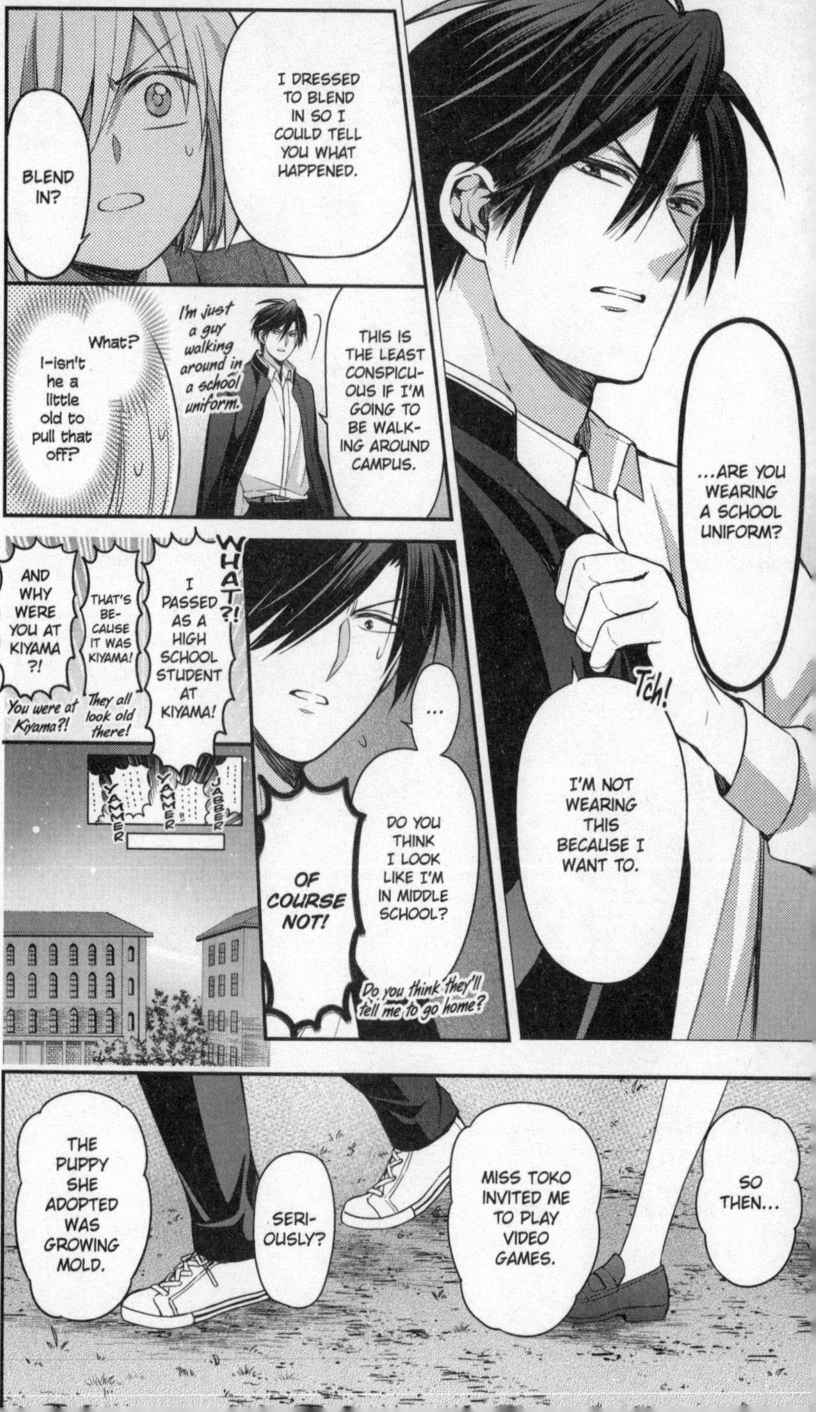
...ARE YOU WEARING A SCHOOL UNIFORM?
Tch!
I'M NOT WEARING THIS BECAUSE I WANT TO.
I DRESSED TO BLEND IN SO I COULD TELL YOU WHAT HAPPENED.
BLEND IN?
THIS IS THE LEAST CONSPICUOUS IF I'M GOING TO BE WALKING AROUND CAMPUS.
I'm just a guy walking around in a school uniform.
What?
I-isn't he a little old to pull that off?
WHAT?!
I PASSED AS A HIGH SCHOOL STUDENT AT KIYAMA!
...
DO YOU THINK I LOOK LIKE I'M IN MIDDLE SCHOOL?
Do you think they'll tell me to go home?
OF COURSE NOT!
THAT'S BECAUSE IT WAS KIYAMA!
They all look old there!
AND WHY WERE YOU AT KIYAMA?!
You were at Kiyama?!
JABBER
YAMMER
YAMMER
SO THEN...
MISS TOKO INVITED ME TO PLAY VIDEO GAMES.
SERIOUSLY?
THE PUPPY SHE ADOPTED WAS GROWING MOLD.

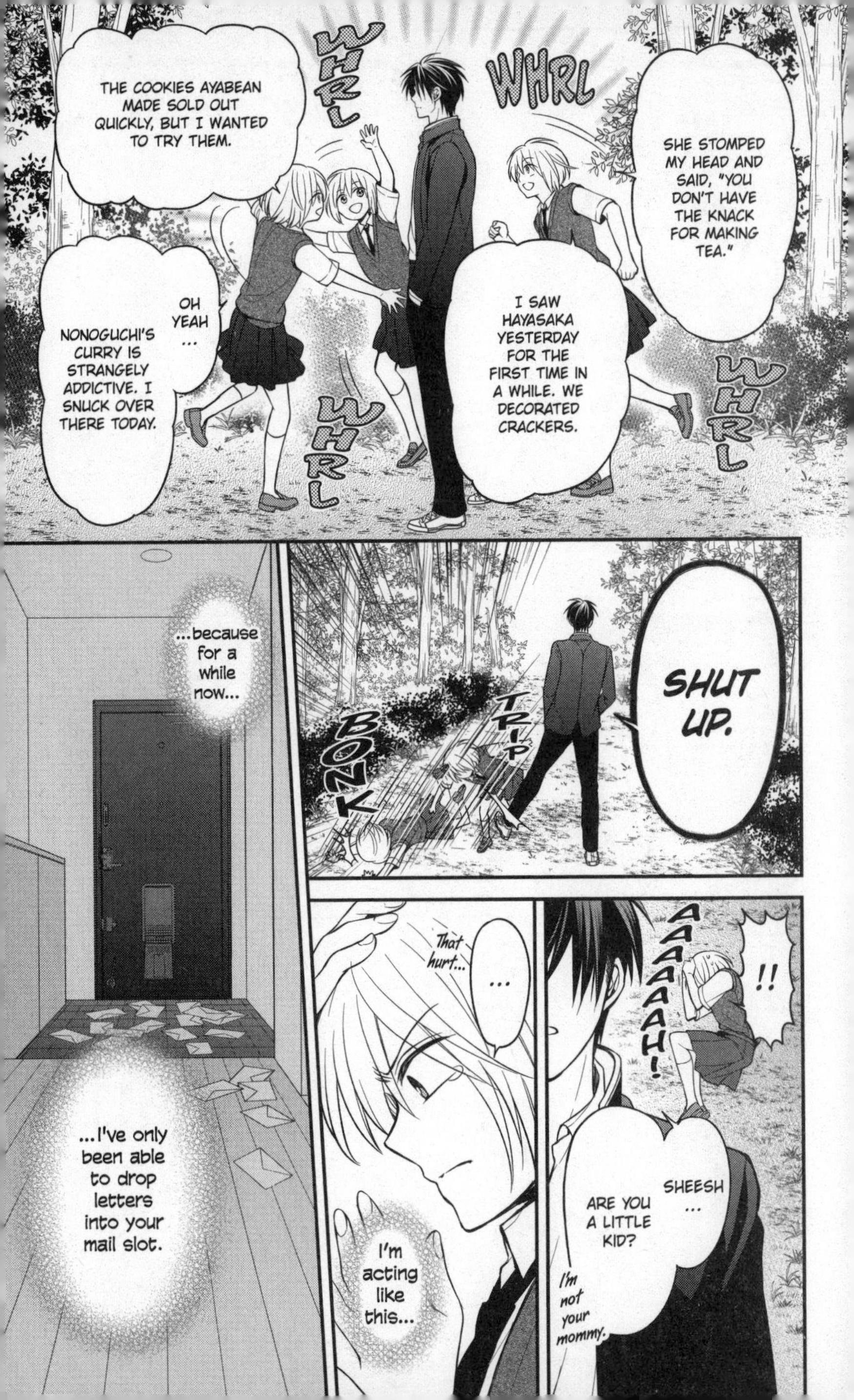
SHE STOMPED MY HEAD AND SAID, "YOU DON'T HAVE THE KNACK FOR MAKING TEA."
WHRL
WHRL
I SAW HAYASAKA YESTERDAY FOR THE FIRST TIME IN A WHILE. WE DECORATED CRACKERS.
WHRL
THE COOKIES AYABEAN MADE SOLD OUT QUICKLY, BUT I WANTED TO TRY THEM.
OH YEAH ...
NONOGUCHI'S CURRY IS STRANGELY ADDICTIVE. I SNUCK OVER THERE TODAY.
WHRL
SHUT UP.
TRIP
BONK
AAAAAAH!
!!
SHEESH ...
ARE YOU A LITTLE KID?
I'm not your mommy.
That hurt...
...
I'm acting like this...
...because for a while now...
...I've only been able to drop letters into your mail slot.

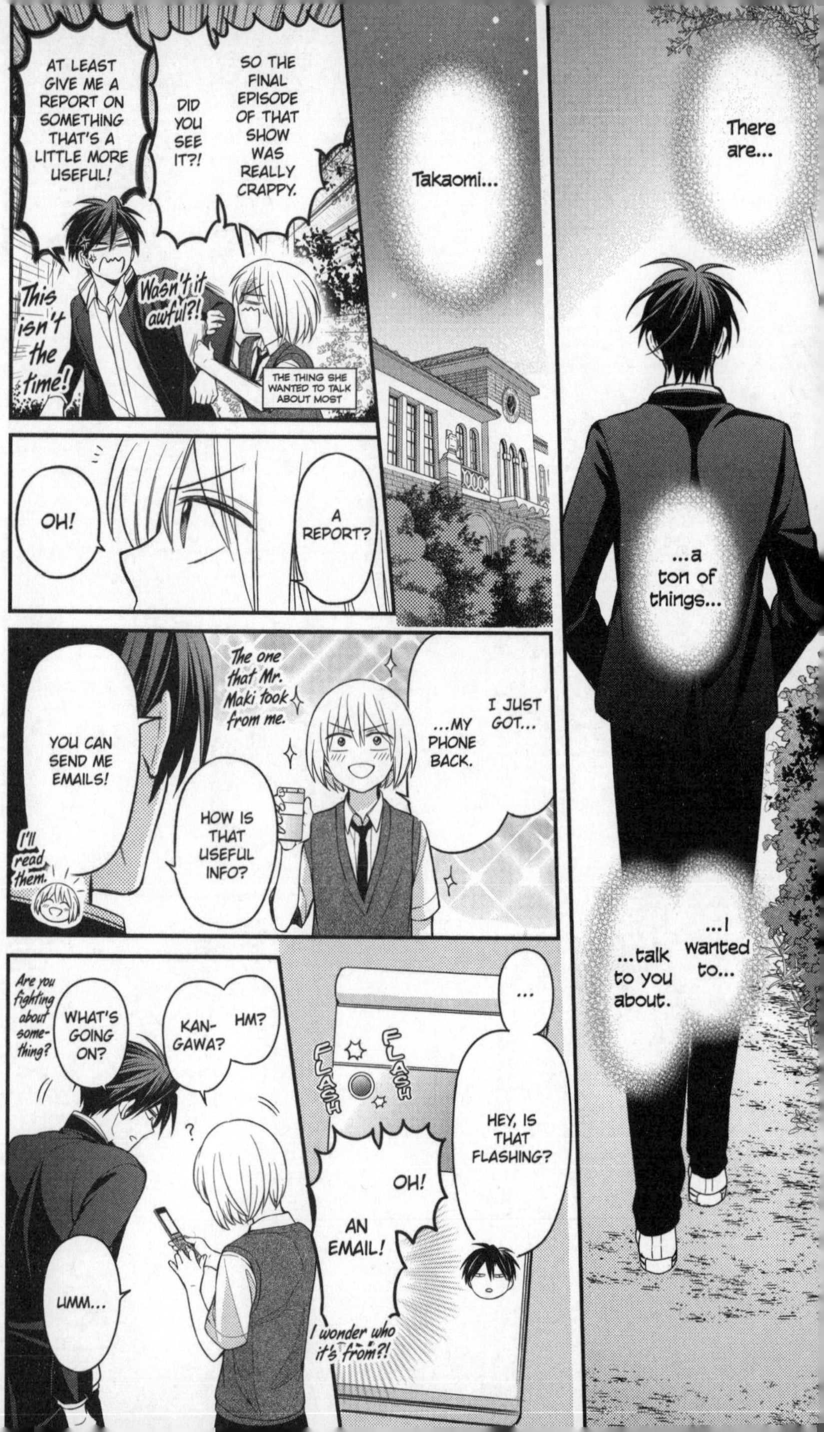
There are...
...a ton of things...
...I wanted to...
...talk to you about.
Takaomi...
SO THE FINAL EPISODE OF THAT SHOW WAS REALLY CRAPPY.
DID YOU SEE IT?!
AT LEAST GIVE ME A REPORT ON SOMETHING THAT'S A LITTLE MORE USEFUL!
Wasn't it awful?!
This isn't the time!
THE THING SHE WANTED TO TALK ABOUT MOST
A REPORT?
OH!
I JUST GOT...
...MY PHONE BACK.
The one that Mr. Maki took from me.
HOW IS THAT USEFUL INFO?
YOU CAN SEND ME EMAILS!
I'll read them.
...
HEY, IS THAT FLASHING?
FLASH
FLASH
OH!
AN EMAIL!
I wonder who it's from?!
HM?
KAN-GAWA?
WHAT'S GOING ON?
Are you fighting about something?
UMM...

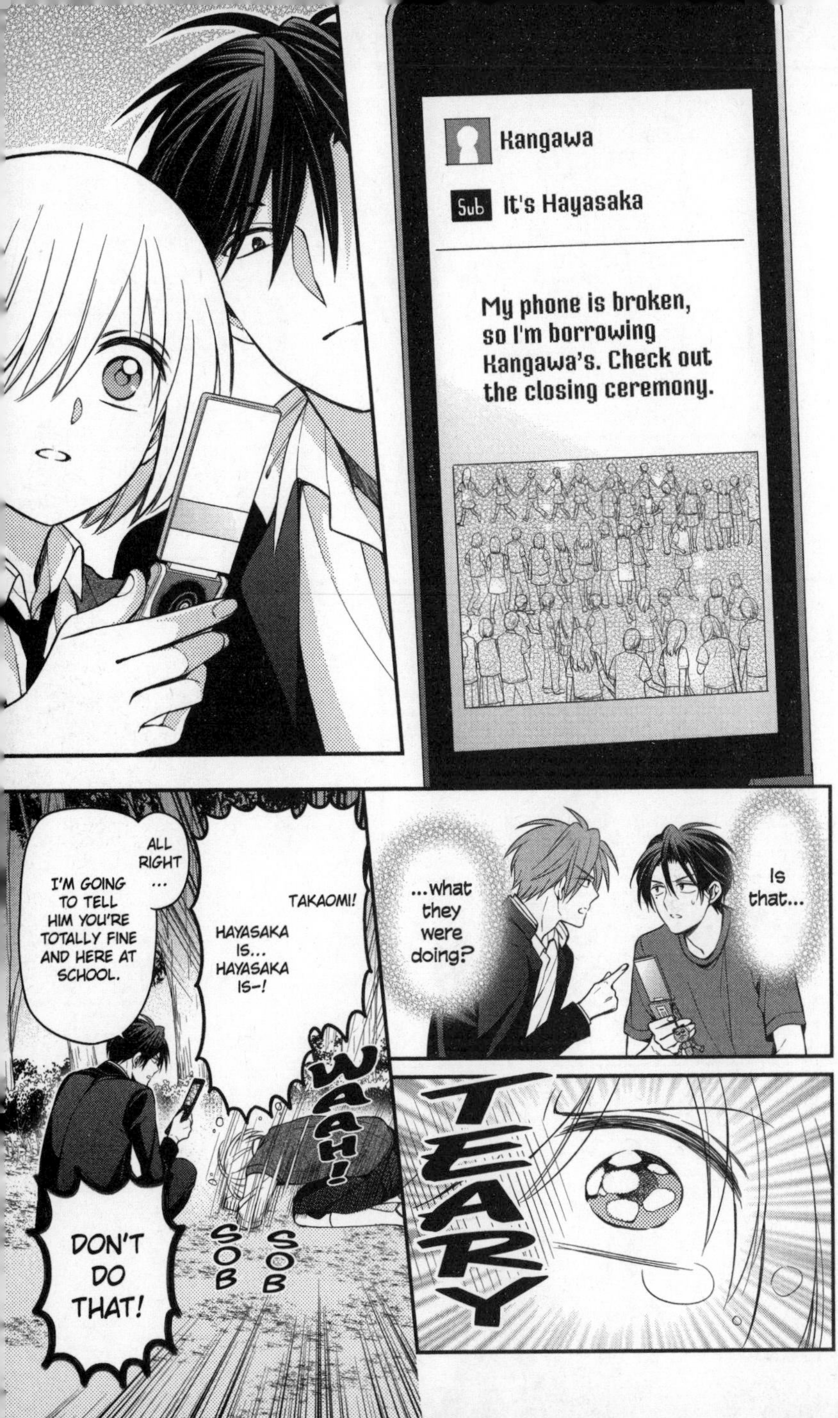
Kangawa
Sub It's Hayasaka
My phone is broken, so I'm borrowing Kangawa's. Check out the closing ceremony.
Is that...
...what they were doing?
TEARY
TAKAOMI!
HAYASAKA IS... HAYASAKA IS-!
ALL RIGHT ...
I'M GOING TO TELL HIM YOU'RE TOTALLY FINE AND HERE AT SCHOOL.
WAAH!
SOB SOB
DON'T DO THAT!

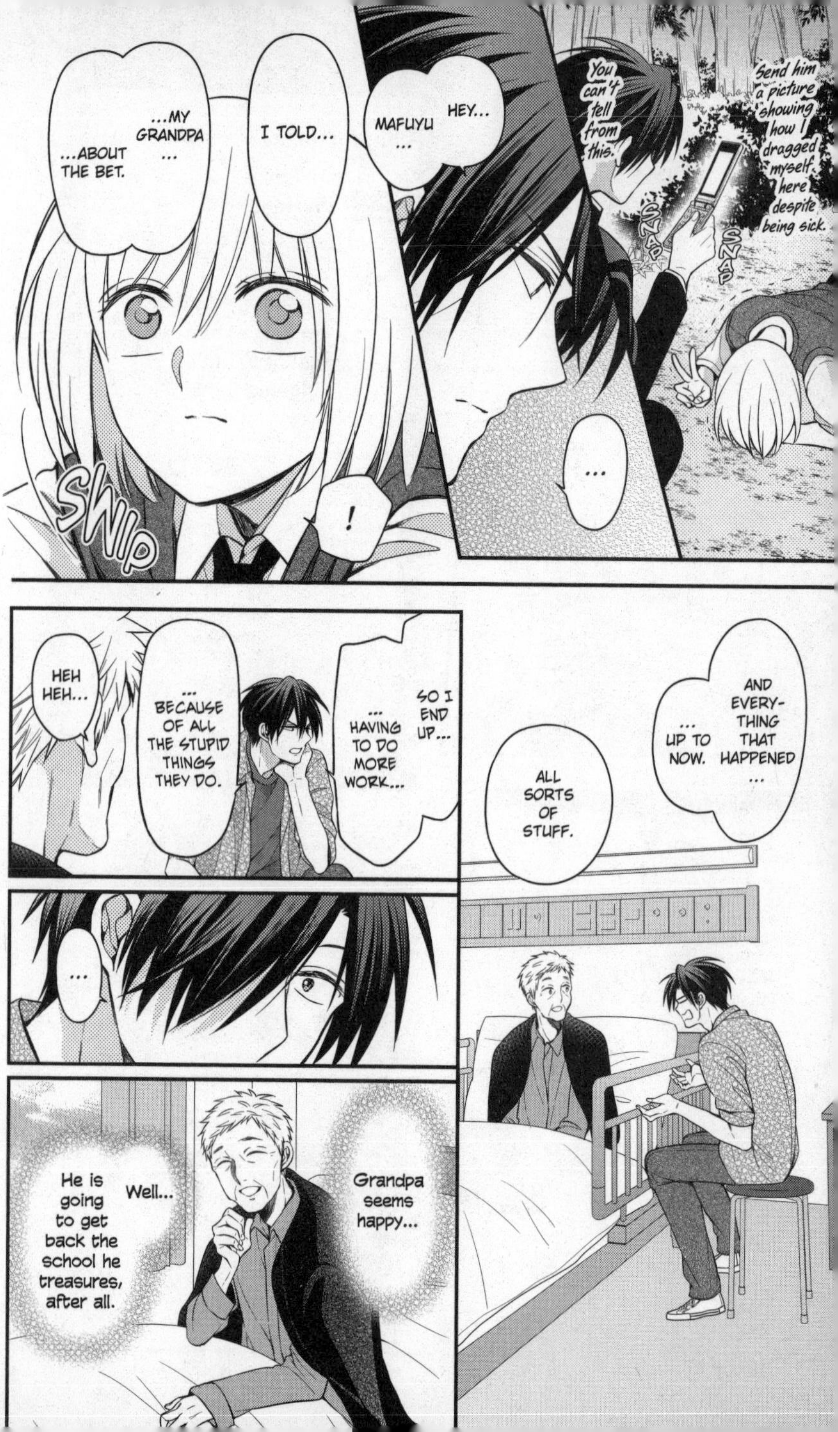
Send him a picture showing how I dragged myself here despite being sick.
You can't tell from this.
SNAP
SNAP
HEY... MAFUYU...
...
I TOLD...
...MY GRANDPA...
...ABOUT THE BET.
!
SWIP
AND EVERYTHING THAT HAPPENED...
...UP TO NOW.
ALL SORTS OF STUFF.
SO I END UP...
...HAVING TO DO MORE WORK...
...BECAUSE OF ALL THE STUPID THINGS THEY DO.
HEH HEH...
...
Grandpa seems happy...
Well...
He is going to get back the school he treasures, after all.

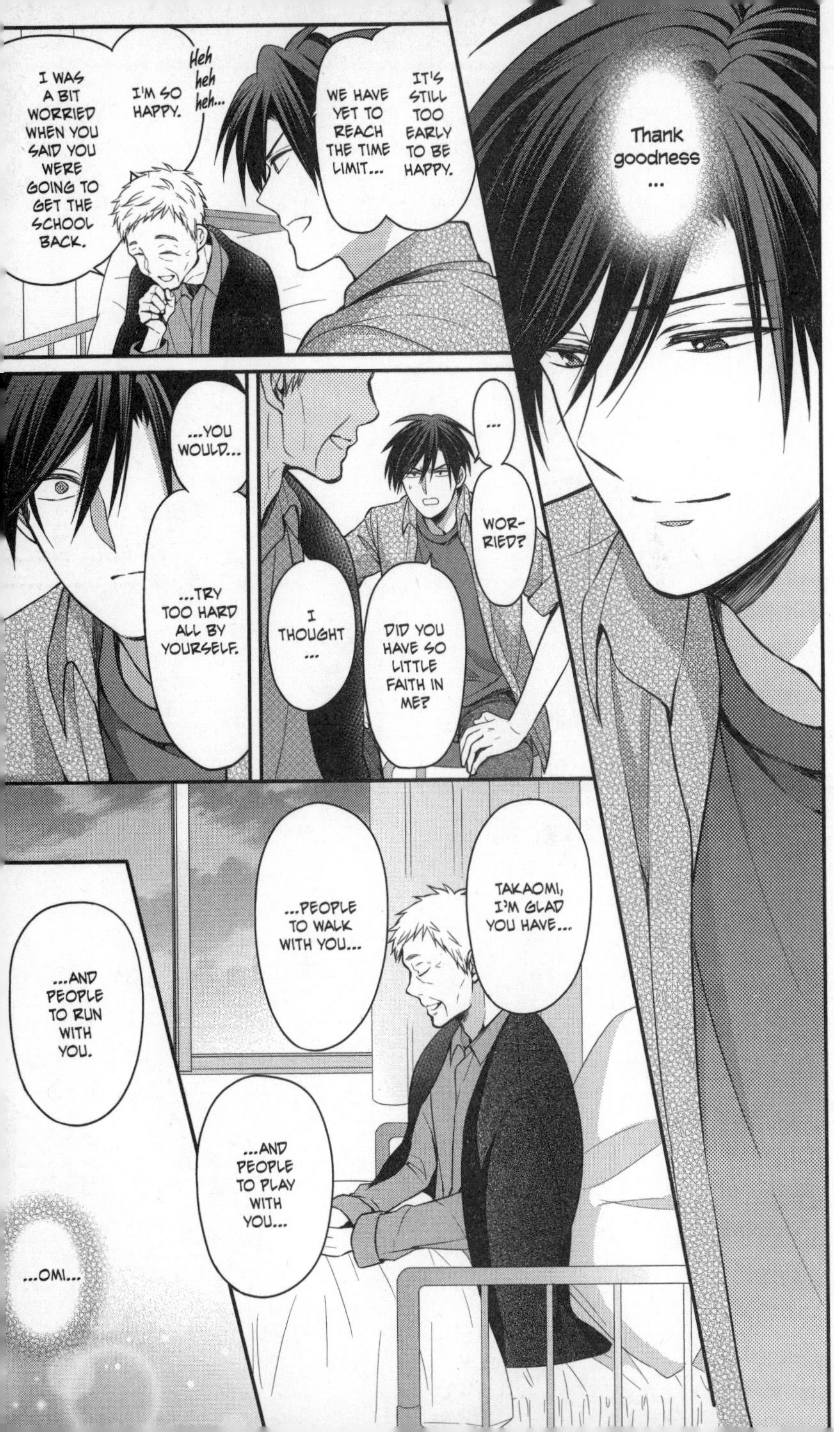
Thank goodness ...
IT'S STILL TOO EARLY TO BE HAPPY.
WE HAVE YET TO REACH THE TIME LIMIT...
Heh heh heh...
I'M SO HAPPY.
I WAS A BIT WORRIED WHEN YOU SAID YOU WERE GOING TO GET THE SCHOOL BACK.
...
WOR-RIED?
DID YOU HAVE SO LITTLE FAITH IN ME?
I THOUGHT ...
...YOU WOULD...
...TRY TOO HARD ALL BY YOURSELF.
TAKAOMI, I'M GLAD YOU HAVE...
...PEOPLE TO WALK WITH YOU...
...AND PEOPLE TO RUN WITH YOU.
...AND PEOPLE TO PLAY WITH YOU...
...OMI...

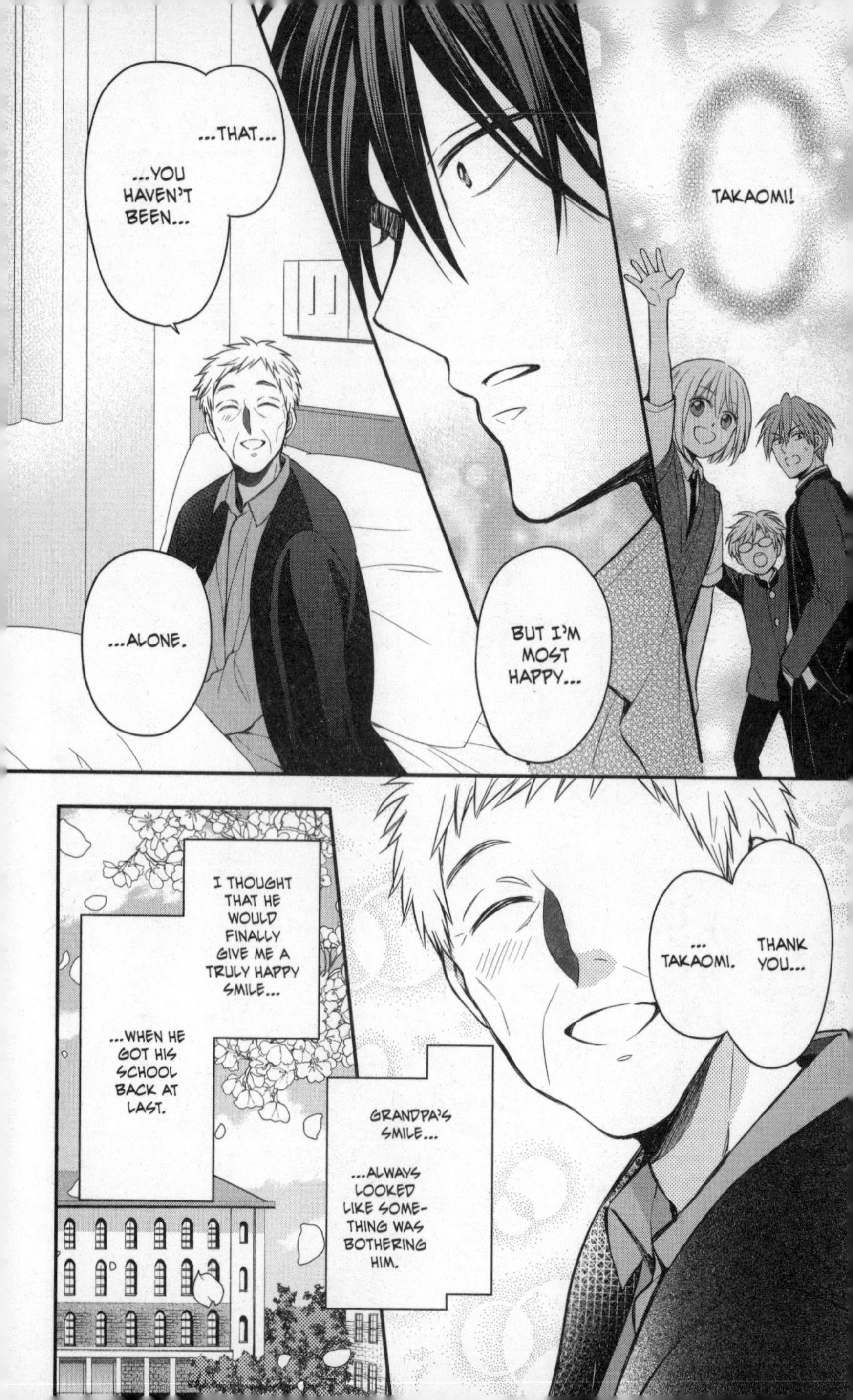
TAKAOMI!
BUT I'M MOST HAPPY...
...THAT...
...YOU HAVEN'T BEEN...
...ALONE.
THANK YOU...
...TAKAOMI.
GRANDPA'S SMILE...
...ALWAYS LOOKED LIKE SOME-THING WAS BOTHERING HIM.
I THOUGHT THAT HE WOULD FINALLY GIVE ME A TRULY HAPPY SMILE...
...WHEN HE GOT HIS SCHOOL BACK AT LAST.

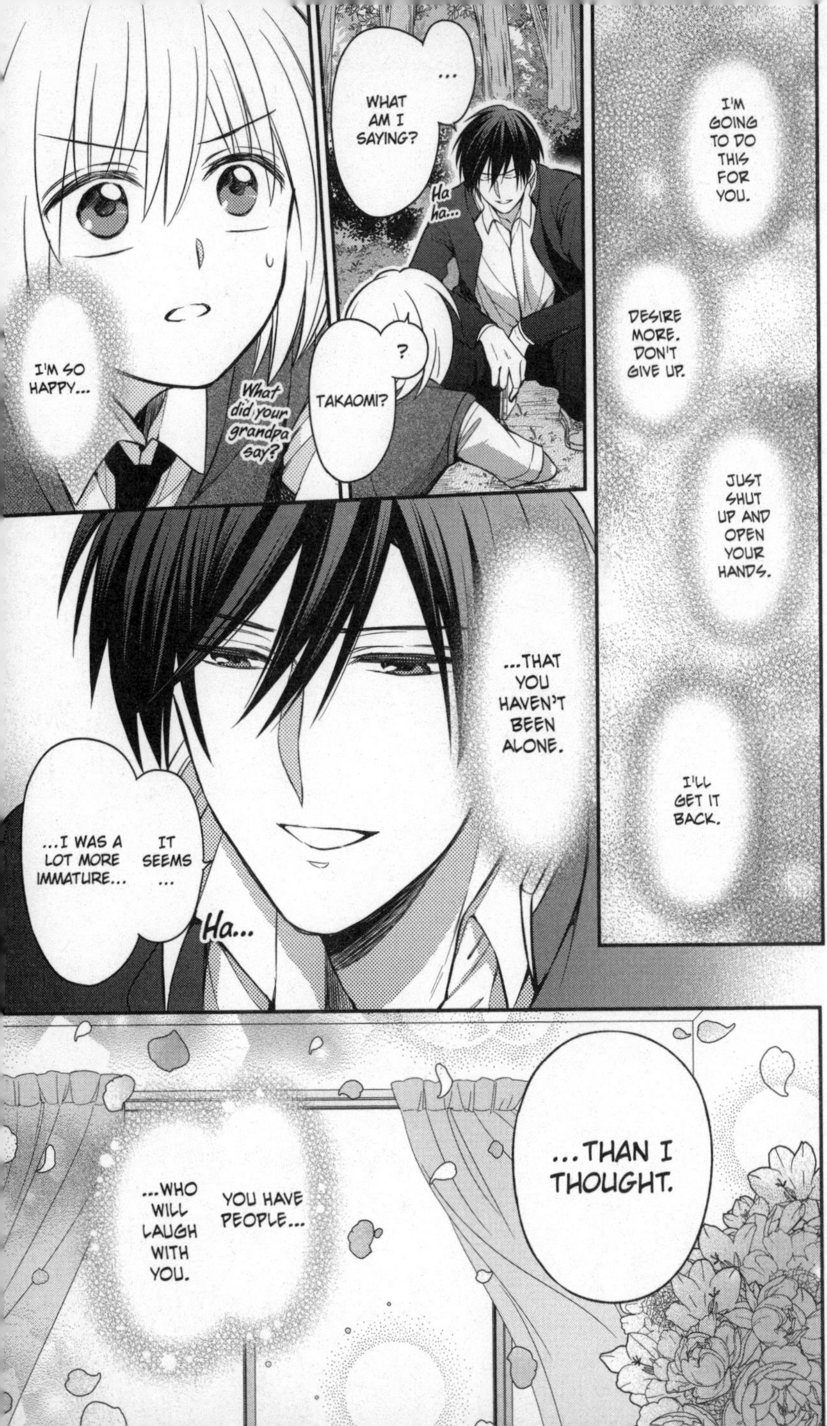
I'M GOING TO DO THIS FOR YOU.
DESIRE MORE. DON'T GIVE UP.
JUST SHUT UP AND OPEN YOUR HANDS.
I'LL GET IT BACK.
...
WHAT AM I SAYING?
Ha ha...
?
TAKAOMI?
What did your grandpa say?
I'M SO HAPPY...
...THAT YOU HAVEN'T BEEN ALONE.
IT SEEMS...
...I WAS A LOT MORE IMMATURE...
Ha...
...THAN I THOUGHT.
YOU HAVE PEOPLE...
...WHO WILL LAUGH WITH YOU.

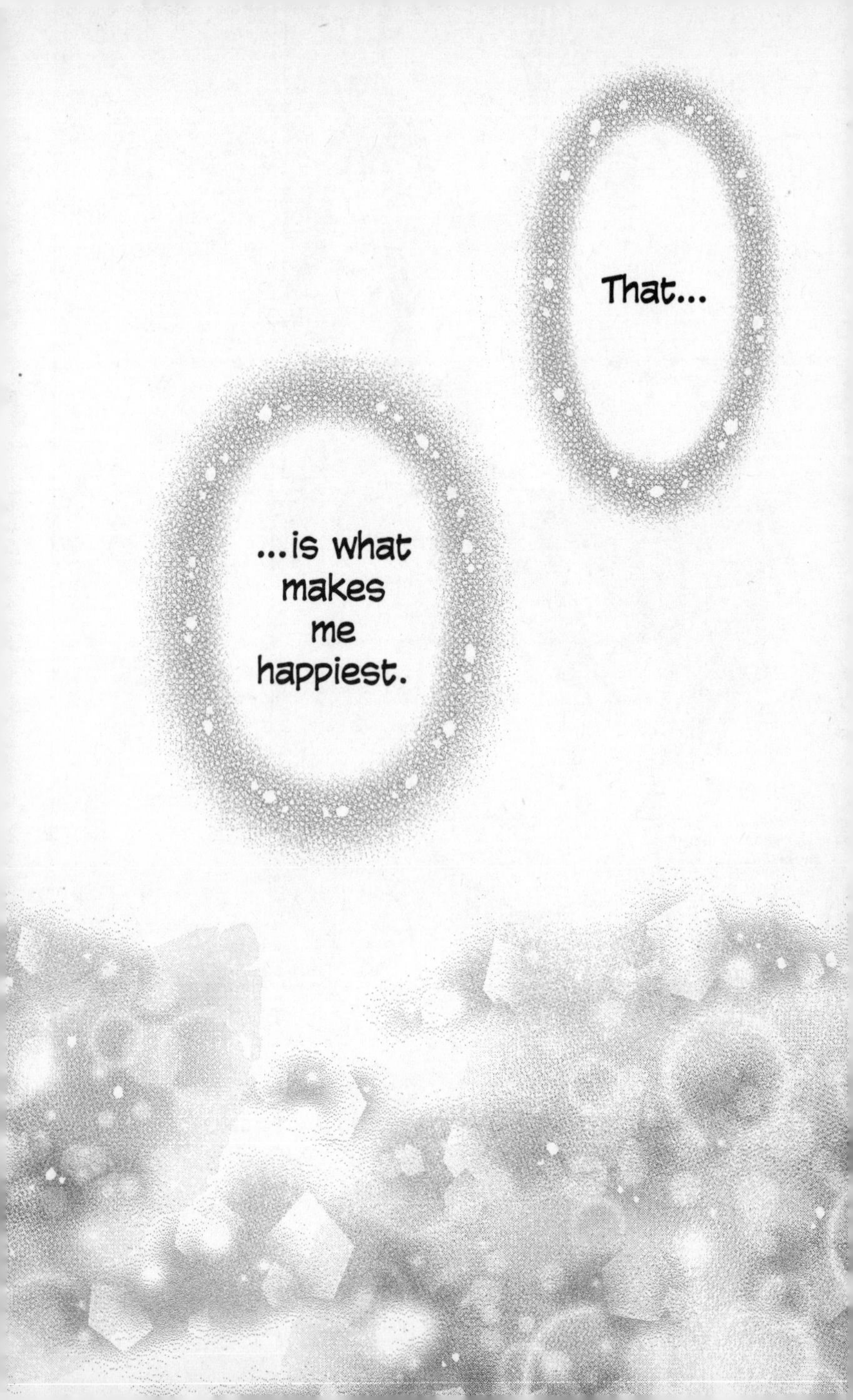
That...
...is what makes me happiest.

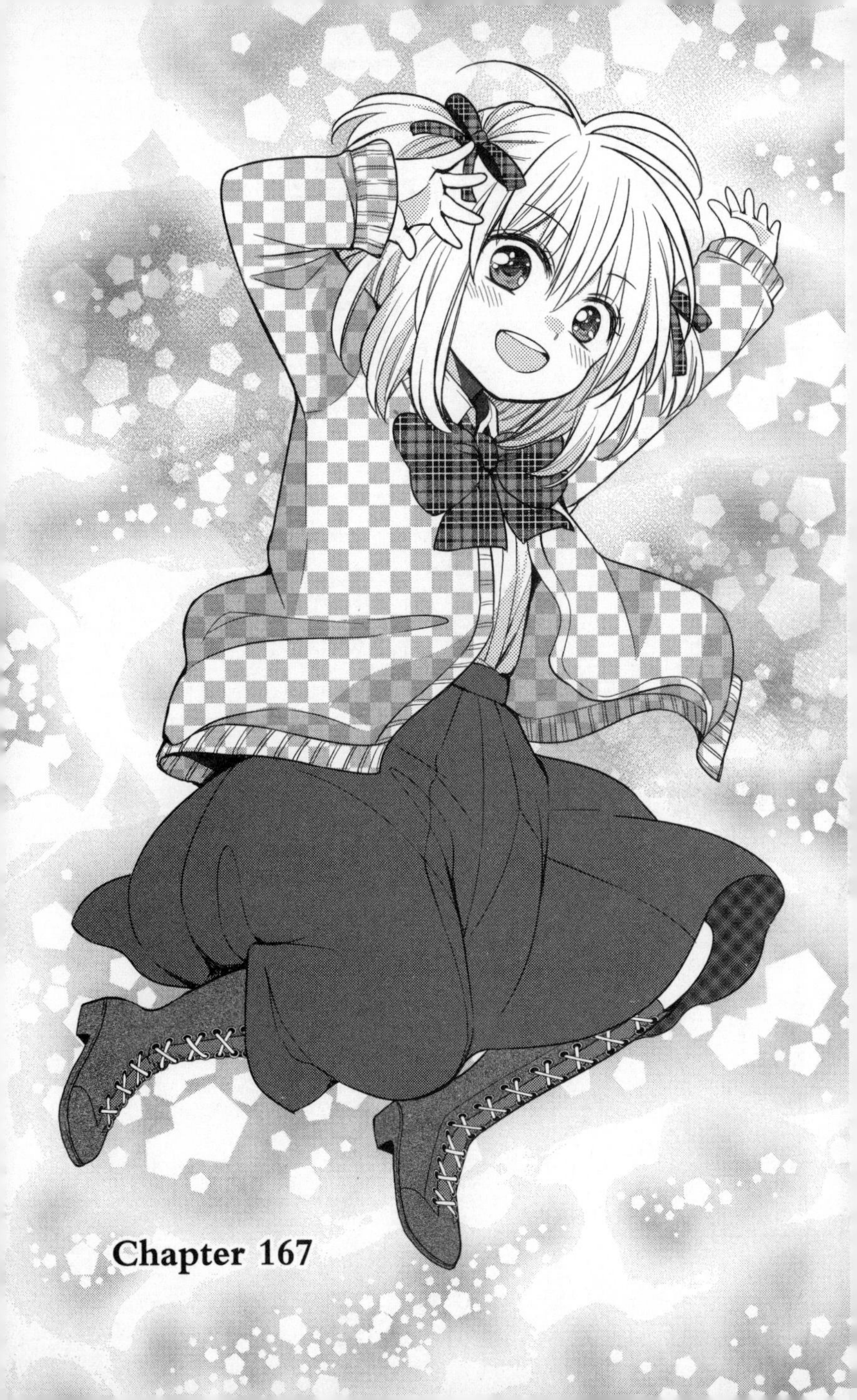
Chapter 167

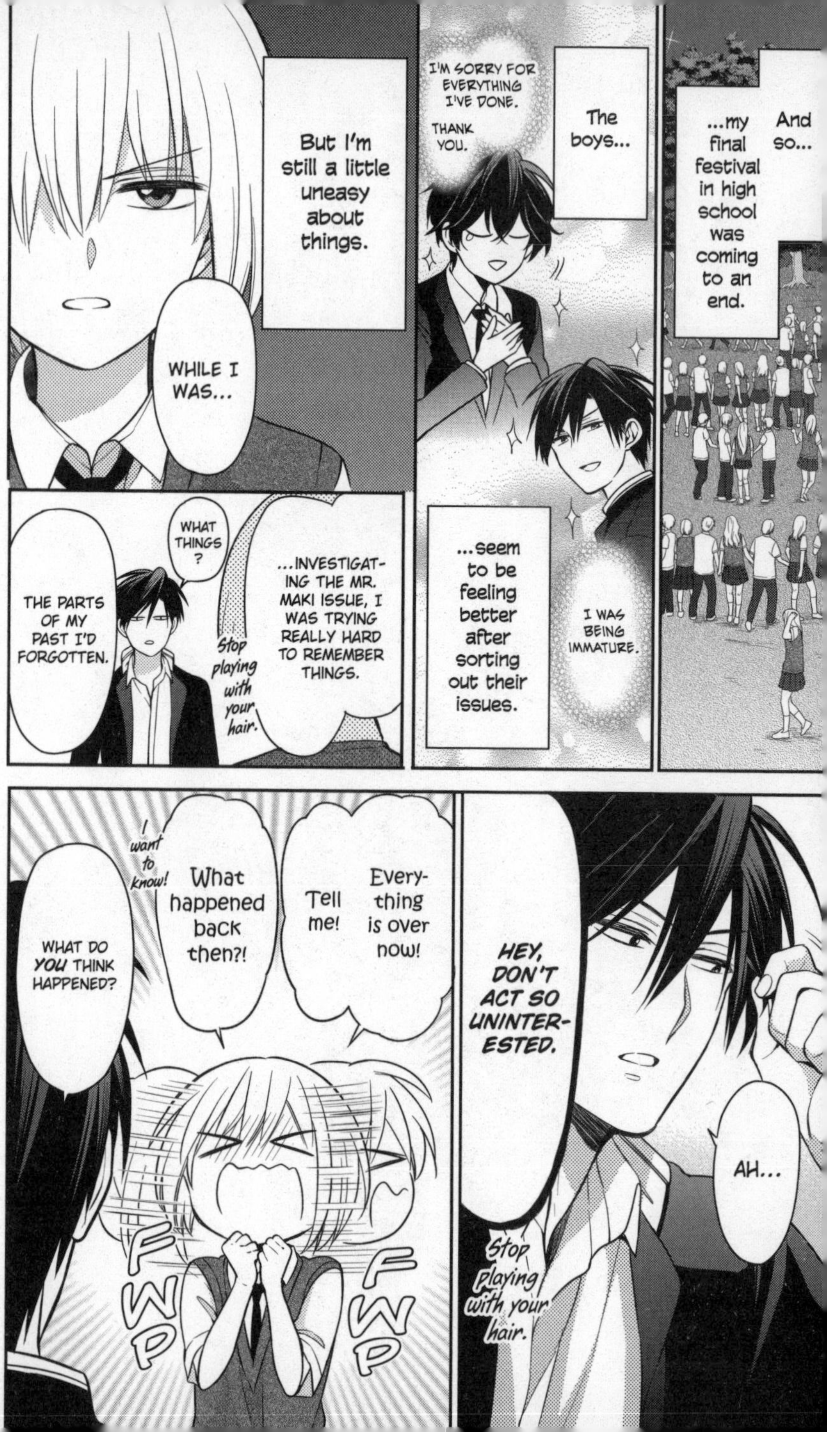
And so...
...my final festival in high school was coming to an end.
The boys...
I'M SORRY FOR EVERYTHING I'VE DONE.
THANK YOU.
...seem to be feeling better after sorting out their issues.
I WAS BEING IMMATURE.
But I'm still a little uneasy about things.
WHILE I WAS...
...INVESTIGAT-ING THE MR. MAKI ISSUE, I WAS TRYING REALLY HARD TO REMEMBER THINGS.
Stop playing with your hair.
WHAT THINGS?
THE PARTS OF MY PAST I'D FORGOTTEN.
HEY, DON'T ACT SO UNINTER-ESTED.
AH...
Stop playing with your hair.
Every-thing is over now!
Tell me!
What happened back then?!
I want to know!
WHAT DO *YOU* THINK HAPPENED?
FWP
FWP

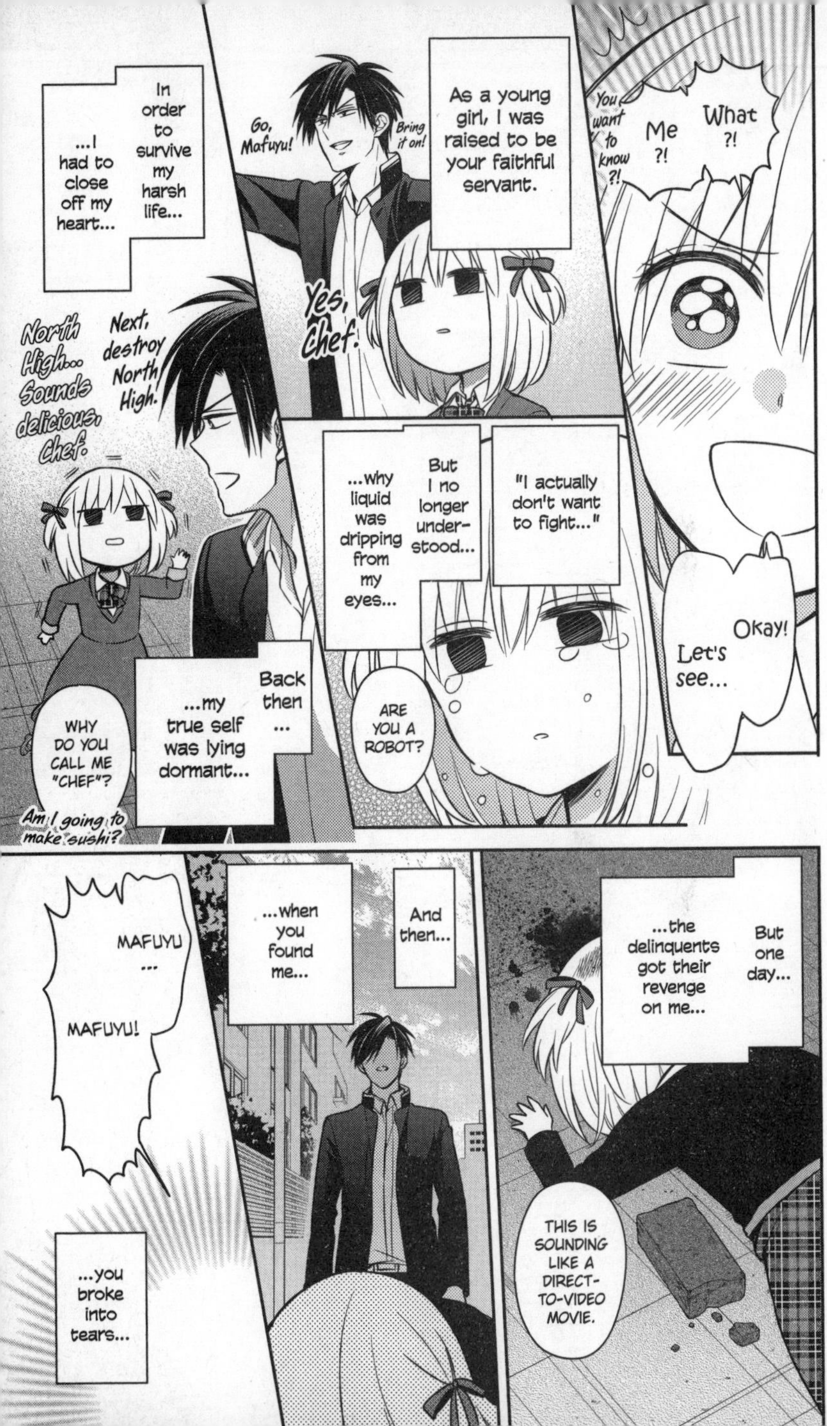
What ?!
Me ?!
You want to know ?!
Okay! Let's see...
As a young girl, I was raised to be your faithful servant.
Bring it on!
Go, Mafuyu!
Yes, Chef.
In order to survive my harsh life...
...I had to close off my heart...
Next, destroy North High.
North High... Sounds delicious, Chef.
WHY DO YOU CALL ME "CHEF"?
Am I going to make sushi?
"I actually don't want to fight..."
But I no longer under-stood...
...why liquid was dripping from my eyes...
ARE YOU A ROBOT?
Back then...
...my true self was lying dormant...
But one day...
...the delinquents got their revenge on me...
THIS IS SOUNDING LIKE A DIRECT-TO-VIDEO MOVIE.
And then...
...when you found me...
MAFUYU...
MAFUYU!
...you broke into tears...

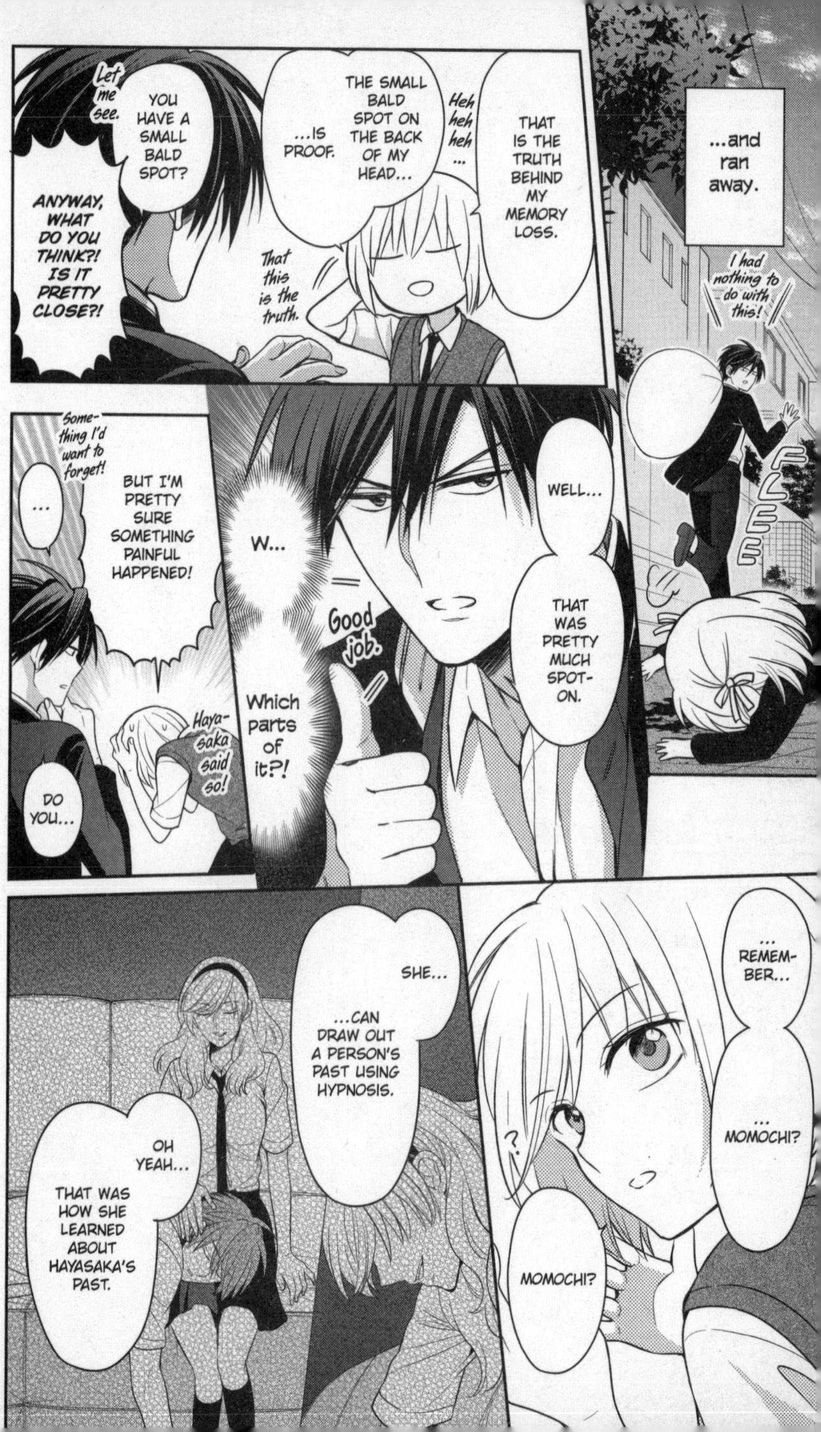
...and ran away.
I had nothing to do with this!
FLEE
THAT IS THE TRUTH BEHIND MY MEMORY LOSS.
Heh heh heh...
THE SMALL BALD SPOT ON THE BACK OF MY HEAD...
...IS PROOF.
Let me see.
YOU HAVE A SMALL BALD SPOT?
ANYWAY, WHAT DO YOU THINK?! IS IT PRETTY CLOSE?!
That this is the truth.
WELL...
THAT WAS PRETTY MUCH SPOT-ON.
W...
Good job.
Which parts of it?!
Some-thing I'd want to forget!
...
BUT I'M PRETTY SURE SOMETHING PAINFUL HAPPENED!
Haya-saka said so!
DO YOU...
...REMEM-BER...
...MOMOCHI?
MOMOCHI?
?
SHE...
...CAN DRAW OUT A PERSON'S PAST USING HYPNOSIS.
OH YEAH...
THAT WAS HOW SHE LEARNED ABOUT HAYASAKA'S PAST.

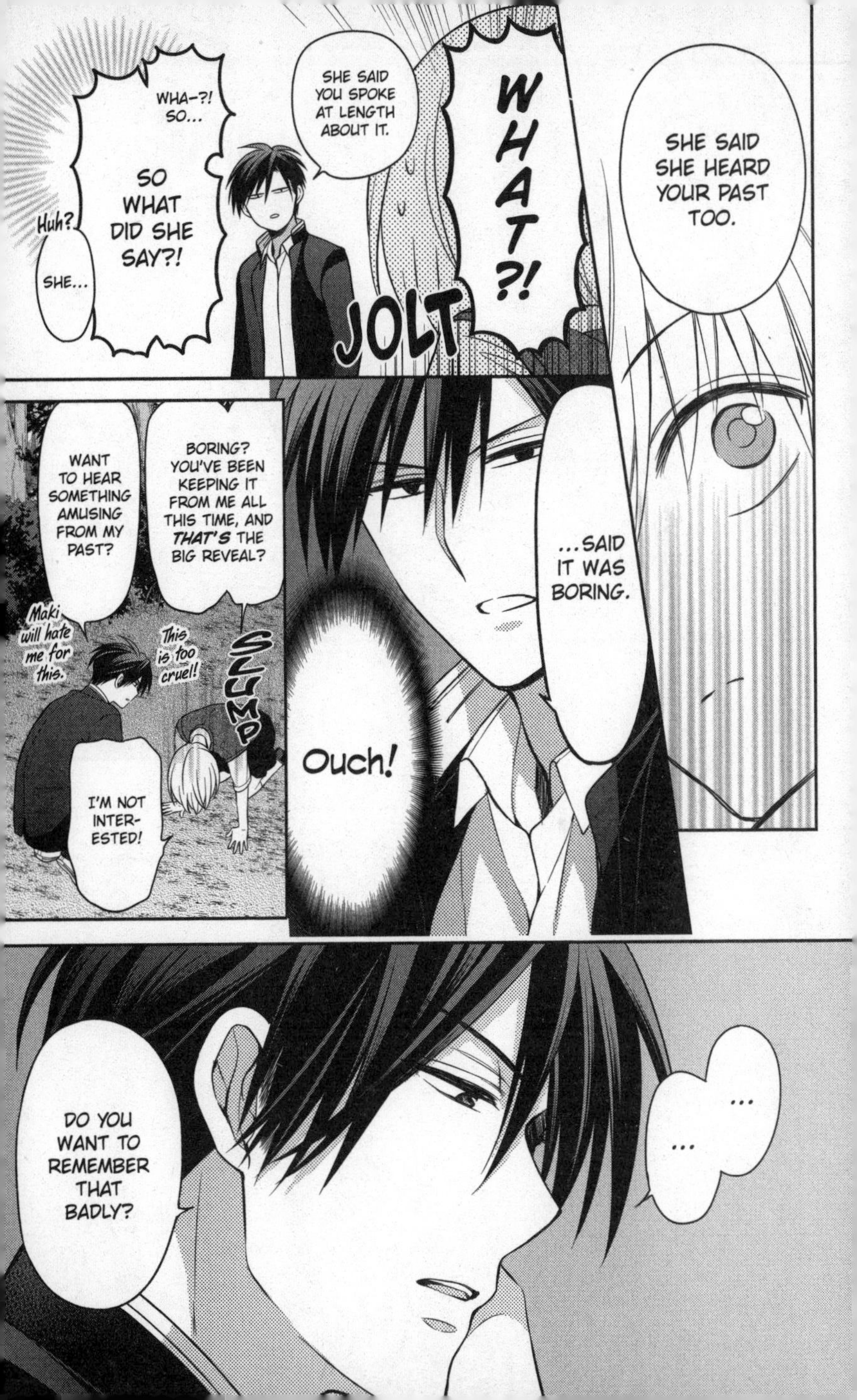
SHE SAID SHE HEARD YOUR PAST TOO.
WHAT?!
JOLT
SHE SAID YOU SPOKE AT LENGTH ABOUT IT.
WHA-?! SO...
SO WHAT DID SHE SAY?!
Huh?
SHE...
...SAID IT WAS BORING.
Ouch!
BORING? YOU'VE BEEN KEEPING IT FROM ME ALL THIS TIME, AND *THAT'S* THE BIG REVEAL?
WANT TO HEAR SOMETHING AMUSING FROM MY PAST?
SLUMP
This is too cruel!
Maki will hate me for this.
I'M NOT INTERESTED!
...
...
DO YOU WANT TO REMEMBER THAT BADLY?

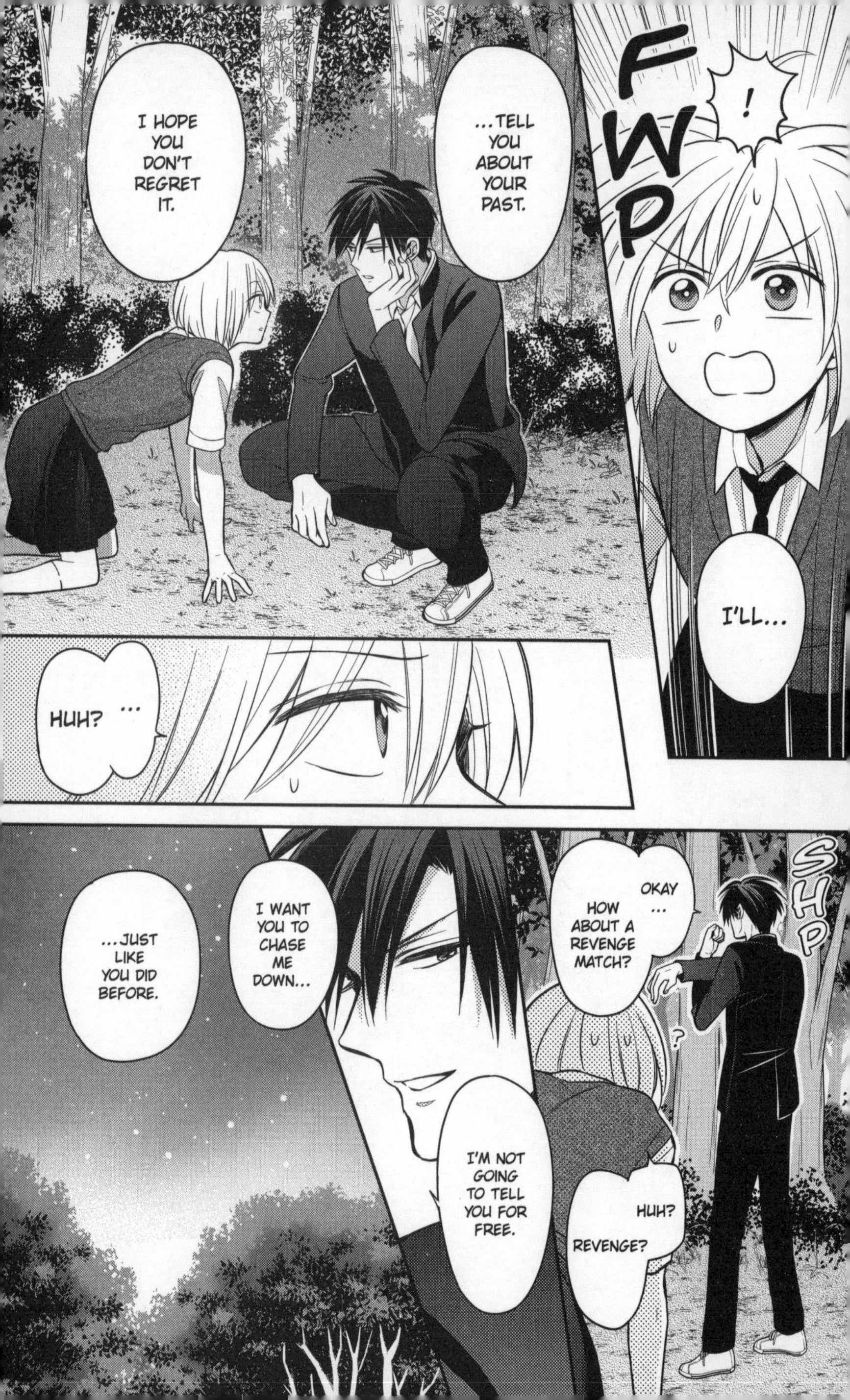
FWP
!
I'LL...
...TELL YOU ABOUT YOUR PAST.
I HOPE YOU DON'T REGRET IT.
HUH? ...
SHP
OKAY...
HOW ABOUT A REVENGE MATCH?
?
HUH?
REVENGE?
I'M NOT GOING TO TELL YOU FOR FREE.
I WANT YOU TO CHASE ME DOWN...
...JUST LIKE YOU DID BEFORE.

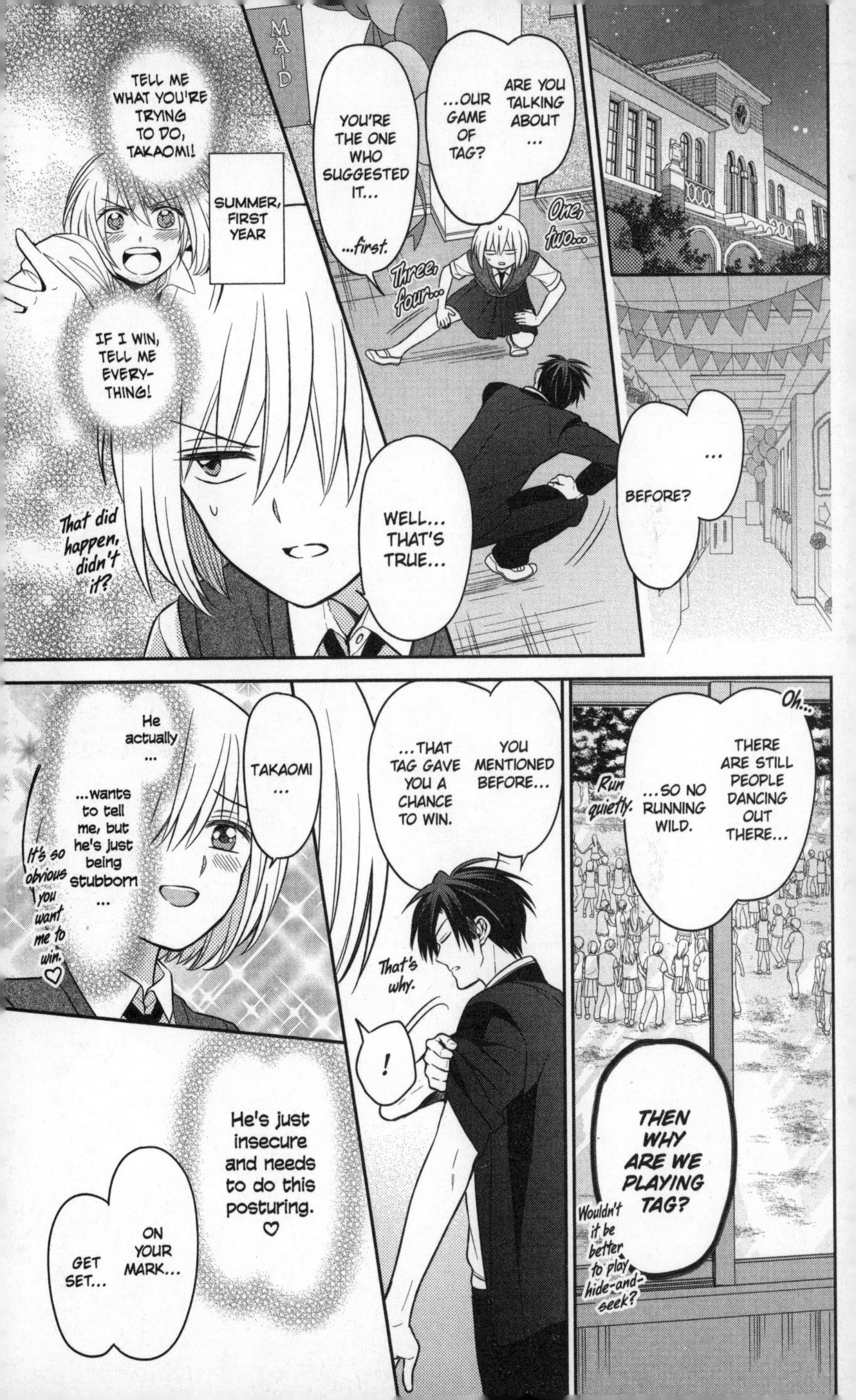
MAID
...
BEFORE?
ARE YOU TALKING ABOUT ...
...OUR GAME OF TAG?
YOU'RE THE ONE WHO SUGGESTED IT...
...first.
One, two...
Three, four...
SUMMER, FIRST YEAR
TELL ME WHAT YOU'RE TRYING TO DO, TAKAOMI!
IF I WIN, TELL ME EVERY-THING!
WELL... THAT'S TRUE...
That did happen, didn't it?
Oh...
THERE ARE STILL PEOPLE DANCING OUT THERE...
...SO NO RUNNING WILD.
Run quietly.
THEN WHY ARE WE PLAYING TAG?
Wouldn't it be better to play hide-and-seek?
YOU MENTIONED BEFORE...
...THAT TAG GAVE YOU A CHANCE TO WIN.
That's why.
!
TAKAOMI ...
He actually ...
...wants to tell me, but he's just being stubborn ...
It's so obvious you want me to win. ♡
He's just insecure and needs to do this posturing. ♡
ON YOUR MARK...
GET SET...

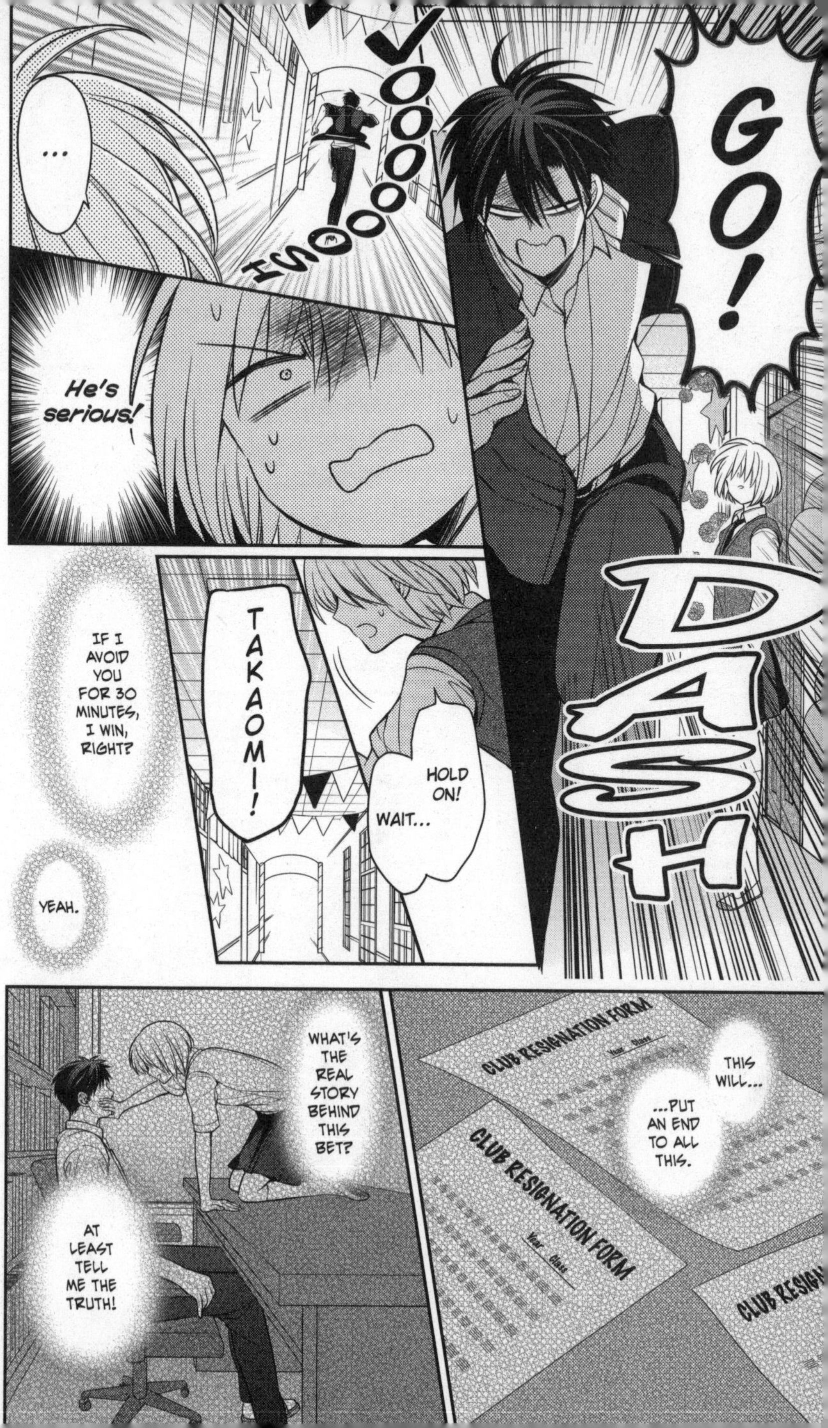
GO!
VOOOOOOSH
...
He's serious!
DASH
TAKAOMI!
HOLD ON! WAIT...
IF I AVOID YOU FOR 30 MINUTES, I WIN, RIGHT?
YEAH.
CLUB RESIGNATION FORM
THIS WILL...
...PUT AN END TO ALL THIS.
WHAT'S THE REAL STORY BEHIND THIS BET?
AT LEAST TELL ME THE TRUTH!

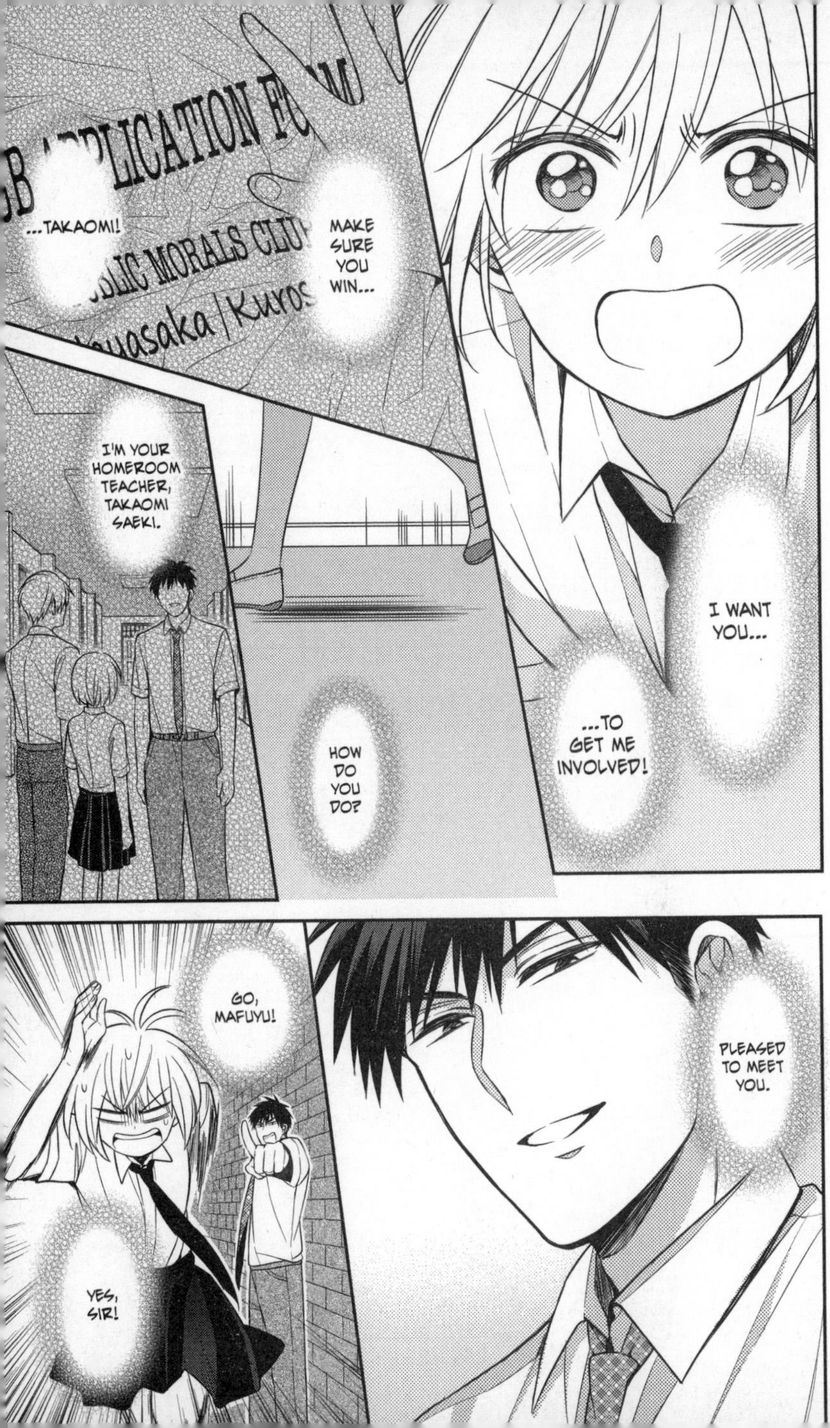
I WANT YOU...
...TO GET ME INVOLVED!
MAKE SURE YOU WIN...
...TAKAOMI!
HOW DO YOU DO?
I'M YOUR HOMEROOM TEACHER, TAKAOMI SAEKI.
PLEASED TO MEET YOU.
GO, MAFUYU!
YES, SIR!

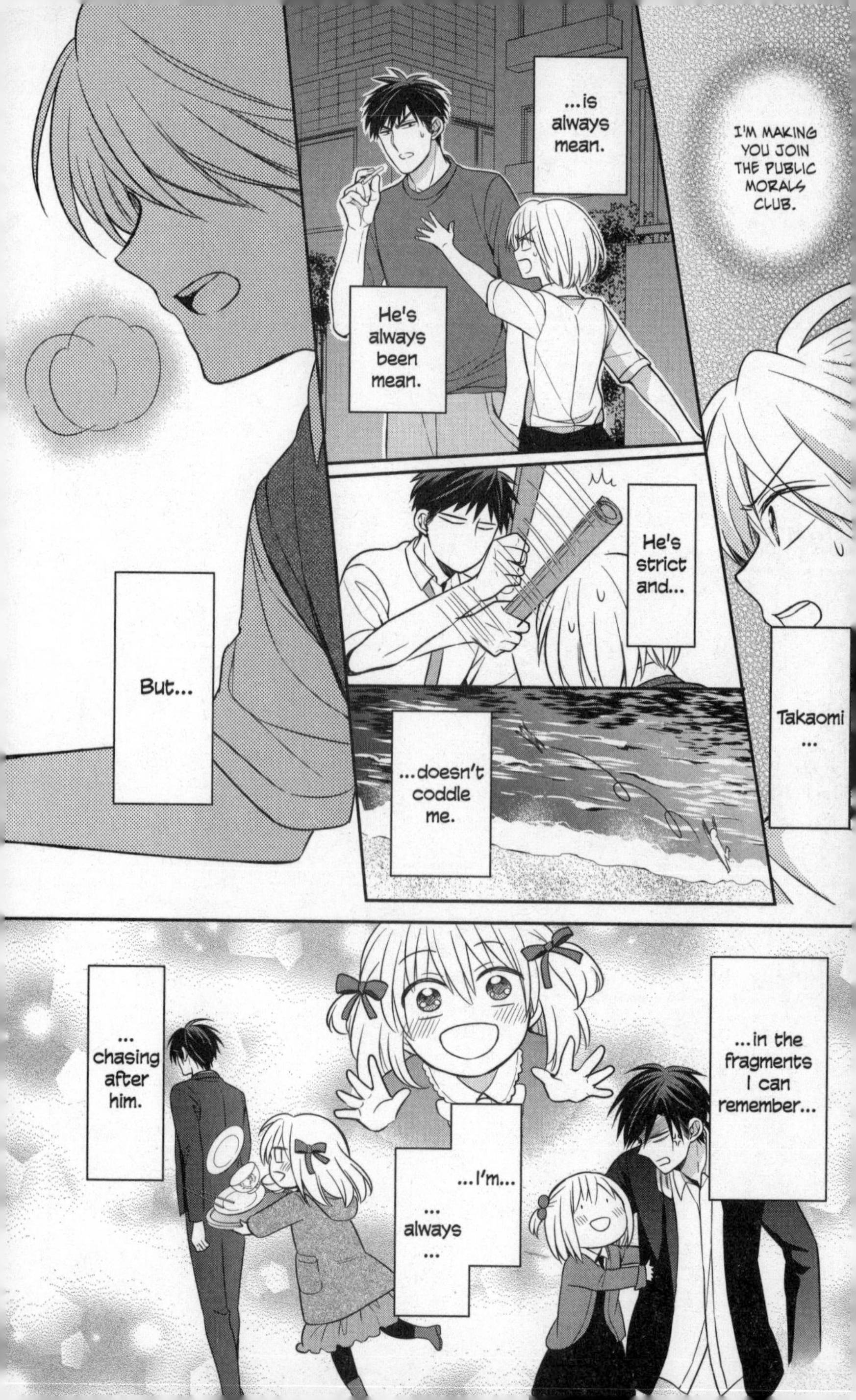
I'M MAKING YOU JOIN THE PUBLIC MORALS CLUB.
Takaomi ...
...is always mean.
He's always been mean.
He's strict and...
...doesn't coddle me.
But...
...in the fragments I can remember...
...I'm...
... always ...
... chasing after him.

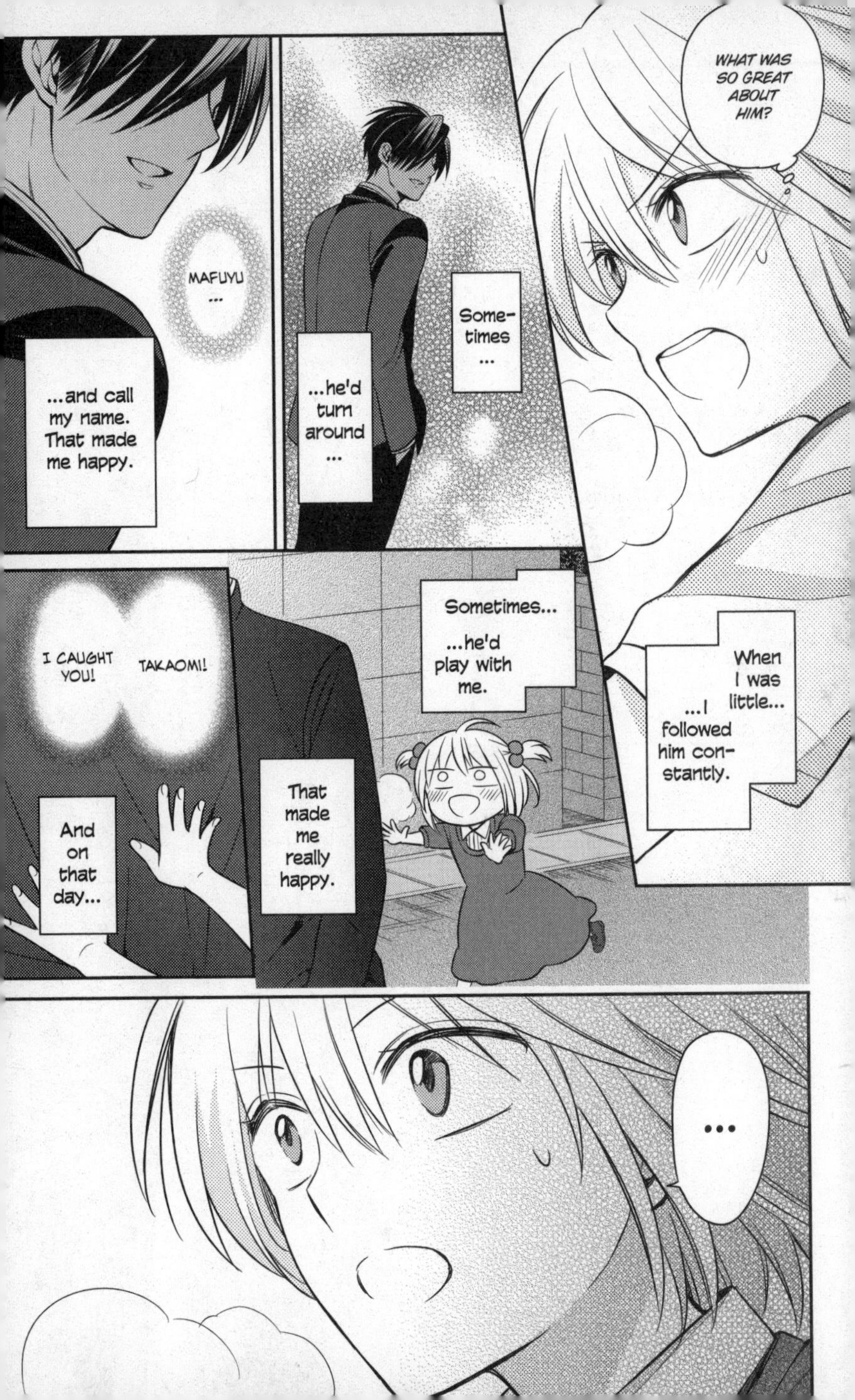
WHAT WAS SO GREAT ABOUT HIM?
When I was little...
...I followed him con-stantly.
Some-times ...
...he'd turn around ...
MAFUYU ...
...and call my name. That made me happy.
Sometimes...
...he'd play with me.
That made me really happy.
TAKAOMI!
I CAUGHT YOU!
And on that day...
...

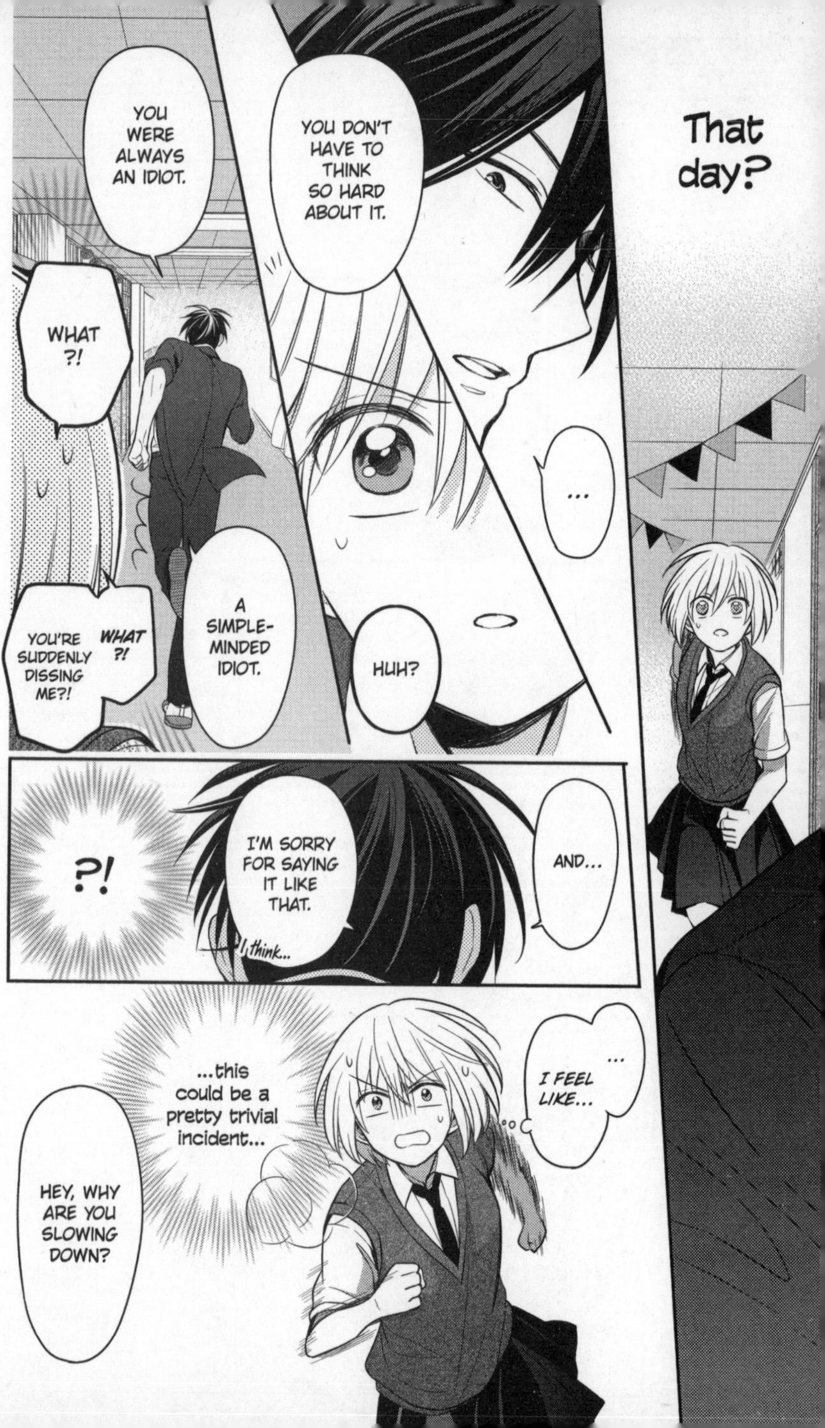

That day?
YOU DON'T HAVE TO THINK SO HARD ABOUT IT.
...
HUH?
YOU WERE ALWAYS AN IDIOT.
WHAT ?!
A SIMPLE-MINDED IDIOT.
WHAT ?!
YOU'RE SUDDENLY DISSING ME?!
AND...
I'M SORRY FOR SAYING IT LIKE THAT.
I, think...
?!
... I FEEL LIKE...
...this could be a pretty trivial incident...
HEY, WHY ARE YOU SLOWING DOWN?

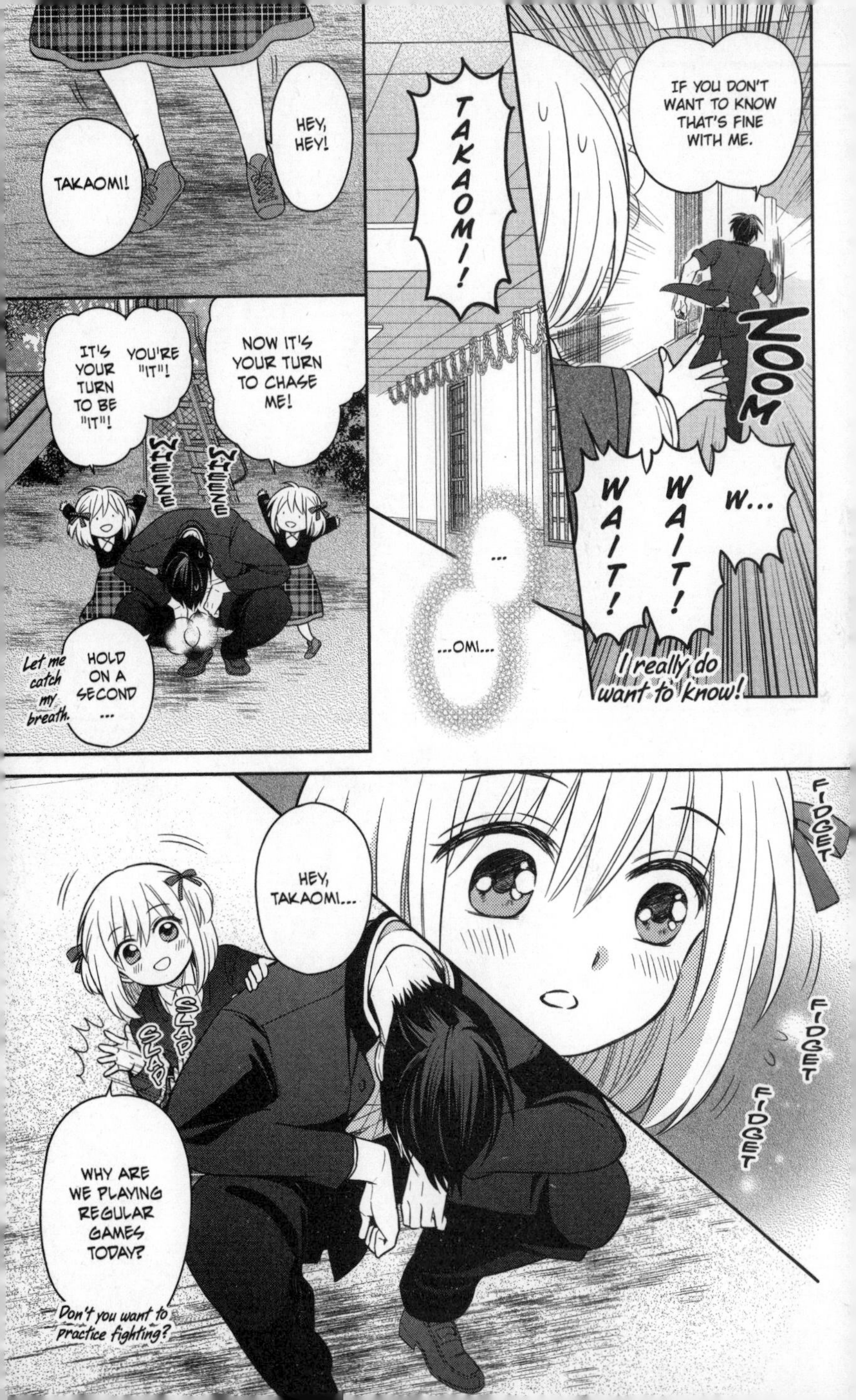

IF YOU DON'T WANT TO KNOW THAT'S FINE WITH ME.
ZOOM
W...
WAIT!
WAIT!
I really do want to know!
TAKAOMI!!
...
...OMI...
HEY, HEY!
TAKAOMI!
NOW IT'S YOUR TURN TO CHASE ME!
YOU'RE "IT"!
IT'S YOUR TURN TO BE "IT"!
WHEEZE
WHEEZE
HOLD ON A SECOND ...
Let me catch my breath.
FIDGET
FIDGET
FIDGET
HEY, TAKAOMI...
SLAP
SLAP
WHY ARE WE PLAYING REGULAR GAMES TODAY?
Don't you want to practice fighting?

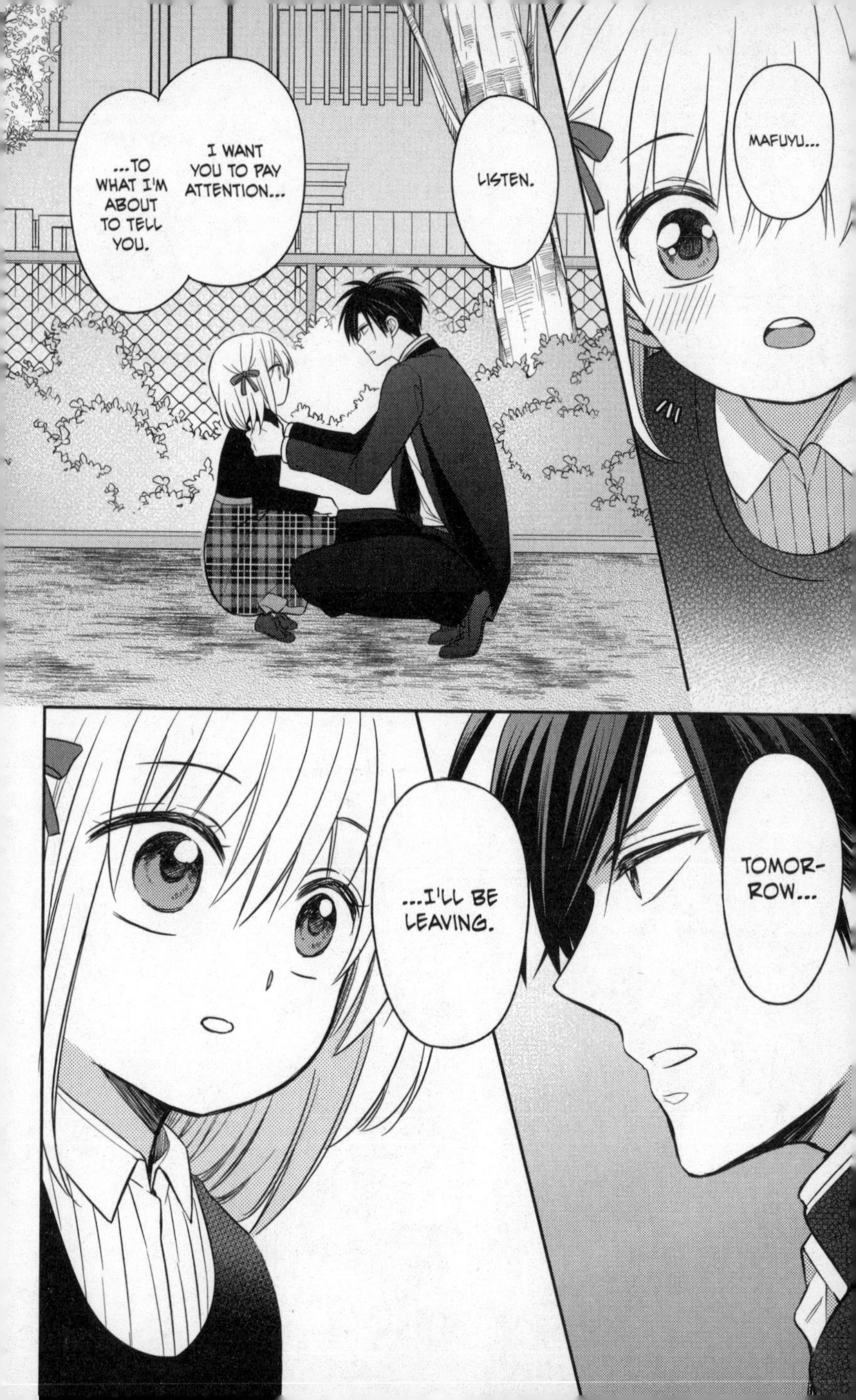
MAFUYU...
LISTEN.
I WANT YOU TO PAY ATTENTION...
...TO WHAT I'M ABOUT TO TELL YOU.
TOMOR-ROW...
...I'LL BE LEAVING.

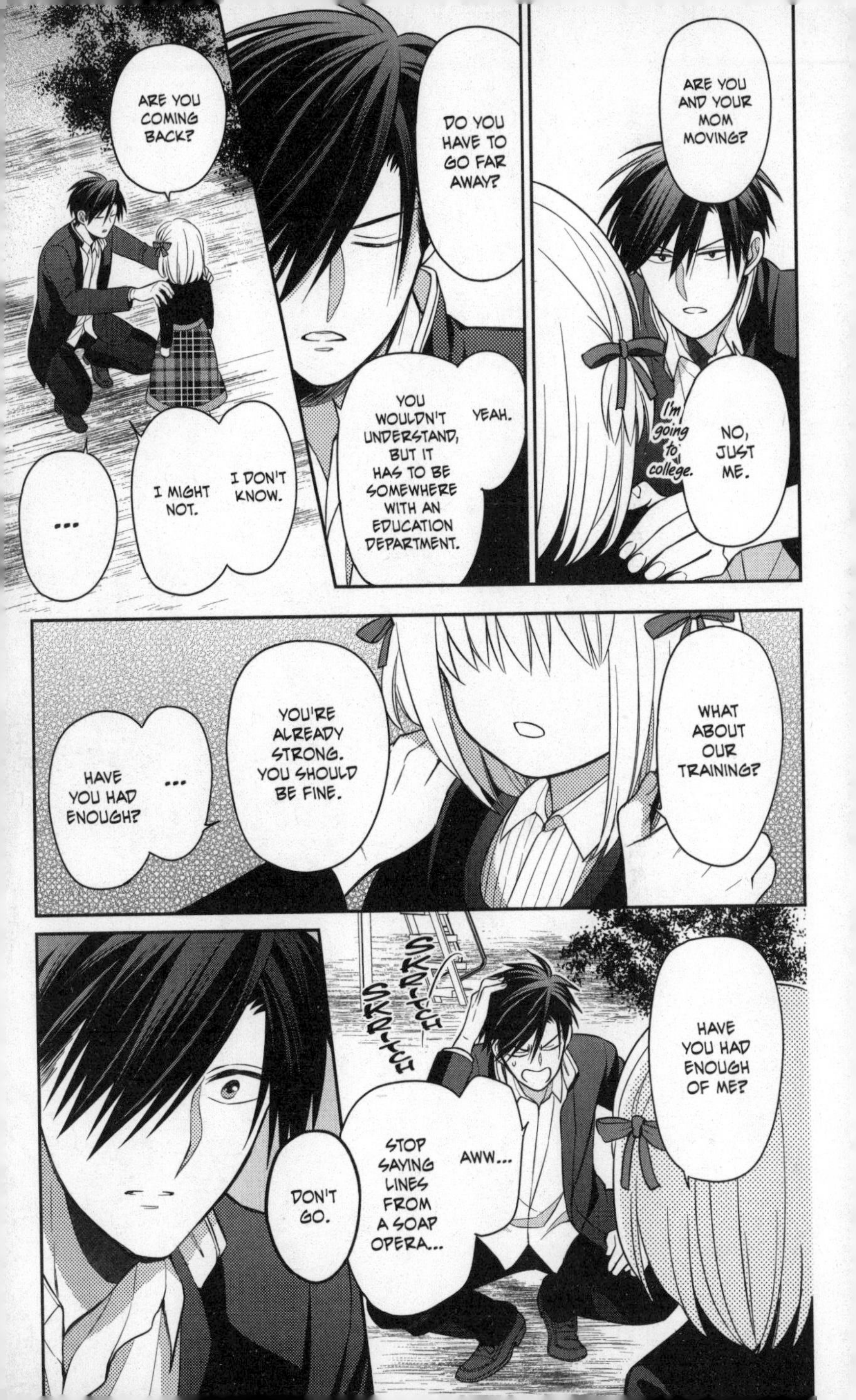
ARE YOU AND YOUR MOM MOVING?
NO, JUST ME.
I'm going to college.
DO YOU HAVE TO GO FAR AWAY?
YEAH.
YOU WOULDN'T UNDERSTAND, BUT IT HAS TO BE SOMEWHERE WITH AN EDUCATION DEPARTMENT.
ARE YOU COMING BACK?
I DON'T KNOW.
I MIGHT NOT.
...
WHAT ABOUT OUR TRAINING?
YOU'RE ALREADY STRONG. YOU SHOULD BE FINE.
...
HAVE YOU HAD ENOUGH?
HAVE YOU HAD ENOUGH OF ME?
AWW...
STOP SAYING LINES FROM A SOAP OPERA...
SKRITCH SKRITCH
DON'T GO.

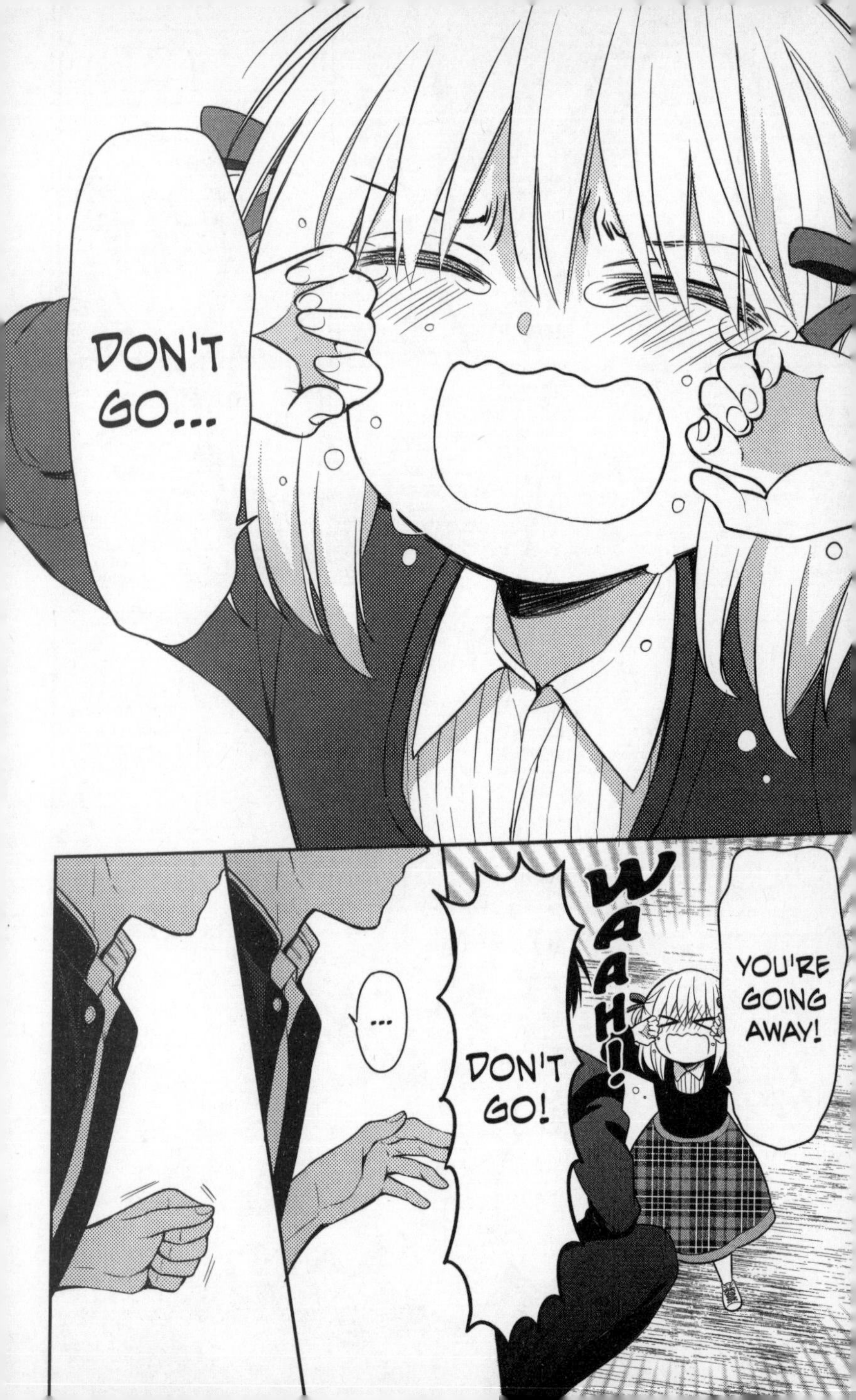
DON'T GO...
YOU'RE GOING AWAY!
WAAH!!
DON'T GO!
...

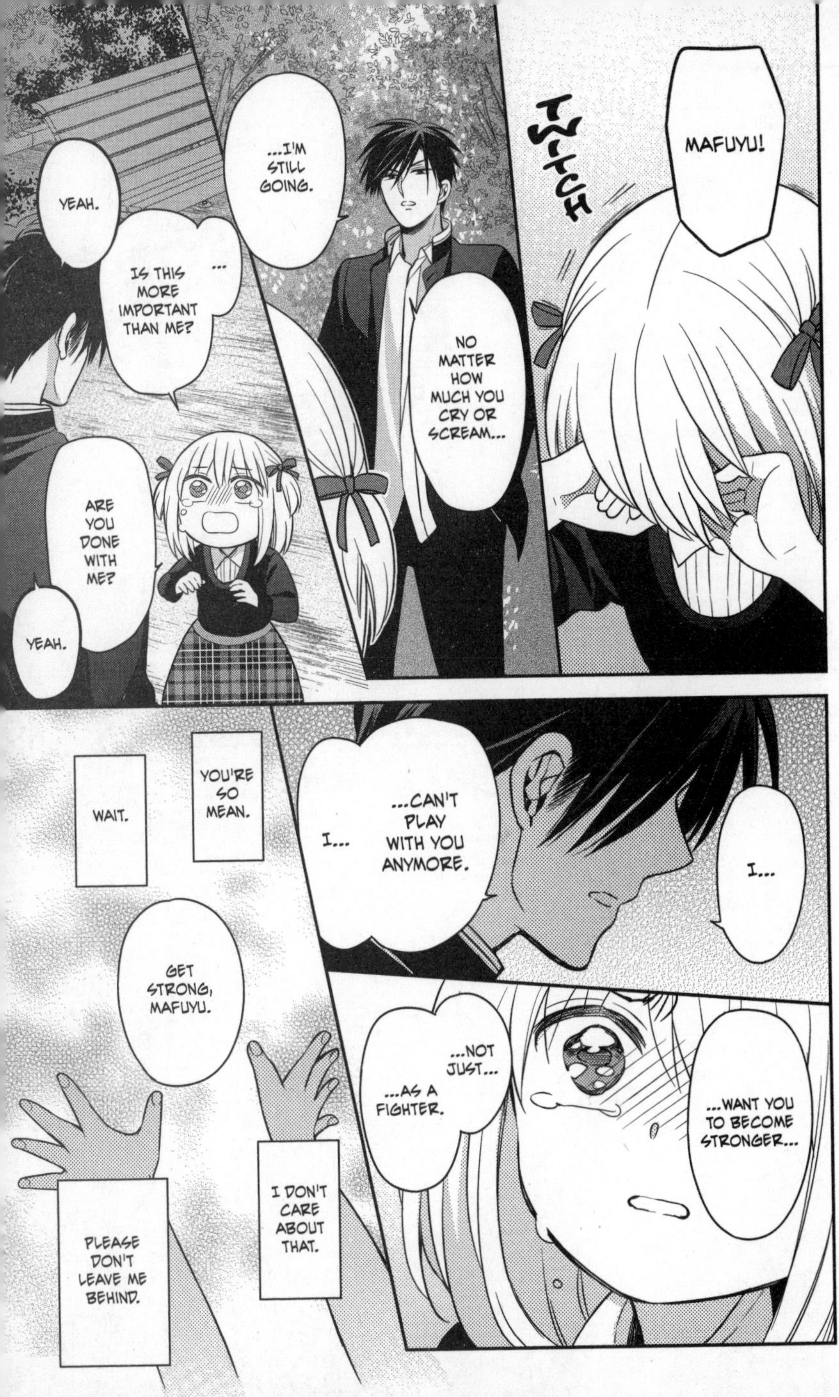
MAFUYU!
TWITCH
NO MATTER HOW MUCH YOU CRY OR SCREAM...
...I'M STILL GOING.
...
IS THIS MORE IMPORTANT THAN ME?
YEAH.
ARE YOU DONE WITH ME?
YEAH.
I...
...CAN'T PLAY WITH YOU ANYMORE.
I...
...WANT YOU TO BECOME STRONGER...
...NOT JUST...
...AS A FIGHTER.
YOU'RE SO MEAN.
WAIT.
GET STRONG, MAFUYU.
I DON'T CARE ABOUT THAT.
PLEASE DON'T LEAVE ME BEHIND.

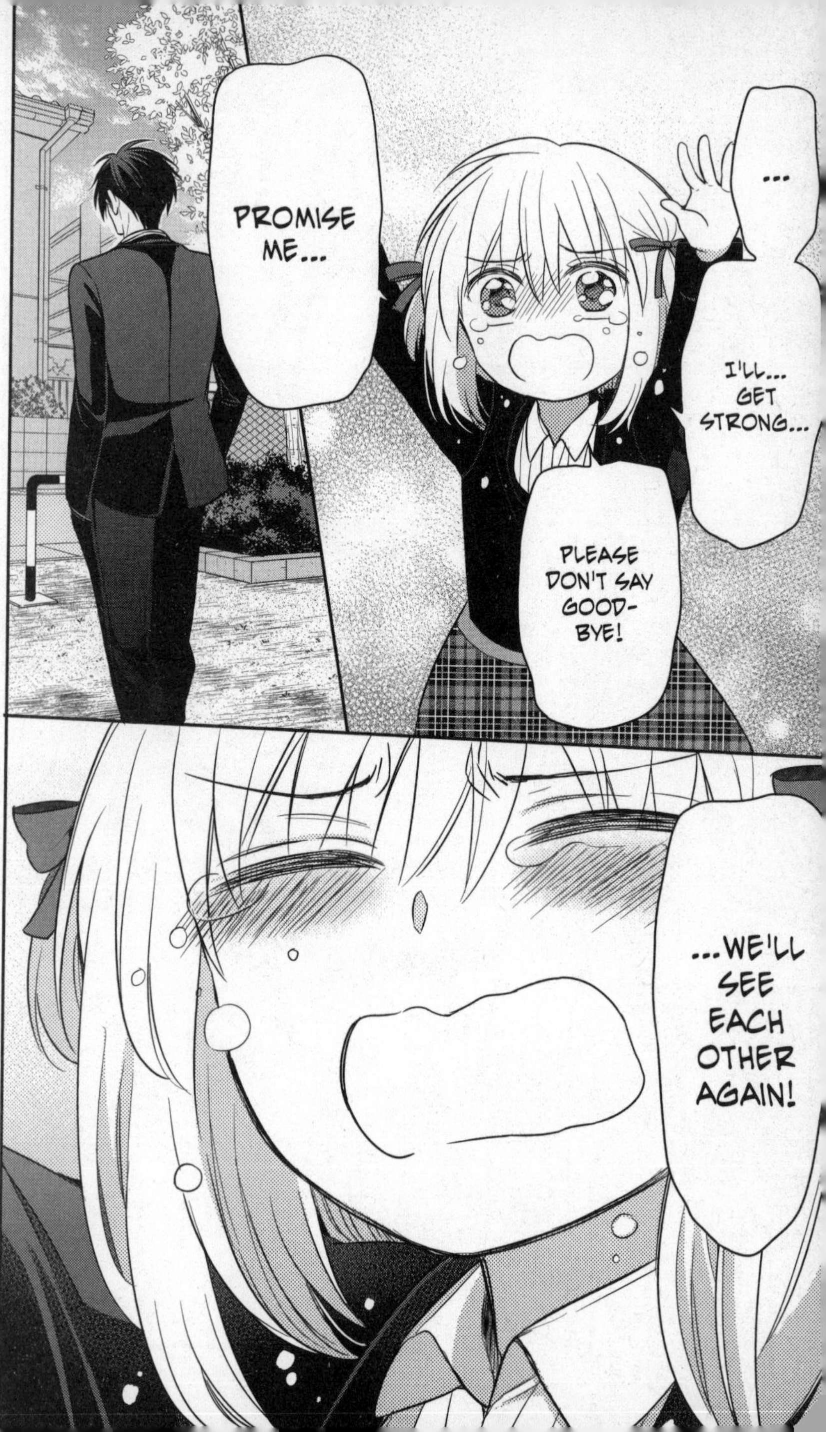
...
I'LL... GET STRONG...
PLEASE DON'T SAY GOOD-BYE!
PROMISE ME...
...WE'LL SEE EACH OTHER AGAIN!

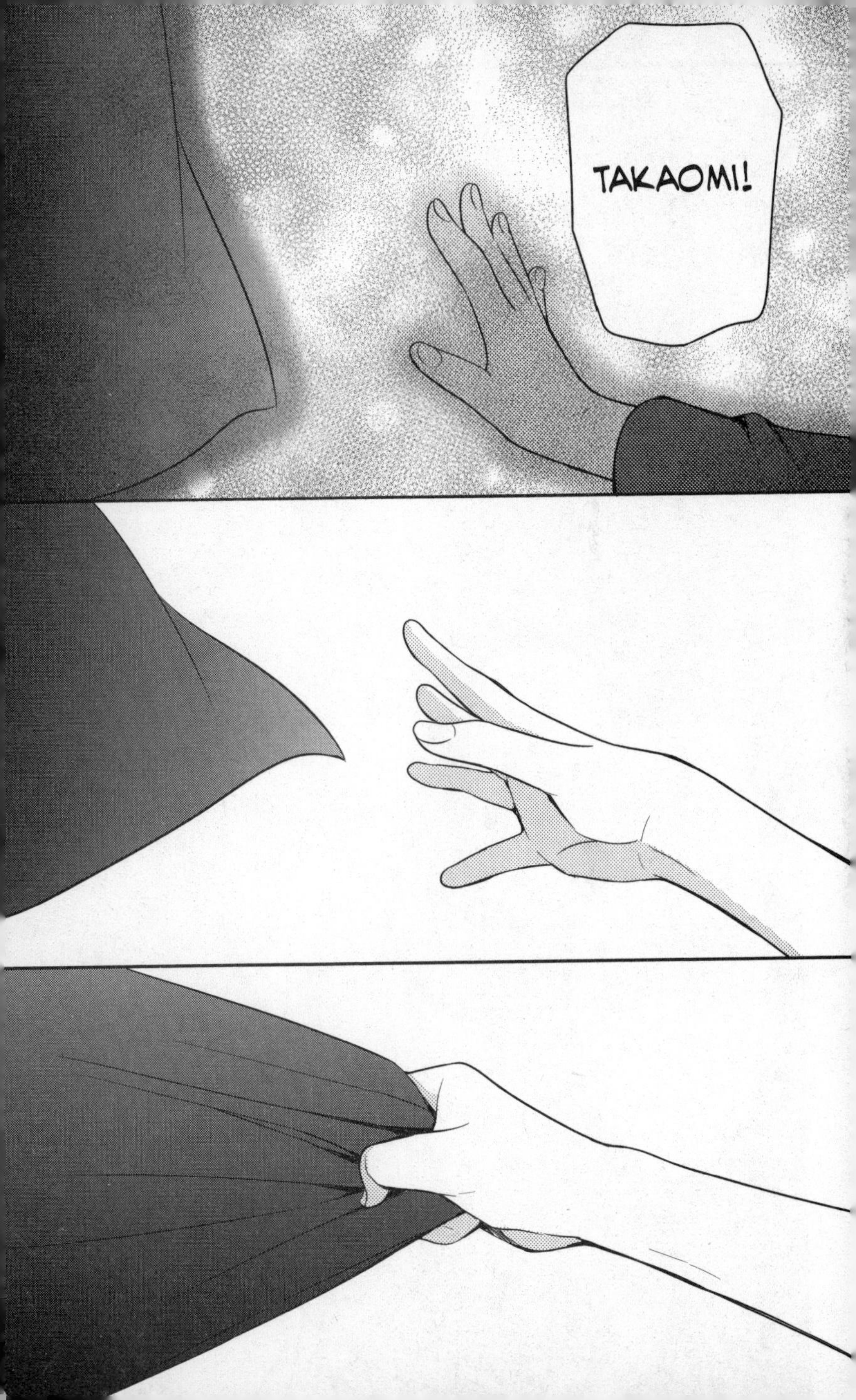
TAKAOMI!

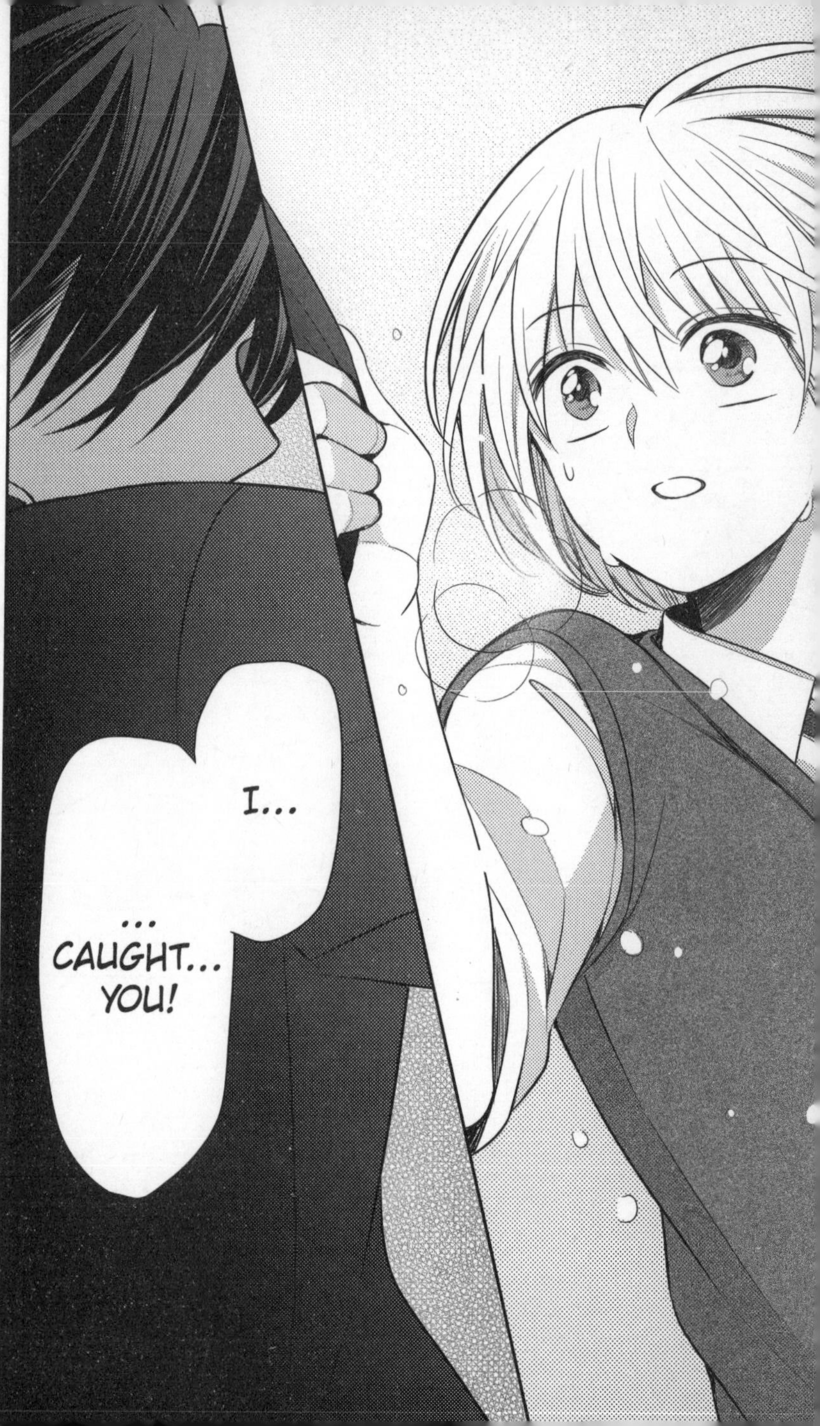
I...
...CAUGHT... YOU!

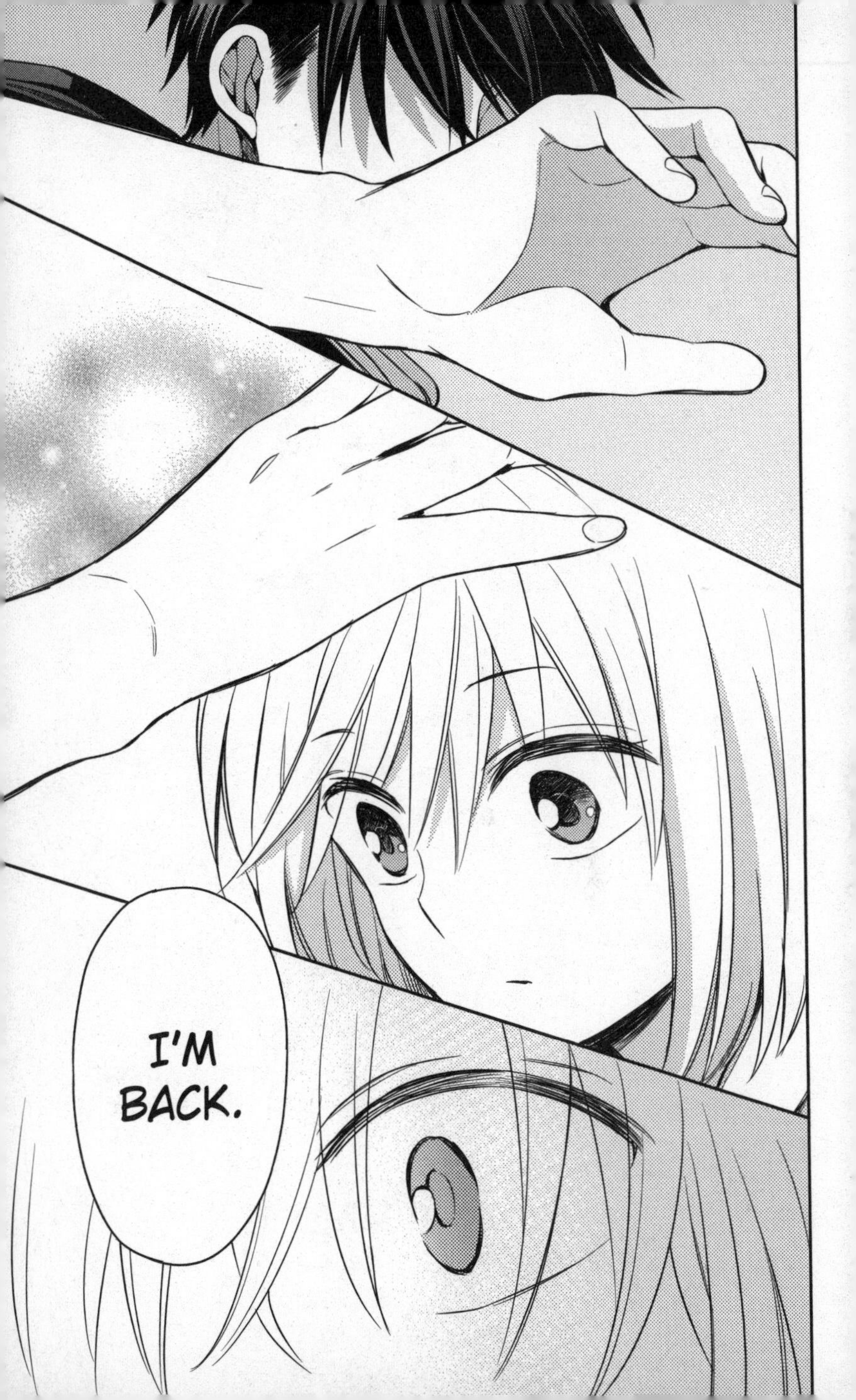
I'M BACK.

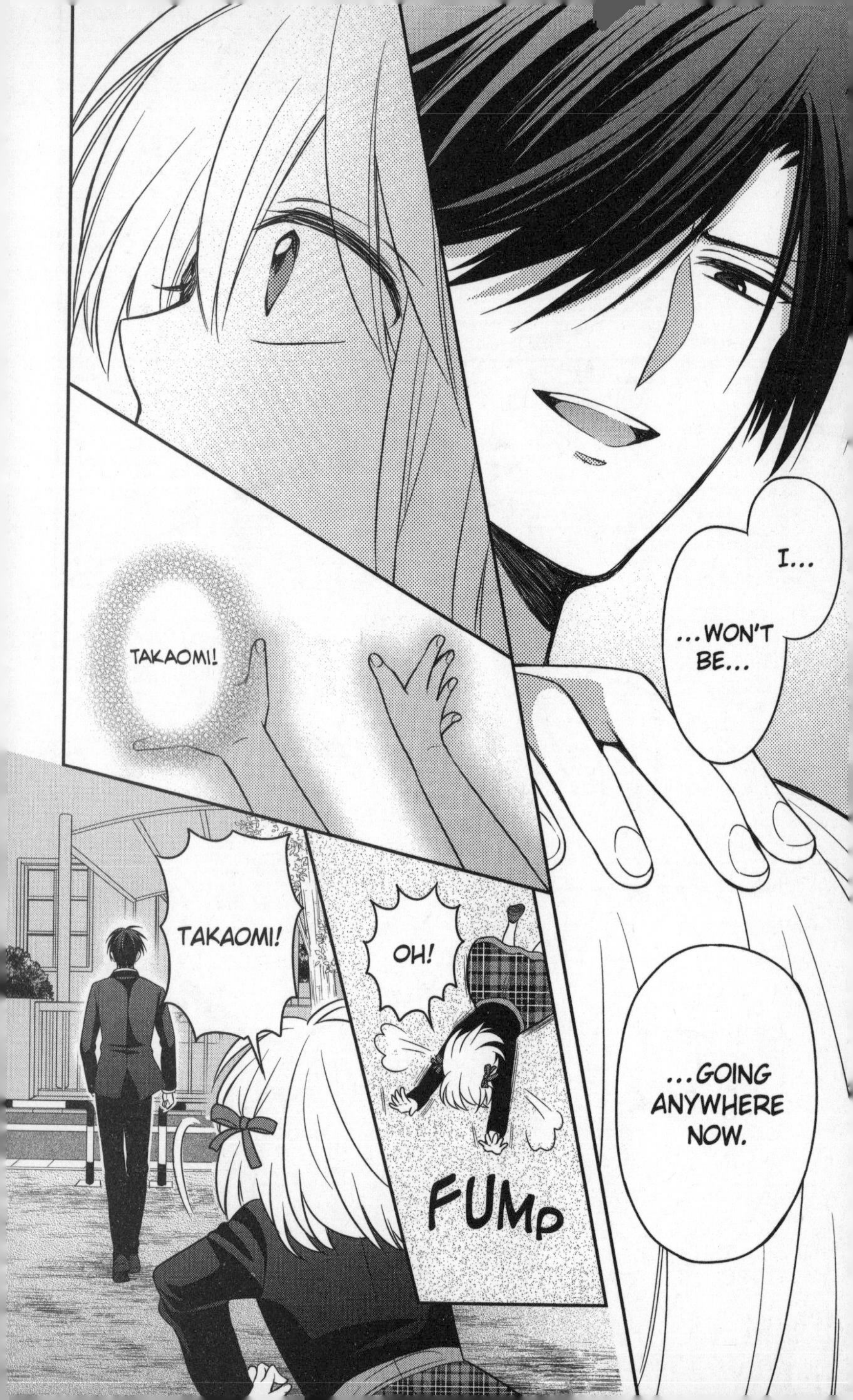
I...
...WON'T BE...
...GOING ANYWHERE NOW.
TAKAOMI!
OH!
FUMP
TAKAOMI!

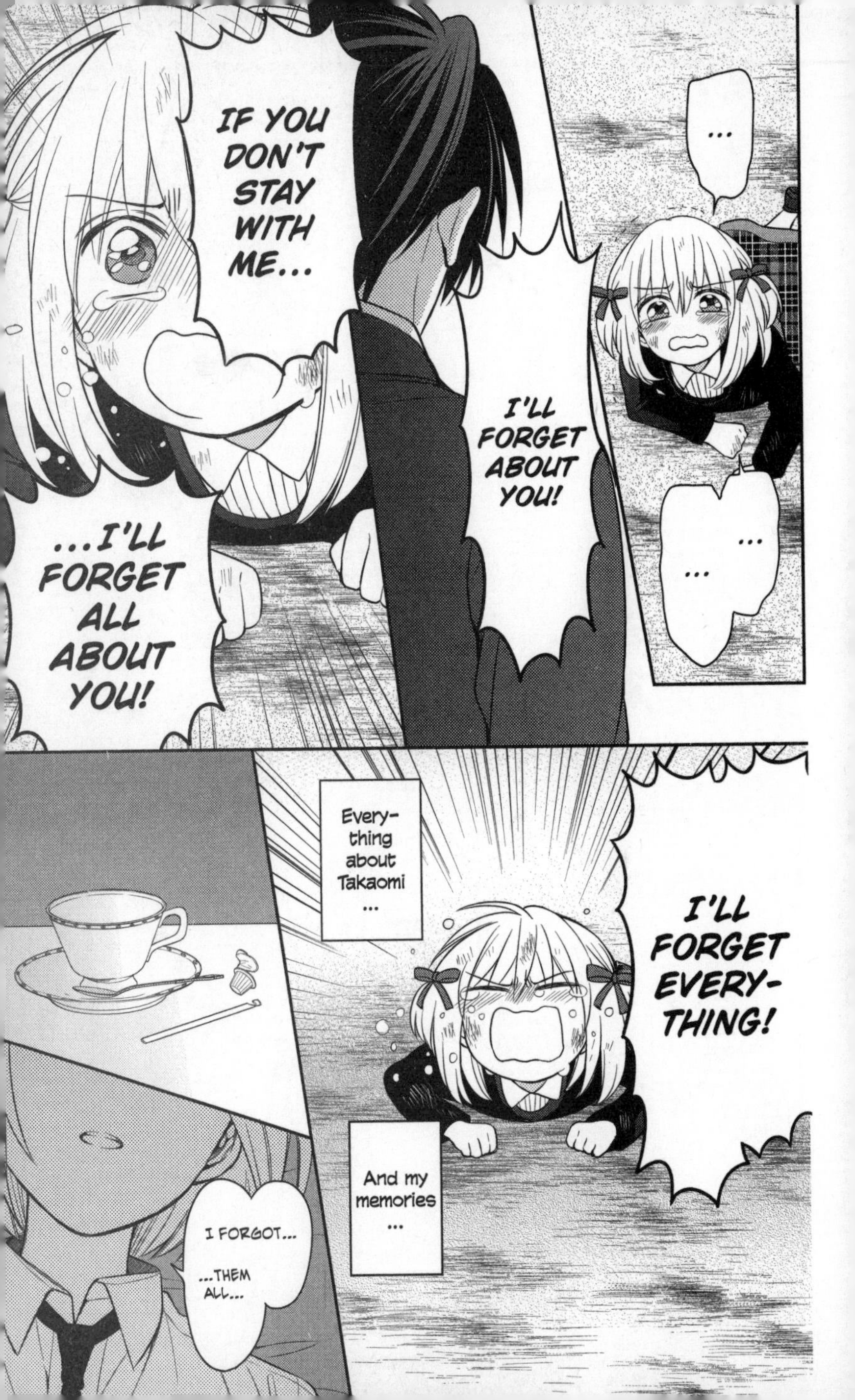
...
... ...
IF YOU DON'T STAY WITH ME...
I'LL FORGET ABOUT YOU!
...I'LL FORGET ALL ABOUT YOU!
I'LL FORGET EVERY-THING!
Every-thing about Takaomi ...
And my memories ...
I FORGOT...
...THEM ALL...

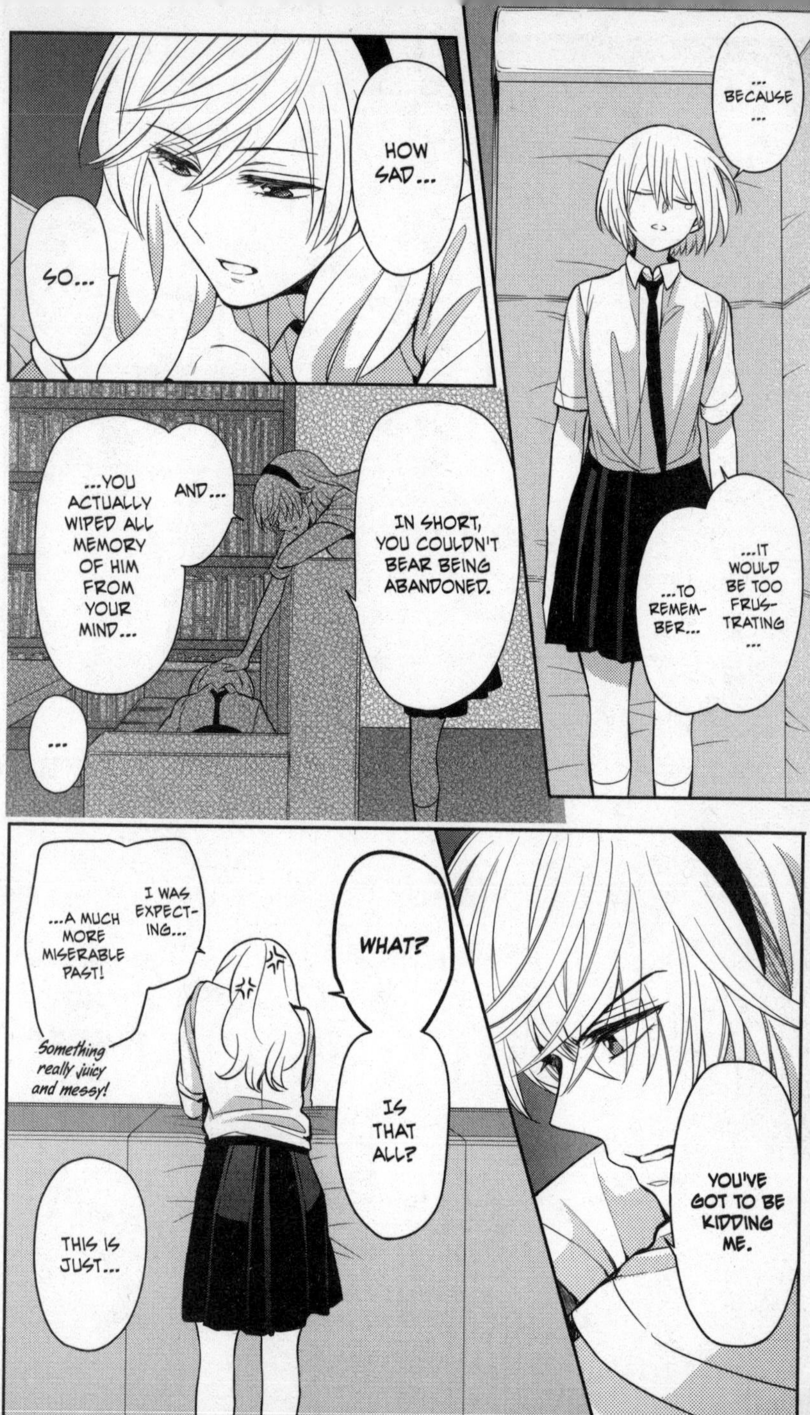

... BECAUSE ...
...IT WOULD BE TOO FRUS-TRATING ...
...TO REMEM-BER...
HOW SAD...
SO...
IN SHORT, YOU COULDN'T BEAR BEING ABANDONED.
AND...
...YOU ACTUALLY WIPED ALL MEMORY OF HIM FROM YOUR MIND...
...
YOU'VE GOT TO BE KIDDING ME.
WHAT?
IS THAT ALL?
I WAS EXPECT-ING...
...A MUCH MORE MISERABLE PAST!
Something really juicy and messy!
THIS IS JUST...

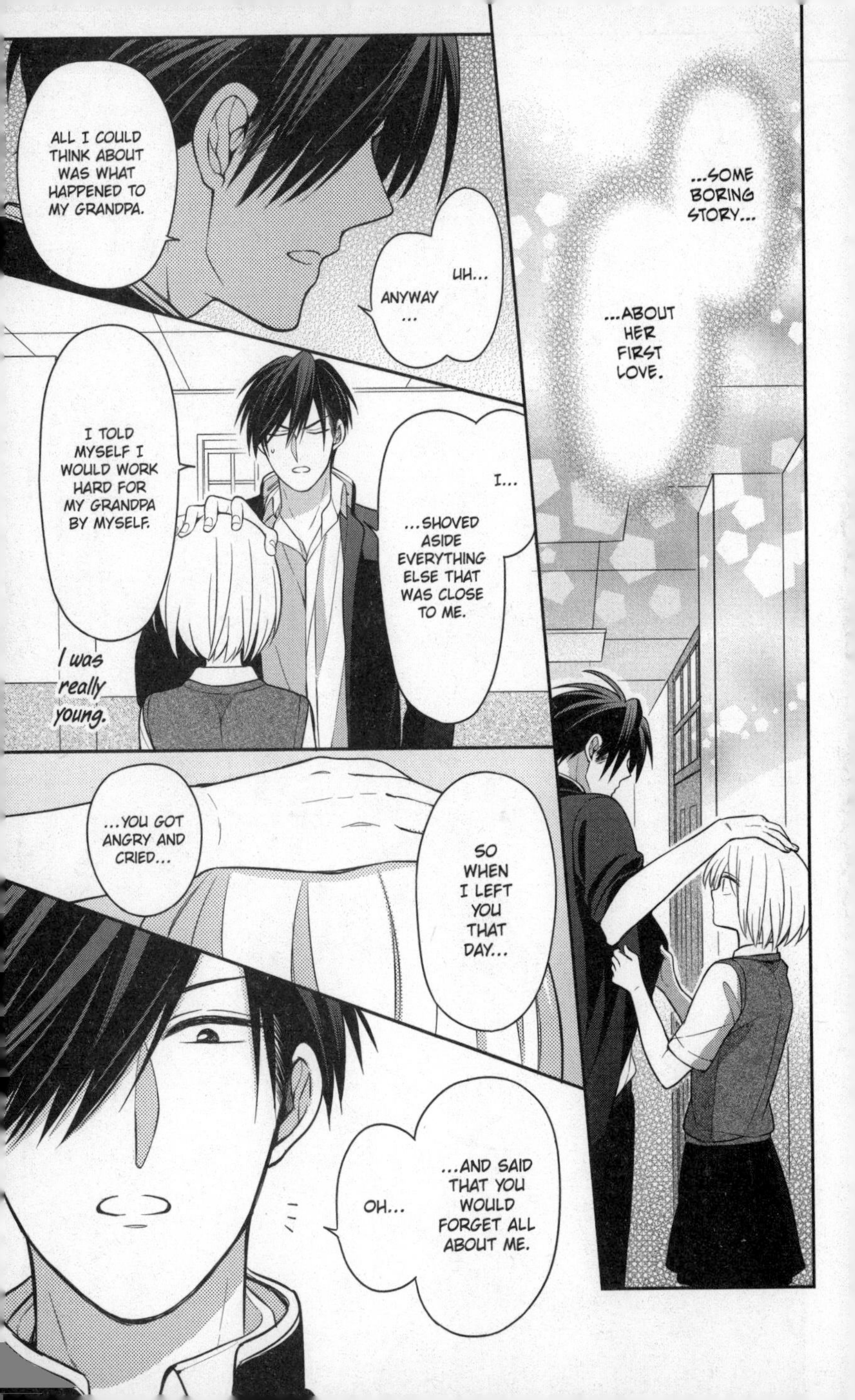
...SOME BORING STORY...
...ABOUT HER FIRST LOVE.
ALL I COULD THINK ABOUT WAS WHAT HAPPENED TO MY GRANDPA.
UH... ANYWAY...
I...
...SHOVED ASIDE EVERYTHING ELSE THAT WAS CLOSE TO ME.
I TOLD MYSELF I WOULD WORK HARD FOR MY GRANDPA BY MYSELF.
I was really young.
SO WHEN I LEFT YOU THAT DAY...
...YOU GOT ANGRY AND CRIED...
...AND SAID THAT YOU WOULD FORGET ALL ABOUT ME.
OH...

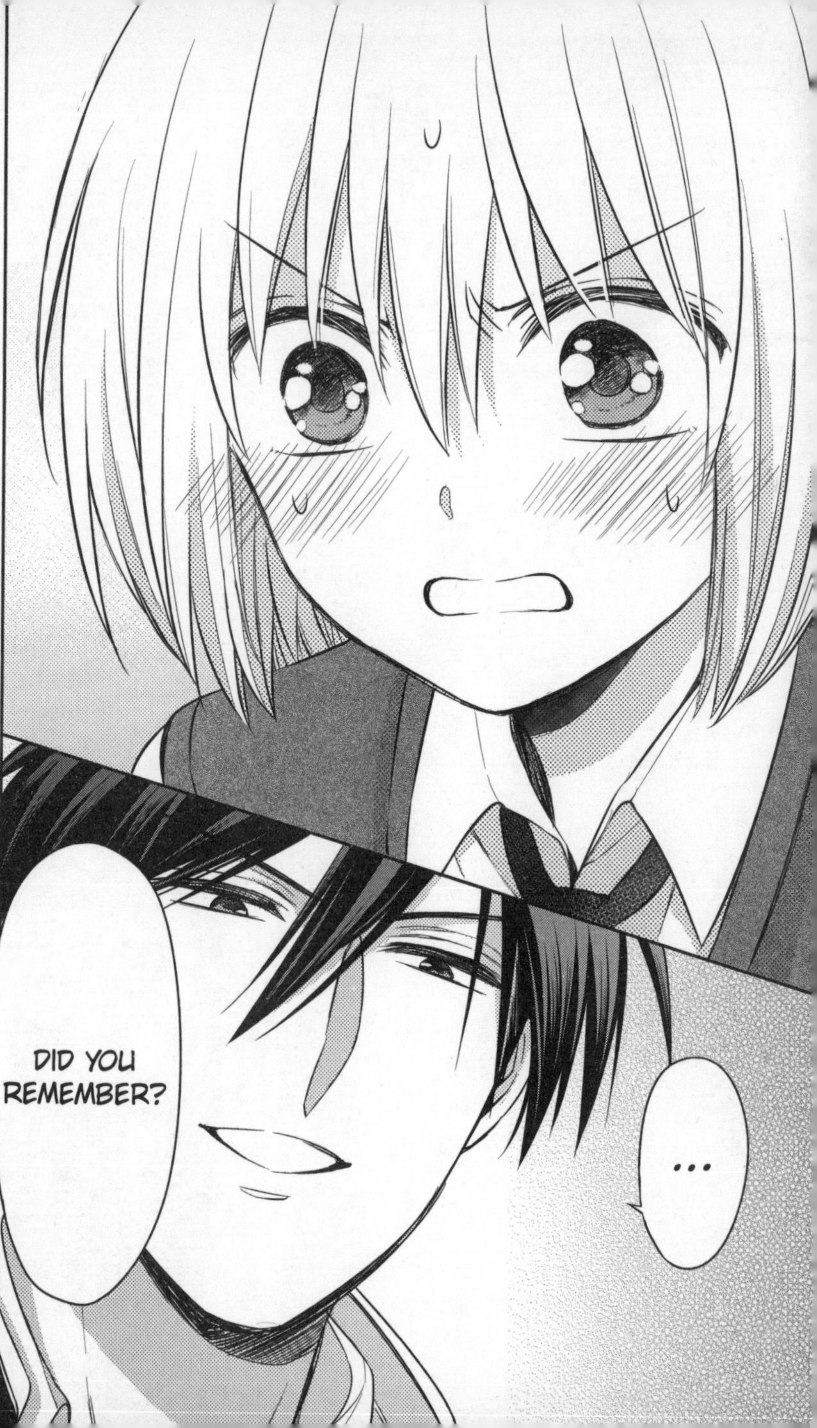
...
DID YOU REMEMBER?

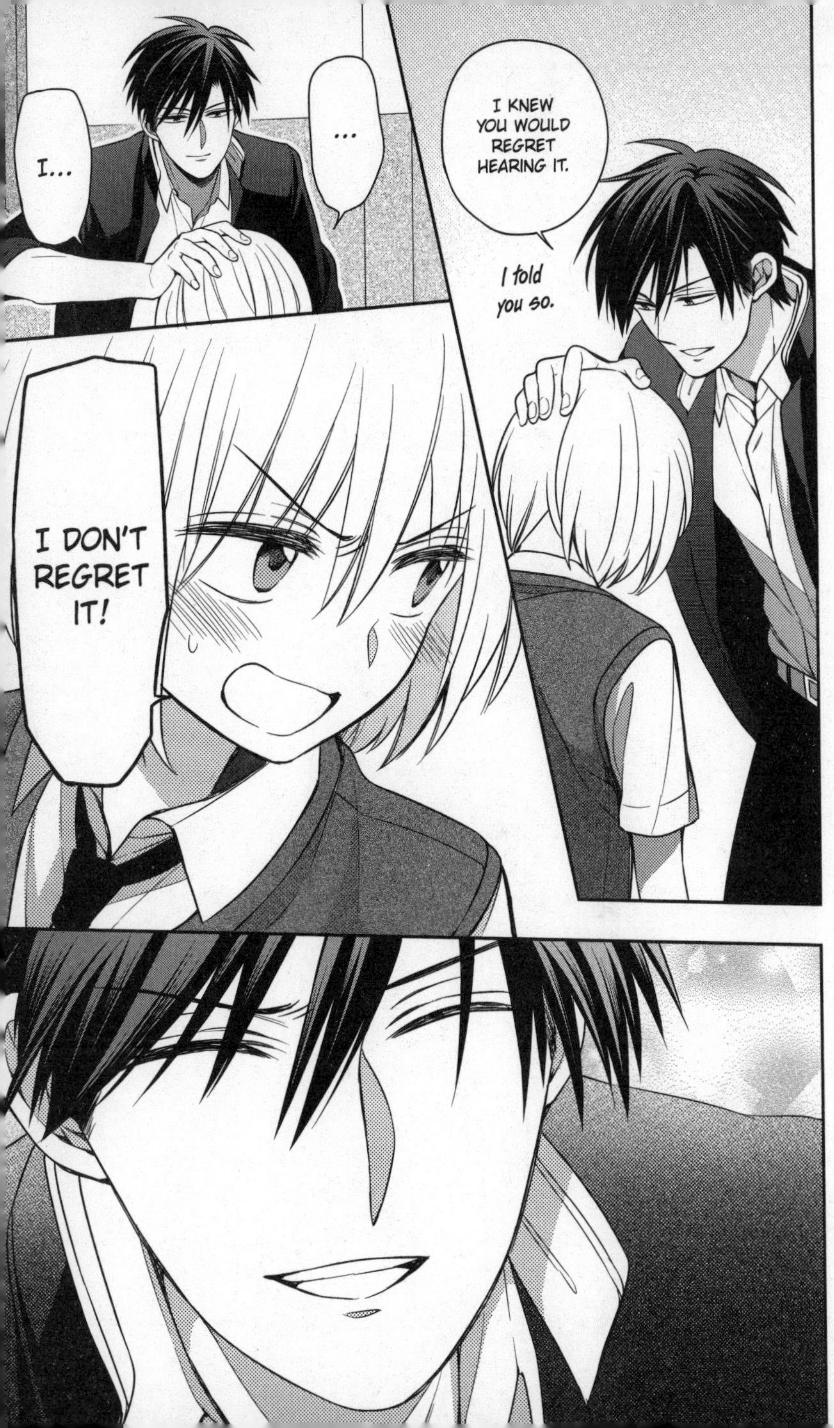
I KNEW YOU WOULD REGRET HEARING IT.
I told you so.
...
I...
I DON'T REGRET IT!

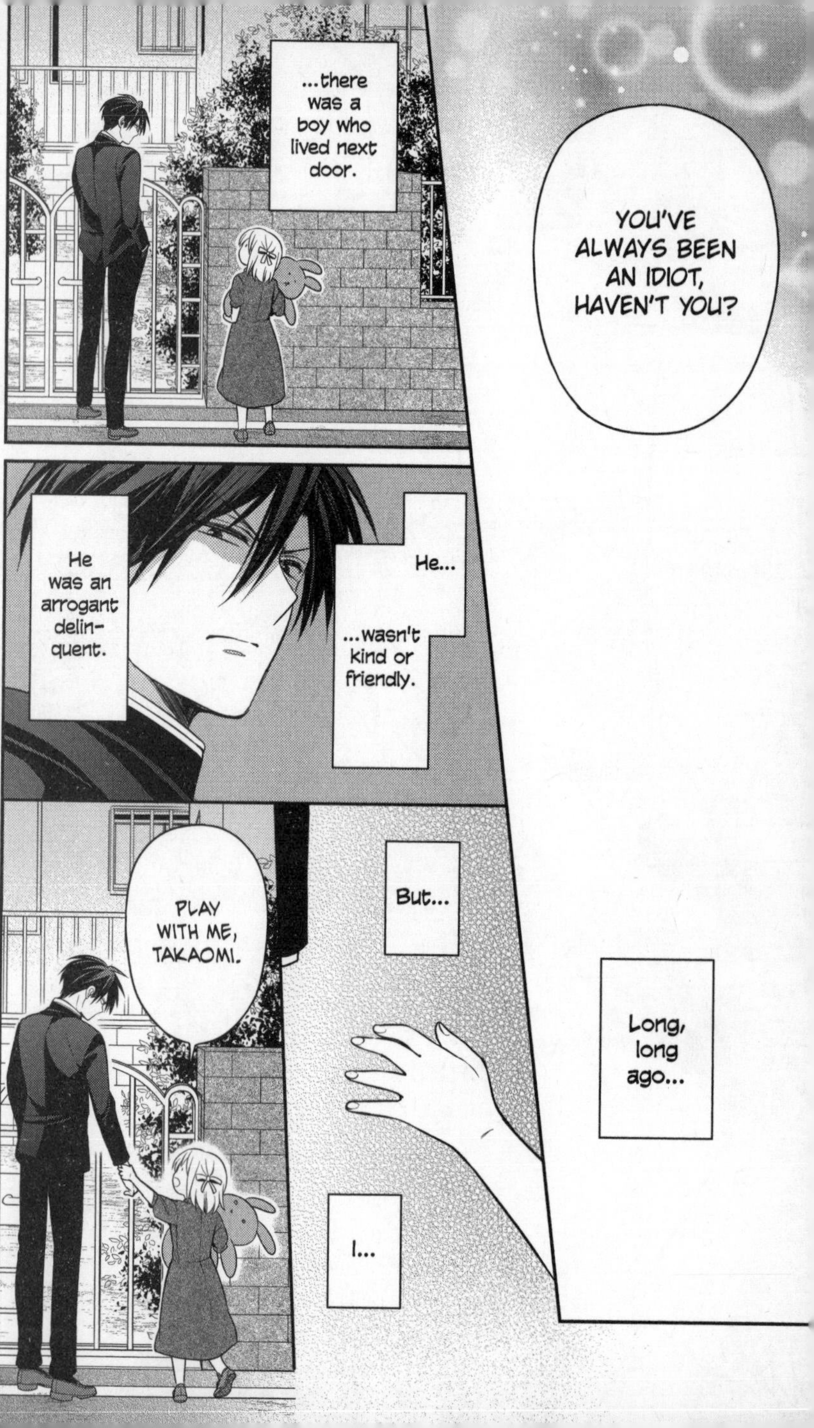
YOU'VE ALWAYS BEEN AN IDIOT, HAVEN'T YOU?
Long, long ago...
...there was a boy who lived next door.
He...
...wasn't kind or friendly.
He was an arrogant delinquent.
But...
I...
PLAY WITH ME, TAKAOMI.

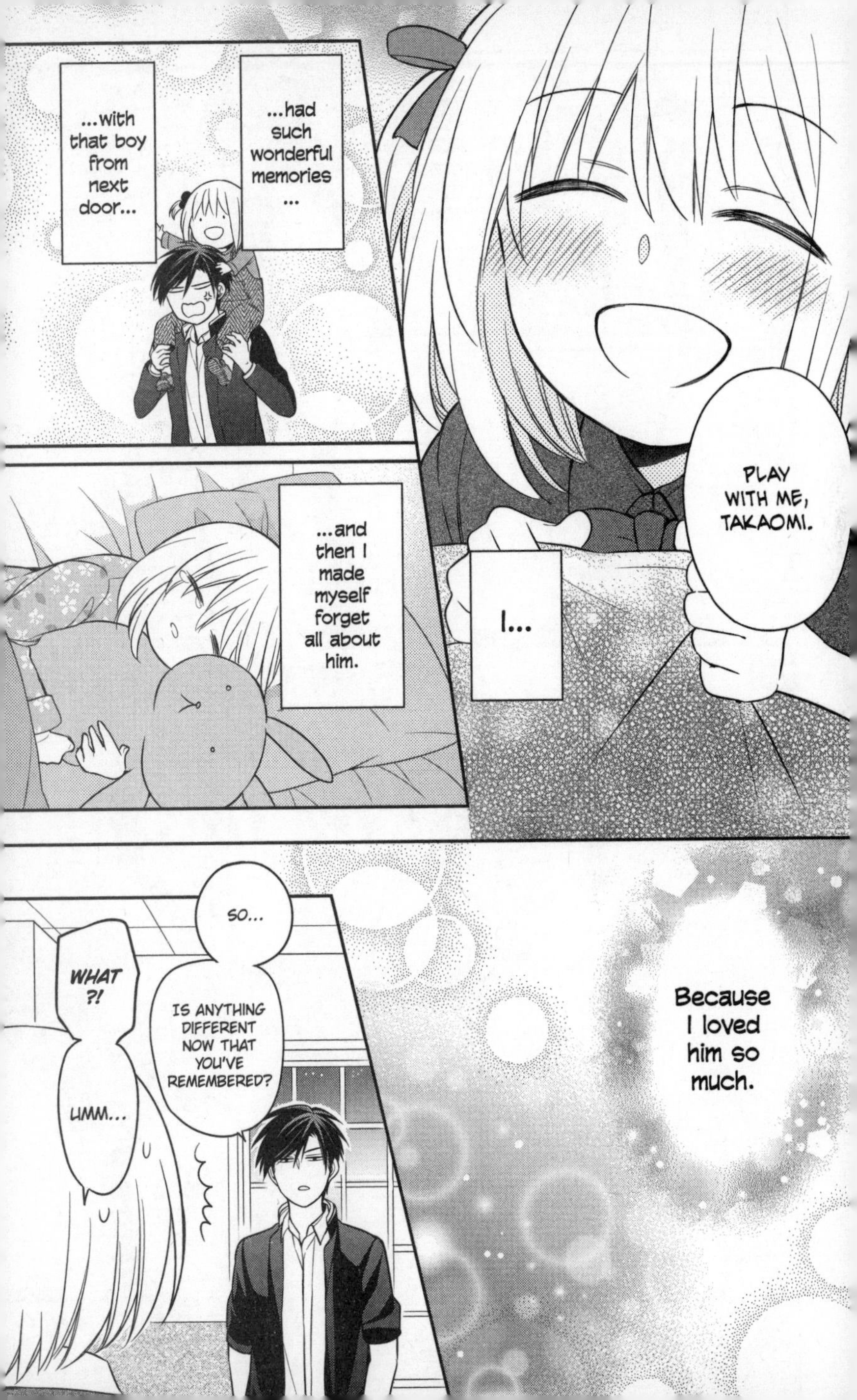
PLAY WITH ME, TAKAOMI.
I...
...had such wonderful memories...
...with that boy from next door...
...and then I made myself forget all about him.
Because I loved him so much.
SO...
IS ANYTHING DIFFERENT NOW THAT YOU'VE REMEMBERED?
WHAT?!
UMM...

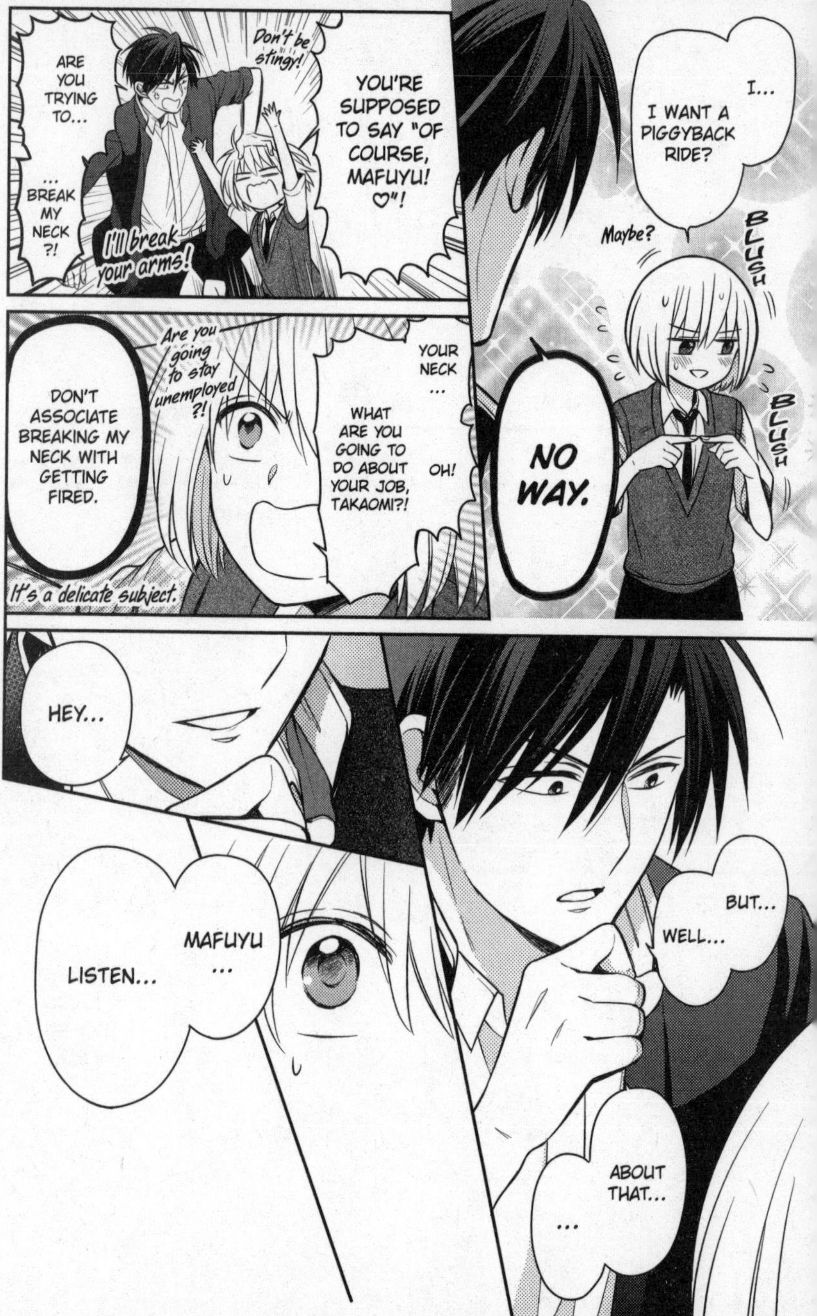
I...
I WANT A PIGGYBACK RIDE?
Maybe?
BLUSH
BLUSH
NO WAY.
YOU'RE SUPPOSED TO SAY "OF COURSE, MAFUYU! ♡"!
Don't be stingy!
ARE YOU TRYING TO...
... BREAK MY NECK ?!
I'll break your arms!
YOUR NECK ...
OH!
WHAT ARE YOU GOING TO DO ABOUT YOUR JOB, TAKAOMI?!
Are you going to stay unemployed ?!
DON'T ASSOCIATE BREAKING MY NECK WITH GETTING FIRED.
It's a delicate subject.
HEY...
BUT... WELL...
MAFUYU ...
LISTEN...
ABOUT THAT...
...

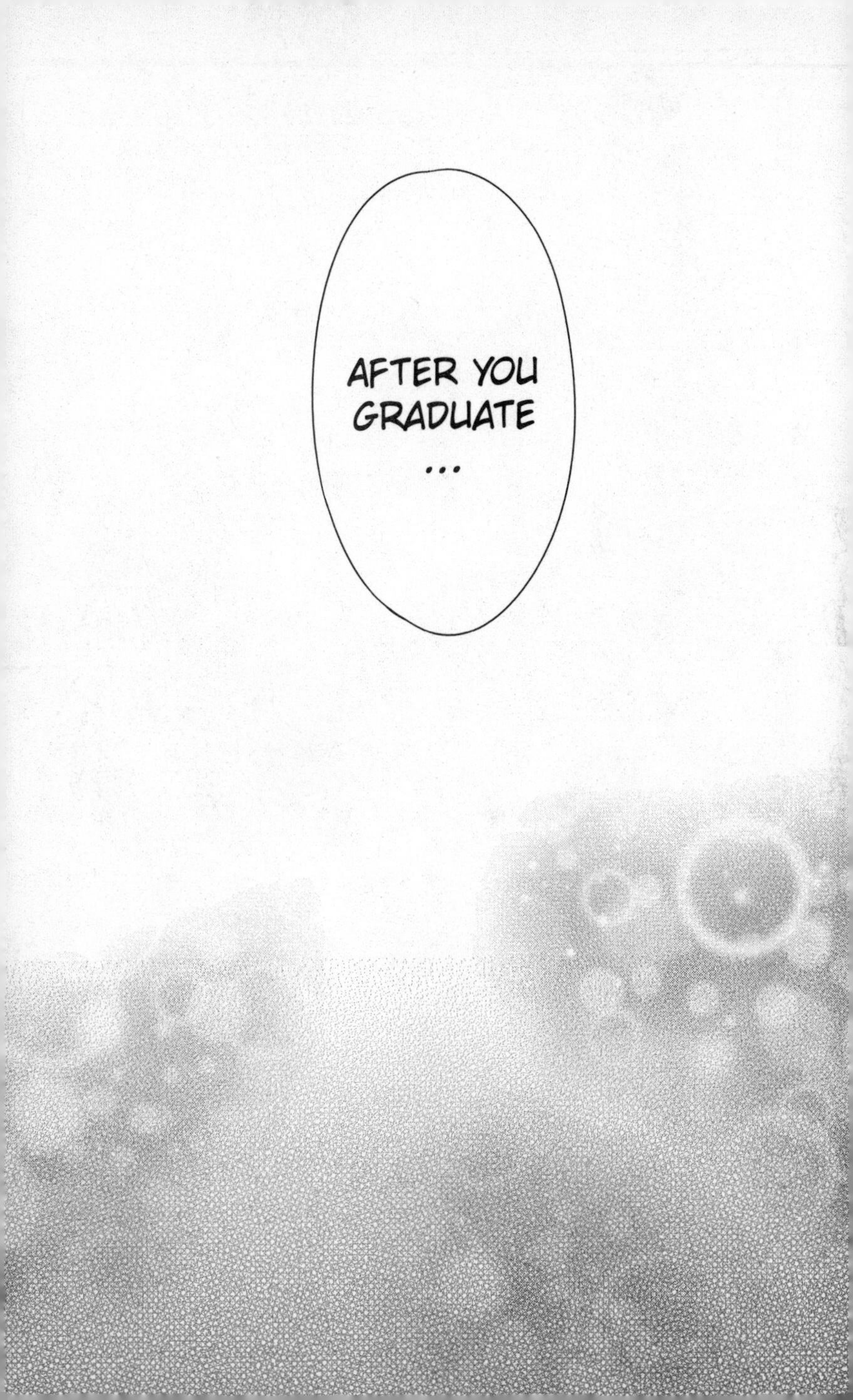
AFTER YOU GRADUATE ...

Chapter 168—The End

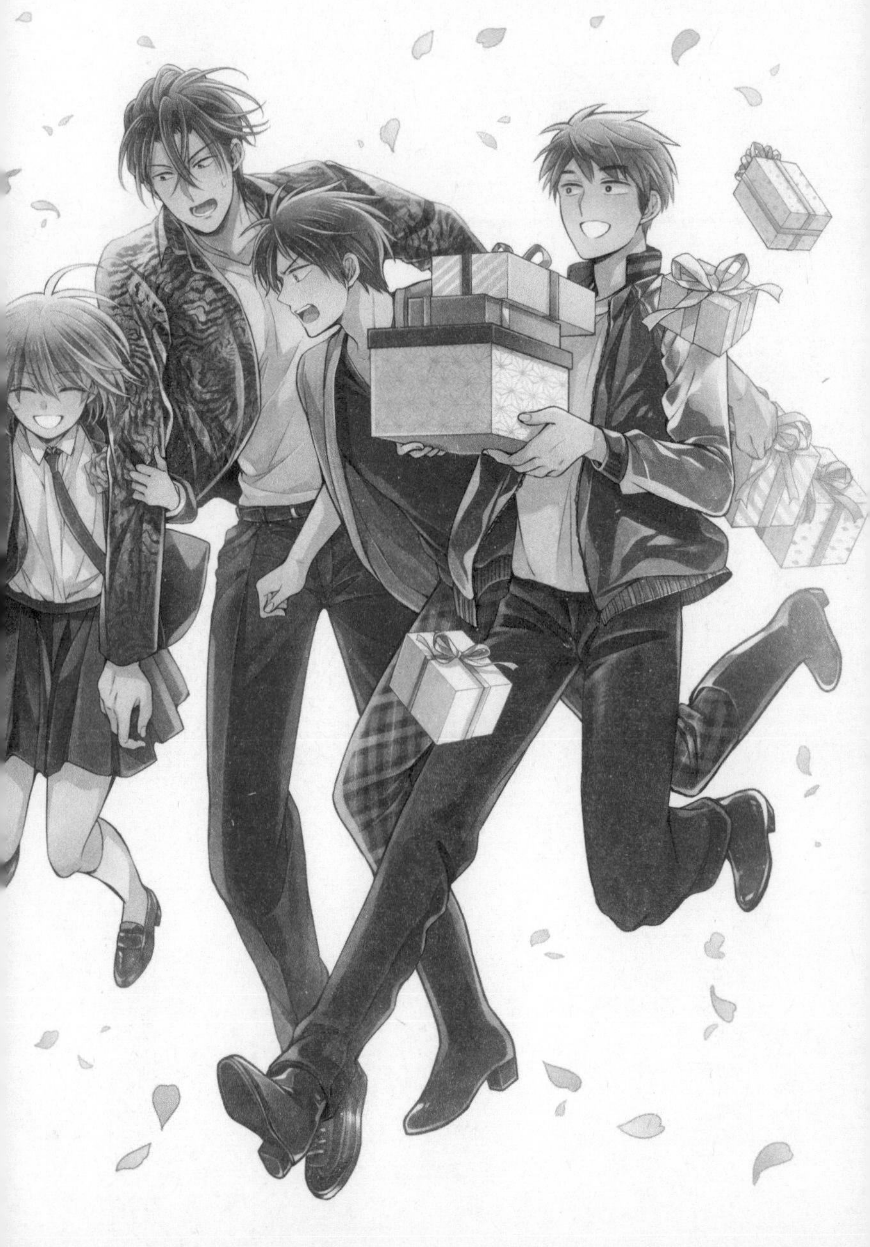

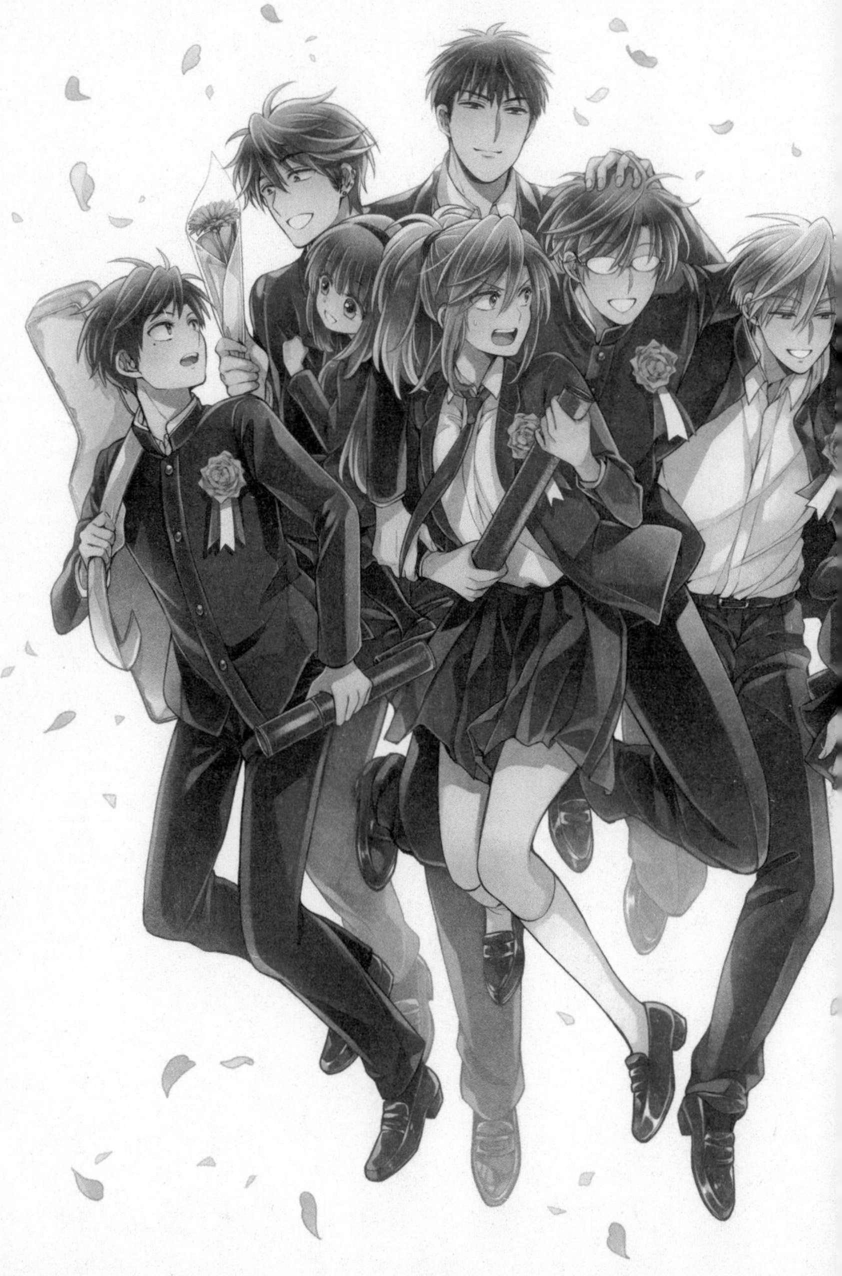

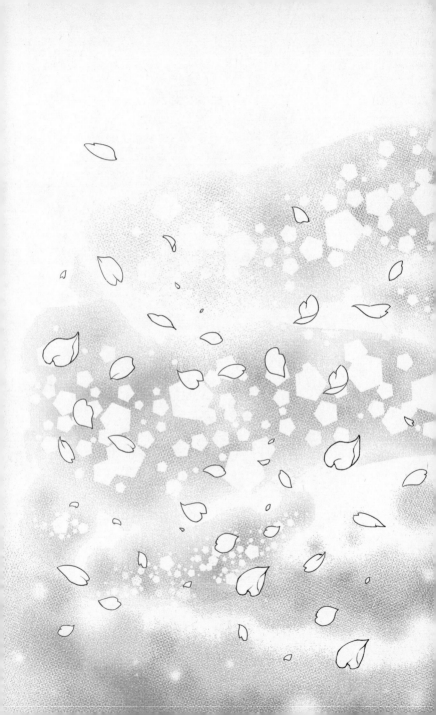

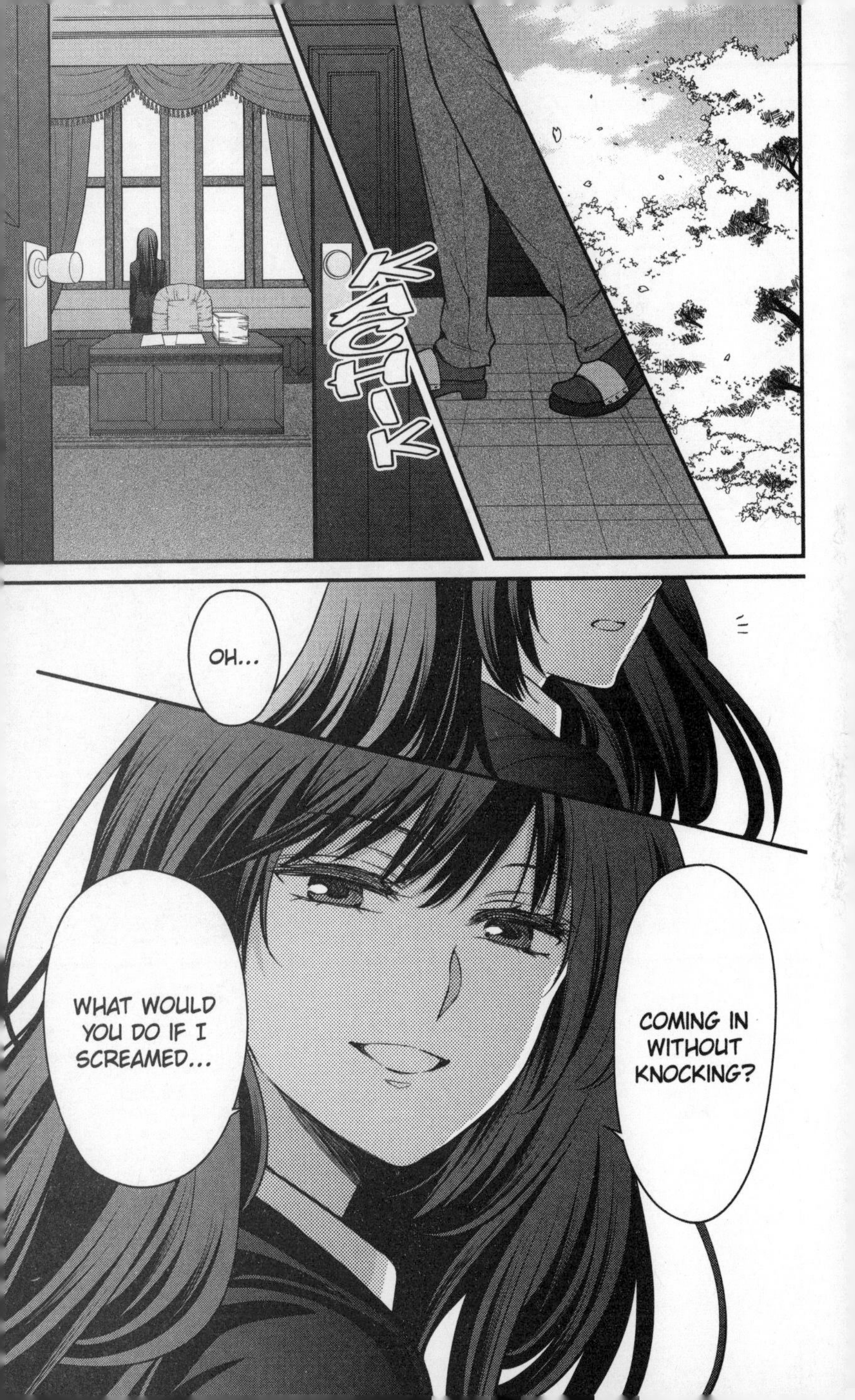
KACHI-K
OH...
COMING IN WITHOUT KNOCKING?
WHAT WOULD YOU DO IF I SCREAMED...

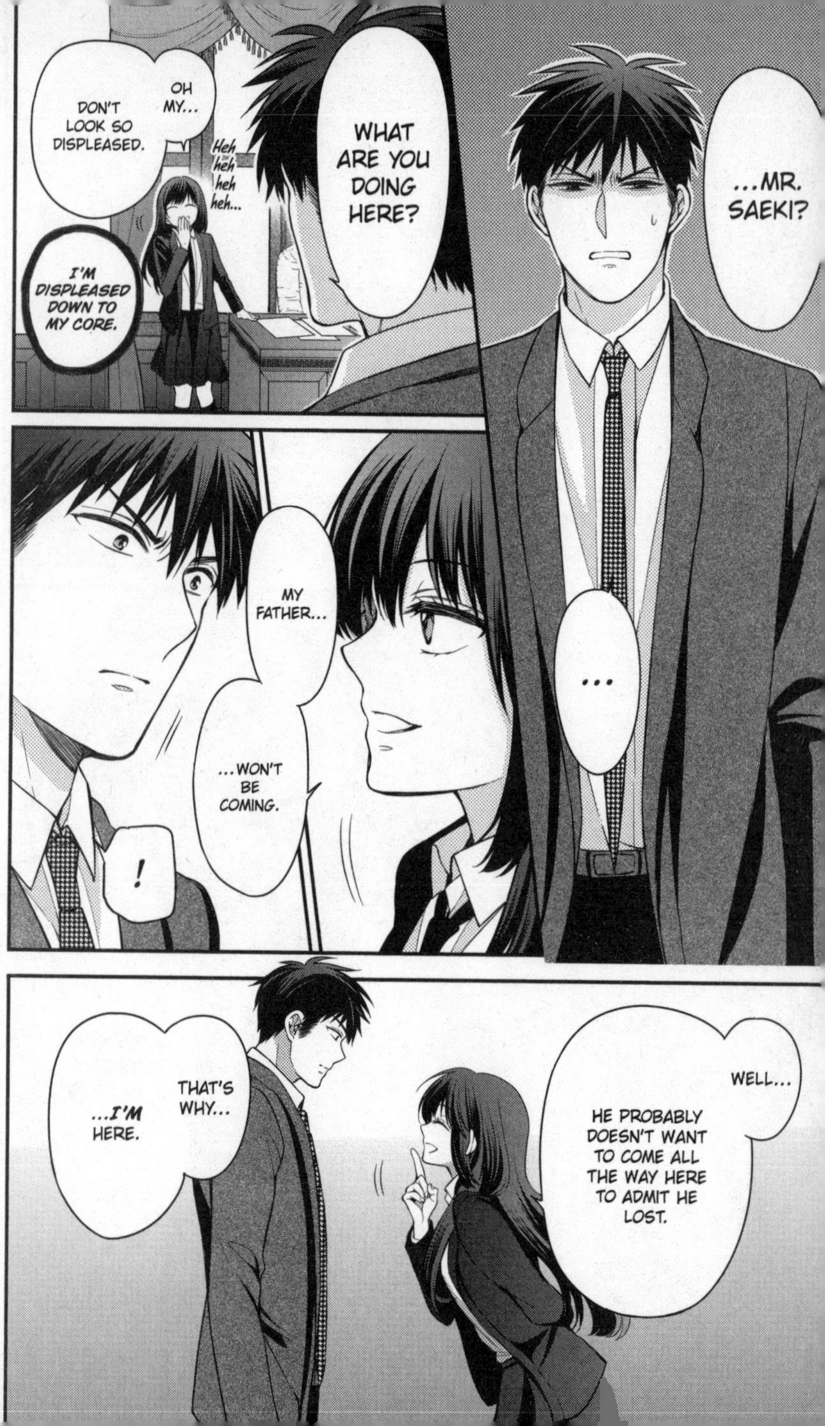
...MR. SAEKI?
...
WHAT ARE YOU DOING HERE?
OH MY...
DON'T LOOK SO DISPLEASED.
Heh heh heh heh...
I'M DISPLEASED DOWN TO MY CORE.
MY FATHER...
...WON'T BE COMING.
!
WELL...
HE PROBABLY DOESN'T WANT TO COME ALL THE WAY HERE TO ADMIT HE LOST.
THAT'S WHY...
...I'M HERE.

Midorigaoka Academy
THIS PLACE FELL INTO RUIN BECAUSE OF MY FATHER'S INEXPERIENCE AT RUNNING A HIGH SCHOOL.
BUT DESPITE THE SHARP DROP IN ENROLL-MENT...
...YOU MANAGED TO TURN THAT AROUND.
THE NUMBER OF APPLICANTS HAS DOUBLED THIS YEAR.
JUST AS YOU PROMISED.
MY FATHER...
...LOST THIS WAGER.
THE RIGHTS TO OPERATE MIDORIGAOKA ACADEMY...
...SHALL BE HANDED OVER TO YOU, MR. SAEKI.

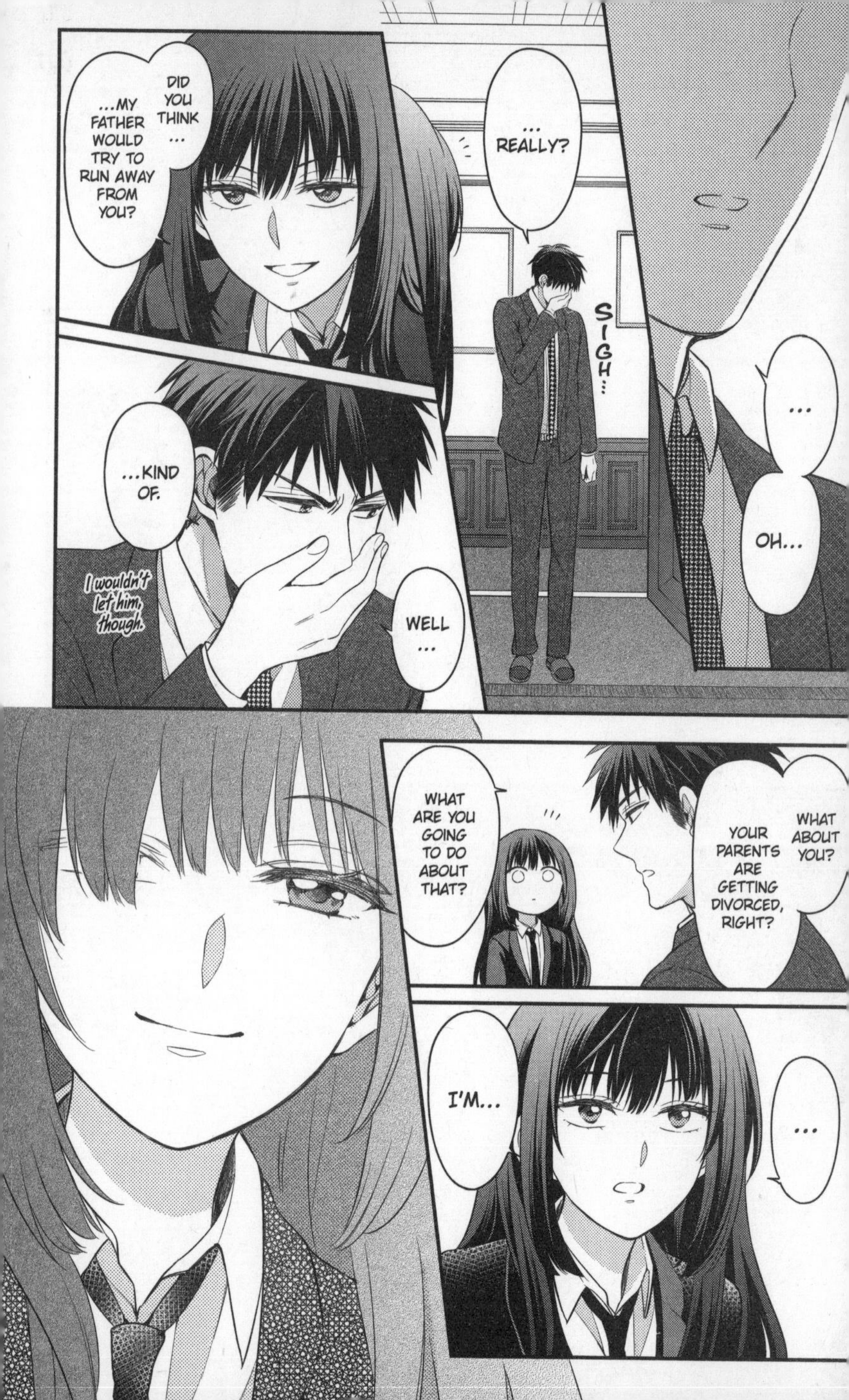
...
OH...
...REALLY?
SIGH...
DID YOU THINK...
...MY FATHER WOULD TRY TO RUN AWAY FROM YOU?
WELL...
...KIND OF.
I wouldn't let him, though.
WHAT ABOUT YOU?
YOUR PARENTS ARE GETTING DIVORCED, RIGHT?
WHAT ARE YOU GOING TO DO ABOUT THAT?
...
I'M...

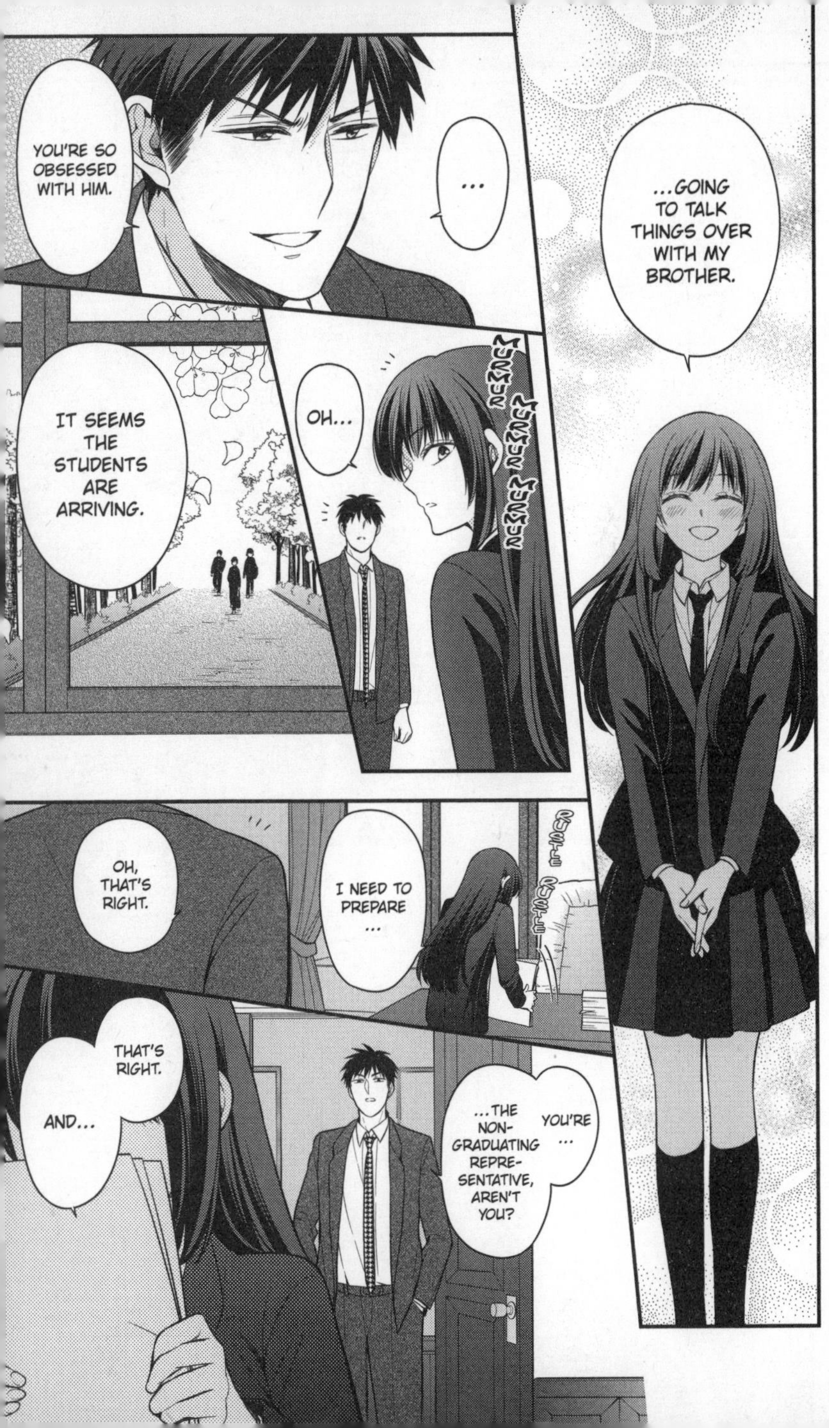
...GOING TO TALK THINGS OVER WITH MY BROTHER.
...
YOU'RE SO OBSESSED WITH HIM.
MURMUR MURMUR MURMUR MURMUR
OH...
IT SEEMS THE STUDENTS ARE ARRIVING.
RUSTLE RUSTLE
I NEED TO PREPARE ...
OH, THAT'S RIGHT.
YOU'RE ...
...THE NON-GRADUATING REPRE-SENTATIVE, AREN'T YOU?
THAT'S RIGHT.
AND...

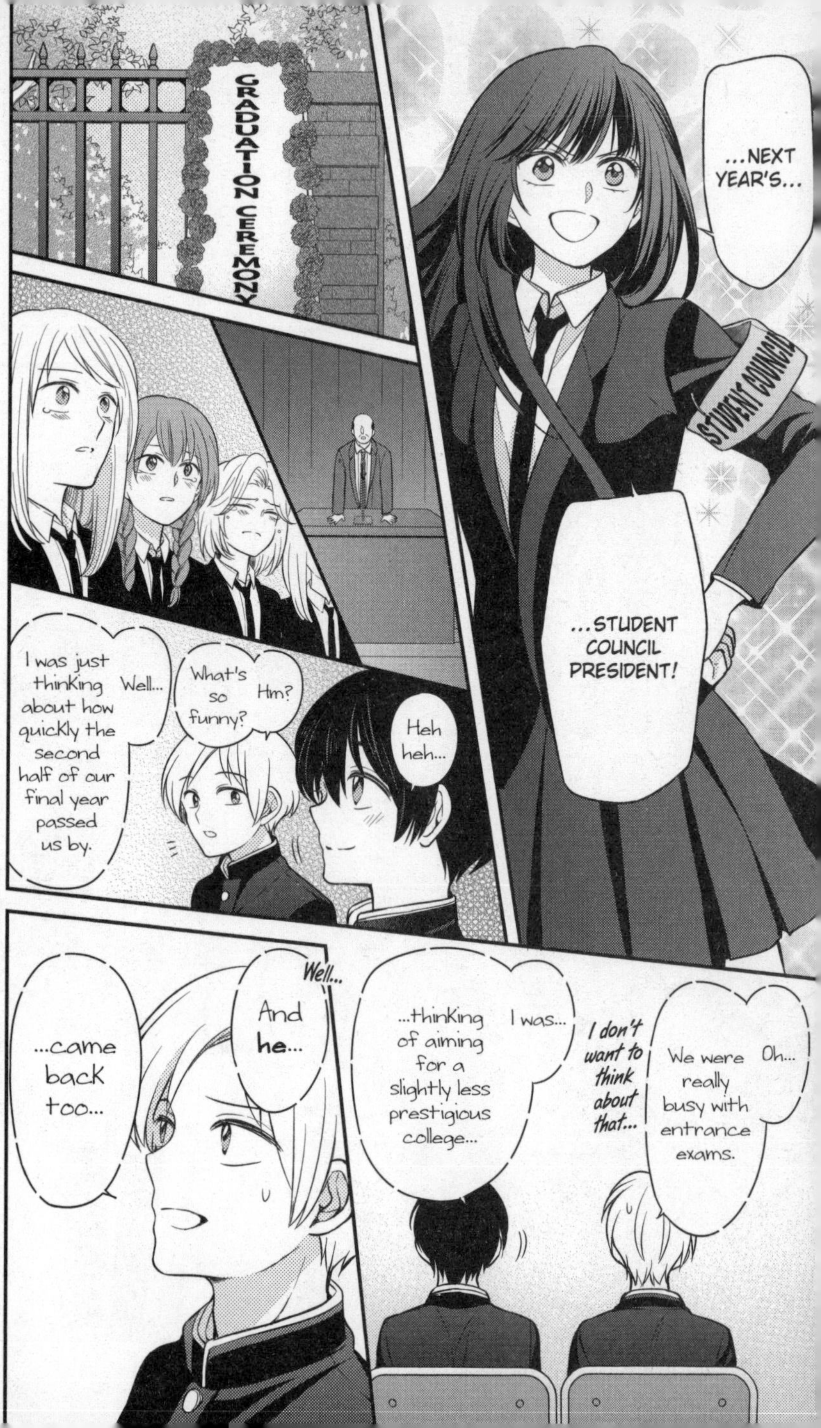
...NEXT YEAR'S...
...STUDENT COUNCIL PRESIDENT!
STUDENT COUNCIL
GRADUATION CEREMONY
Heh heh...
Hm?
What's so funny?
Well...
I was just thinking about how quickly the second half of our final year passed us by.
Oh...
We were really busy with entrance exams.
I don't want to think about that...
I was...
...thinking of aiming for a slightly less prestigious college...
Well...
And he...
...came back too...

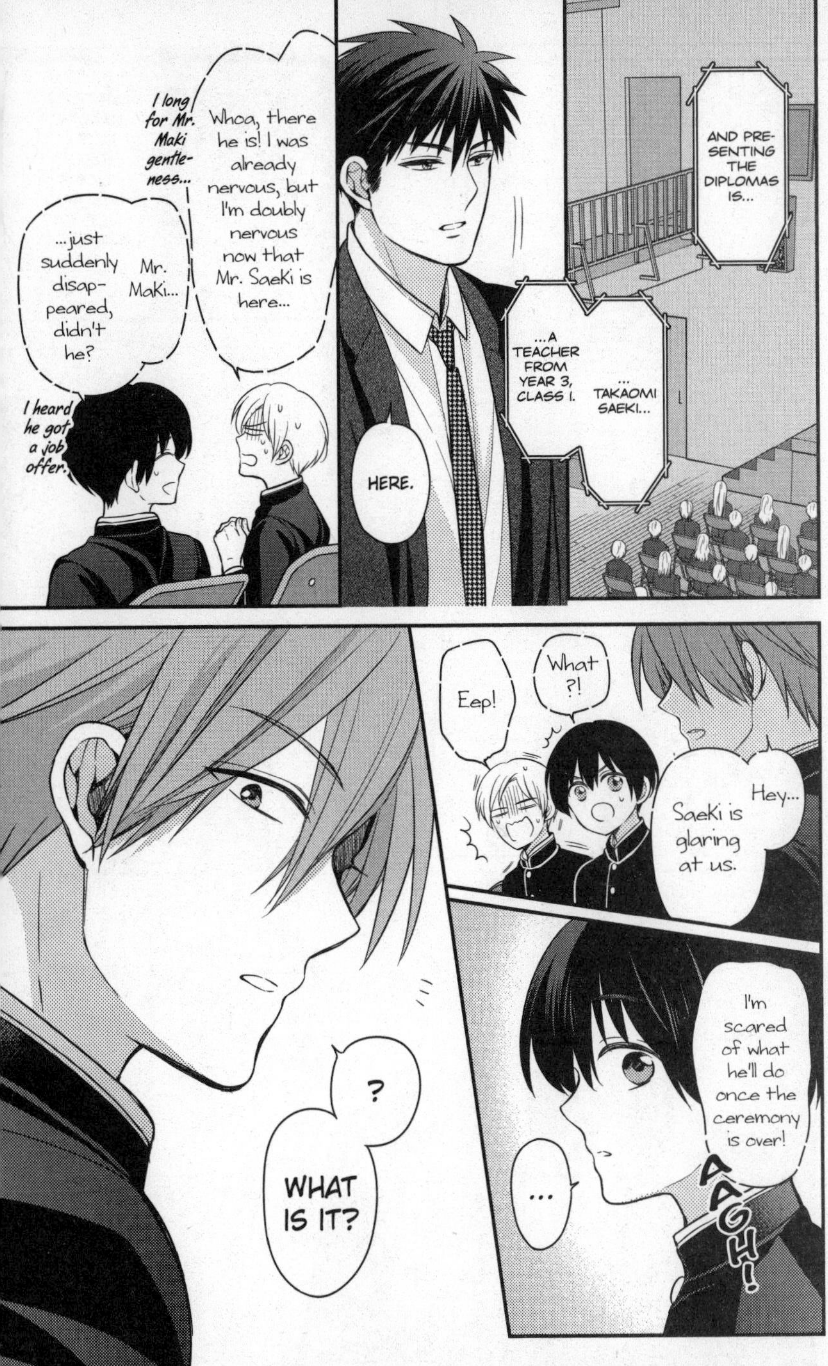
AND PRESENTING THE DIPLOMAS IS...
...A TEACHER FROM YEAR 3, CLASS 1.
...TAKAOMI SAEKI...
HERE.
Whoa, there he is! I was already nervous, but I'm doubly nervous now that Mr. Saeki is here...
I long for Mr. Maki gentleness...
Mr. Maki...
...just suddenly disappeared, didn't he?
I heard he got a job offer.
Hey... Saeki is glaring at us.
What?!
Eep!
I'm scared of what he'll do once the ceremony is over!
AAGH!
...
?
WHAT IS IT?

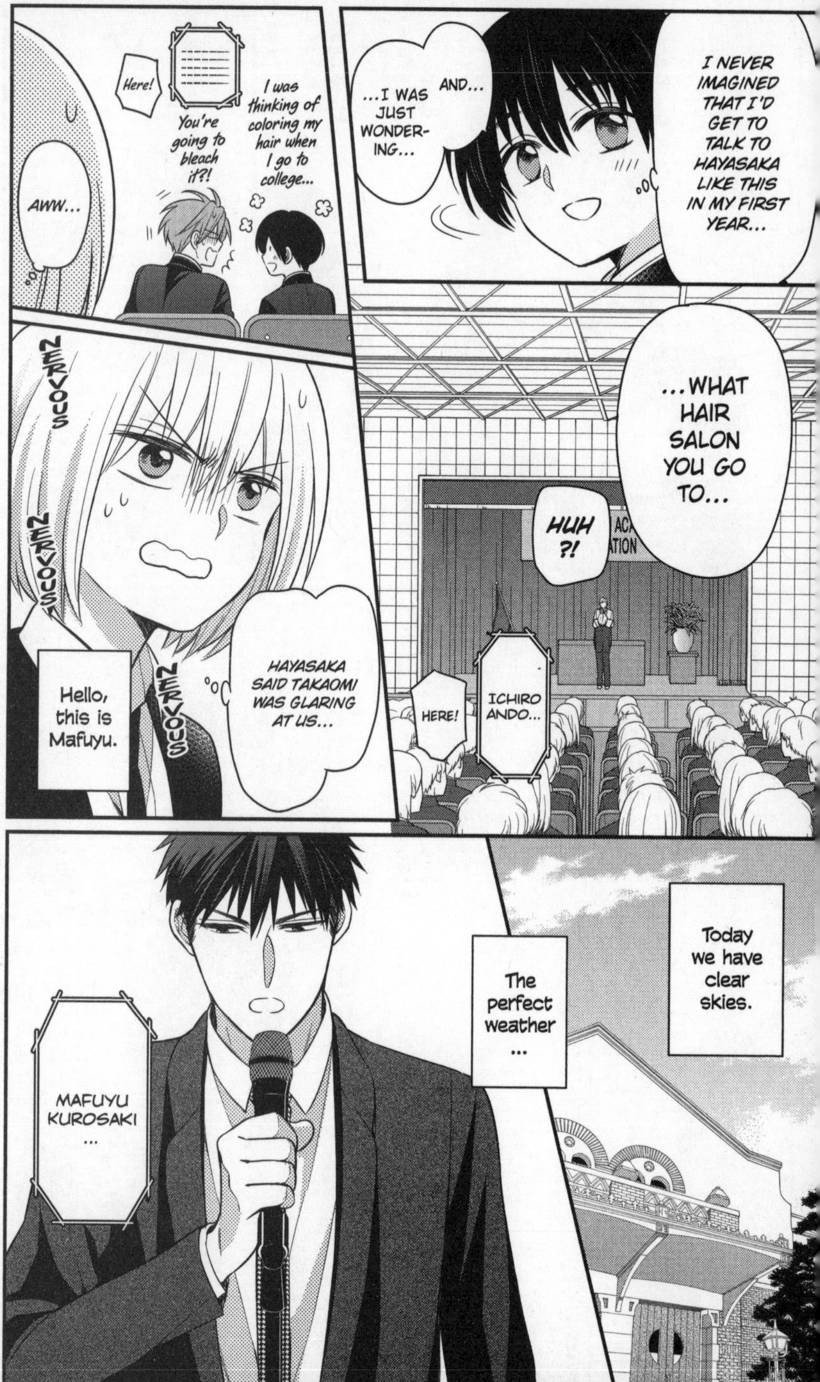
I NEVER IMAGINED THAT I'D GET TO TALK TO HAYASAKA LIKE THIS IN MY FIRST YEAR...
AND...
...I WAS JUST WONDERING...
I was thinking of coloring my hair when I go to college...
You're going to bleach it?!
Here!
AWW...
...WHAT HAIR SALON YOU GO TO...
HUH?!
ICHIRO ANDO...
HERE!
NERVOUS
NERVOUS
HAYASAKA SAID TAKAOMI WAS GLARING AT US...
NERVOUS
Hello, this is Mafuyu.
Today we have clear skies.
The perfect weather...
MAFUYU KUROSAKI...

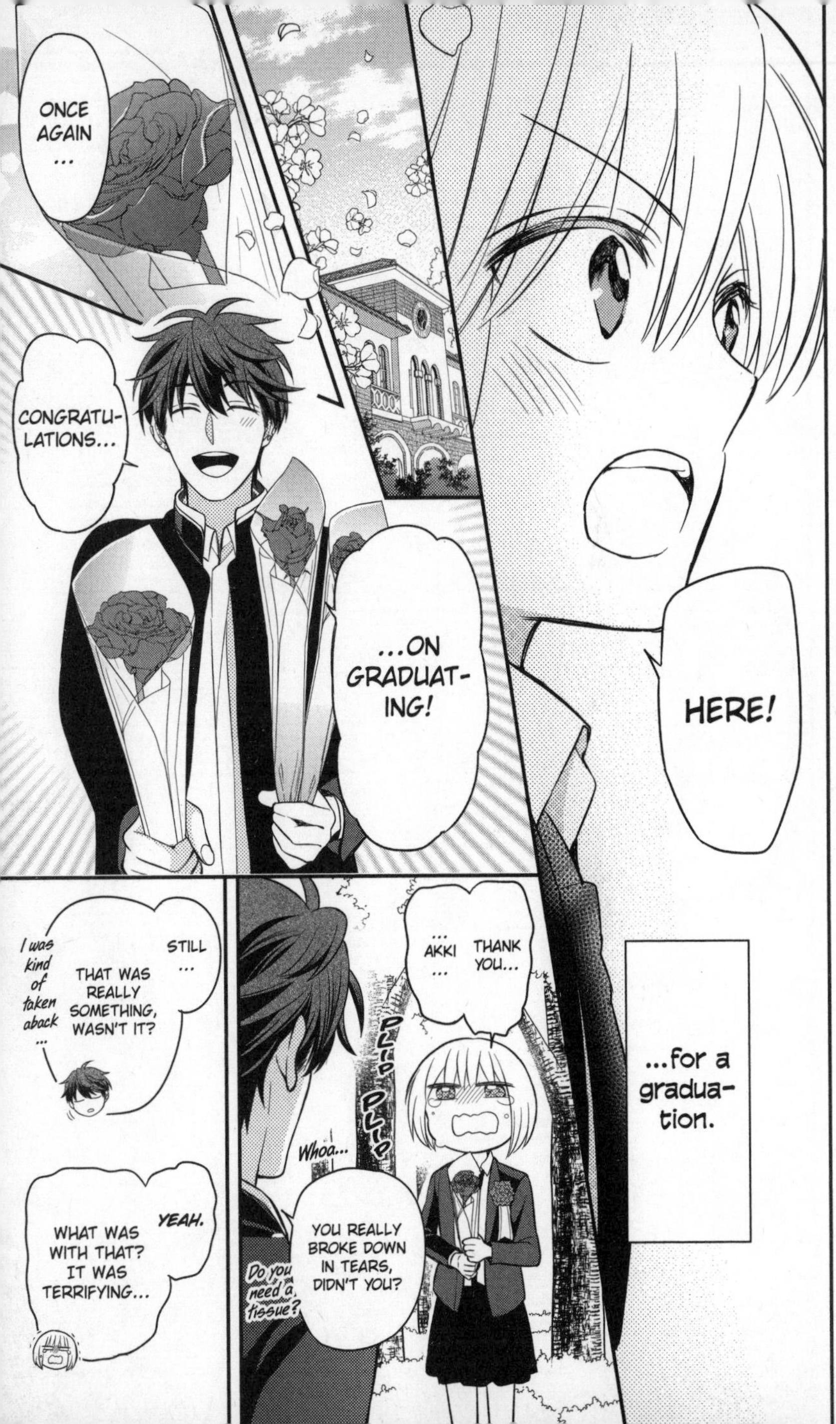
HERE!
...for a graduation.
ONCE AGAIN ...
CONGRATULATIONS...
...ON GRADUATING!
... AKKI ... THANK YOU...
PLIP PLIP
Whoa...
YOU REALLY BROKE DOWN IN TEARS, DIDN'T YOU?
Do you need a tissue?
STILL ...
THAT WAS REALLY SOMETHING, WASN'T IT?
I was kind of taken aback ...
YEAH.
WHAT WAS WITH THAT? IT WAS TERRIFYING...

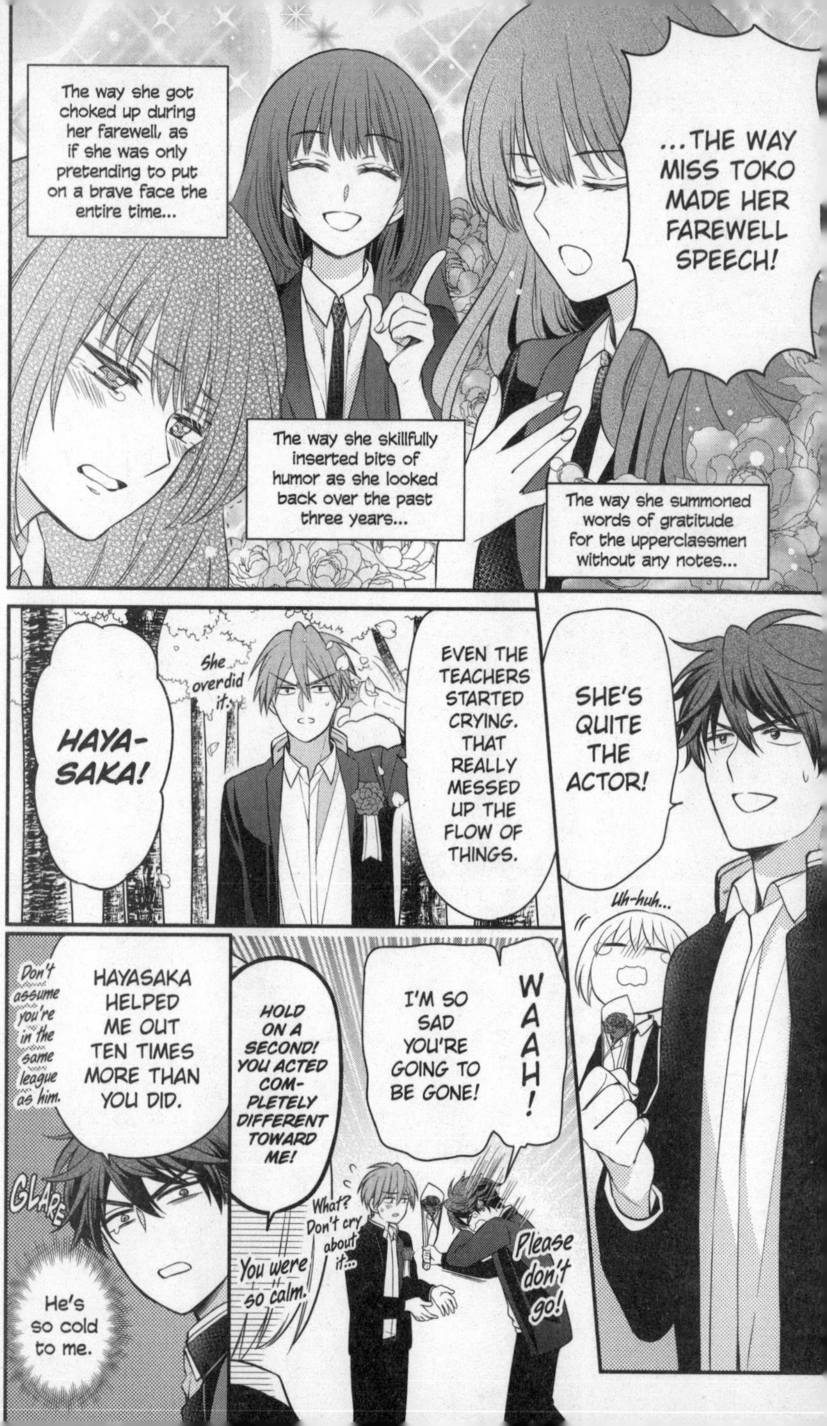
...THE WAY MISS TOKO MADE HER FAREWELL SPEECH!
The way she summoned words of gratitude for the upperclassmen without any notes...
The way she skillfully inserted bits of humor as she looked back over the past three years...
The way she got choked up during her farewell, as if she was only pretending to put on a brave face the entire time...
SHE'S QUITE THE ACTOR!
Uh-huh...
EVEN THE TEACHERS STARTED CRYING. THAT REALLY MESSED UP THE FLOW OF THINGS.
She overdid it.
HAYA-SAKA!
WAAH!
I'M SO SAD YOU'RE GOING TO BE GONE!
Please don't go!
What? Don't cry about it...
HOLD ON A SECOND! YOU ACTED COM-PLETELY DIFFERENT TOWARD ME!
You were so calm.
HAYASAKA HELPED ME OUT TEN TIMES MORE THAN YOU DID.
Don't assume you're in the same league as him.
GLARE
He's so cold to me.

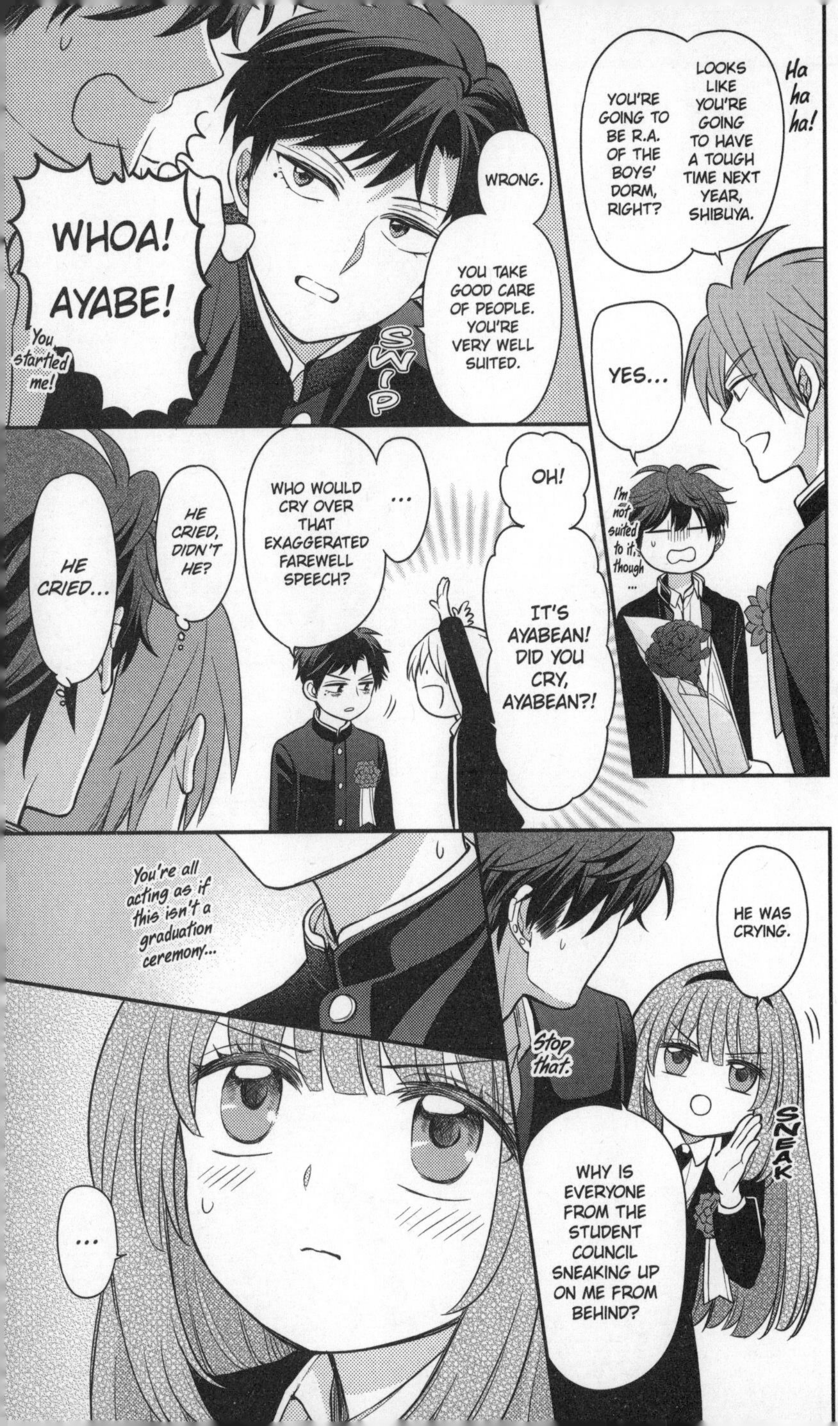
Ha ha ha!
LOOKS LIKE YOU'RE GOING TO HAVE A TOUGH TIME NEXT YEAR, SHIBUYA.
YOU'RE GOING TO BE R.A. OF THE BOYS' DORM, RIGHT?
YES...
I'm not suited to it, though...
WRONG.
YOU TAKE GOOD CARE OF PEOPLE. YOU'RE VERY WELL SUITED.
SWIP
WHOA! AYABE!
You startled me!
OH!
IT'S AYABEAN! DID YOU CRY, AYABEAN?!
...
WHO WOULD CRY OVER THAT EXAGGERATED FAREWELL SPEECH?
HE CRIED, DIDN'T HE?
HE CRIED...
HE WAS CRYING.
SNEAK
WHY IS EVERYONE FROM THE STUDENT COUNCIL SNEAKING UP ON ME FROM BEHIND?
Stop that.
You're all acting as if this isn't a graduation ceremony...
...

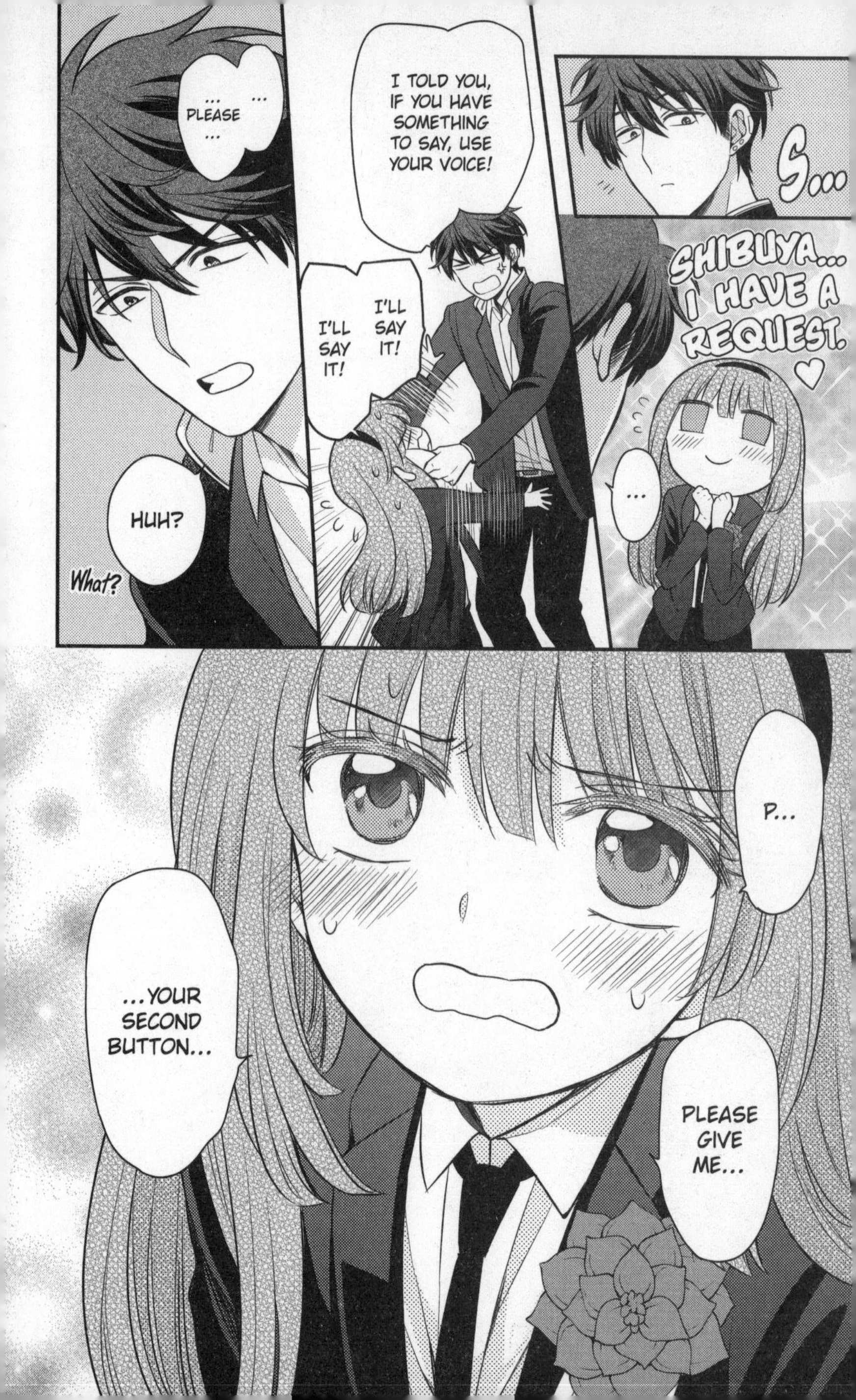
S...
SHIBUYA... I HAVE A REQUEST. ♥
...
I TOLD YOU, IF YOU HAVE SOMETHING TO SAY, USE YOUR VOICE!
I'LL SAY IT!
I'LL SAY IT!
... ... PLEASE ...
HUH?
What?
P...
PLEASE GIVE ME...
...YOUR SECOND BUTTON...

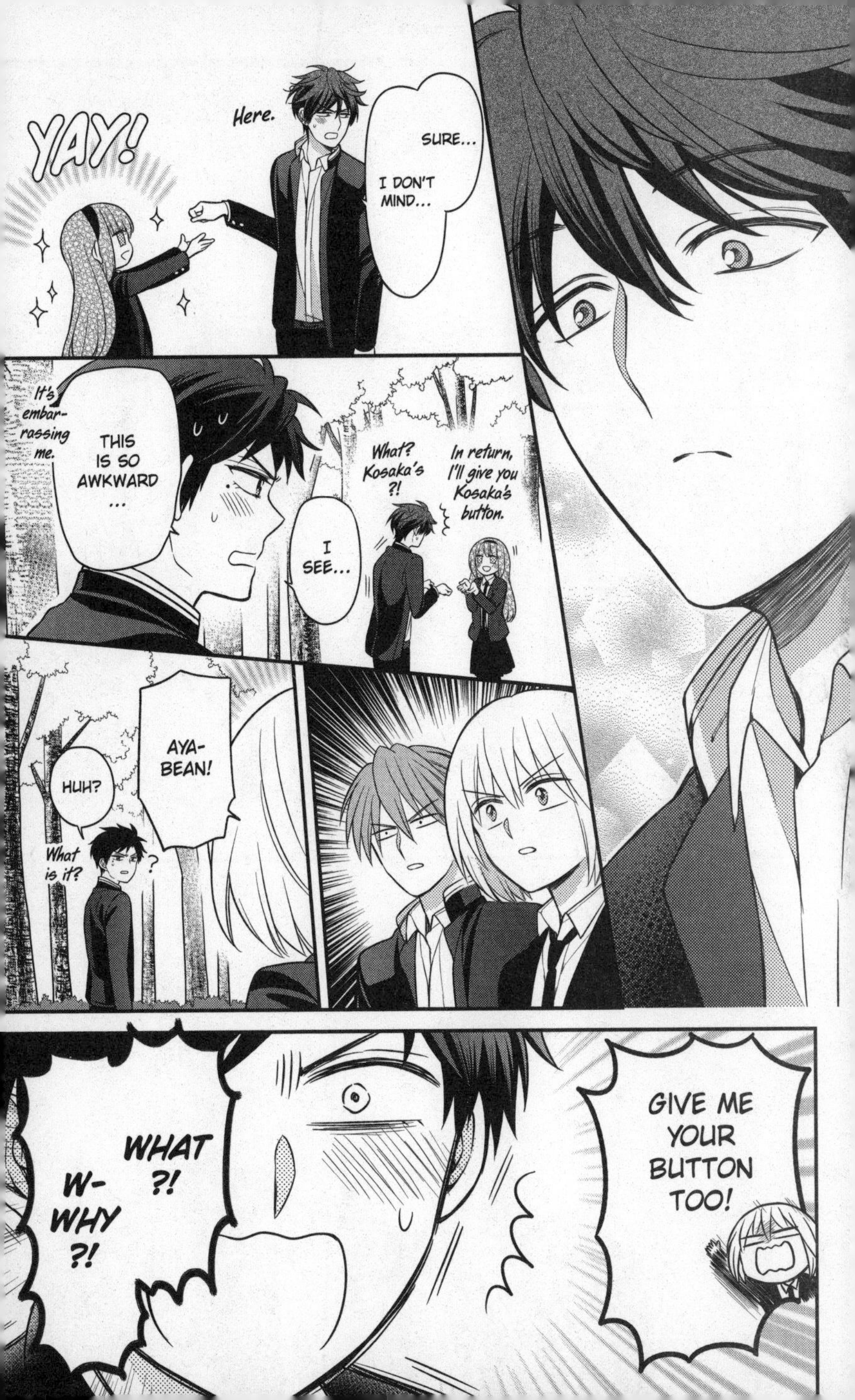
SURE... I DON'T MIND...
Here.
YAY!
In return, I'll give you Kosaka's button.
What? Kosaka's ?!
I SEE...
THIS IS SO AWKWARD ...
It's embarrassing me.
AYA-BEAN!
HUH?
What is it?
GIVE ME YOUR BUTTON TOO!
WHAT ?!
W-WHY ?!

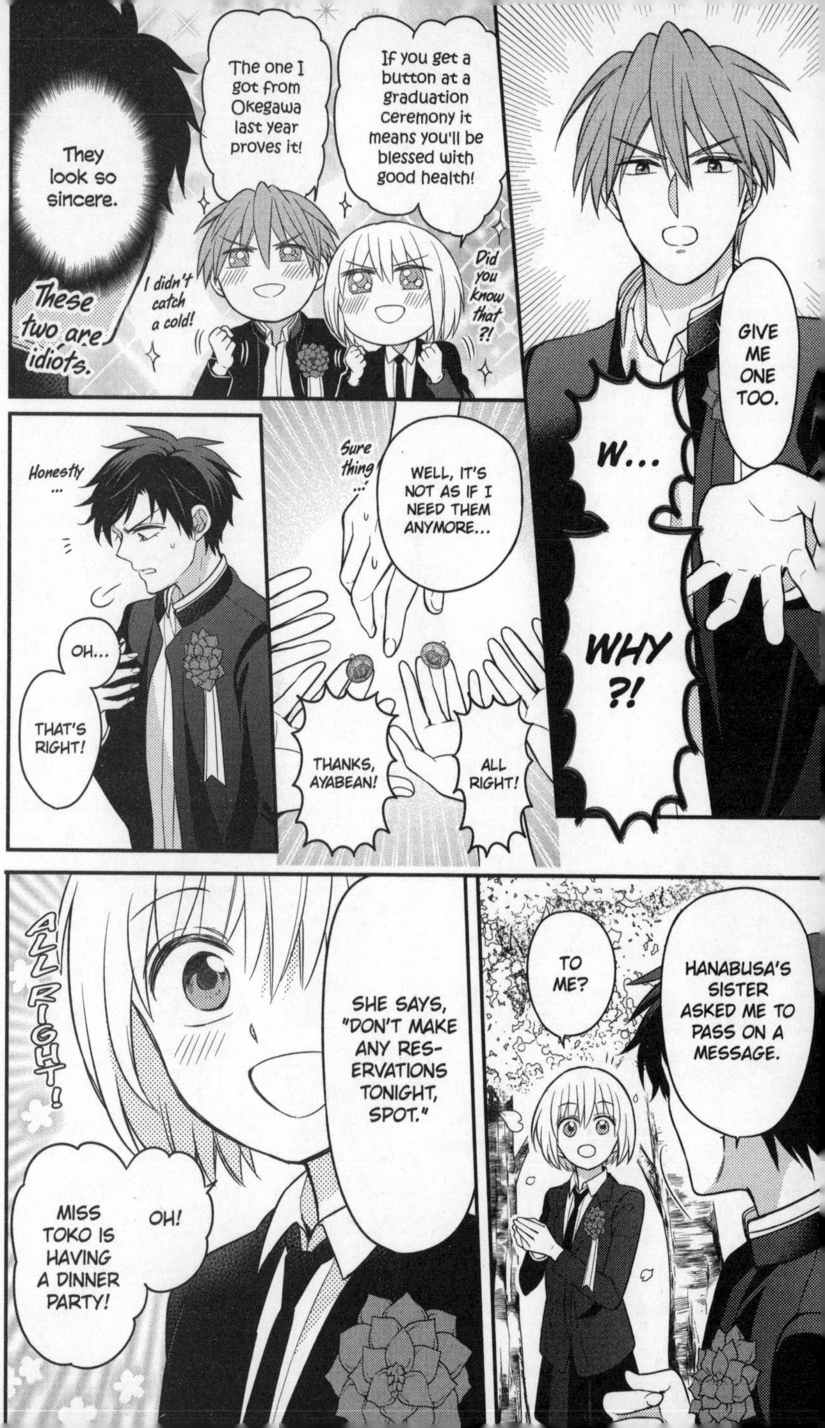
GIVE ME ONE TOO.
W... WHY?!
If you get a button at a graduation ceremony it means you'll be blessed with good health!
The one I got from Okegawa last year proves it!
Did you know that?!
I didn't catch a cold!
They look so sincere.
These two are idiots.
Sure thing...
WELL, IT'S NOT AS IF I NEED THEM ANYMORE...
ALL RIGHT!
THANKS, AYABEAN!
Honestly...
OH...
THAT'S RIGHT!
HANABUSA'S SISTER ASKED ME TO PASS ON A MESSAGE.
TO ME?
SHE SAYS, "DON'T MAKE ANY RES-ERVATIONS TONIGHT, SPOT."
ALL RIGHT!
OH!
MISS TOKO IS HAVING A DINNER PARTY!

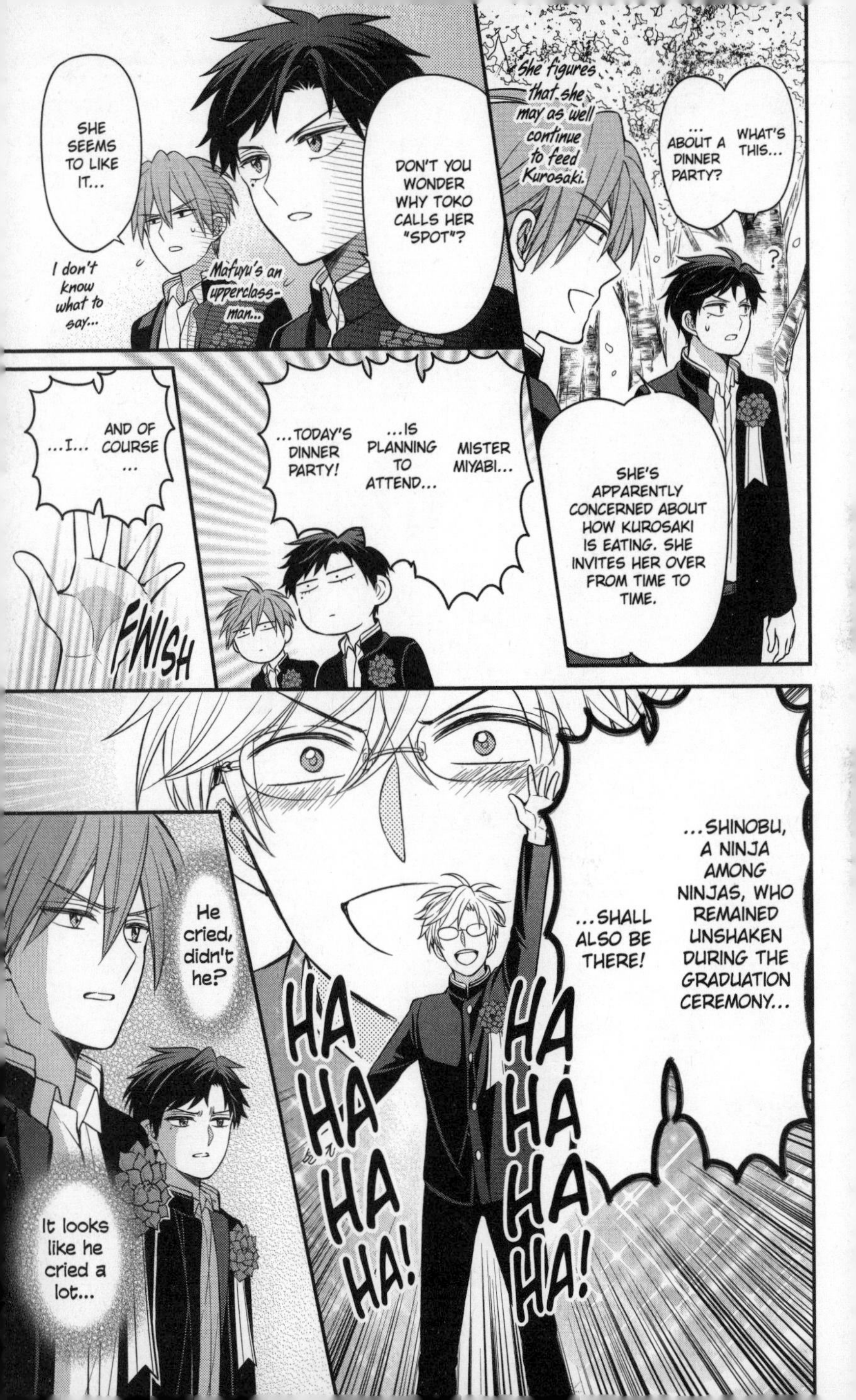
WHAT'S THIS... ...ABOUT A DINNER PARTY?
She figures that she may as well continue to feed Kurosaki.
SHE'S APPARENTLY CONCERNED ABOUT HOW KUROSAKI IS EATING. SHE INVITES HER OVER FROM TIME TO TIME.
DON'T YOU WONDER WHY TOKO CALLS HER "SPOT"?
SHE SEEMS TO LIKE IT...
Mafuyu's an upperclassman...
I don't know what to say...
MISTER MIYABI...
...IS PLANNING TO ATTEND...
...TODAY'S DINNER PARTY!
AND OF COURSE...
...I...
FWISH
...SHINOBU, A NINJA AMONG NINJAS, WHO REMAINED UNSHAKEN DURING THE GRADUATION CEREMONY...
...SHALL ALSO BE THERE!
HA HA HA HA HA!
HA HA HA HA HA!
He cried, didn't he?
It looks like he cried a lot...

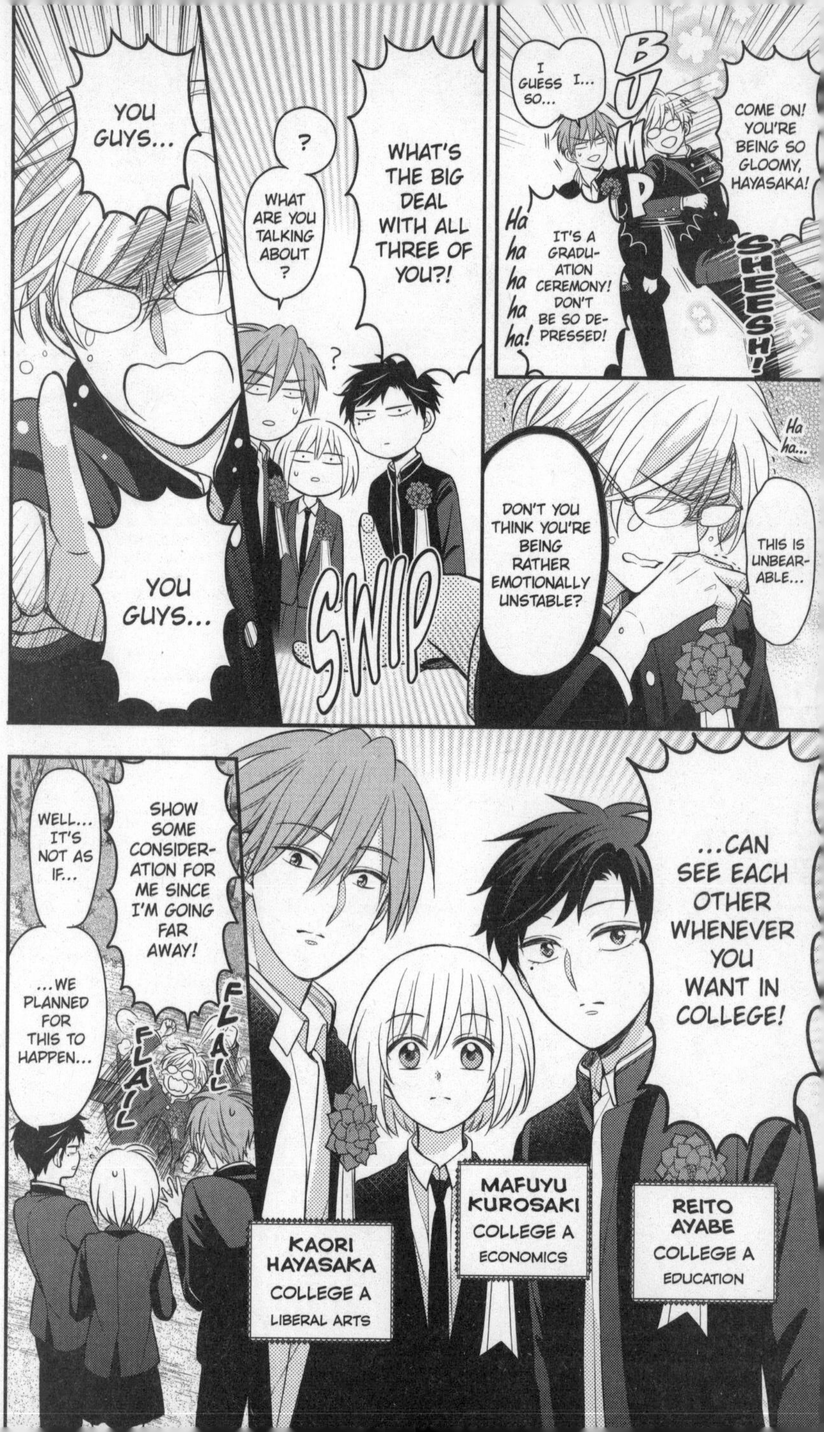
COME ON! YOU'RE BEING SO GLOOMY, HAYASAKA!
BUMP
SHEESH!
I... I GUESS SO...
IT'S A GRADU-ATION CEREMONY! DON'T BE SO DE-PRESSED!
Ha ha ha ha ha!
Ha ha...
THIS IS UNBEAR-ABLE...
DON'T YOU THINK YOU'RE BEING RATHER EMOTIONALLY UNSTABLE?
WHAT'S THE BIG DEAL WITH ALL THREE OF YOU?!
?
WHAT ARE YOU TALKING ABOUT?
?
SWIP
YOU GUYS...
YOU GUYS...
...CAN SEE EACH OTHER WHENEVER YOU WANT IN COLLEGE!
REITO AYABE
COLLEGE A
EDUCATION
MAFUYU KUROSAKI
COLLEGE A
ECONOMICS
KAORI HAYASAKA
COLLEGE A
LIBERAL ARTS
SHOW SOME CONSIDER-ATION FOR ME SINCE I'M GOING FAR AWAY!
FLAIL
FLAIL
WELL... IT'S NOT AS IF...
...WE PLANNED FOR THIS TO HAPPEN...

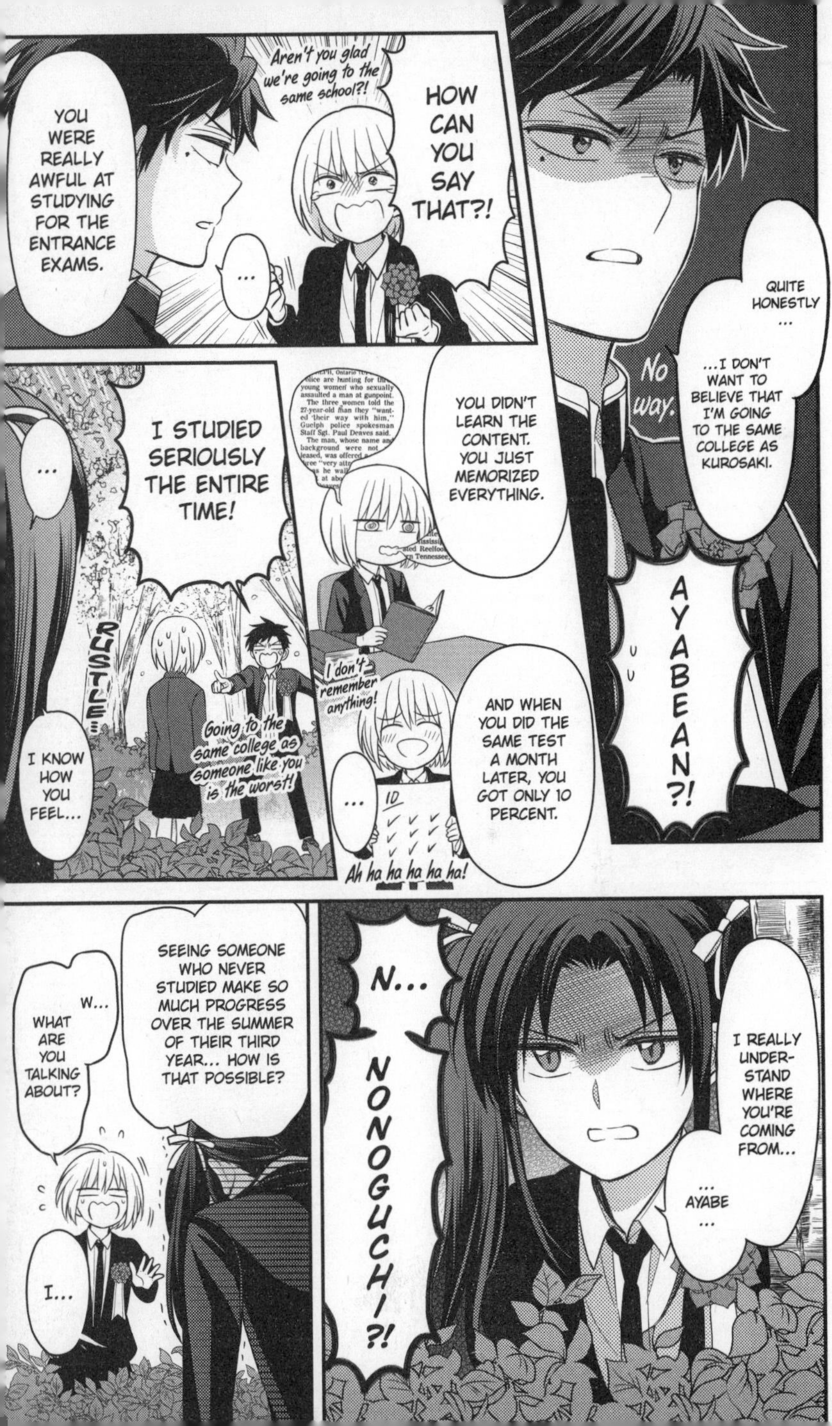
QUITE HONESTLY ...
No way.
...I DON'T WANT TO BELIEVE THAT I'M GOING TO THE SAME COLLEGE AS KUROSAKI.
AYABEAN?!
Aren't you glad we're going to the same school?!
HOW CAN YOU SAY THAT?!
...
YOU WERE REALLY AWFUL AT STUDYING FOR THE ENTRANCE EXAMS.
YOU DIDN'T LEARN THE CONTENT. YOU JUST MEMORIZED EVERYTHING.
AND WHEN YOU DID THE SAME TEST A MONTH LATER, YOU GOT ONLY 10 PERCENT.
I don't remember anything!
...
Ah ha ha ha ha ha!
I STUDIED SERIOUSLY THE ENTIRE TIME!
...
RUSTLE...
Going to the same college as someone like you is the worst!
I KNOW HOW YOU FEEL...
N... NONOGUCHI?!
I REALLY UNDER-STAND WHERE YOU'RE COMING FROM...
... AYABE ...
SEEING SOMEONE WHO NEVER STUDIED MAKE SO MUCH PROGRESS OVER THE SUMMER OF THEIR THIRD YEAR... HOW IS THAT POSSIBLE?
W... WHAT ARE YOU TALKING ABOUT?
I...

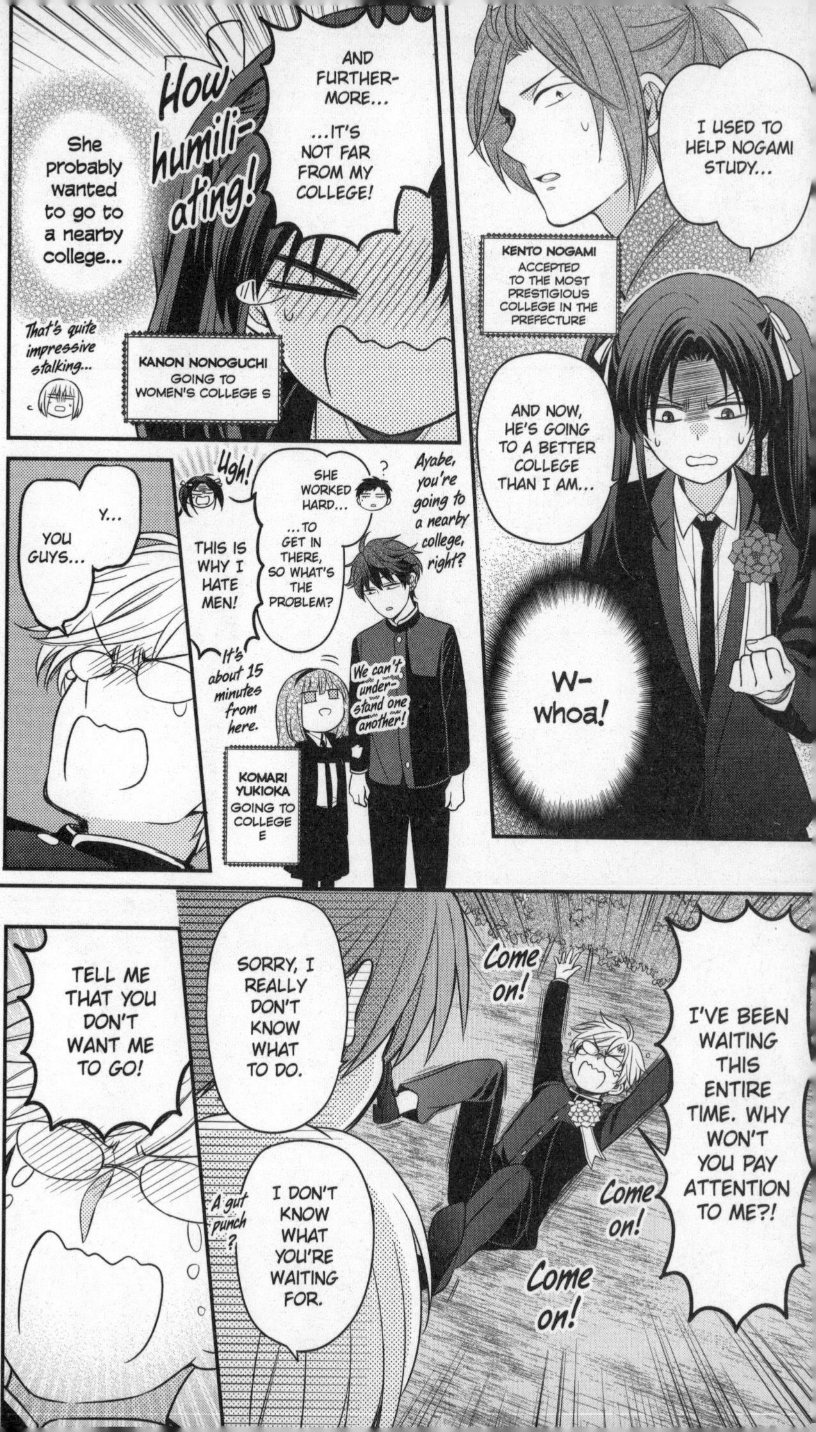

I USED TO HELP NOGAMI STUDY...
KENTO NOGAMI ACCEPTED TO THE MOST PRESTIGIOUS COLLEGE IN THE PREFECTURE
AND NOW, HE'S GOING TO A BETTER COLLEGE THAN I AM...
W-whoa!
AND FURTHERMORE...
...IT'S NOT FAR FROM MY COLLEGE!
How humiliating!
She probably wanted to go to a nearby college...
KANON NONOGUCHI GOING TO WOMEN'S COLLEGE S
That's quite impressive stalking...
Ayabe, you're going to a nearby college, right?
?
SHE WORKED HARD...
...TO GET IN THERE, SO WHAT'S THE PROBLEM?
Ugh!
THIS IS WHY I HATE MEN!
It's about 15 minutes from here.
We can't understand one another!
KOMARI YUKIOKA GOING TO COLLEGE E
Y...
YOU GUYS...
I'VE BEEN WAITING THIS ENTIRE TIME. WHY WON'T YOU PAY ATTENTION TO ME?!
Come on!
Come on!
Come on!
SORRY, I REALLY DON'T KNOW WHAT TO DO.
I DON'T KNOW WHAT YOU'RE WAITING FOR.
A gut punch?
TELL ME THAT YOU DON'T WANT ME TO GO!

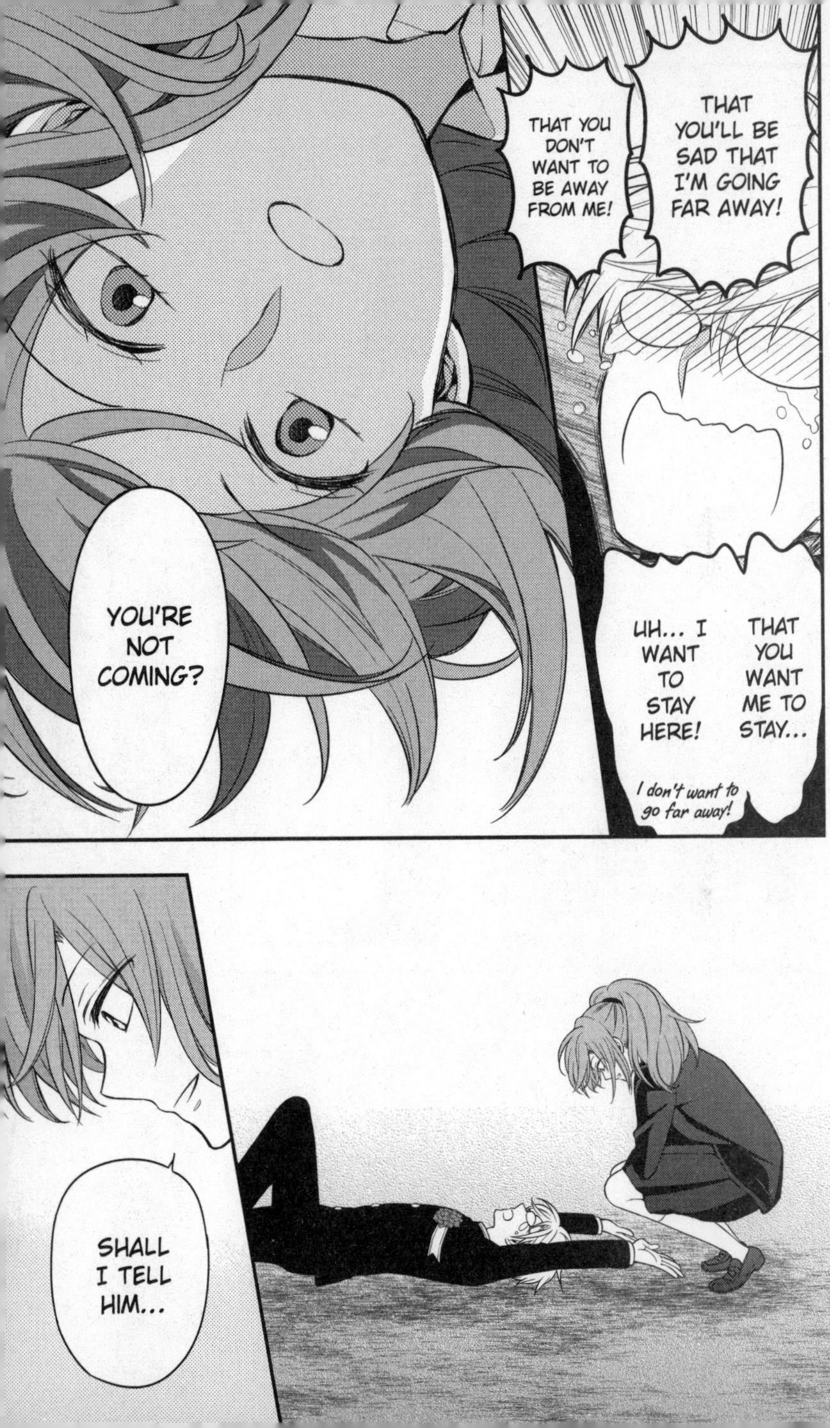
THAT YOU'LL BE SAD THAT I'M GOING FAR AWAY!
THAT YOU DON'T WANT TO BE AWAY FROM ME!
THAT YOU WANT ME TO STAY...
UH... I WANT TO STAY HERE!
I don't want to go far away!
YOU'RE NOT COMING?
SHALL I TELL HIM...

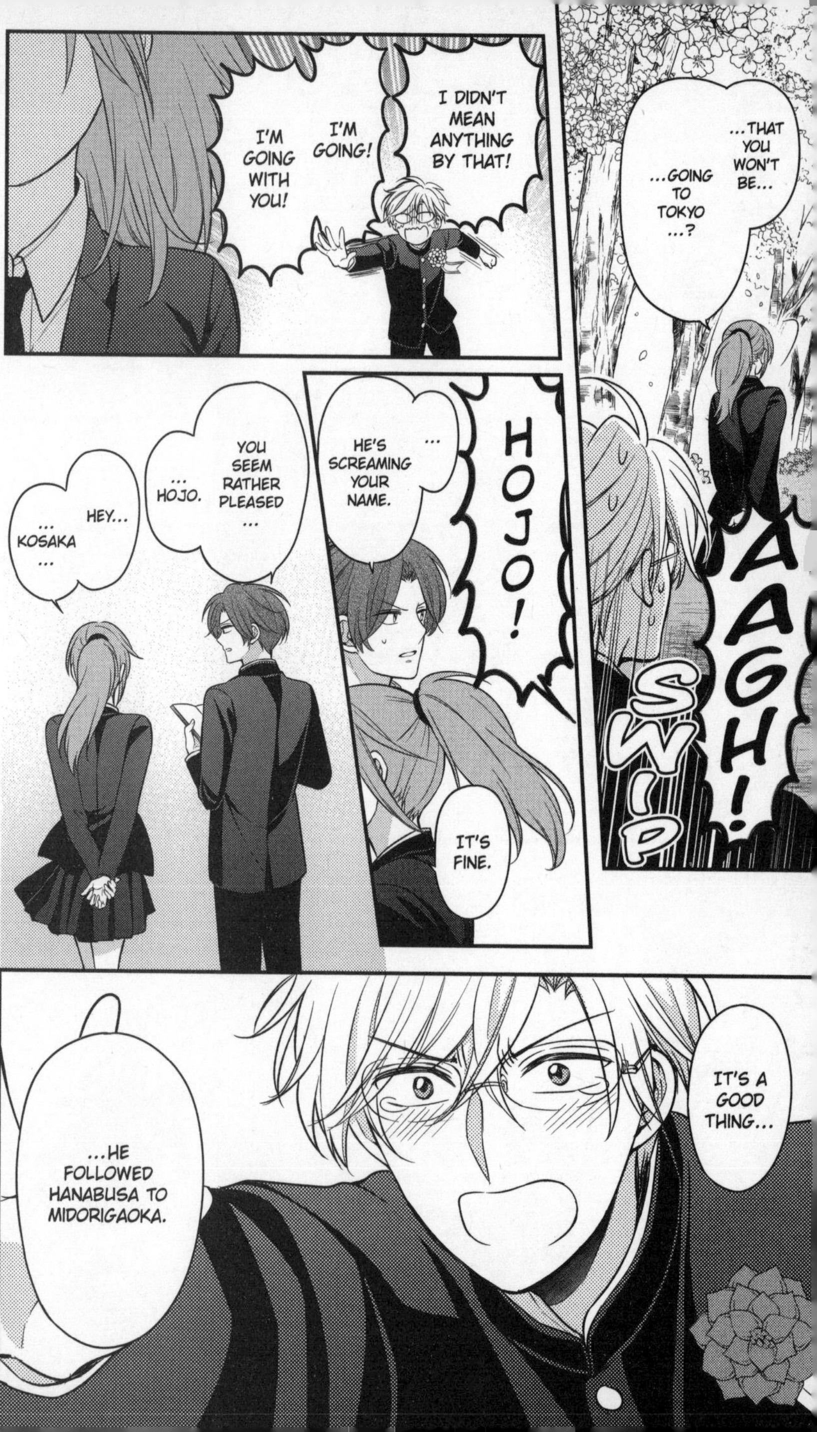
...THAT YOU WON'T BE...
...GOING TO TOKYO ...?
AAGH!
SWIP
I DIDN'T MEAN ANYTHING BY THAT!
I'M GOING!
I'M GOING WITH YOU!
HOJO!
...
HE'S SCREAMING YOUR NAME.
IT'S FINE.
YOU SEEM RATHER PLEASED ...
... HOJO.
HEY... ...KOSAKA ...
IT'S A GOOD THING...
...HE FOLLOWED HANABUSA TO MIDORIGAOKA.

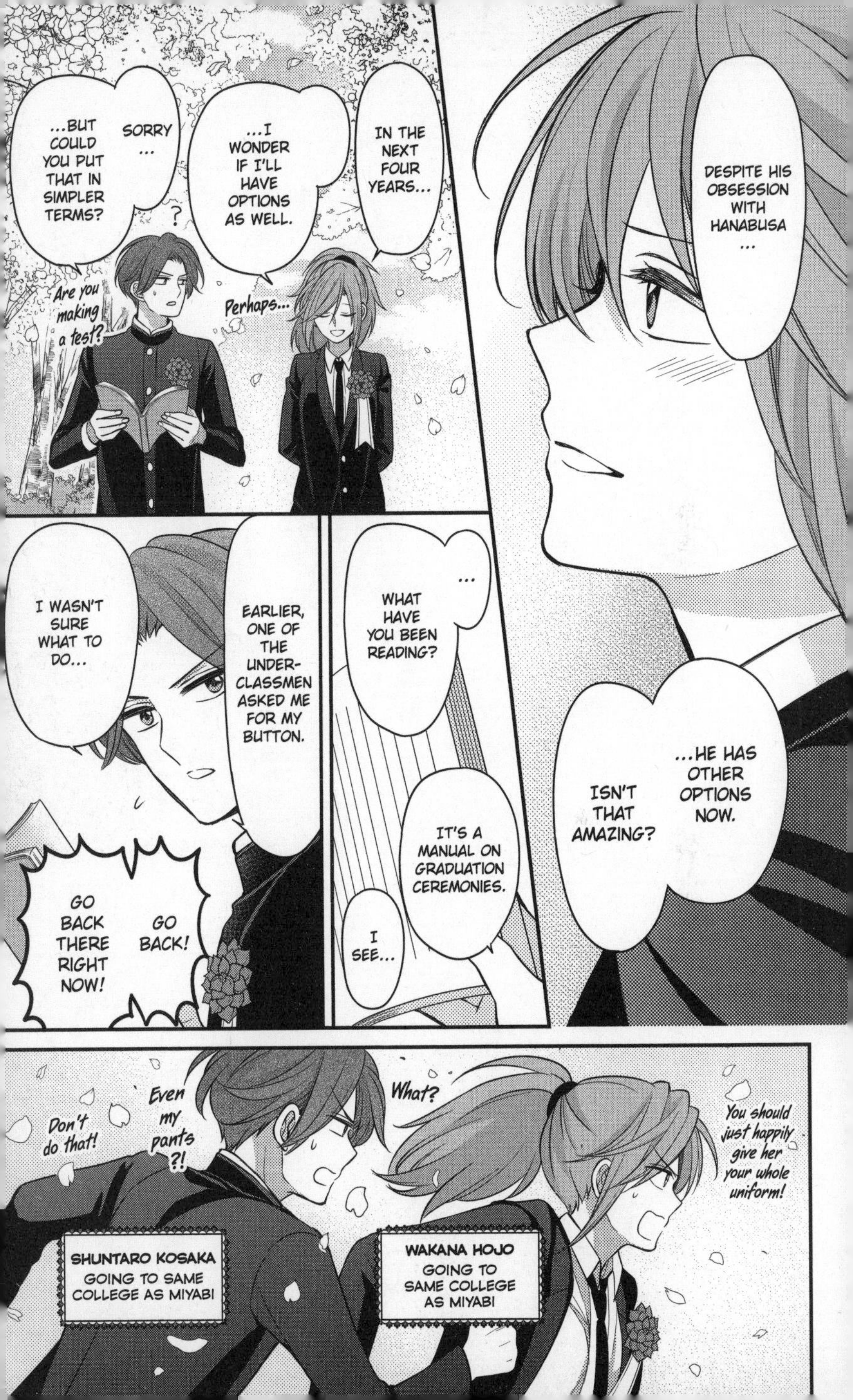
DESPITE HIS OBSESSION WITH HANABUSA ...
...HE HAS OTHER OPTIONS NOW.
ISN'T THAT AMAZING?
IN THE NEXT FOUR YEARS...
...I WONDER IF I'LL HAVE OPTIONS AS WELL.
Perhaps...
SORRY ...
...BUT COULD YOU PUT THAT IN SIMPLER TERMS?
?
Are you making a test?
...
WHAT HAVE YOU BEEN READING?
IT'S A MANUAL ON GRADUATION CEREMONIES.
I SEE...
EARLIER, ONE OF THE UNDER-CLASSMEN ASKED ME FOR MY BUTTON.
I WASN'T SURE WHAT TO DO...
GO BACK!
GO BACK THERE RIGHT NOW!
You should just happily give her your whole uniform!
What?
Even my pants?!
Don't do that!
WAKANA HOJO
GOING TO SAME COLLEGE AS MIYABI
SHUNTARO KOSAKA
GOING TO SAME COLLEGE AS MIYABI

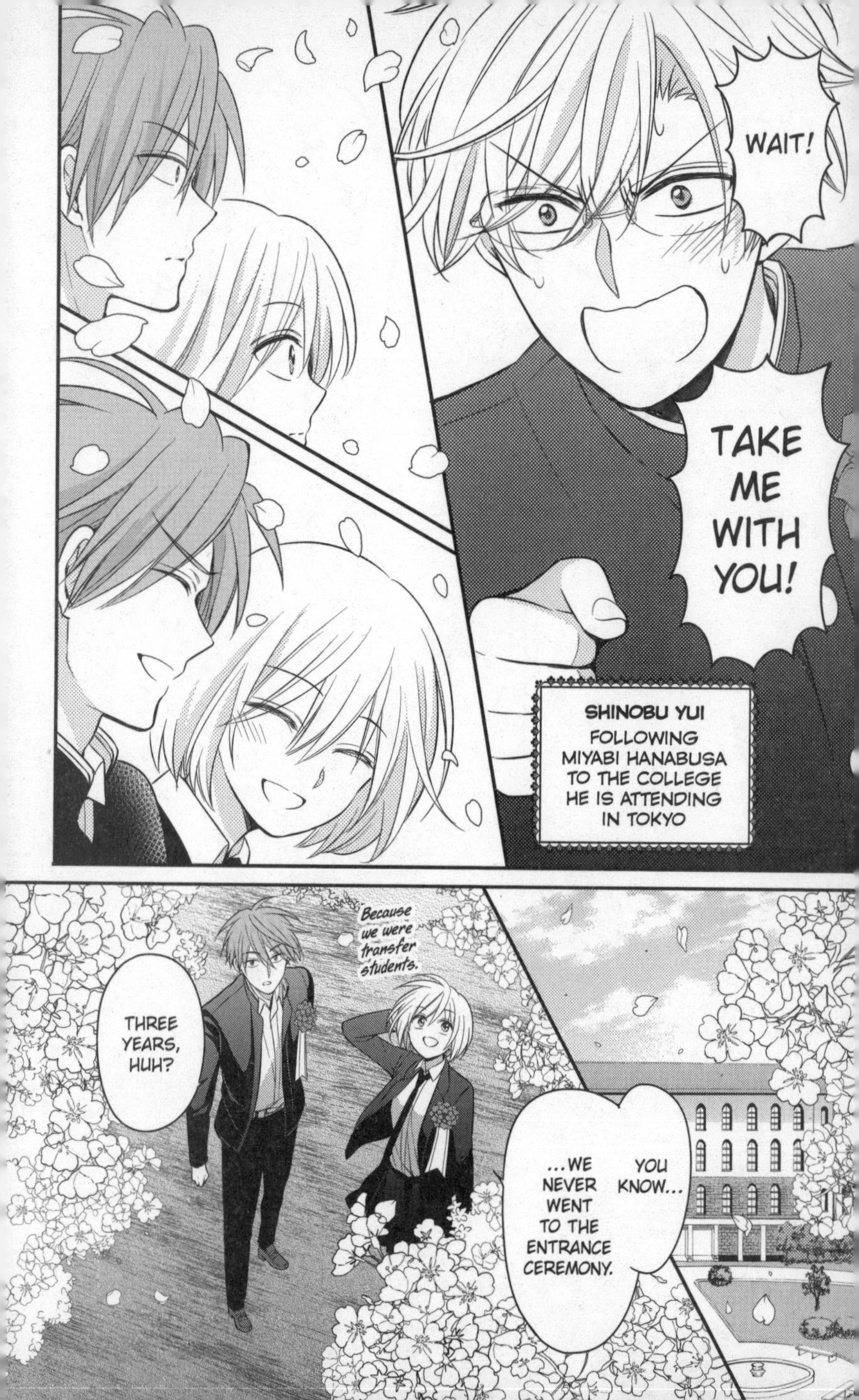
WAIT!
TAKE ME WITH YOU!
SHINOBU YUI
FOLLOWING MIYABI HANABUSA TO THE COLLEGE HE IS ATTENDING IN TOKYO
YOU KNOW...
...WE NEVER WENT TO THE ENTRANCE CEREMONY.
Because we were transfer students.
THREE YEARS, HUH?

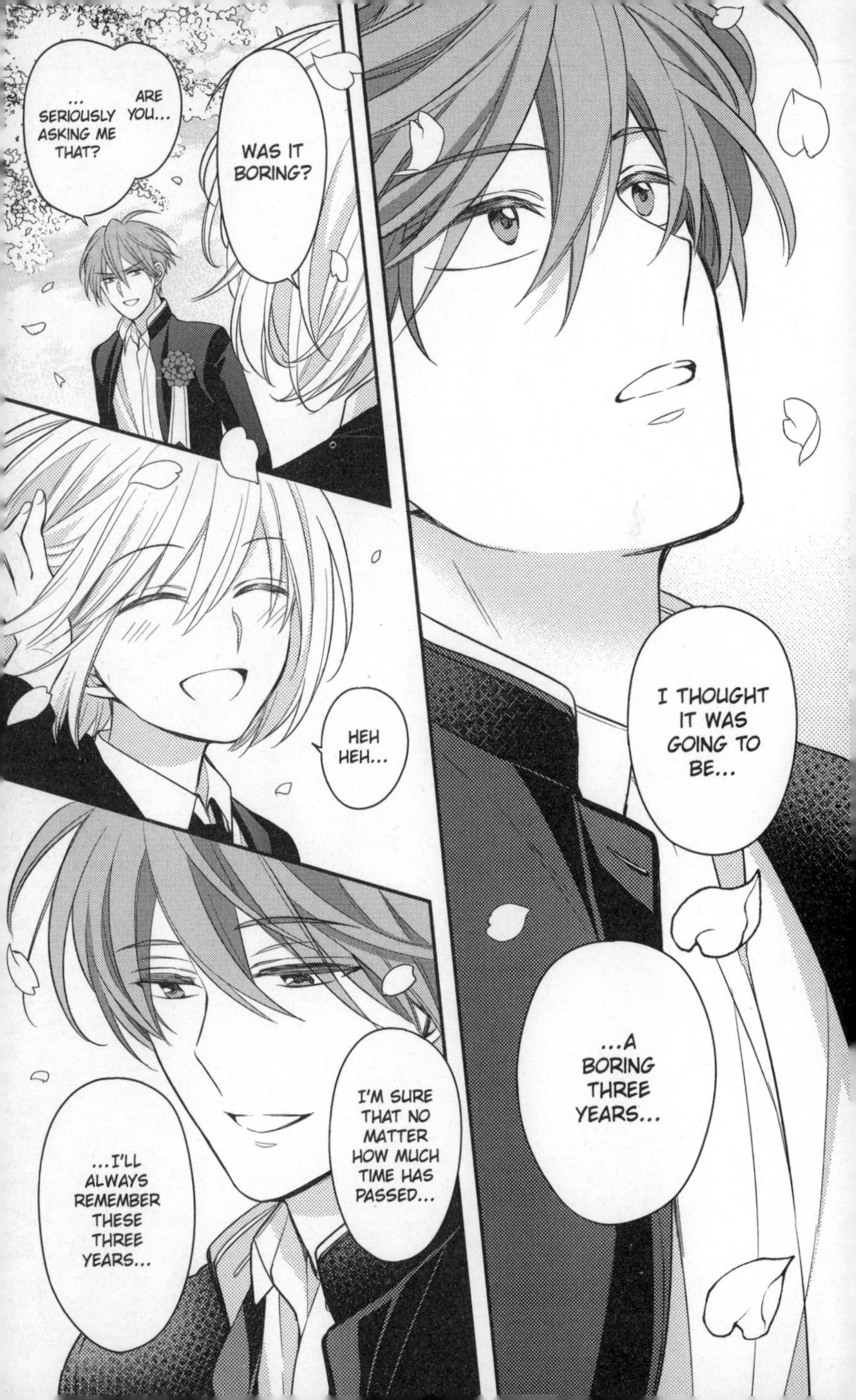
I THOUGHT IT WAS GOING TO BE...
...A BORING THREE YEARS...
WAS IT BORING?
ARE YOU... ...SERIOUSLY ASKING ME THAT?
HEH HEH...
I'M SURE THAT NO MATTER HOW MUCH TIME HAS PASSED...
...I'LL ALWAYS REMEMBER THESE THREE YEARS...

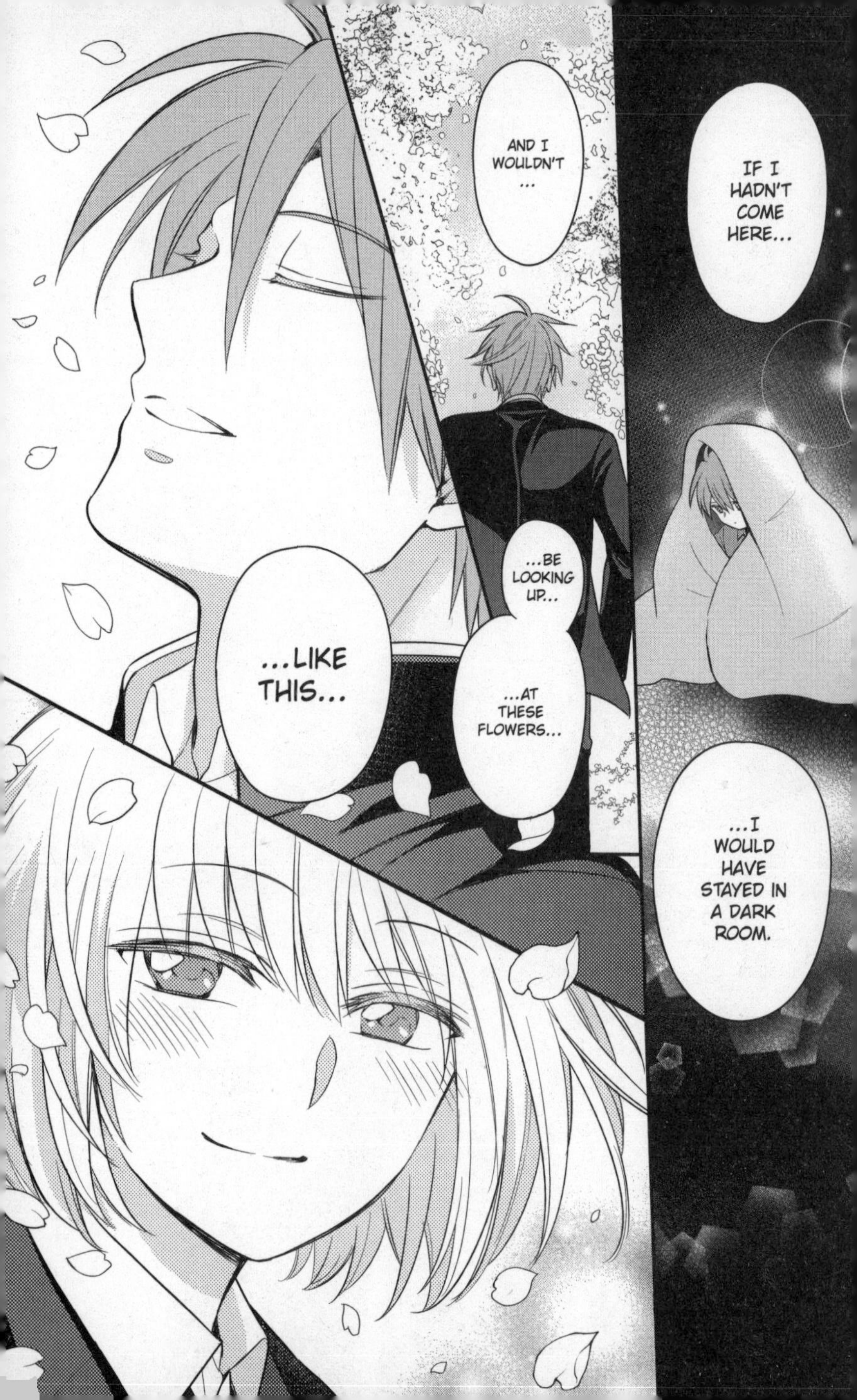
IF I HADN'T COME HERE...
...I WOULD HAVE STAYED IN A DARK ROOM.
AND I WOULDN'T ...
...BE LOOKING UP...
...AT THESE FLOWERS...
...LIKE THIS...

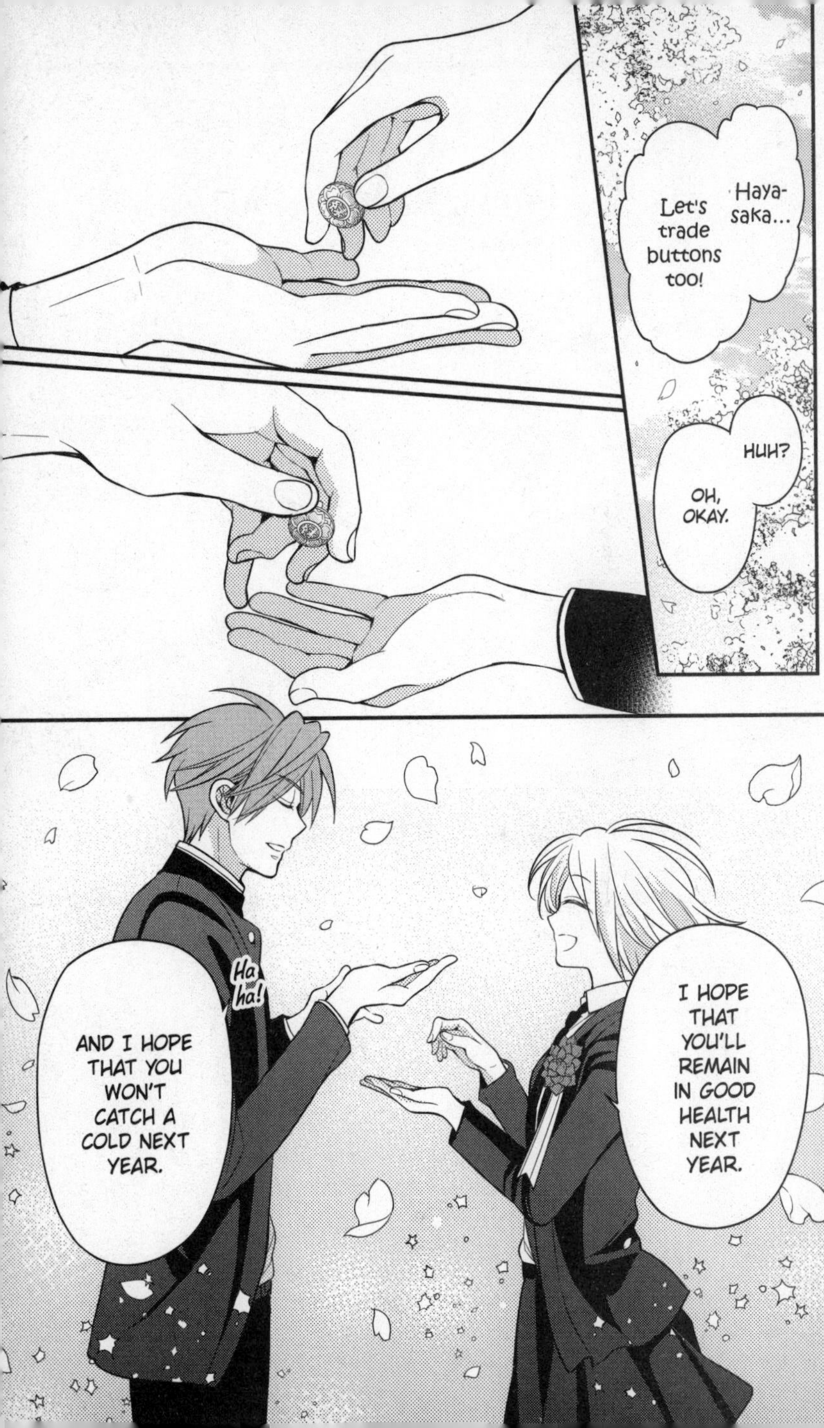
Haya-saka...
Let's trade buttons too!
HUH?
OH, OKAY.
I HOPE THAT YOU'LL REMAIN IN GOOD HEALTH NEXT YEAR.
Ha ha!
AND I HOPE THAT YOU WON'T CATCH A COLD NEXT YEAR.

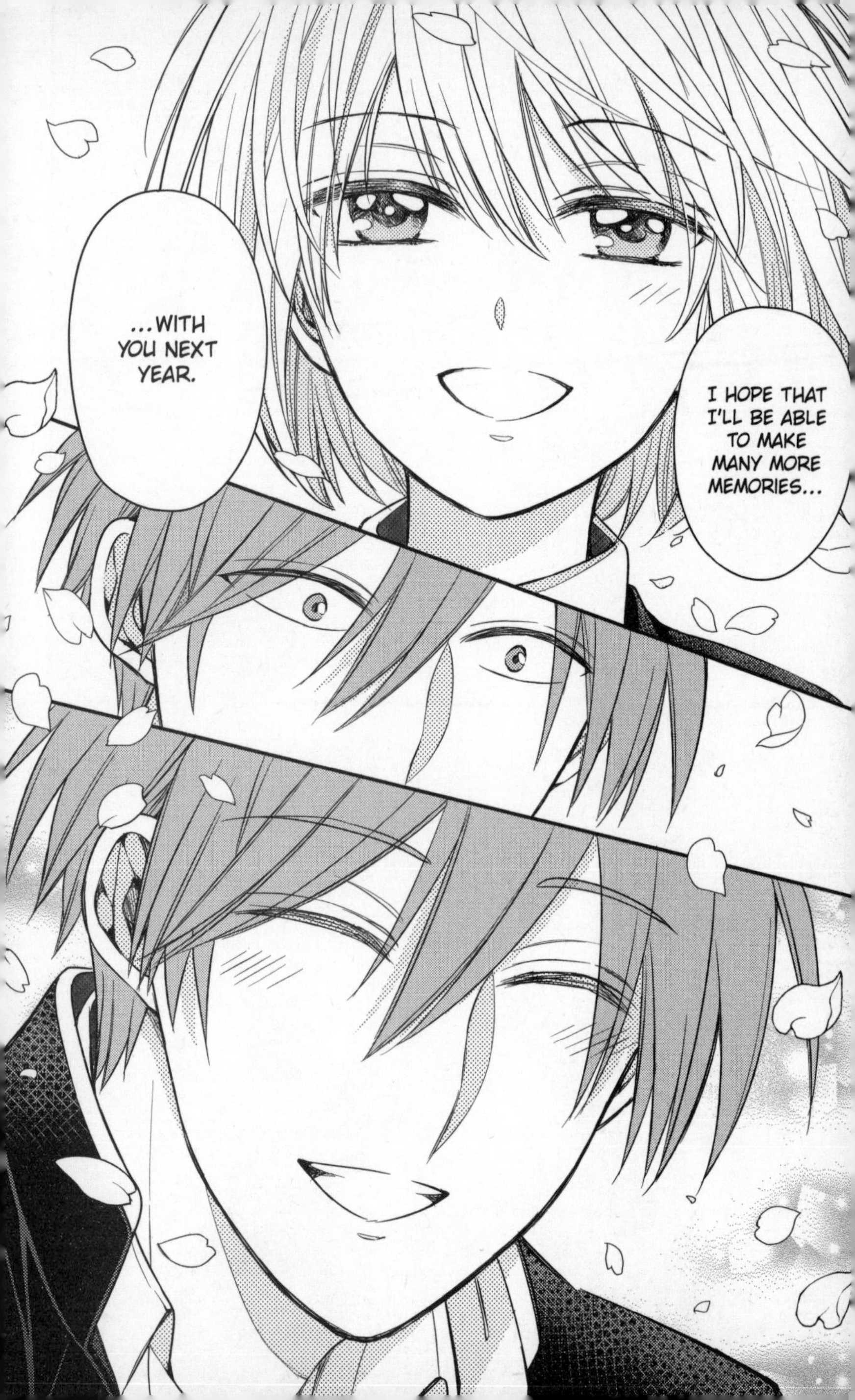
I HOPE THAT I'LL BE ABLE TO MAKE MANY MORE MEMORIES...
...WITH YOU NEXT YEAR.

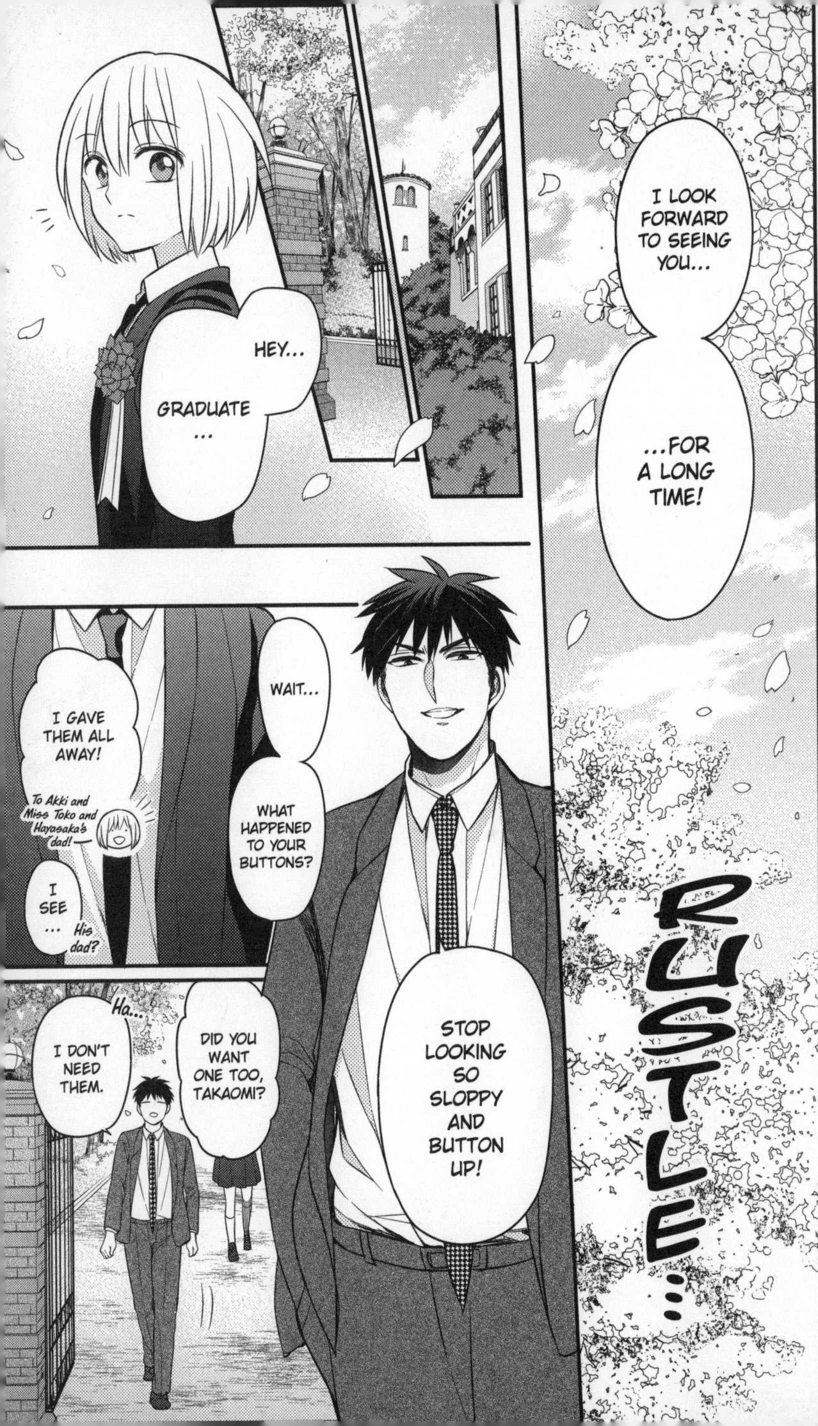

I LOOK FORWARD TO SEEING YOU...
...FOR A LONG TIME!
RUSTLE...
HEY...
GRADUATE ...
WAIT...
WHAT HAPPENED TO YOUR BUTTONS?
I GAVE THEM ALL AWAY!
To Akki and Miss Toko and Hayasaka's dad!
I SEE ...
His dad?
STOP LOOKING SO SLOPPY AND BUTTON UP!
DID YOU WANT ONE TOO, TAKAOMI?
Ha...
I DON'T NEED THEM.

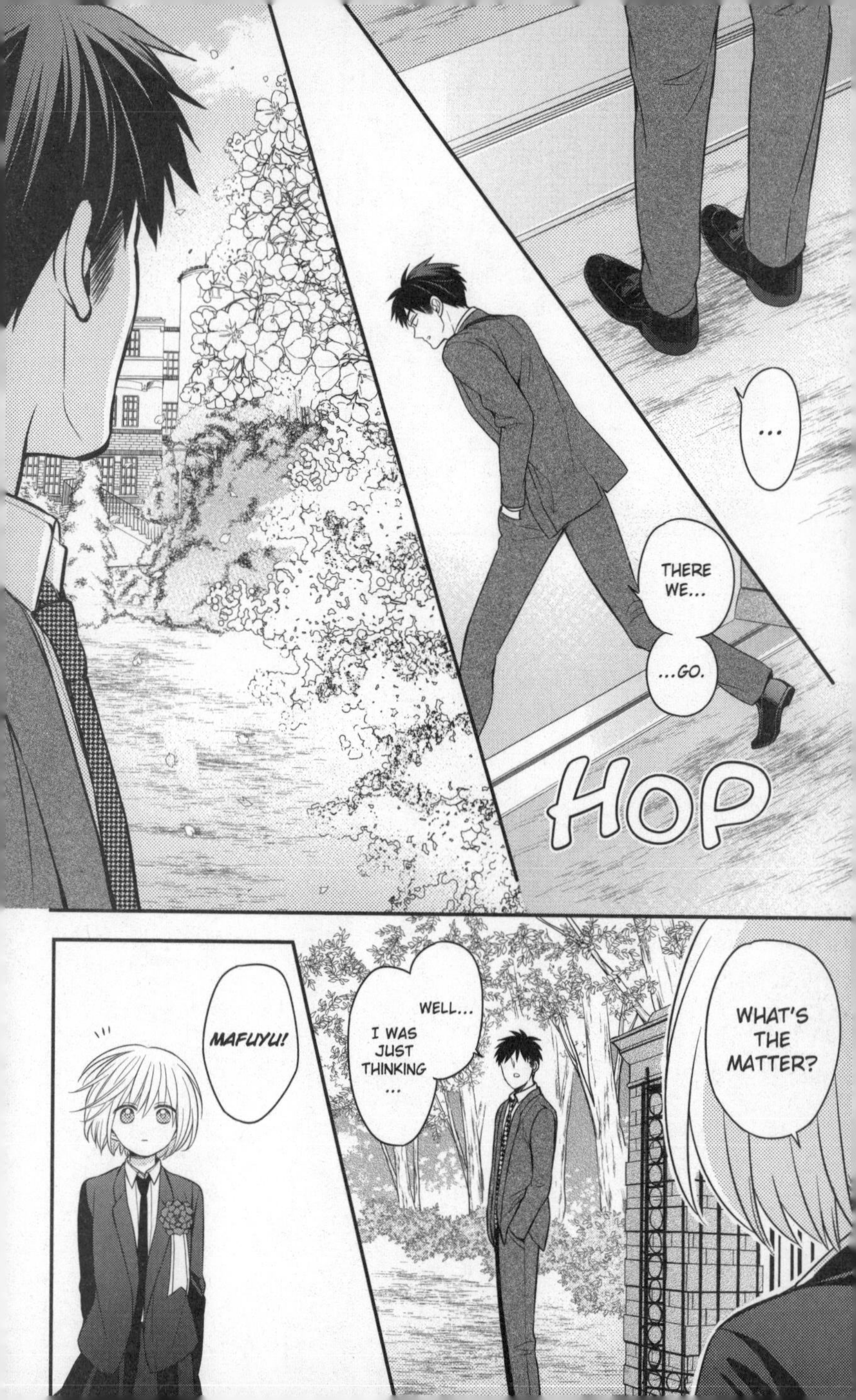
...
THERE WE...
...GO.
HOP
WHAT'S THE MATTER?
WELL...
I WAS JUST THINKING ...
MAFUYU!

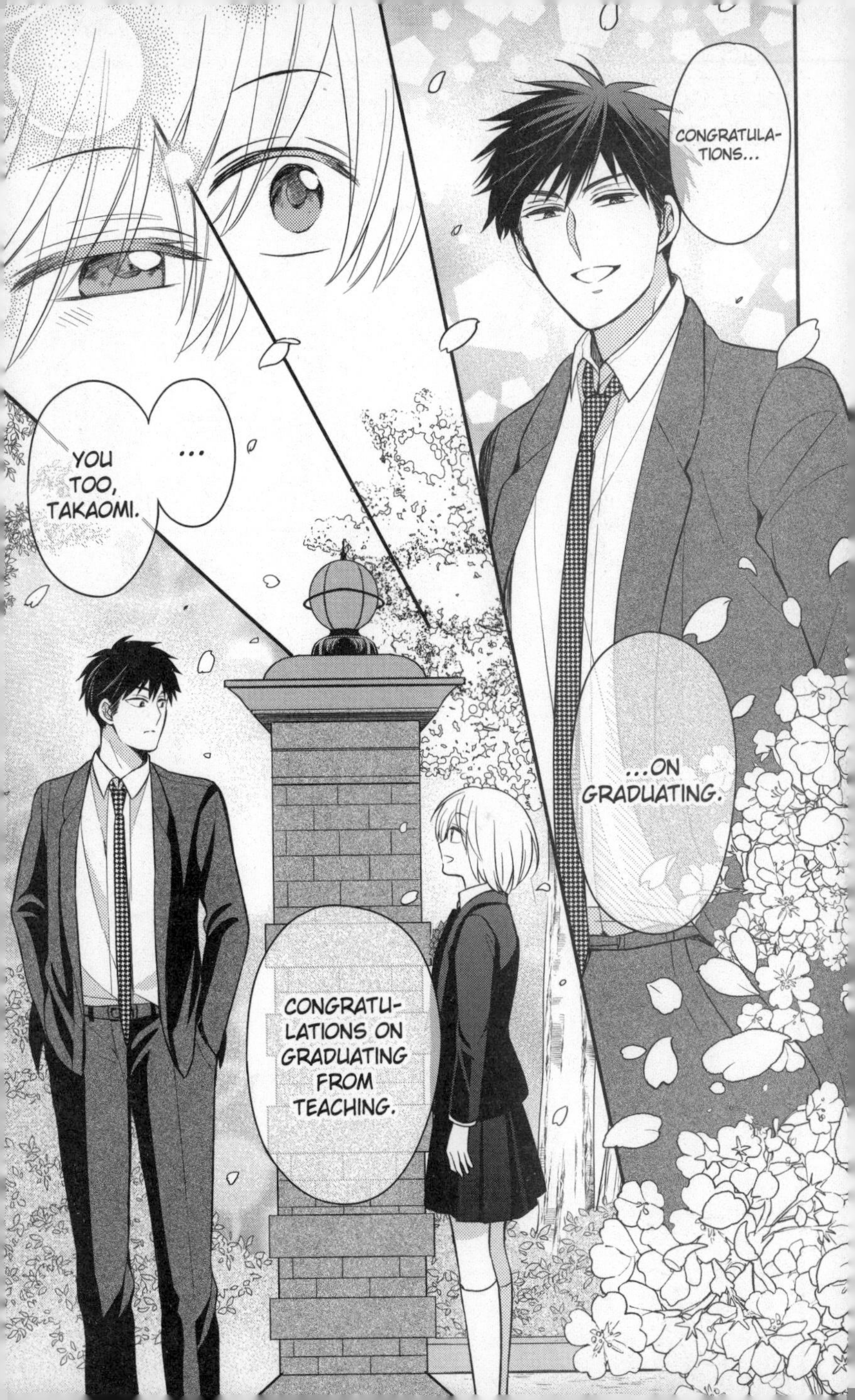
CONGRATULA-TIONS...
...ON GRADUATING.
...
YOU TOO, TAKAOMI.
CONGRATU-LATIONS ON GRADUATING FROM TEACHING.

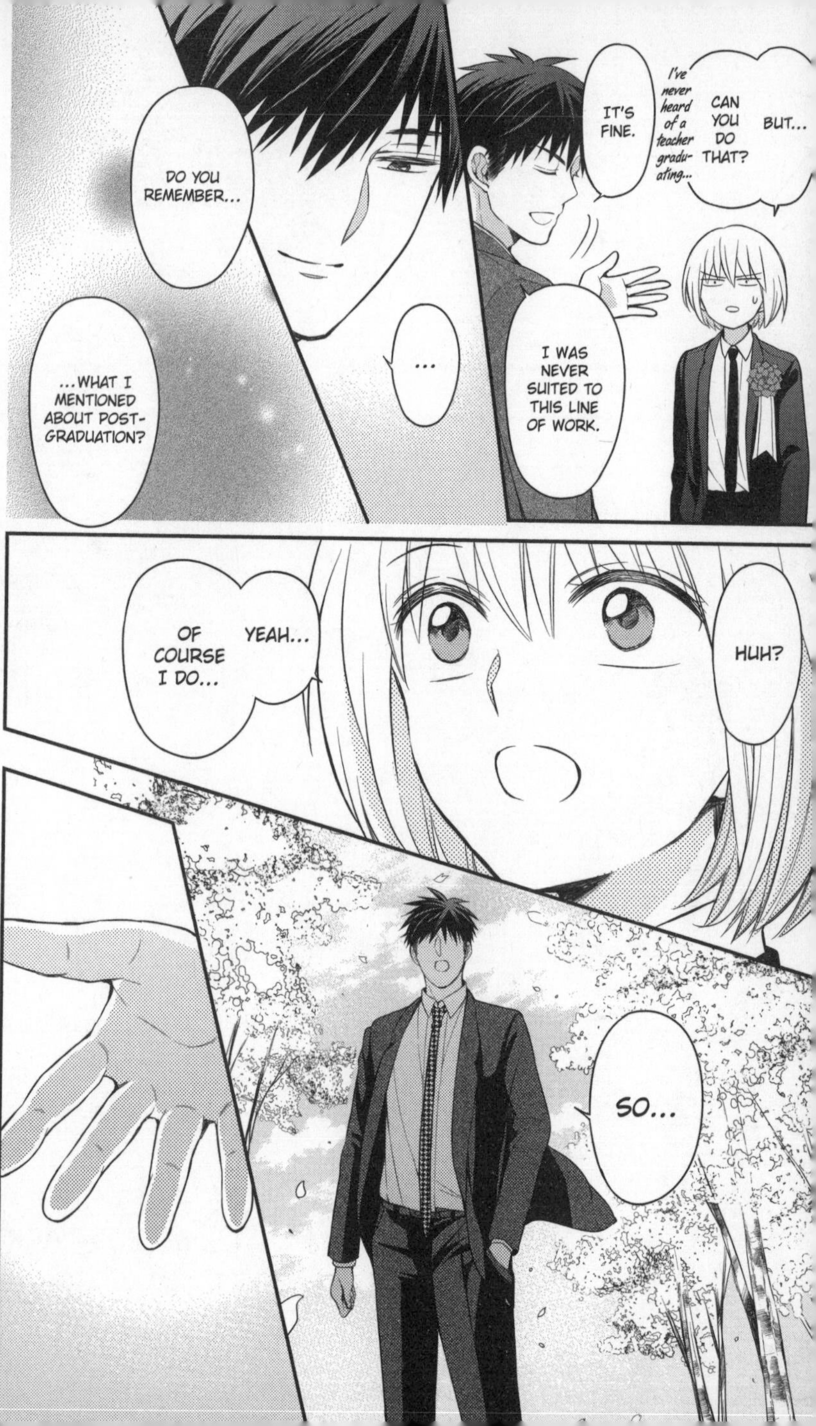
BUT... CAN YOU DO THAT?
I've never heard of a teacher graduating...
IT'S FINE.
I WAS NEVER SUITED TO THIS LINE OF WORK.
...
DO YOU REMEMBER...
...WHAT I MENTIONED ABOUT POST-GRADUATION?
HUH?
YEAH... OF COURSE I DO...
SO...

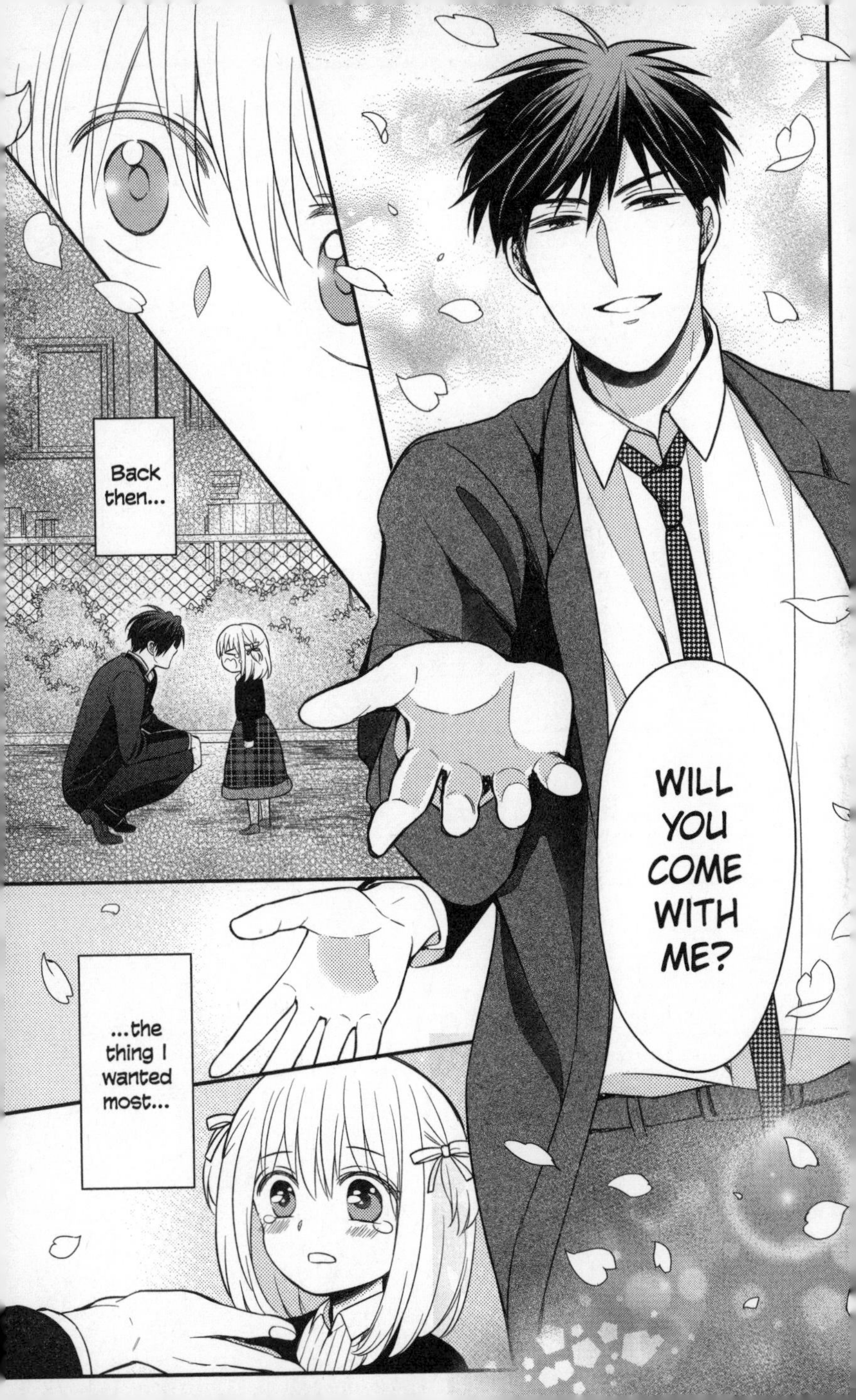
WILL YOU COME WITH ME?
Back then...
...the thing I wanted most...

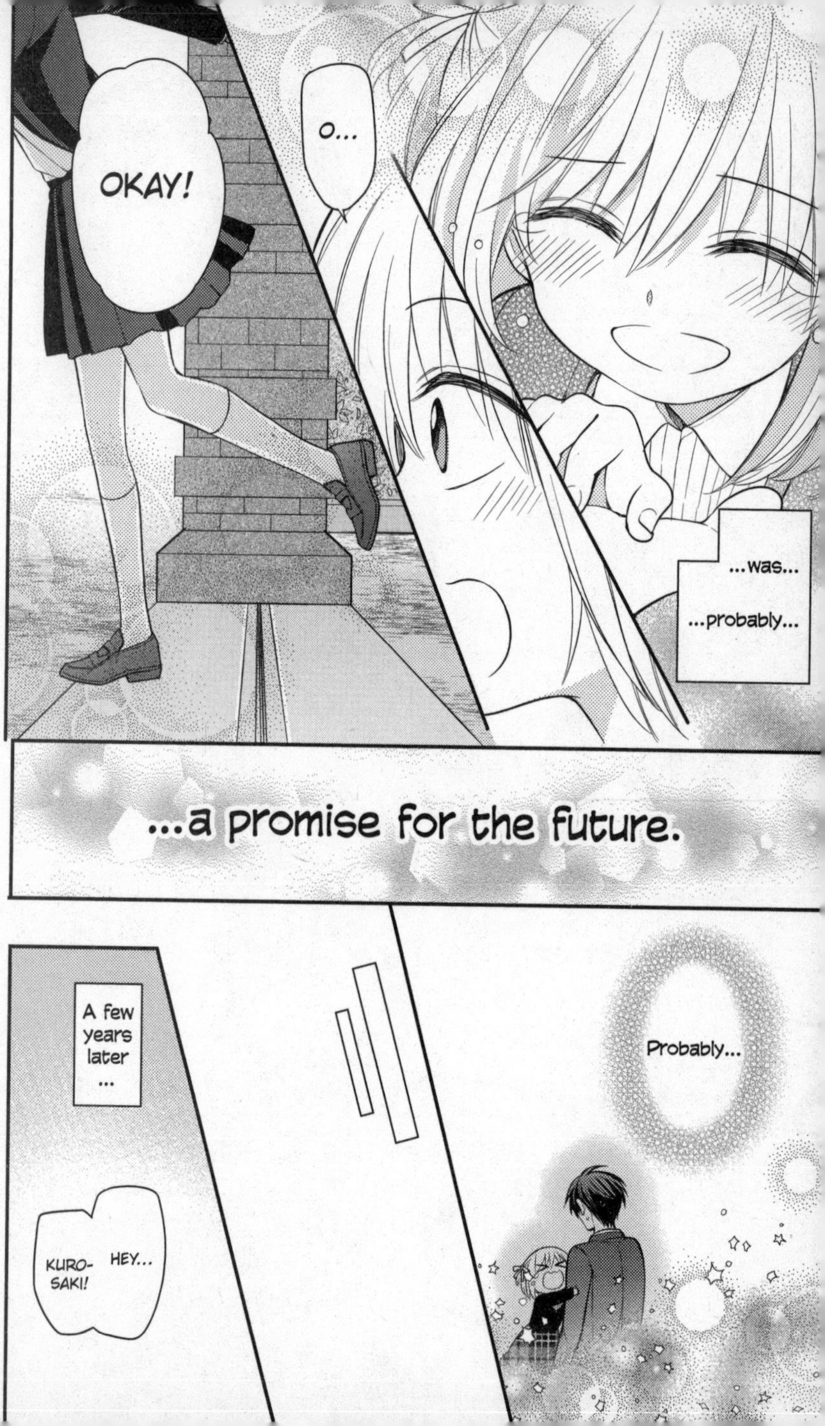
...was...
...probably...
O...
OKAY!
...a promise for the future.
Probably...
A few years later ...
HEY... KURO-SAKI!

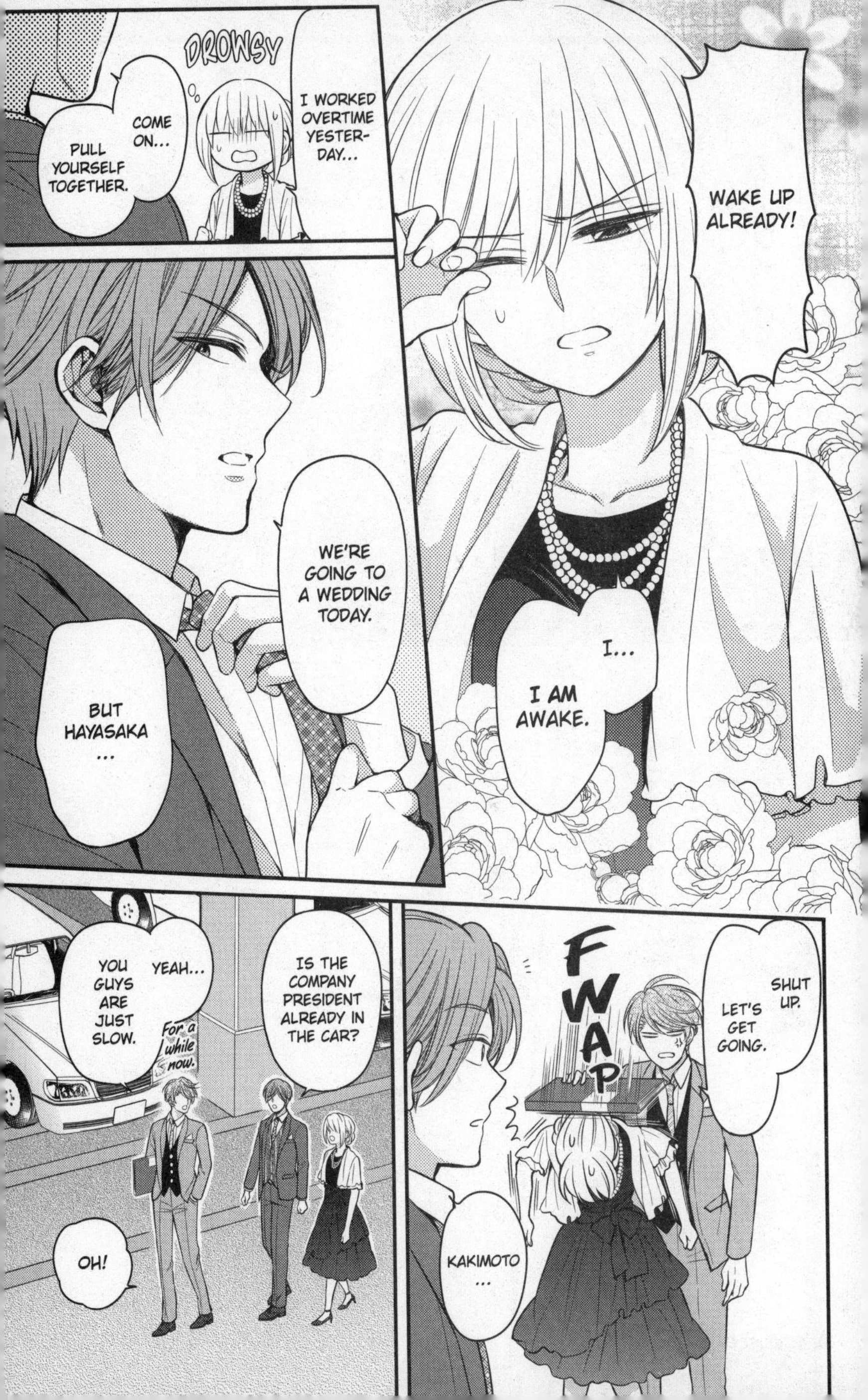
WAKE UP ALREADY!
I...
I AM AWAKE.
DROWSY
I WORKED OVERTIME YESTER-DAY...
COME ON...
PULL YOURSELF TOGETHER.
WE'RE GOING TO A WEDDING TODAY.
BUT HAYASAKA...
SHUT UP.
LET'S GET GOING.
FWAP
KAKIMOTO...
IS THE COMPANY PRESIDENT ALREADY IN THE CAR?
YEAH...
YOU GUYS ARE JUST SLOW.
For a while now.
OH!

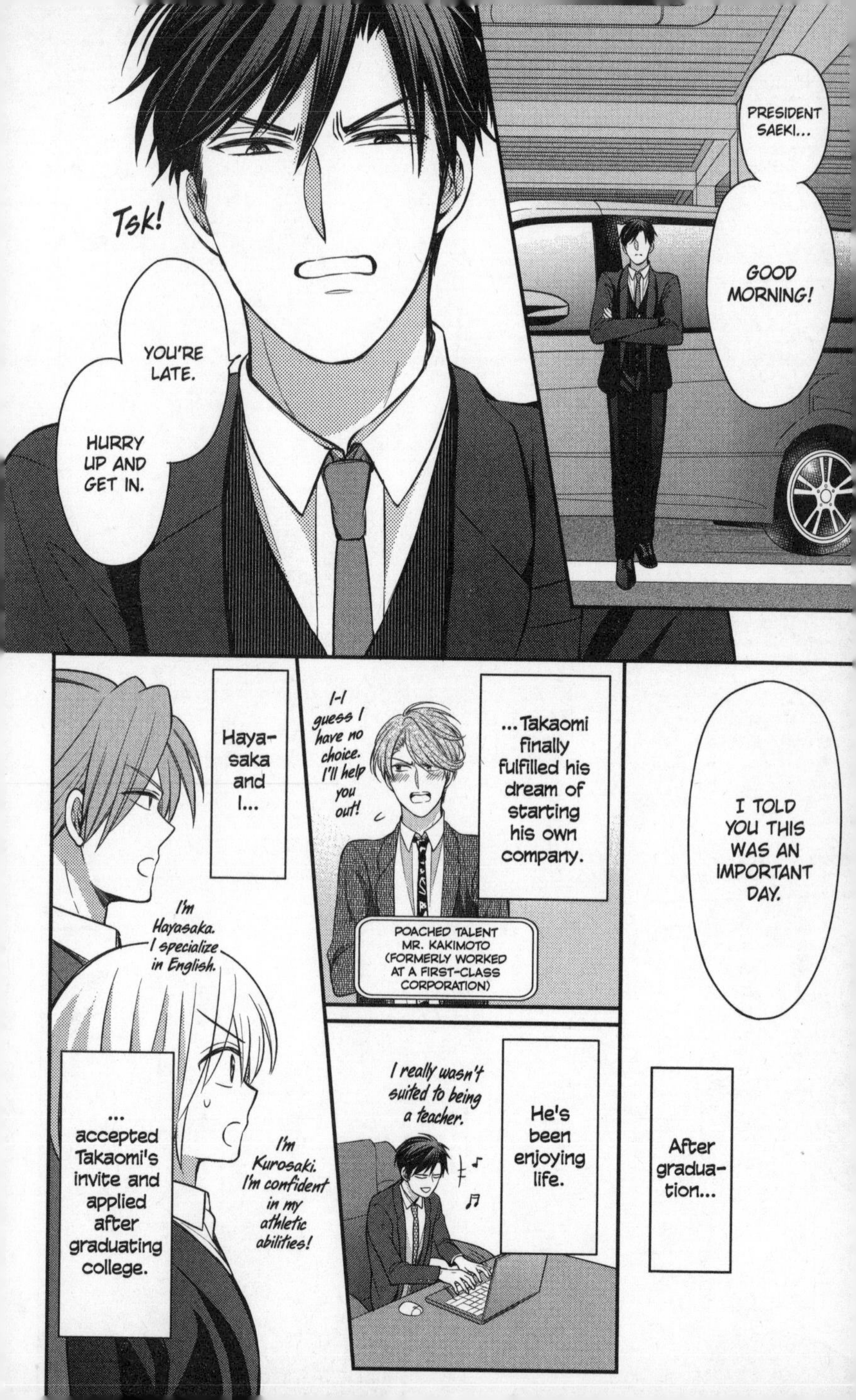
PRESIDENT SAEKI...
GOOD MORNING!
Tsk!
YOU'RE LATE.
HURRY UP AND GET IN.
I TOLD YOU THIS WAS AN IMPORTANT DAY.
After graduation...
He's been enjoying life.
I really wasn't suited to being a teacher.
...Takaomi finally fulfilled his dream of starting his own company.
I-I guess I have no choice. I'll help you out!
POACHED TALENT MR. KAKIMOTO (FORMERLY WORKED AT A FIRST-CLASS CORPORATION)
Haya-saka and I...
I'm Hayasaka. I specialize in English.
...accepted Takaomi's invite and applied after graduating college.
I'm Kurosaki. I'm confident in my athletic abilities!

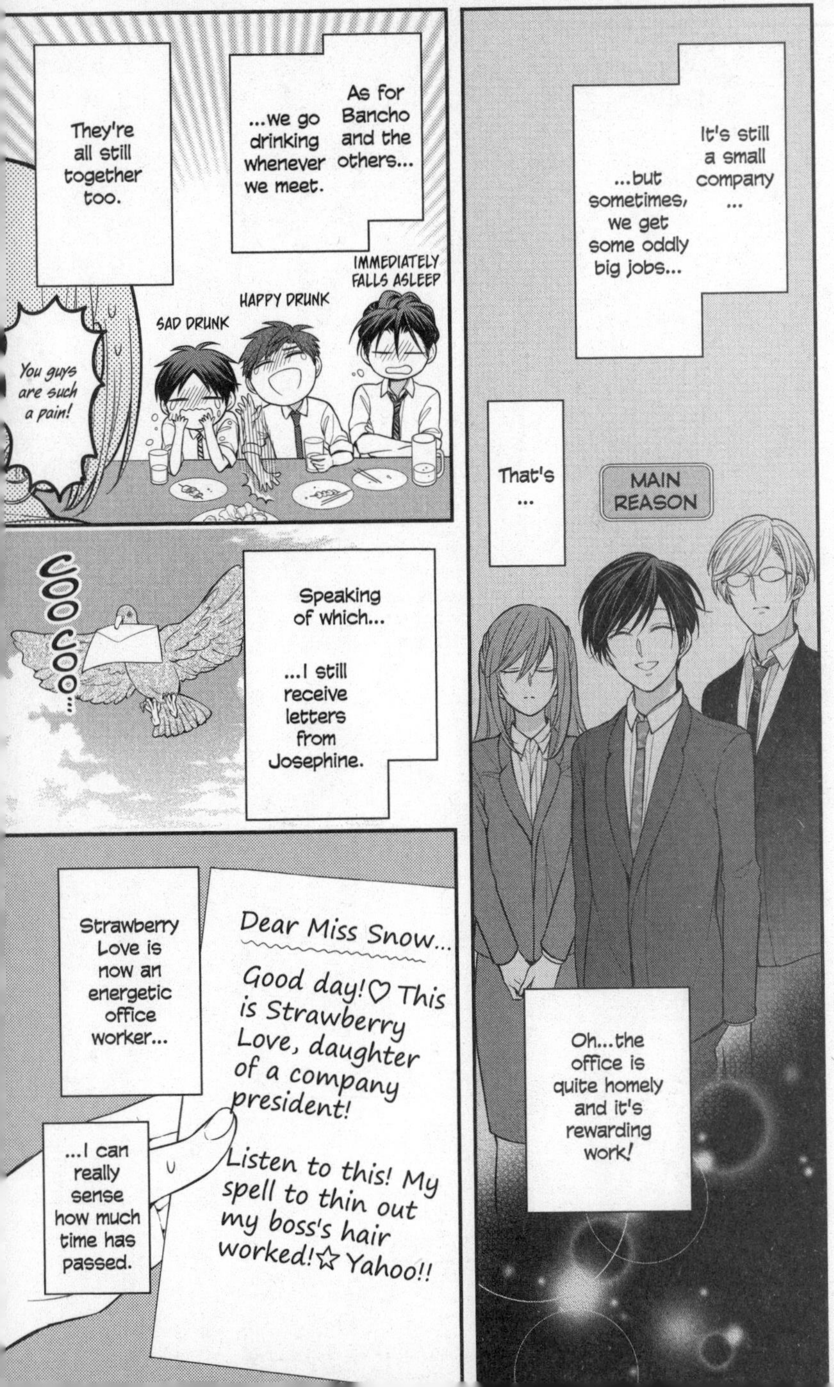
It's still a small company...
...but sometimes, we get some oddly big jobs...
That's...
MAIN REASON
Oh...the office is quite homely and it's rewarding work!
As for Bancho and the others...
...we go drinking whenever we meet.
They're all still together too.
IMMEDIATELY FALLS ASLEEP
HAPPY DRUNK
SAD DRUNK
You guys are such a pain!
Speaking of which...
...I still receive letters from Josephine.
COO COO...
Dear Miss Snow...
Good day!♡ This is Strawberry Love, daughter of a company president!
Listen to this! My spell to thin out my boss's hair worked!☆ Yahoo!!
Strawberry Love is now an energetic office worker...
...I can really sense how much time has passed.

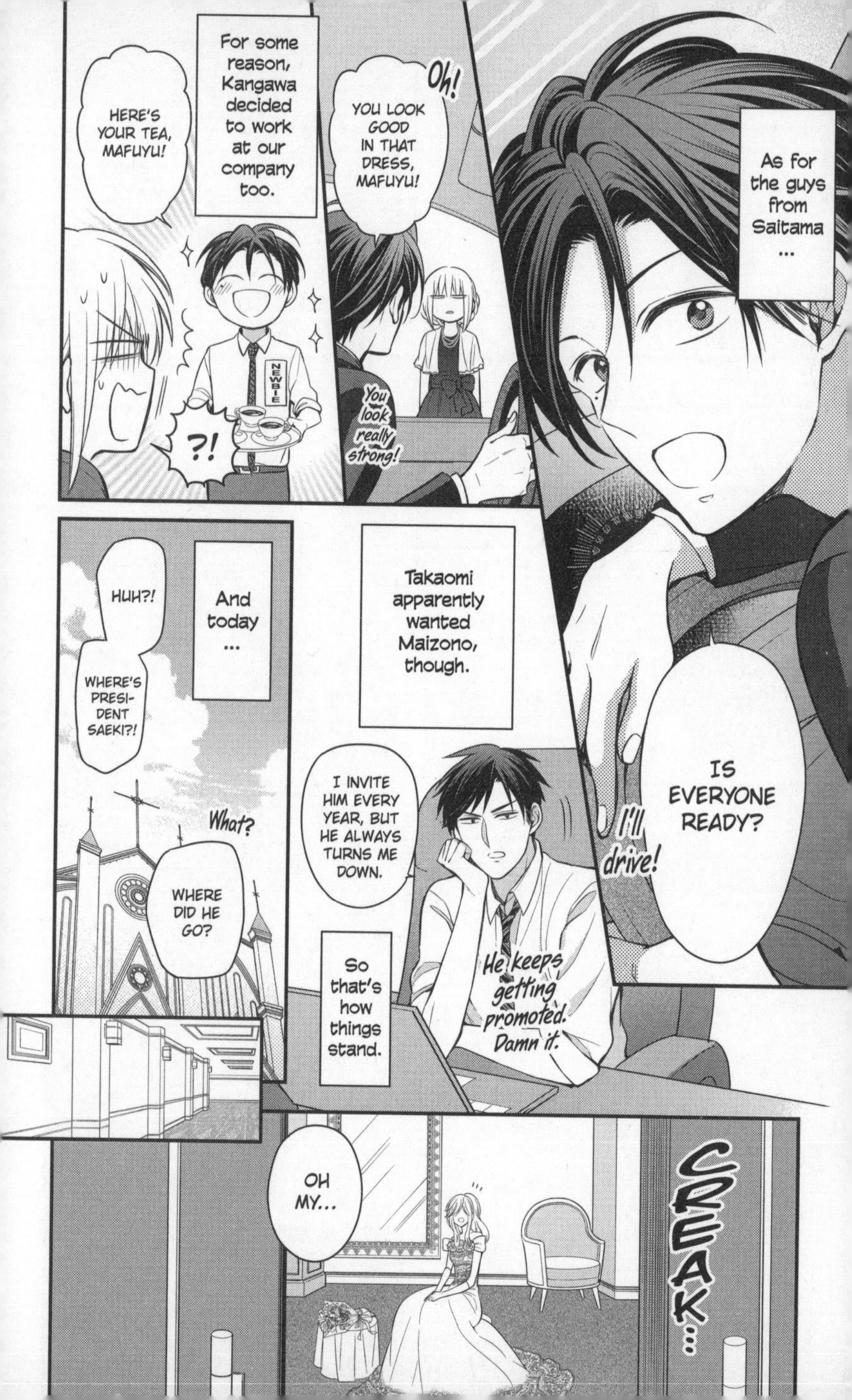
As for the guys from Saitama ...
IS EVERYONE READY?
I'll drive!
Oh!
YOU LOOK GOOD IN THAT DRESS, MAFUYU!
You look really strong!
For some reason, Kangawa decided to work at our company too.
HERE'S YOUR TEA, MAFUYU!
NEWBIE
?!
Takaomi apparently wanted Maizono, though.
I INVITE HIM EVERY YEAR, BUT HE ALWAYS TURNS ME DOWN.
He keeps getting promoted. Damn it.
So that's how things stand.
And today ...
HUH?!
WHERE'S PRESI-DENT SAEKI?!
What?
WHERE DID HE GO?
CREAK...
OH MY...

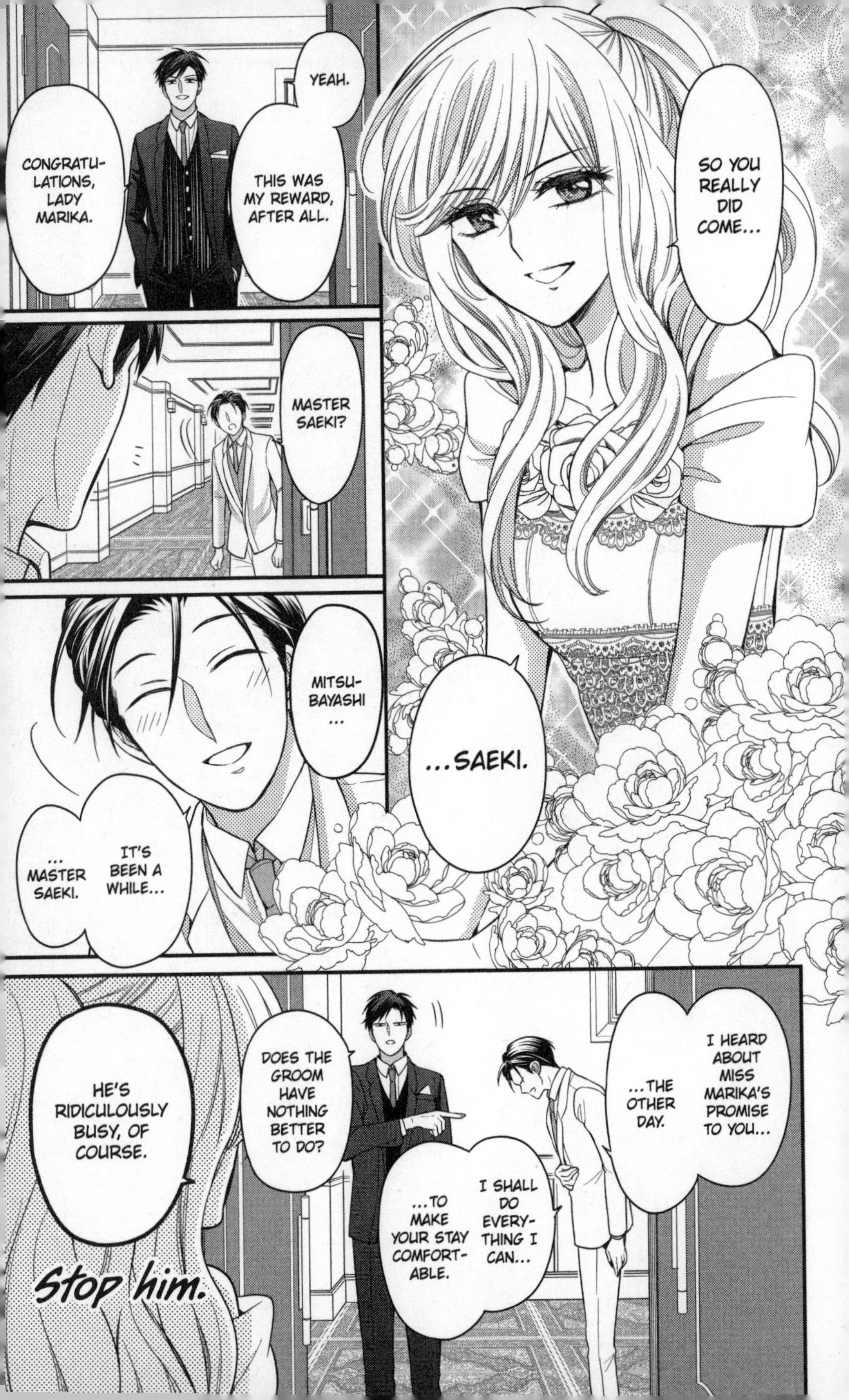
SO YOU REALLY DID COME...
...SAEKI.
YEAH.
THIS WAS MY REWARD, AFTER ALL.
CONGRATULATIONS, LADY MARIKA.
MASTER SAEKI?
MITSUBAYASHI...
IT'S BEEN A WHILE...
...MASTER SAEKI.
I HEARD ABOUT MISS MARIKA'S PROMISE TO YOU...
...THE OTHER DAY.
I SHALL DO EVERYTHING I CAN...
...TO MAKE YOUR STAY COMFORTABLE.
DOES THE GROOM HAVE NOTHING BETTER TO DO?
HE'S RIDICULOUSLY BUSY, OF COURSE.
Stop him.

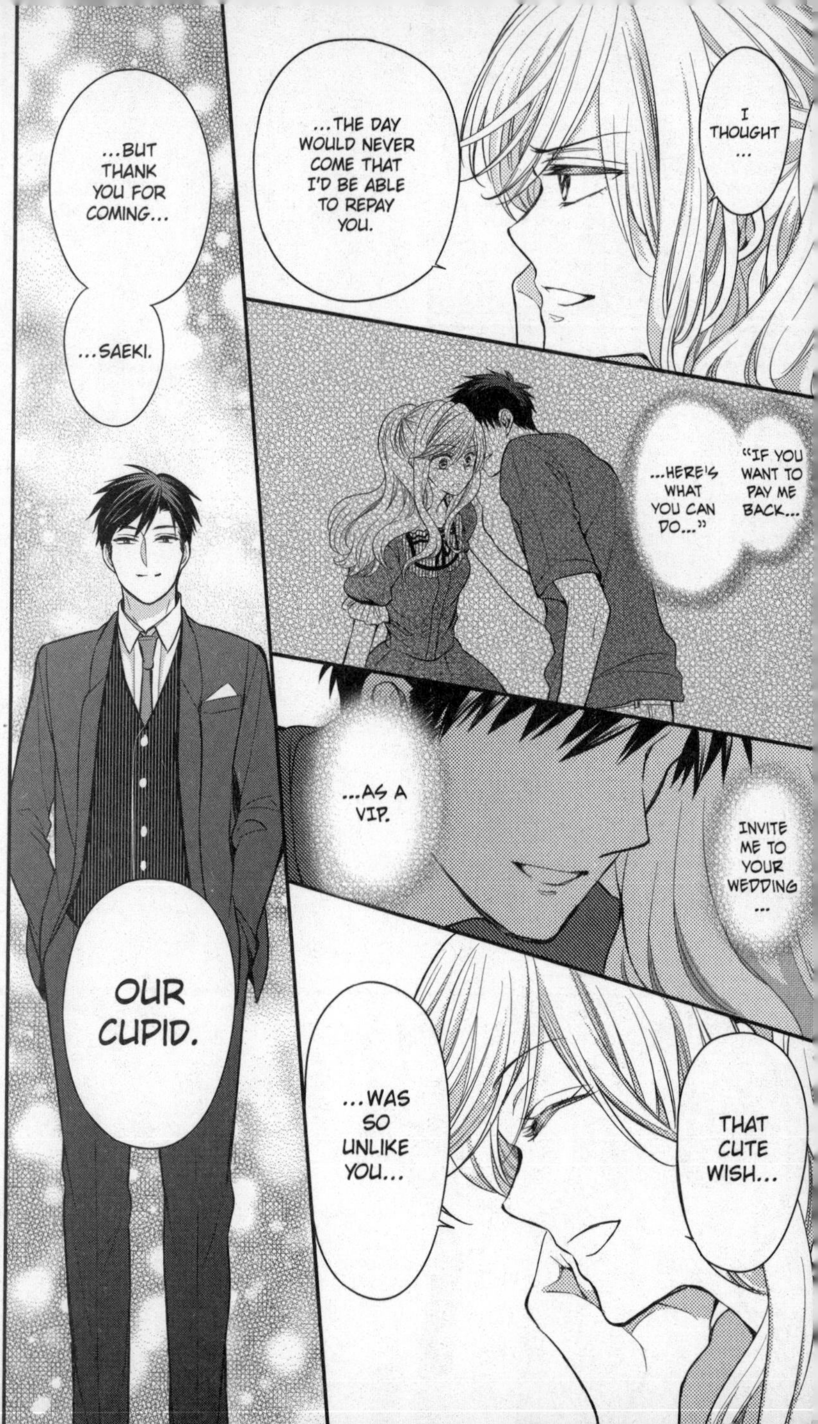
I THOUGHT...
...THE DAY WOULD NEVER COME THAT I'D BE ABLE TO REPAY YOU.
"IF YOU WANT TO PAY ME BACK...
...HERE'S WHAT YOU CAN DO..."
INVITE ME TO YOUR WEDDING...
...AS A VIP.
THAT CUTE WISH...
...WAS SO UNLIKE YOU...
...BUT THANK YOU FOR COMING...
...SAEKI.
OUR CUPID.

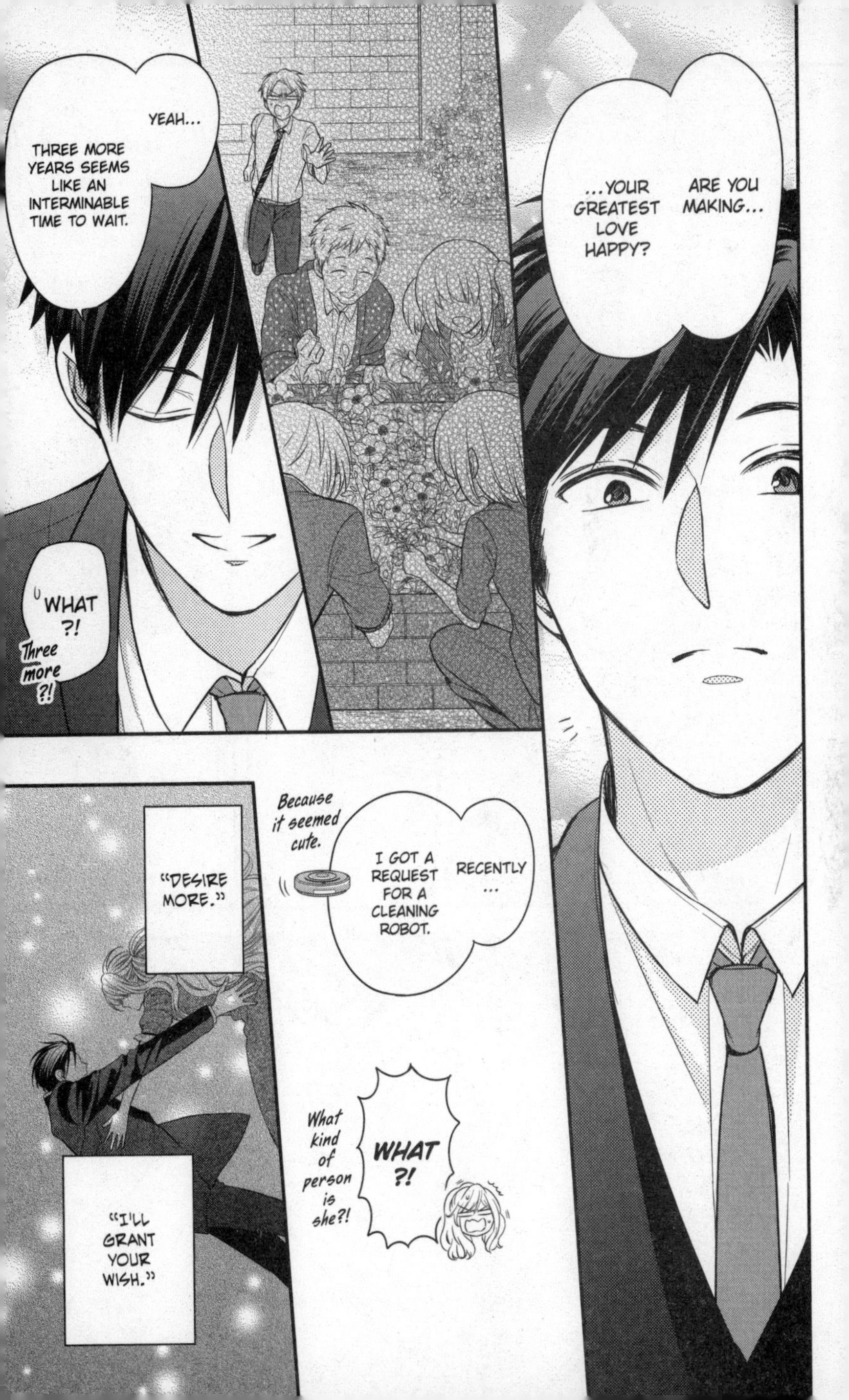
ARE YOU MAKING... ...YOUR GREATEST LOVE HAPPY?
YEAH... THREE MORE YEARS SEEMS LIKE AN INTERMINABLE TIME TO WAIT.
WHAT?!
Three more?!
RECENTLY... I GOT A REQUEST FOR A CLEANING ROBOT.
Because it seemed cute.
WHAT?!
What kind of person is she?!
"DESIRE MORE."
"I'LL GRANT YOUR WISH."

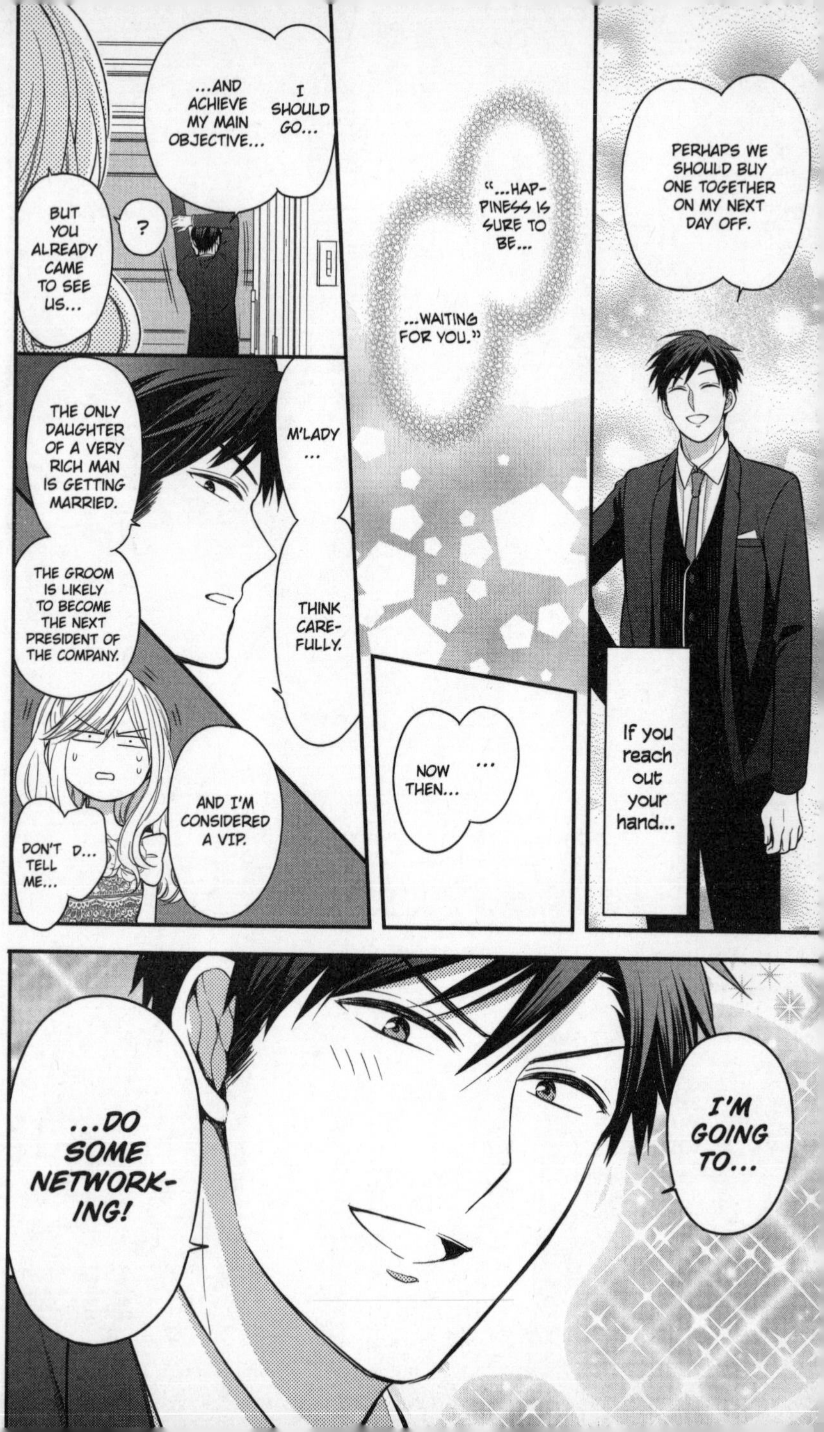
PERHAPS WE SHOULD BUY ONE TOGETHER ON MY NEXT DAY OFF.
If you reach out your hand...
“...HAP-PINESS IS SURE TO BE...
...WAITING FOR YOU.”
...
NOW THEN...
I SHOULD GO...
...AND ACHIEVE MY MAIN OBJECTIVE...
?
BUT YOU ALREADY CAME TO SEE US...
M'LADY...
THE ONLY DAUGHTER OF A VERY RICH MAN IS GETTING MARRIED.
THINK CARE-FULLY.
THE GROOM IS LIKELY TO BECOME THE NEXT PRESIDENT OF THE COMPANY.
AND I'M CONSIDERED A VIP.
D...
DON'T TELL ME...
I'M GOING TO...
...DO SOME NETWORK-ING!

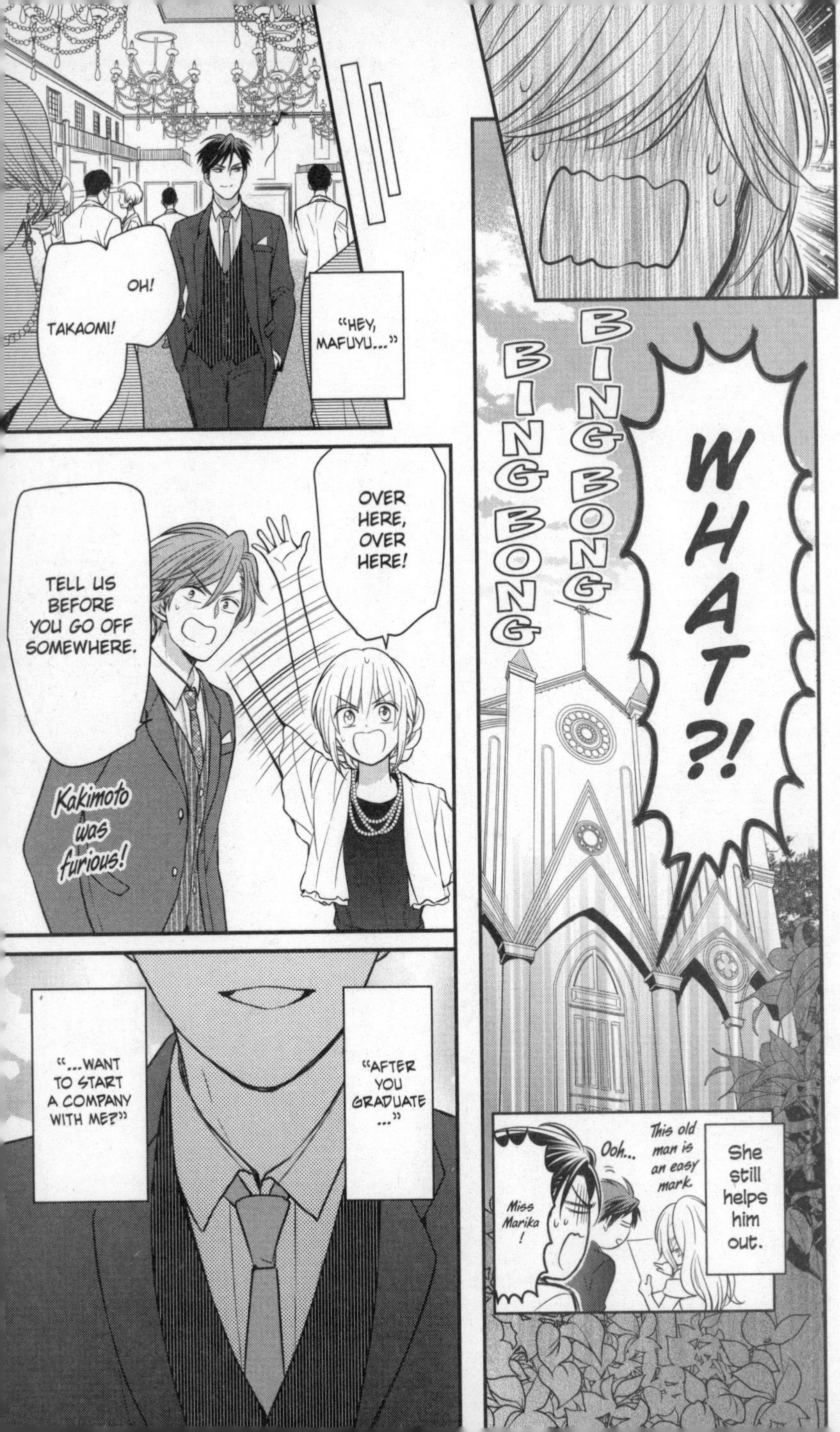
"HEY, MAFUYU..."
OH!
TAKAOMI!
OVER HERE, OVER HERE!
TELL US BEFORE YOU GO OFF SOMEWHERE.
Kakimoto was furious!
"AFTER YOU GRADUATE..."
"...WANT TO START A COMPANY WITH ME?"
WHAT?!
BING BONG
BING BONG
She still helps him out.
This old man is an easy mark.
Ooh...
Miss Marika!

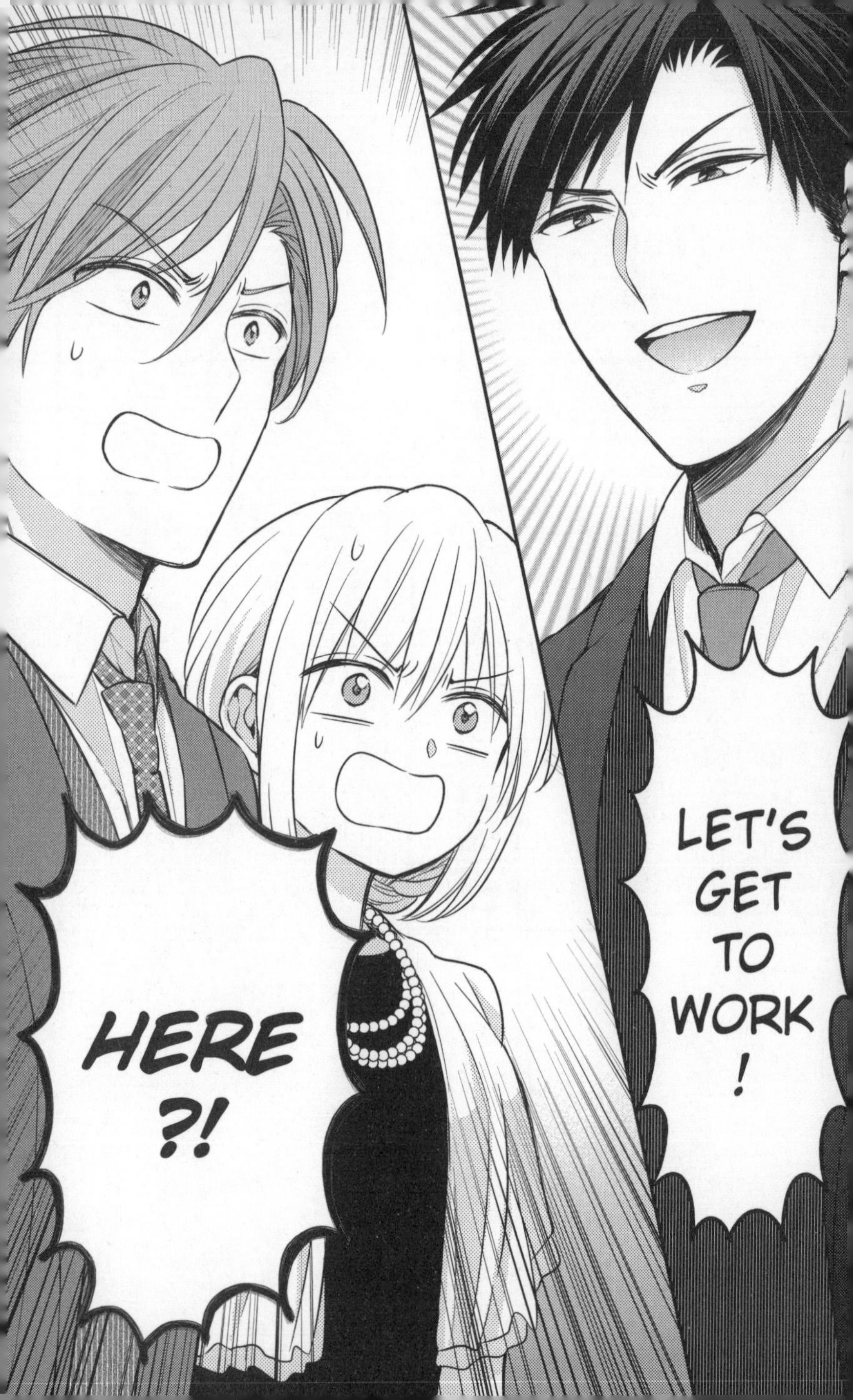
LET'S GET TO WORK!
HERE?!

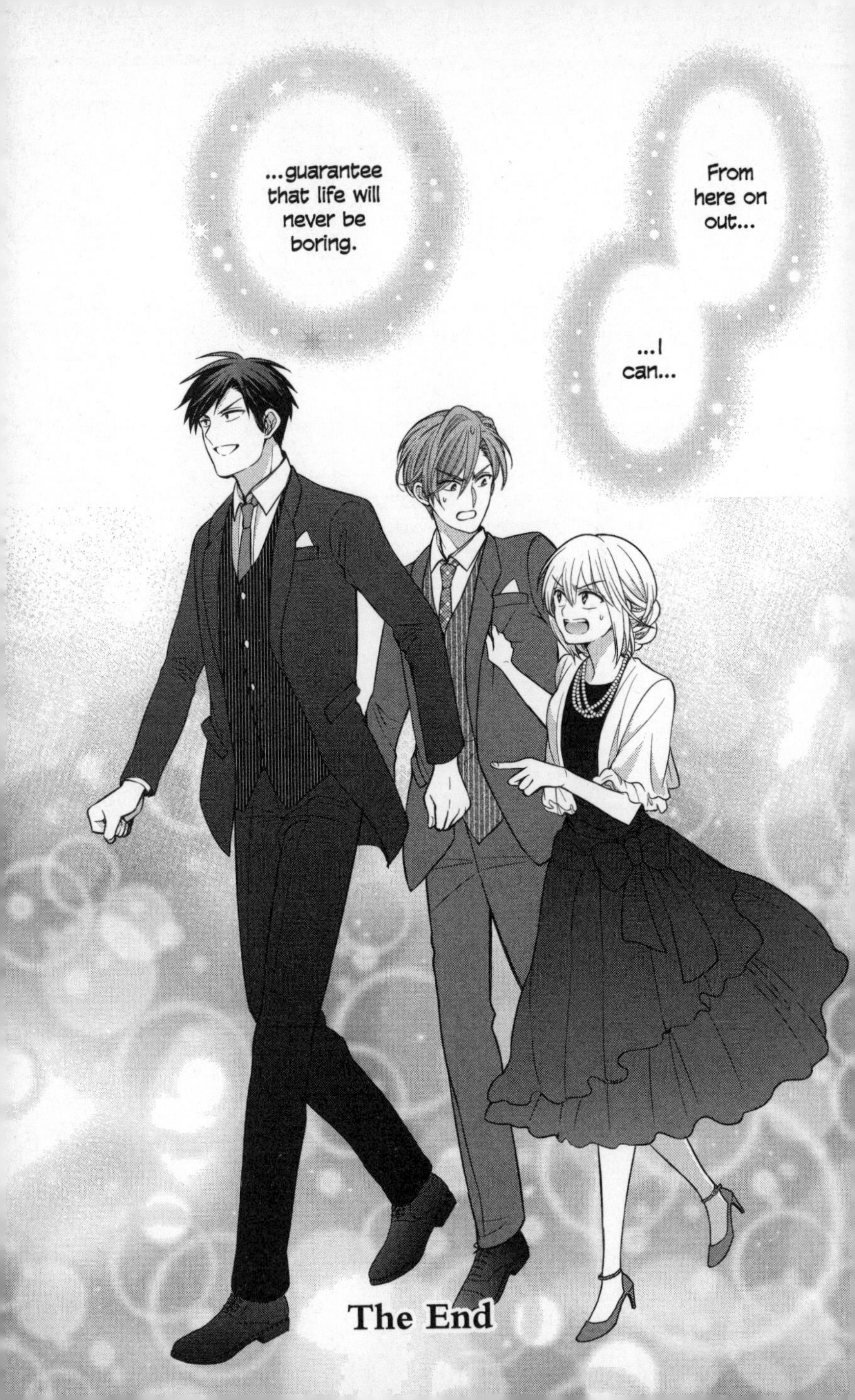
From here on out...
...I can...
...guarantee that life will never be boring.
The End

AFTER THE SCHOOL FESTIVAL

No one's going to know if I show up at the closing ceremonies, right?
I totally look like a student, don't I?
No, there's no way you'd pass as a high school student.
How are you always so confident?

WELCOMING

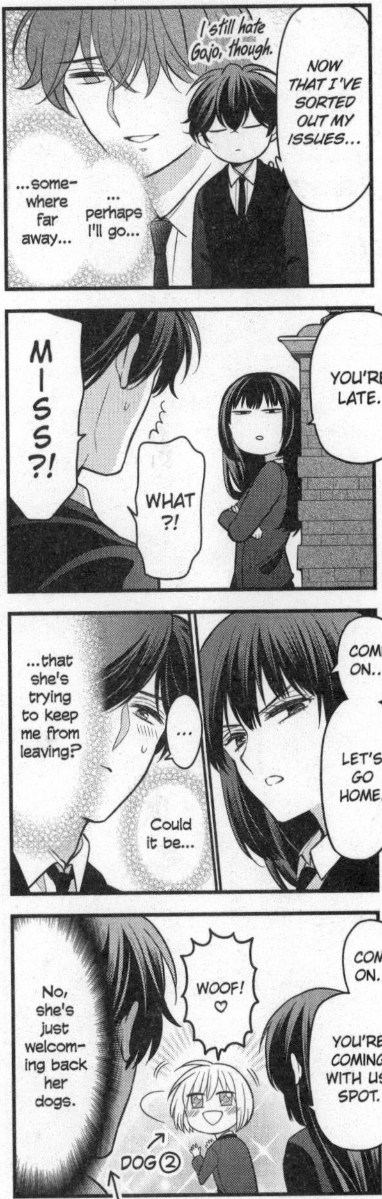
NOW THAT I'VE SORTED OUT MY ISSUES...
I still hate Gojo, though.
... perhaps I'll go...
...somewhere far away...
YOU'RE LATE.
WHAT ?!
MISS ?!
COME ON...
LET'S GO HOME.
...
Could it be...
...that she's trying to keep me from leaving?
COME ON...
YOU'RE COMING WITH US, SPOT.
WOOF! ♡
No, she's just welcoming back her dogs.
DOG②
DOG①

WHAT I WANT TO SAY

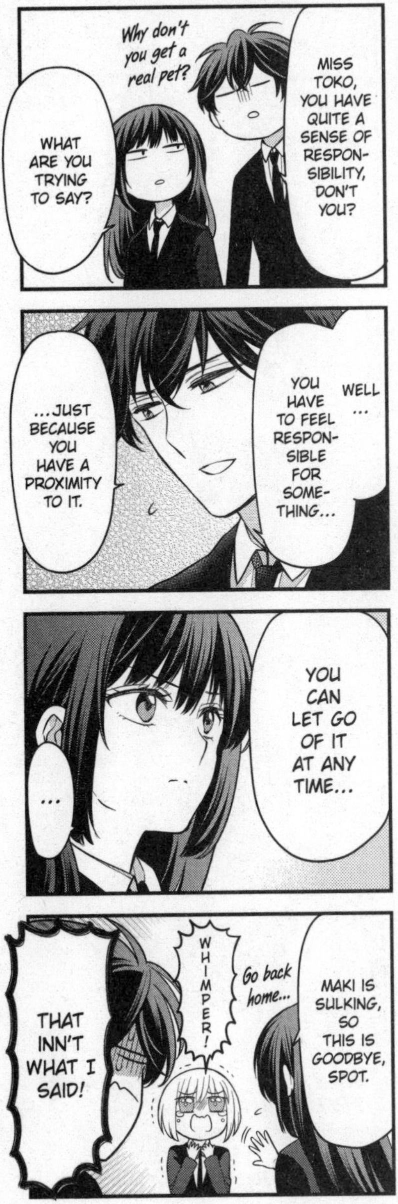
MISS TOKO, YOU HAVE QUITE A SENSE OF RESPONSIBILITY, DON'T YOU?
Why don't you get a real pet?
WHAT ARE YOU TRYING TO SAY?
WELL...
YOU HAVE TO FEEL RESPONSIBLE FOR SOMETHING...
...JUST BECAUSE YOU HAVE A PROXIMITY TO IT.
YOU CAN LET GO OF IT AT ANY TIME...
...
MAKI IS SULKING, SO THIS IS GOODBYE, SPOT.
Go back home...
WHIMPER!
THAT INN'T WHAT I SAID!

NOT FAIR

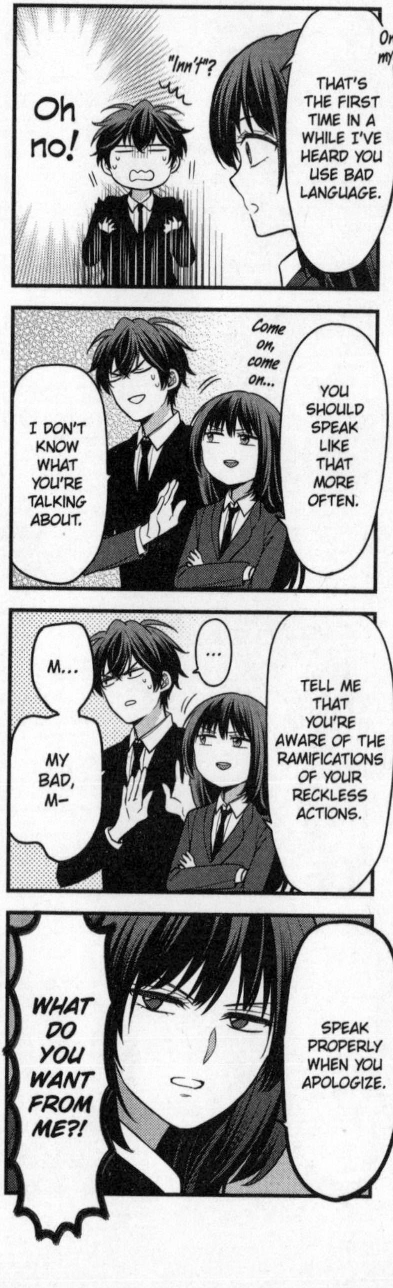
On my...
THAT'S THE FIRST TIME IN A WHILE I'VE HEARD YOU USE BAD LANGUAGE.
"Inn't"?
Oh no!
Come on, come on...
YOU SHOULD SPEAK LIKE THAT MORE OFTEN.
I DON'T KNOW WHAT YOU'RE TALKING ABOUT.
TELL ME THAT YOU'RE AWARE OF THE RAMIFICATIONS OF YOUR RECKLESS ACTIONS.
...
M...
MY BAD, M-
SPEAK PROPERLY WHEN YOU APOLOGIZE.
WHAT DO YOU WANT FROM ME?!

WHILE LOOKING TOWARD THE FUTURE

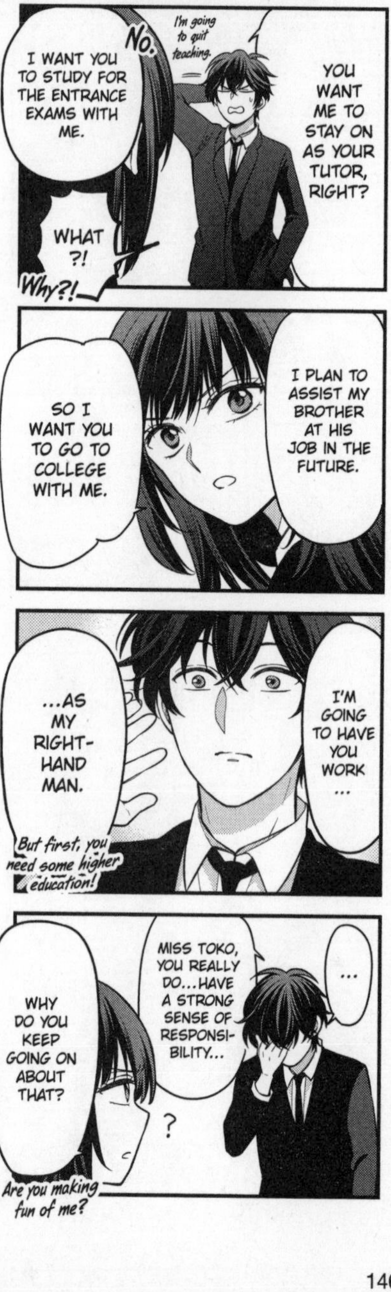
YOU WANT ME TO STAY ON AS YOUR TUTOR, RIGHT?
I'm going to quit teaching.
No.
I WANT YOU TO STUDY FOR THE ENTRANCE EXAMS WITH ME.
WHAT ?!
Why?!
I PLAN TO ASSIST MY BROTHER AT HIS JOB IN THE FUTURE.
SO I WANT YOU TO GO TO COLLEGE WITH ME.
I'M GOING TO HAVE YOU WORK ...
...AS MY RIGHT-HAND MAN.
But first, you need some higher education!
...
MISS TOKO, YOU REALLY DO...HAVE A STRONG SENSE OF RESPONSI-BILITY...
?
WHY DO YOU KEEP GOING ON ABOUT THAT?
Are you making fun of me?

WHAT HAPPENS AFTERWARD

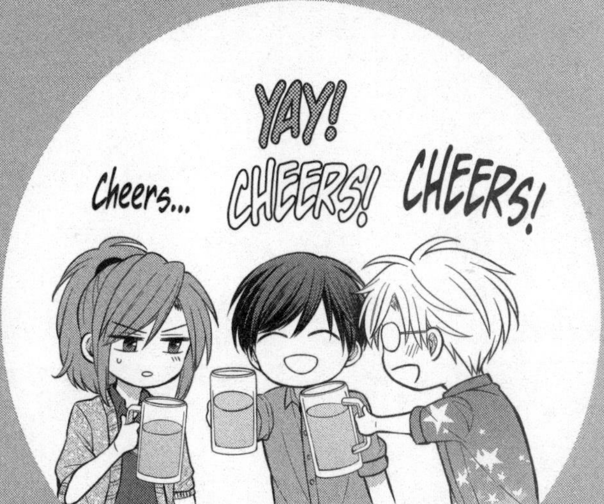
Cheers...
YAY! CHEERS!
CHEERS!
CONGRATULATIONS ON TURNING 20!

STARTING LIFE ON HIS OWN

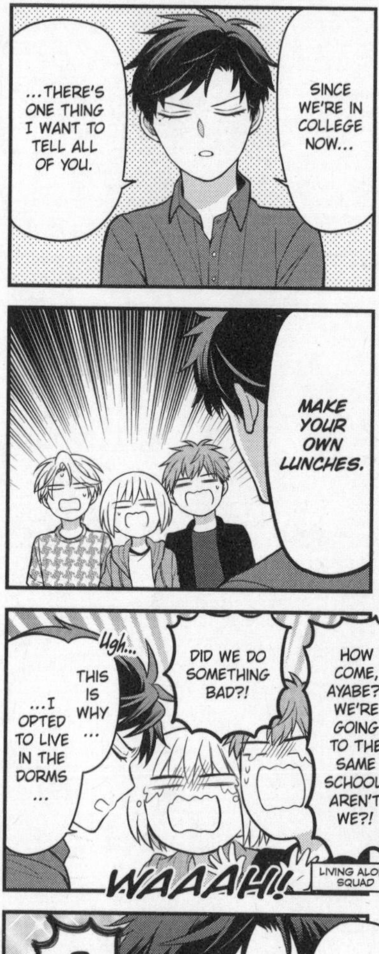
SINCE WE'RE IN COLLEGE NOW...
...THERE'S ONE THING I WANT TO TELL ALL OF YOU.
MAKE YOUR OWN LUNCHES.
HOW COME, AYABE?! WE'RE GOING TO THE SAME SCHOOL, AREN'T WE?!
DID WE DO SOMETHING BAD?!
Ugh...
THIS IS WHY...
...I OPTED TO LIVE IN THE DORMS...
WAAAH!
LIVING ALONE SQUAD
They offer breakfast, lunch and dinner.
For those who request it!
DAMN IT!
He looks so triumphant!

AN UNDERSTANDING FRIEND

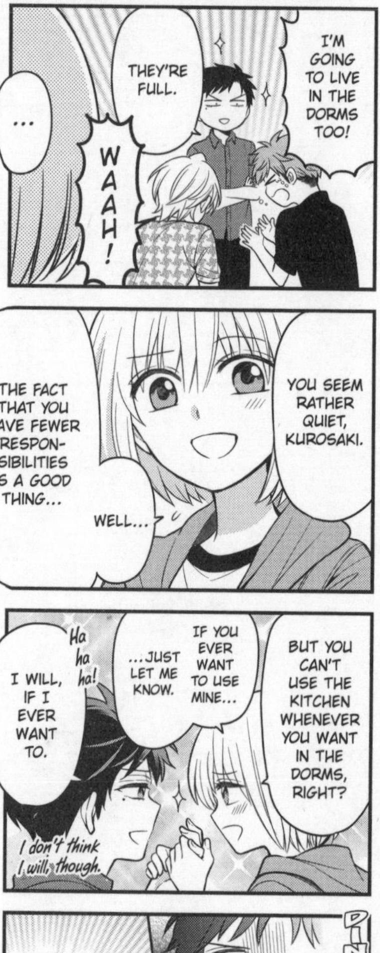
I'M GOING TO LIVE IN THE DORMS TOO!
THEY'RE FULL.
WAAH!
...
YOU SEEM RATHER QUIET, KUROSAKI.
WELL...
THE FACT THAT YOU HAVE FEWER RESPON-SIBILITIES IS A GOOD THING...
BUT YOU CAN'T USE THE KITCHEN WHENEVER YOU WANT IN THE DORMS, RIGHT?
IF YOU EVER WANT TO USE MINE...
...JUST LET ME KNOW.
Ha ha ha!
I WILL, IF I EVER WANT TO.
I don't think I will, though.
DING DONG
WITH-DRAWAL SYMP-TOMS
PLEASE LET ME BORROW YOUR KITCHEN.

THIS HAYASAKA FELLOW

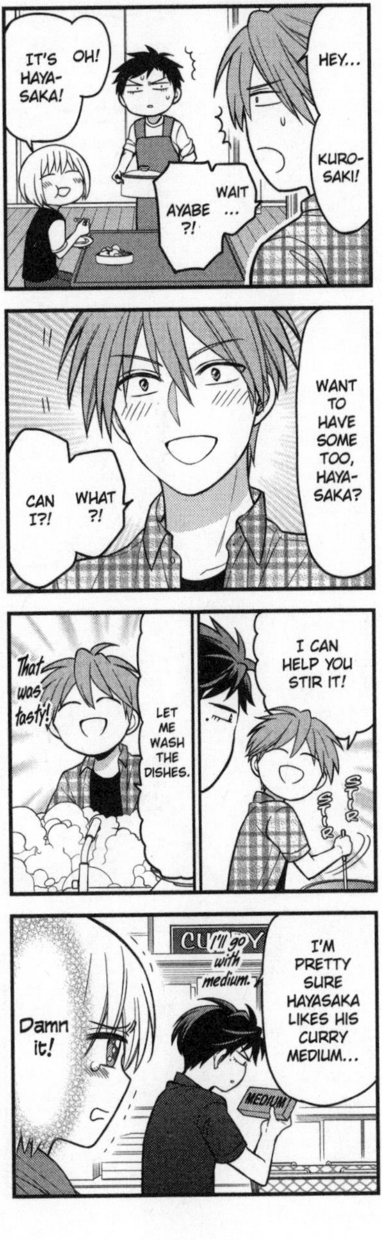
HEY... KURO-SAKI!
WAIT... AYABE?!
OH!
IT'S HAYA-SAKA!
WANT TO HAVE SOME TOO, HAYA-SAKA?
WHAT?!
CAN I?!
I CAN HELP YOU STIR IT!
STIR STIR
LET ME WASH THE DISHES.
That was tasty!
I'M PRETTY SURE HAYASAKA LIKES HIS CURRY MEDIUM...
MEDIUM
I'll go with medium.
Damn it!

FRIENDSHIP BETWEEN MEN AND WOMEN

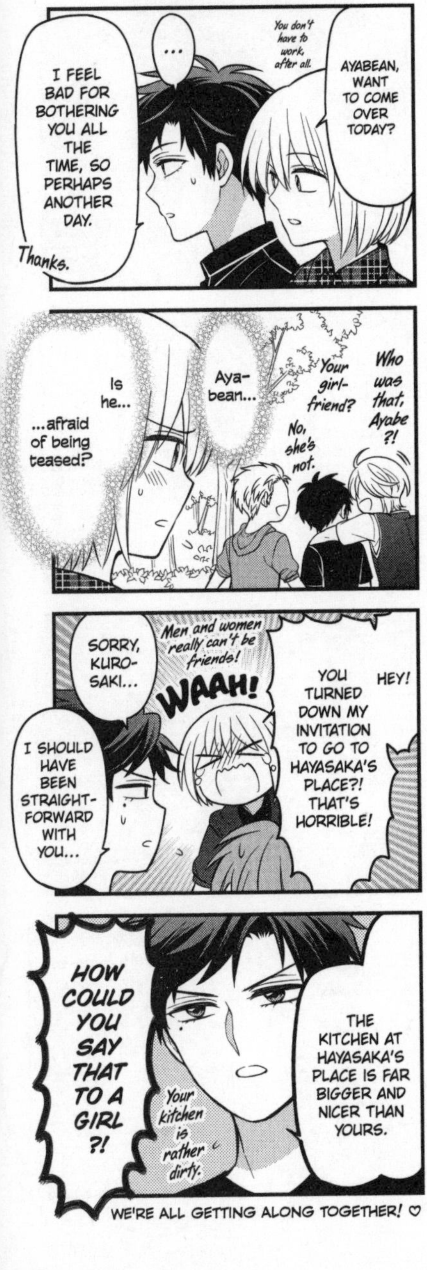
AYABEAN, WANT TO COME OVER TODAY?
You don't have to work, after all.
...
I FEEL BAD FOR BOTHERING YOU ALL THE TIME, SO PERHAPS ANOTHER DAY.
Thanks.
Who was that, Ayabe?!
Your girl-friend?
No, she's not.
Aya-bean...
Is he...
...afraid of being teased?
HEY!
YOU TURNED DOWN MY INVITATION TO GO TO HAYASAKA'S PLACE?! THAT'S HORRIBLE!
Men and women really can't be friends!
WAAH!
SORRY, KURO-SAKI...
I SHOULD HAVE BEEN STRAIGHT-FORWARD WITH YOU...
THE KITCHEN AT HAYASAKA'S PLACE IS FAR BIGGER AND NICER THAN YOURS.
Your kitchen is rather dirty.
HOW COULD YOU SAY THAT TO A GIRL?!

WE'RE ALL GETTING ALONG TOGETHER! ♡

THE ANNOYING TRIO

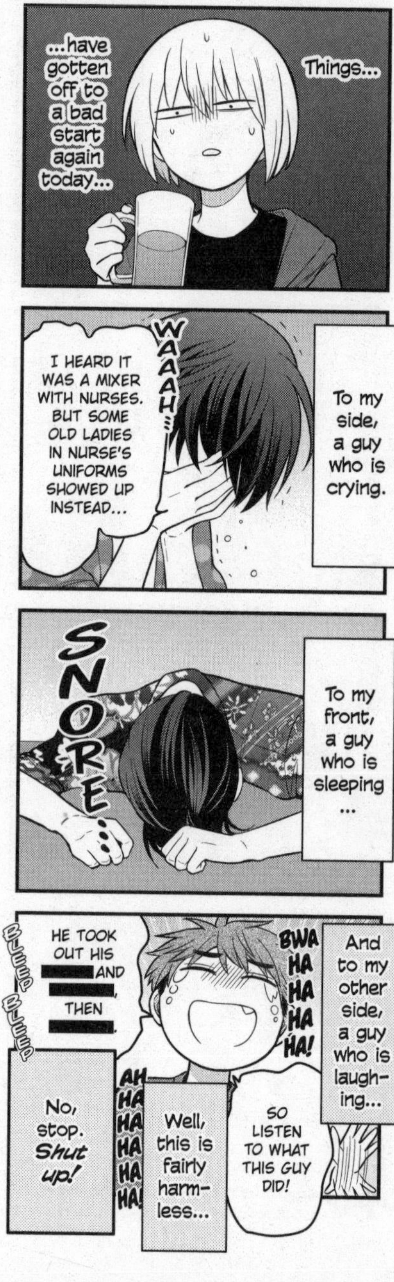
Things...
...have gotten off to a bad start again today...
To my side, a guy who is crying.
WAAAH!!
I HEARD IT WAS A MIXER WITH NURSES. BUT SOME OLD LADIES IN NURSE'S UNIFORMS SHOWED UP INSTEAD...
To my front, a guy who is sleeping ...
SNORE
And to my other side, a guy who is laughing...
BWA HA HA HA HA!
SO LISTEN TO WHAT THIS GUY DID!
HE TOOK OUT HIS [redacted] AND [redacted], THEN [redacted].
BLEEP BLEEP
AH HA HA HA HA HA!
Well, this is fairly harmless...
No, stop. Shut up!

A PRANK

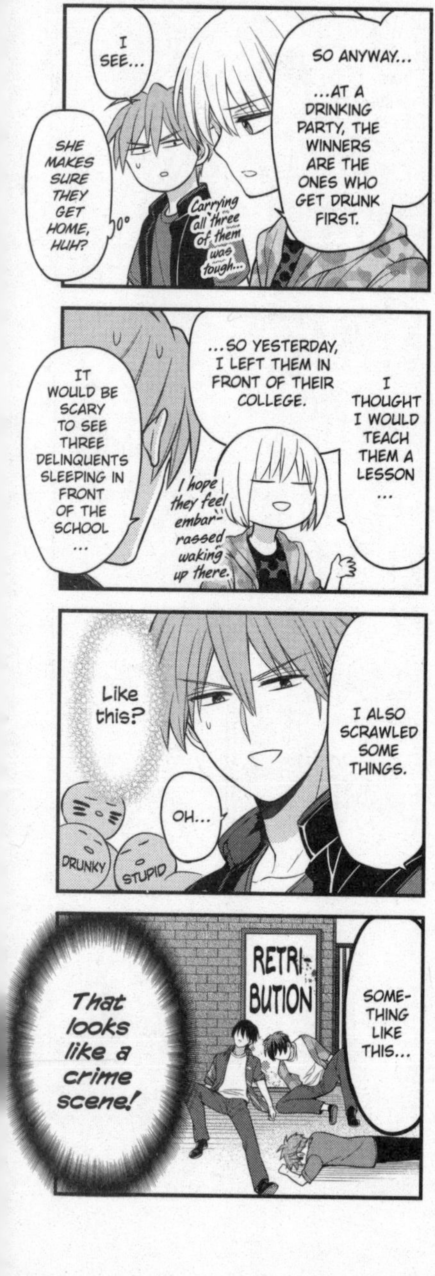
SO ANYWAY...
...AT A DRINKING PARTY, THE WINNERS ARE THE ONES WHO GET DRUNK FIRST.
I SEE...
Carrying all three of them was tough...
SHE MAKES SURE THEY GET HOME, HUH?
I THOUGHT I WOULD TEACH THEM A LESSON ...
...SO YESTERDAY, I LEFT THEM IN FRONT OF THEIR COLLEGE.
I hope they feel embarrassed waking up there.
IT WOULD BE SCARY TO SEE THREE DELINQUENTS SLEEPING IN FRONT OF THE SCHOOL ...
I ALSO SCRAWLED SOME THINGS.
OH...
Like this?
DRUNKY
STUPID
SOME-THING LIKE THIS...
RETRIBUTION
That looks like a crime scene!

ON THE WAY TO OKEGAWA'S COLLEGE

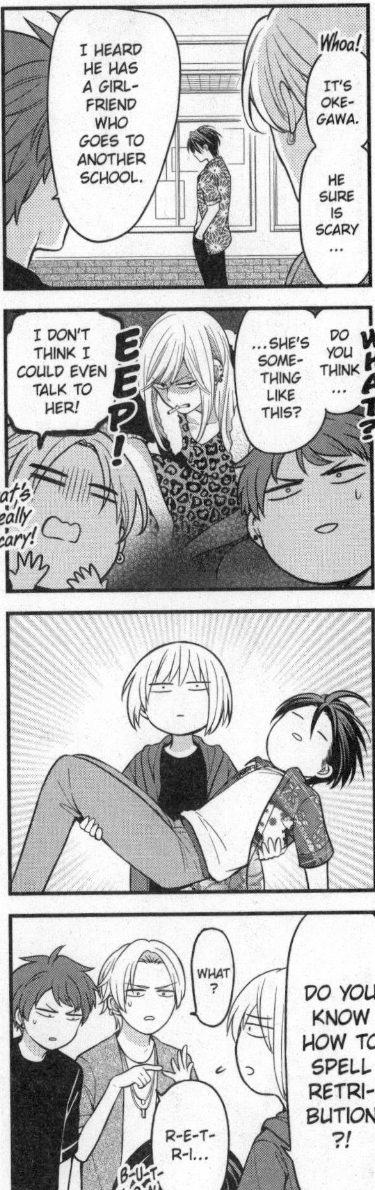
Whoa!
IT'S OKEGAWA.
HE SURE IS SCARY...
I HEARD HE HAS A GIRLFRIEND WHO GOES TO ANOTHER SCHOOL.
WHAT?
DO YOU THINK...
...SHE'S SOMETHING LIKE THIS?
EEP!
I DON'T THINK I COULD EVEN TALK TO HER!
That's really scary!
DO YOU KNOW HOW TO SPELL RETRIBUTION?!
WHAT?
R-E-T-R-I...
B-U-T-I-O-N...

AT KANGAWA'S 20TH BIRTHDAY

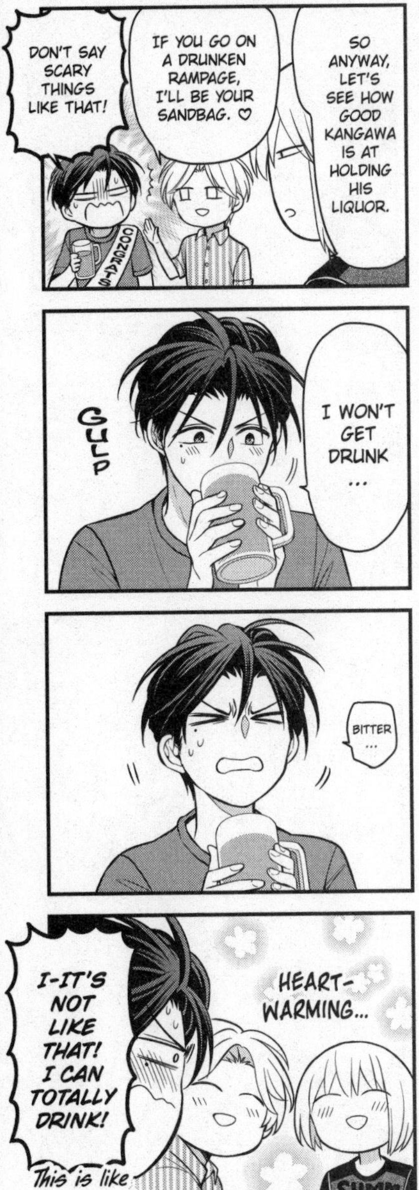
SO ANYWAY, LET'S SEE HOW GOOD KANGAWA IS AT HOLDING HIS LIQUOR.
IF YOU GO ON A DRUNKEN RAMPAGE, I'LL BE YOUR SANDBAG. ♡
DON'T SAY SCARY THINGS LIKE THAT!
CONGRATS
I WON'T GET DRUNK...
GULP
BITTER...
HEART-WARMING...
I-IT'S NOT LIKE THAT! I CAN TOTALLY DRINK!
This is like juice to me!

AT MAIZONO'S PLACE

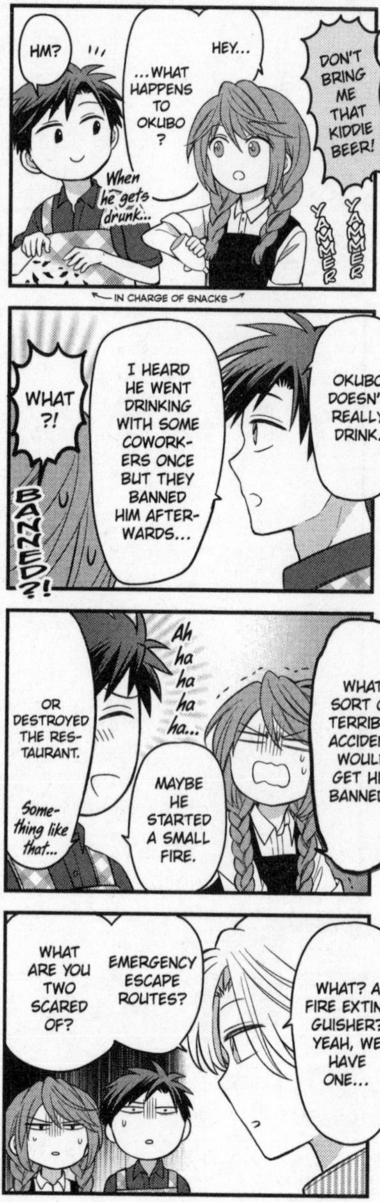
DON'T BRING ME THAT KIDDIE BEER!
YAMMER
YAMMER
HEY...
...WHAT HAPPENS TO OKUBO?
HM?
When he gets drunk...
IN CHARGE OF SNACKS
OKUBO DOESN'T REALLY DRINK.
I HEARD HE WENT DRINKING WITH SOME COWORKERS ONCE BUT THEY BANNED HIM AFTERWARDS...
WHAT?!
BANNED?!
WHAT SORT OF TERRIBLE ACCIDENT WOULD GET HIM BANNED?
Ah ha ha ha ha...
MAYBE HE STARTED A SMALL FIRE.
OR DESTROYED THE RESTAURANT.
Something like that...
WHAT? A FIRE EXTINGUISHER? YEAH, WE HAVE ONE...
EMERGENCY ESCAPE ROUTES?
WHAT ARE YOU TWO SCARED OF?

LUCKY ☆ UNLUCKY

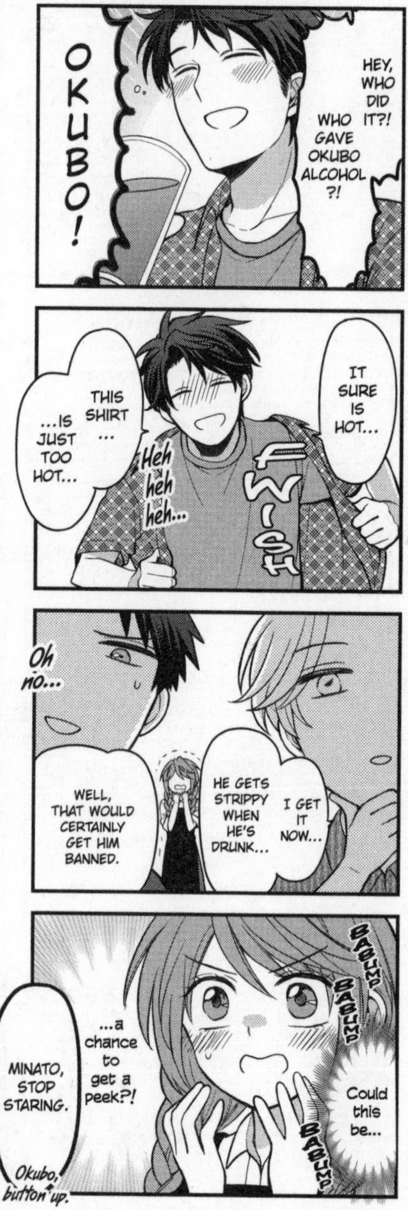
HEY, WHO DID IT?!
WHO GAVE OKUBO ALCOHOL?!
OKUBO!
IT SURE IS HOT...
THIS SHIRT...
...IS JUST TOO HOT...
Heh heh heh...
FWISH
I GET IT NOW...
HE GETS STRIPPY WHEN HE'S DRUNK...
WELL, THAT WOULD CERTAINLY GET HIM BANNED.
Oh no...
BABUMP
BABUMP
Could this be...
BABUMP
...a chance to get a peek?!
MINATO, STOP STARING.
Okubo, button up.

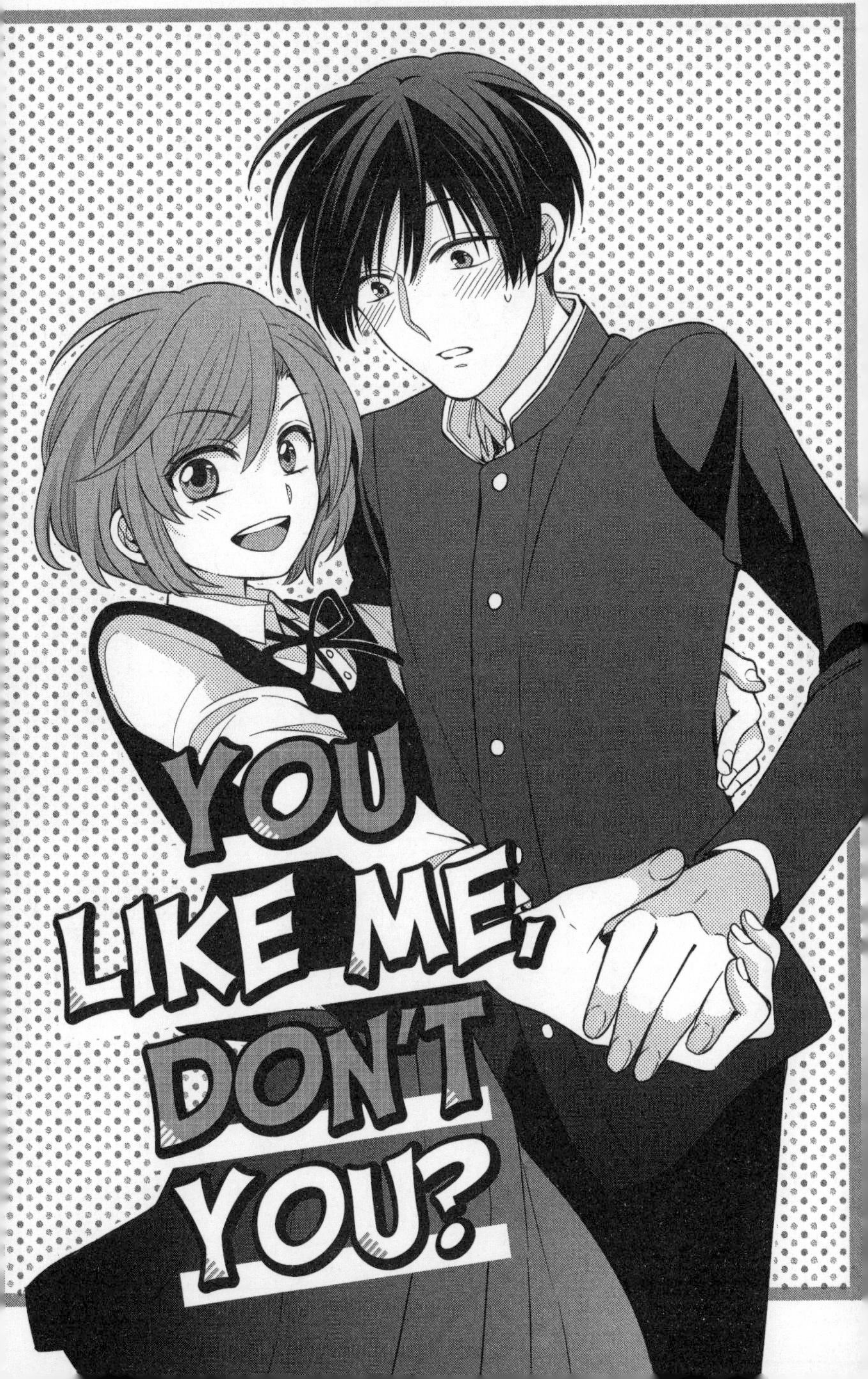
YOU LIKE ME, DON'T YOU?

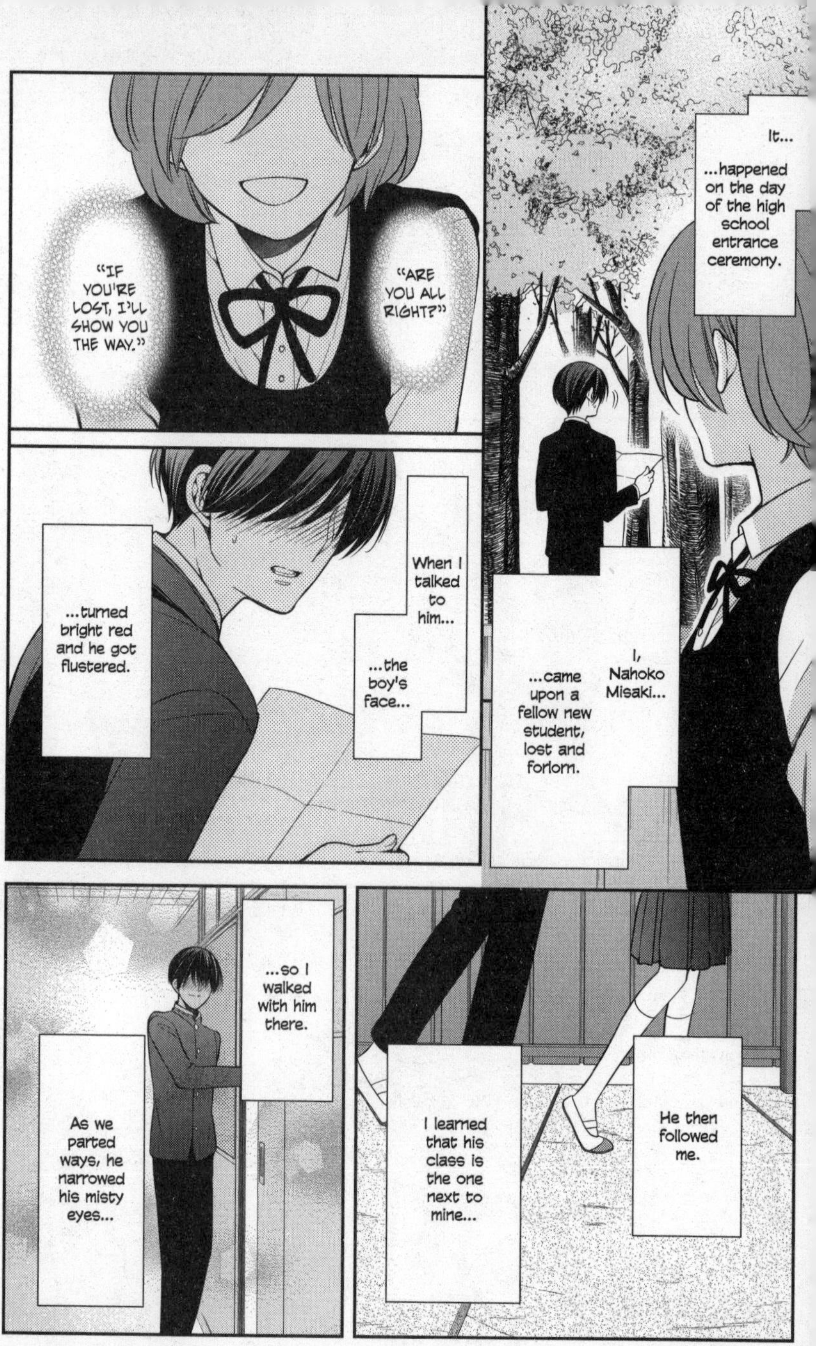
It...
...happened on the day of the high school entrance ceremony.
I, Nahoko Misaki...
...came upon a fellow new student, lost and forlorn.
"ARE YOU ALL RIGHT?"
"IF YOU'RE LOST, I'LL SHOW YOU THE WAY."
When I talked to him...
...the boy's face...
...turned bright red and he got flustered.
He then followed me.
I learned that his class is the one next to mine...
...so I walked with him there.
As we parted ways, he narrowed his misty eyes...

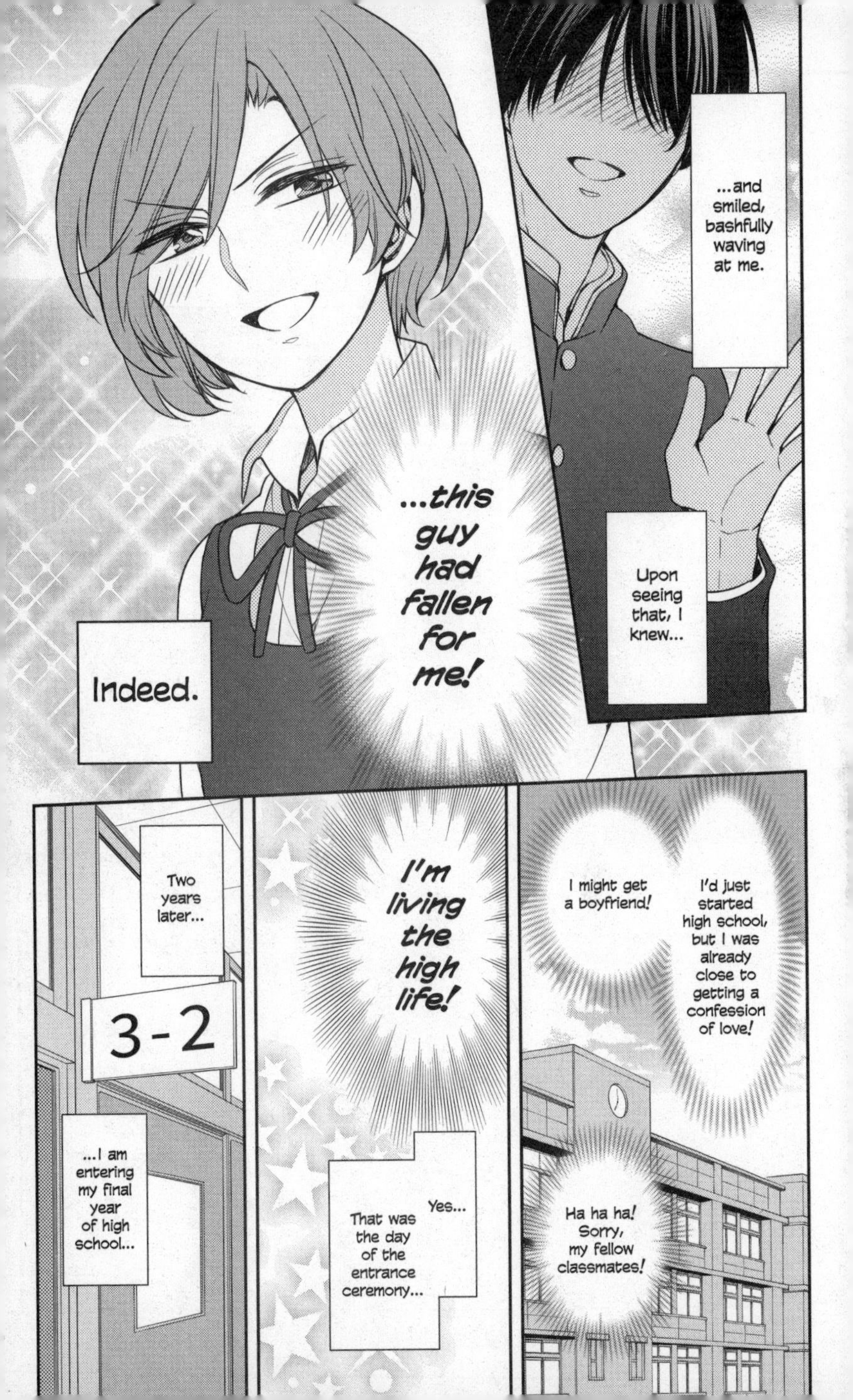
...and smiled, bashfully waving at me.
Upon seeing that, I knew...
...this guy had fallen for me!
Indeed.
I'd just started high school, but I was already close to getting a confession of love!
I might get a boyfriend!
Ha ha ha! Sorry, my fellow classmates!
I'm living the high life!
Yes...
That was the day of the entrance ceremony...
Two years later...
3-2
...I am entering my final year of high school...

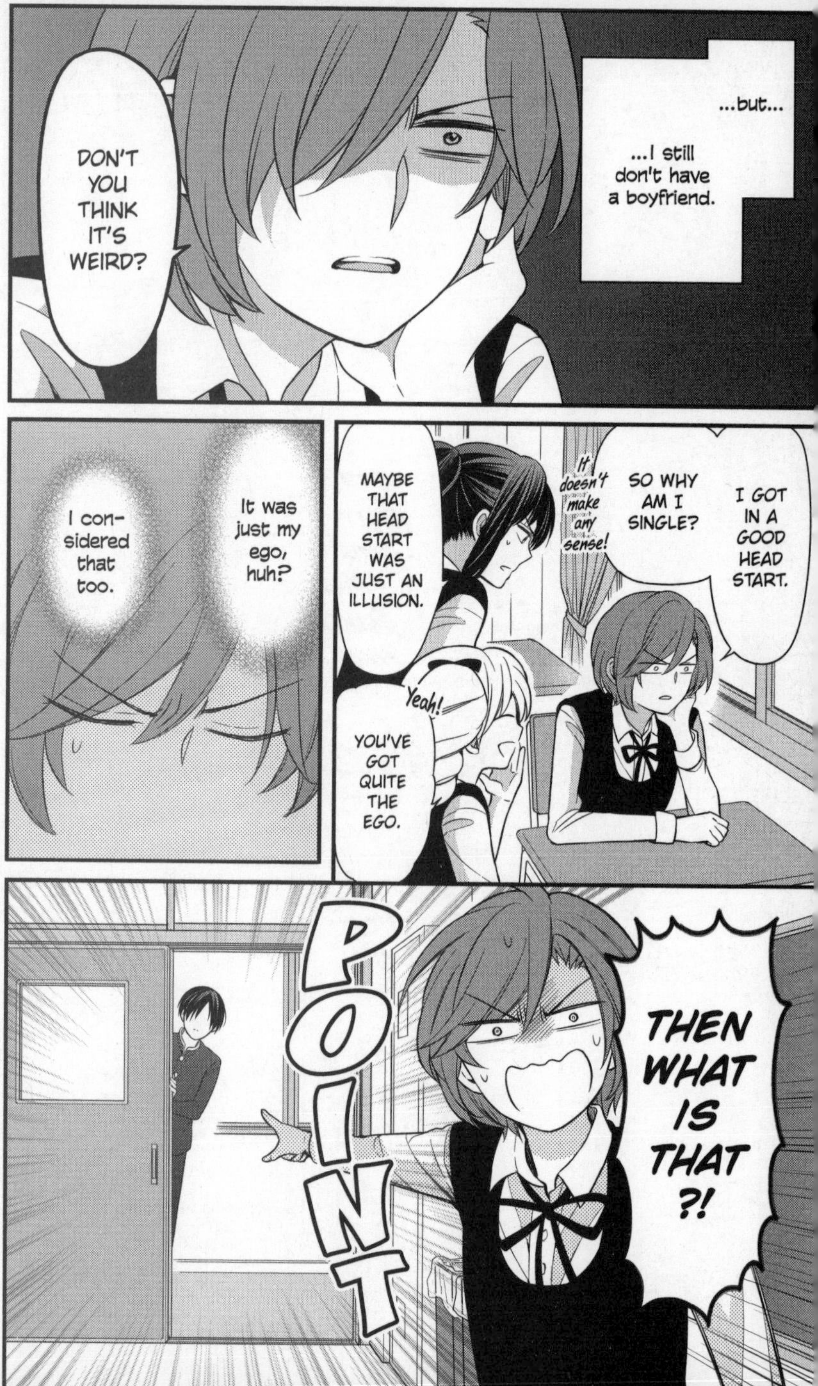
...but...
...I still don't have a boyfriend.
DON'T YOU THINK IT'S WEIRD?
I GOT IN A GOOD HEAD START.
SO WHY AM I SINGLE?
It doesn't make any sense!
MAYBE THAT HEAD START WAS JUST AN ILLUSION.
Yeah!
YOU'VE GOT QUITE THE EGO.
It was just my ego, huh?
I considered that too.
THEN WHAT IS THAT?!
POINT

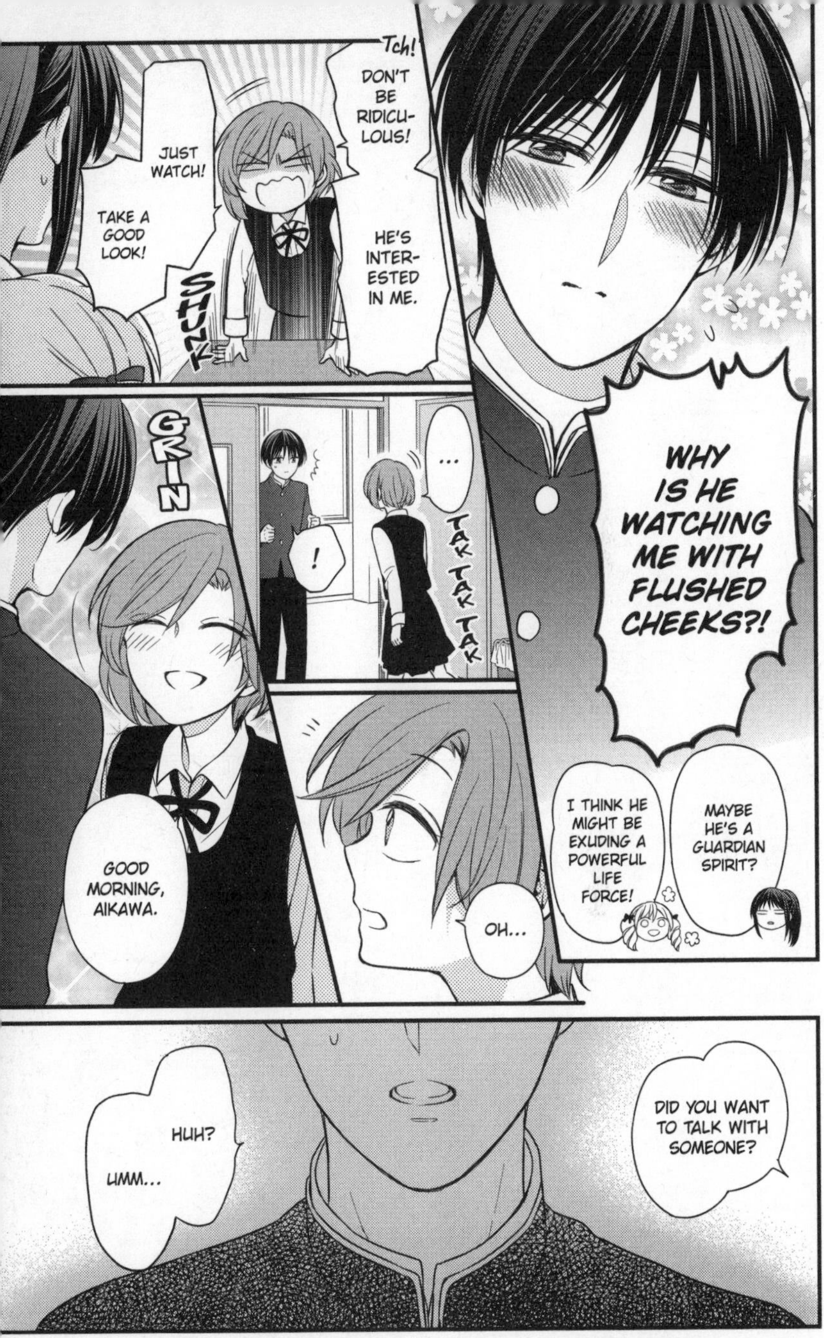
WHY IS HE WATCHING ME WITH FLUSHED CHEEKS?!
MAYBE HE'S A GUARDIAN SPIRIT?
I THINK HE MIGHT BE EXUDING A POWERFUL LIFE FORCE!
Tch!
DON'T BE RIDICU-LOUS!
HE'S INTER-ESTED IN ME.
JUST WATCH!
TAKE A GOOD LOOK!
SHUNK
...
!
TAK TAK TAK
OH...
GRIN
GOOD MORNING, AIKAWA.
DID YOU WANT TO TALK WITH SOMEONE?
HUH?
UMM...

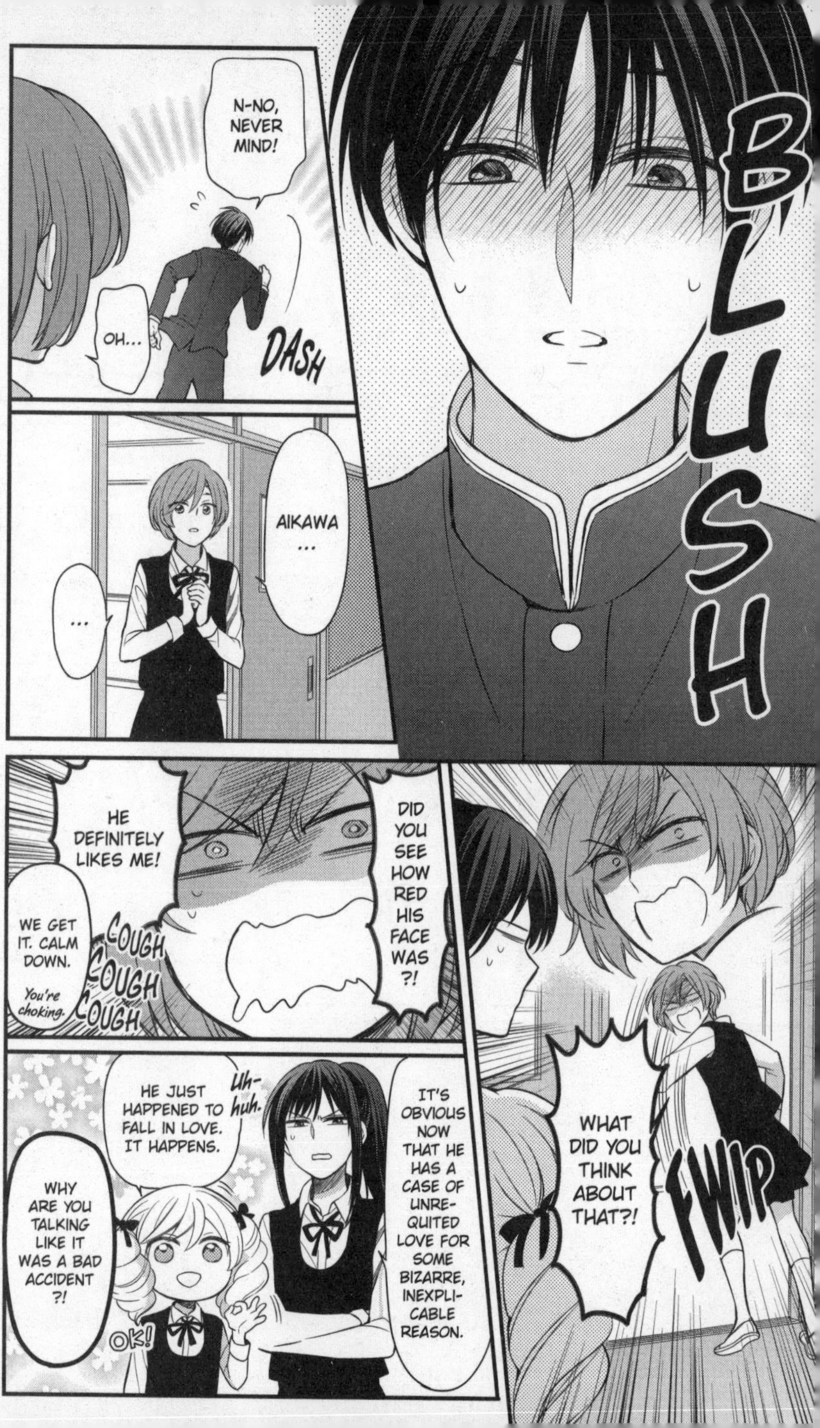
BLUSH
N-NO, NEVER MIND!
DASH
OH...
AIKAWA ...
...
WHAT DID YOU THINK ABOUT THAT?!
FWIP
DID YOU SEE HOW RED HIS FACE WAS?!
HE DEFINITELY LIKES ME!
COUGH COUGH COUGH
WE GET IT. CALM DOWN.
You're choking.
IT'S OBVIOUS NOW THAT HE HAS A CASE OF UNREQUITED LOVE FOR SOME BIZARRE, INEXPLICABLE REASON.
Uh-huh.
HE JUST HAPPENED TO FALL IN LOVE. IT HAPPENS.
WHY ARE YOU TALKING LIKE IT WAS A BAD ACCIDENT?!
OK!

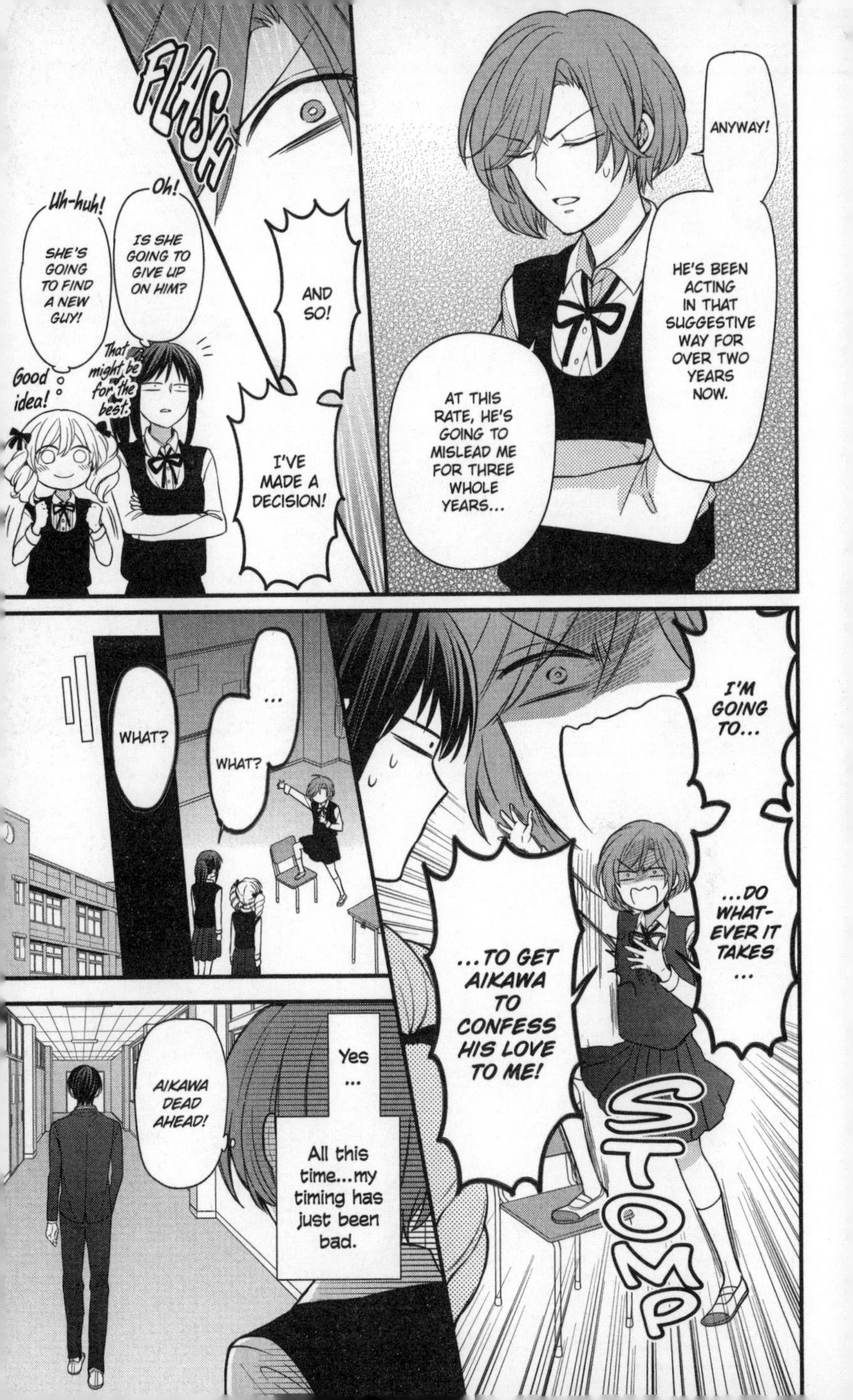
ANYWAY!
HE'S BEEN ACTING IN THAT SUGGESTIVE WAY FOR OVER TWO YEARS NOW.
AT THIS RATE, HE'S GOING TO MISLEAD ME FOR THREE WHOLE YEARS...
FLASH
AND SO!
I'VE MADE A DECISION!
Oh!
IS SHE GOING TO GIVE UP ON HIM?
Uh-huh!
SHE'S GOING TO FIND A NEW GUY!
That might be for the best.
Good idea!
I'M GOING TO...
...DO WHATEVER IT TAKES...
...TO GET AIKAWA TO CONFESS HIS LOVE TO ME!
STOMP
...
WHAT?
WHAT?
Yes...
All this time...my timing has just been bad.
AIKAWA DEAD AHEAD!

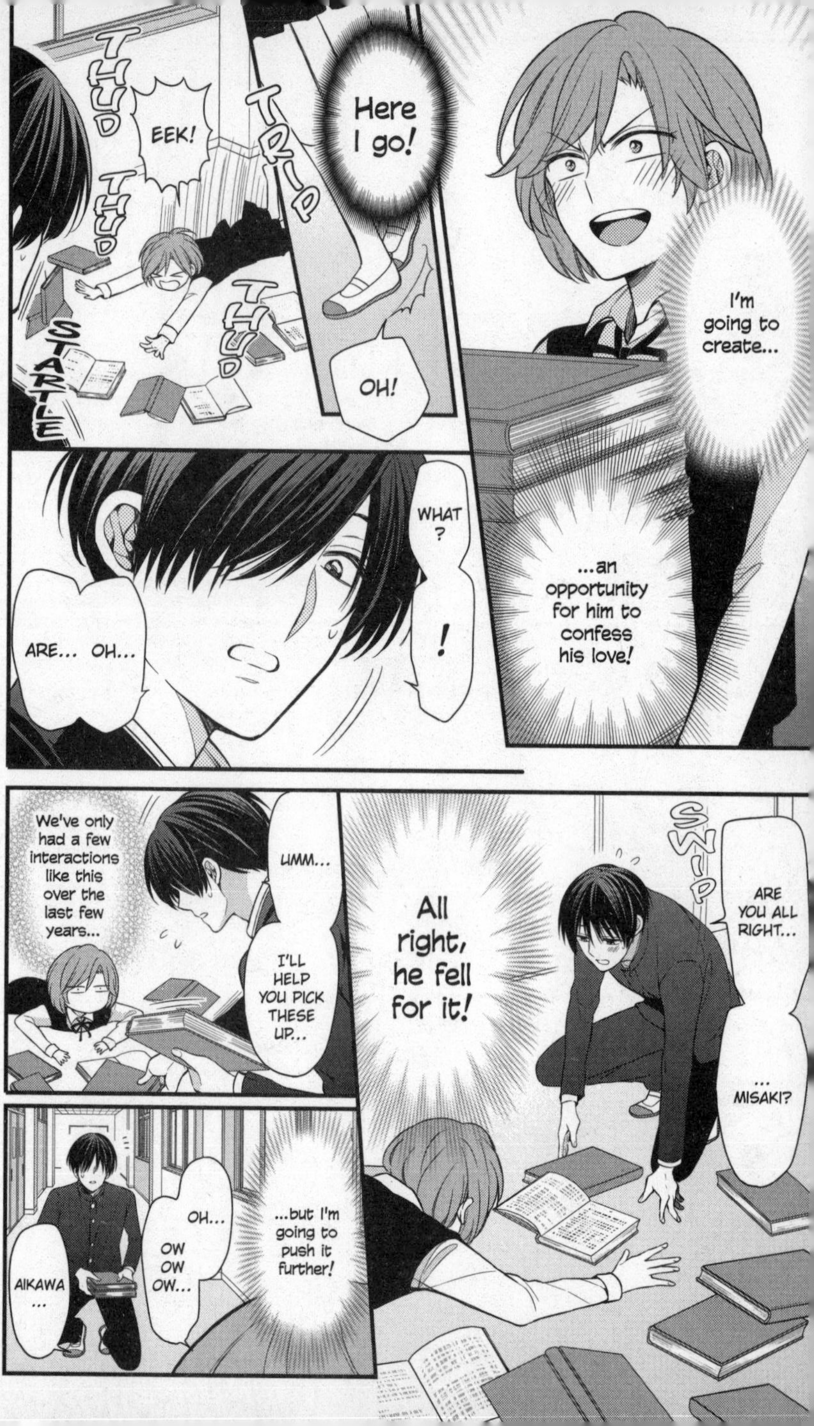
I'm going to create...
...an opportunity for him to confess his love!
Here I go!
TRIP
OH!
THUD
EEK!
THUD THUD
THUD
STARTLE
WHAT?
!
ARE... OH...
SWIP
ARE YOU ALL RIGHT...
...MISAKI?
All right, he fell for it!
We've only had a few interactions like this over the last few years...
UMM...
I'LL HELP YOU PICK THESE UP...
...but I'm going to push it further!
OH...
OW OW OW...
AIKAWA...

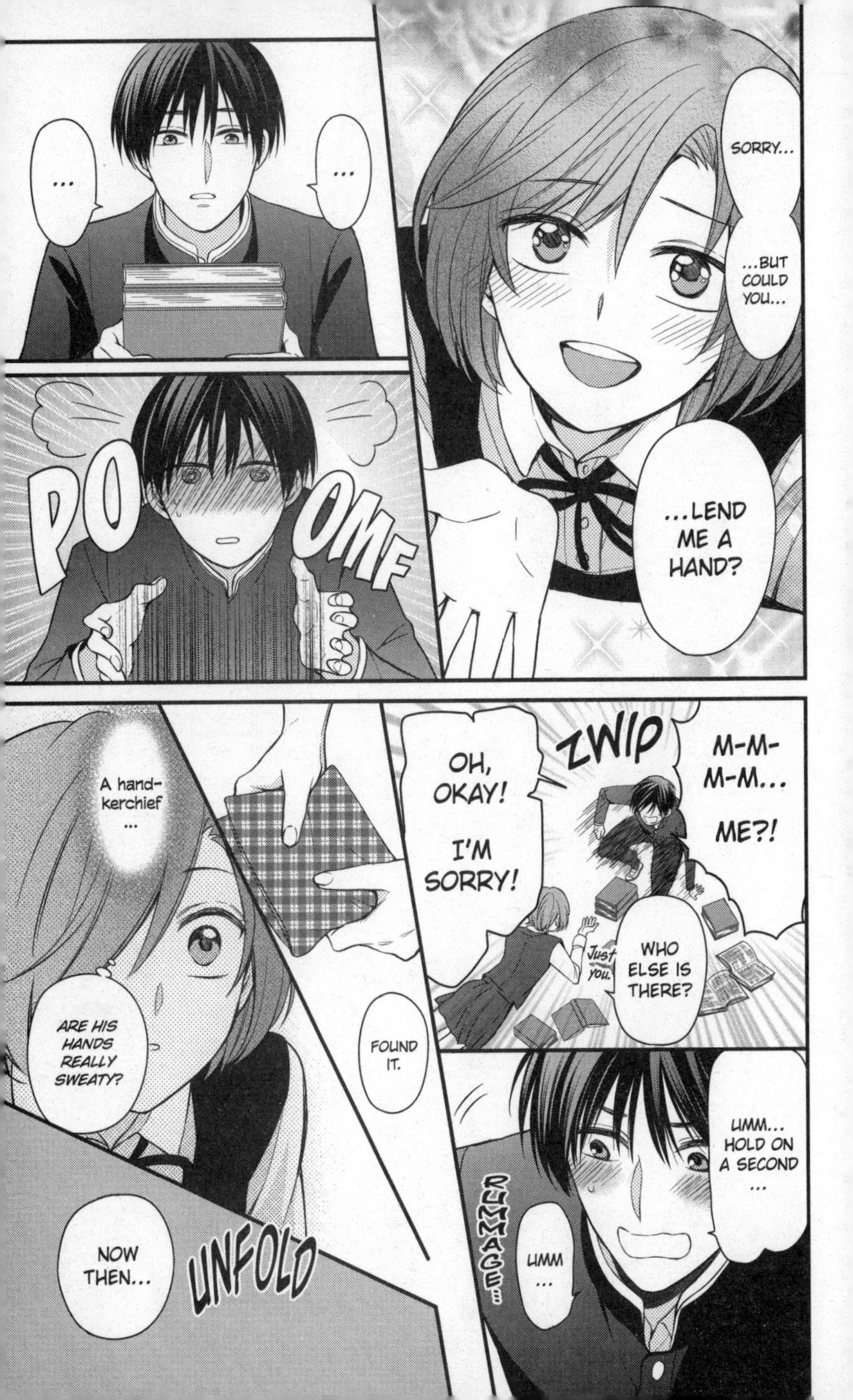
SORRY...
...BUT COULD YOU...
...LEND ME A HAND?
...
...
POOMF
M-M-M-M... ME?!
ZWIP
OH, OKAY! I'M SORRY!
WHO ELSE IS THERE?
Just you.
UMM... HOLD ON A SECOND ...
RUMMAGE...
UMM ...
FOUND IT.
A hand-kerchief ...
ARE HIS HANDS REALLY SWEATY?
NOW THEN...
UNFOLD

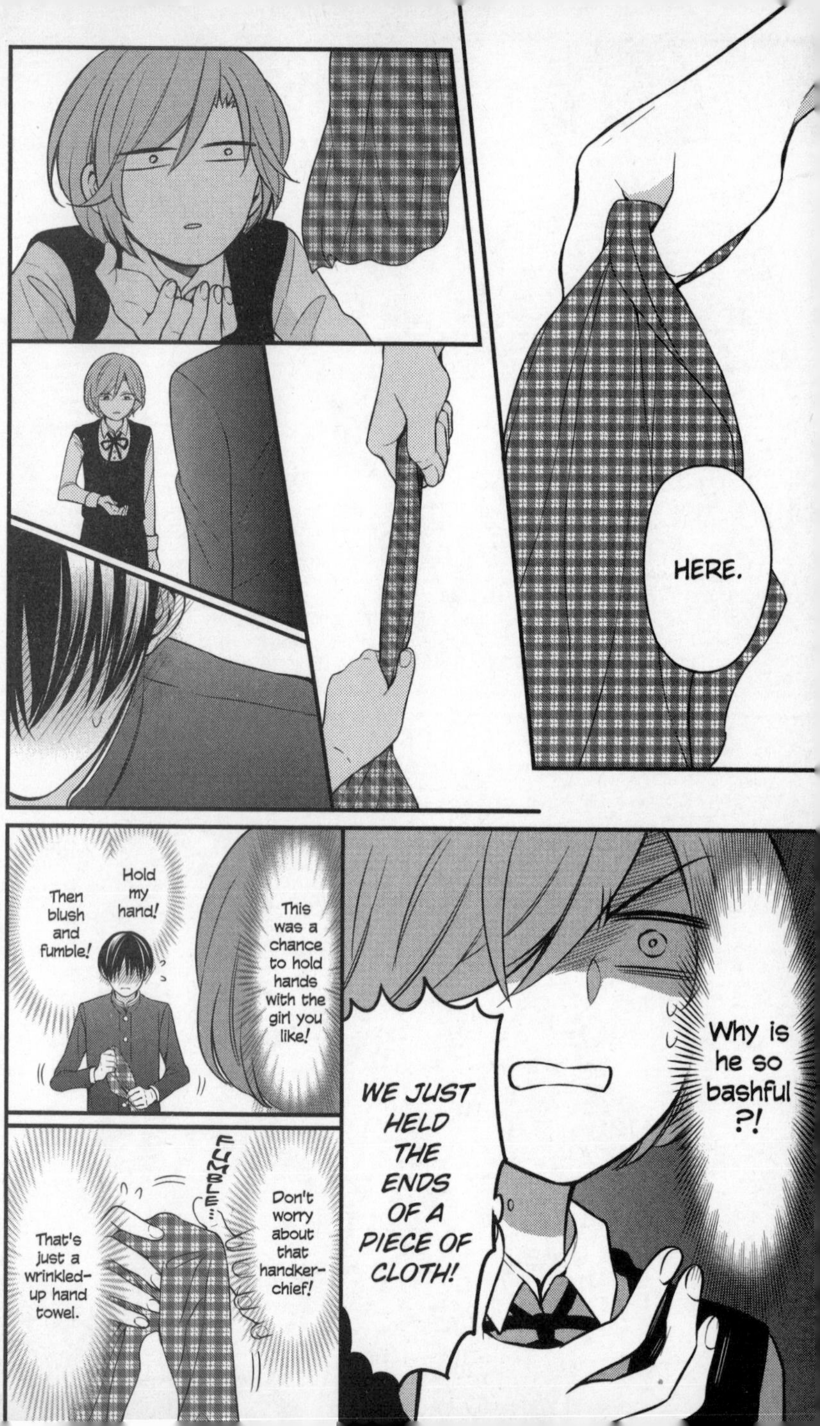
HERE.
Why is he so bashful?!
WE JUST HELD THE ENDS OF A PIECE OF CLOTH!
This was a chance to hold hands with the girl you like!
Hold my hand!
Then blush and fumble!
Don't worry about that handker-chief!
FUMBLE...
That's just a wrinkled-up hand towel.

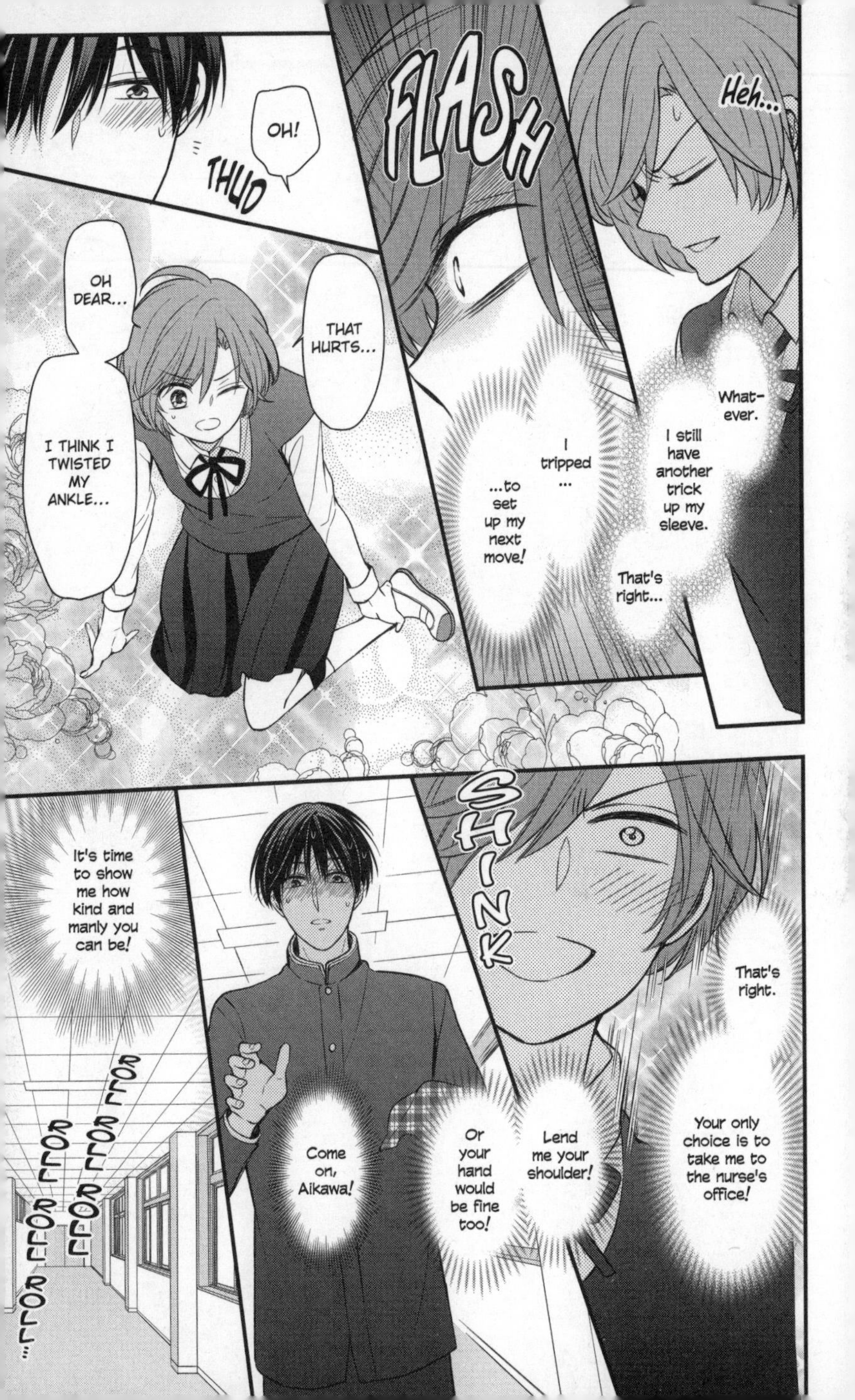
FLASH
Heh...
What-ever.
I still have another trick up my sleeve.
That's right...
I tripped...
...to set up my next move!
OH!
THUD
THAT HURTS...
OH DEAR...
I THINK I TWISTED MY ANKLE...
SHINK
That's right.
Your only choice is to take me to the nurse's office!
Lend me your shoulder!
Or your hand would be fine too!
Come on, Aikawa!
It's time to show me how kind and manly you can be!
ROLL ROLL ROLL
ROLL ROLL ROLL ROLL...

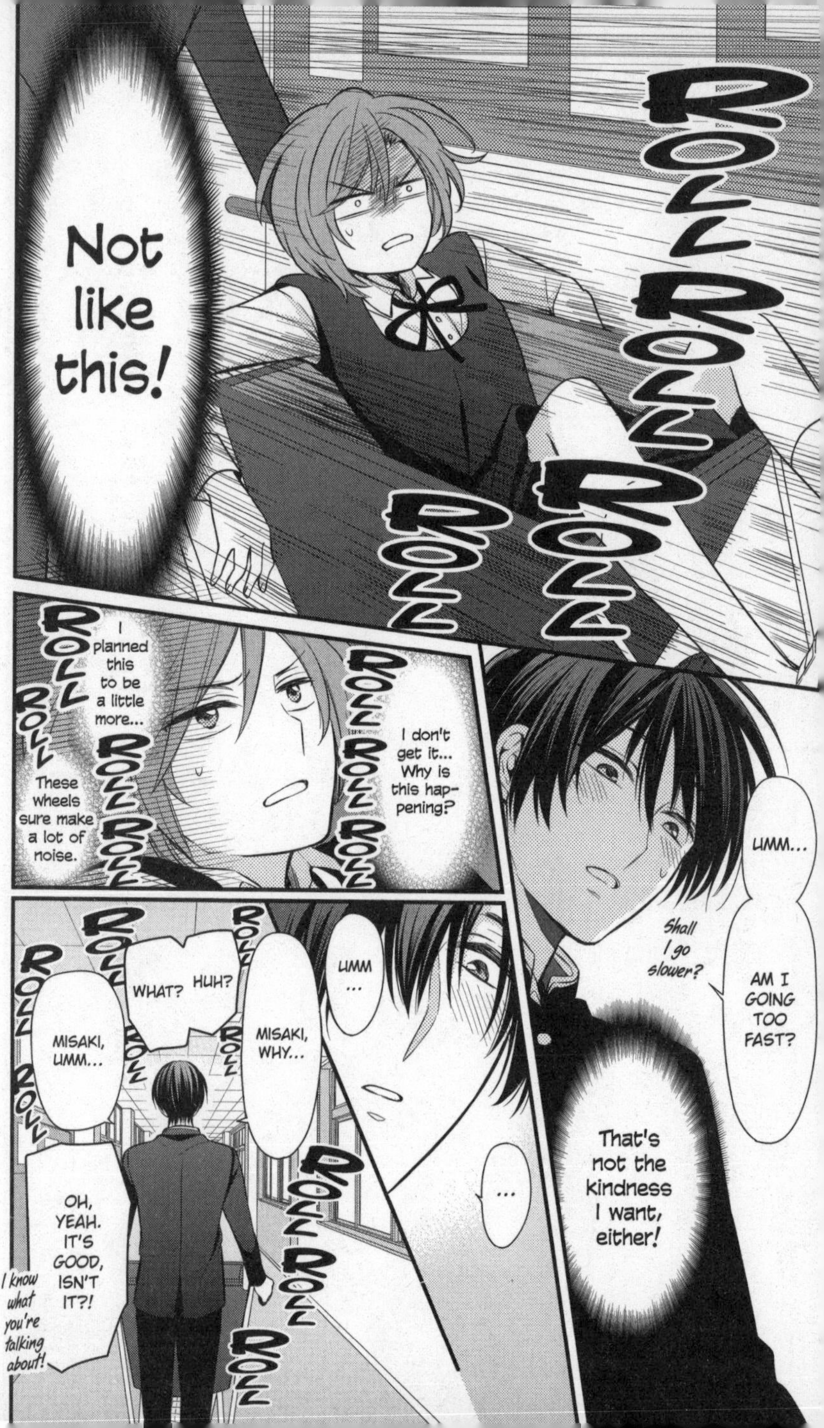
ROLL ROLL ROLL
ROLL ROLL
Not like this!
UMM...
Shall I go slower?
AM I GOING TOO FAST?
That's not the kindness I want, either!
ROLL ROLL ROLL
I don't get it... Why is this hap-pening?
I planned this to be a little more...
ROLL ROLL
These wheels sure make a lot of noise.
ROLL ROLL ROLL
UMM ...
MISAKI, WHY...
...
HUH?
WHAT?
MISAKI, UMM...
ROLL ROLL ROLL
OH, YEAH. IT'S GOOD, ISN'T IT?!
I know what you're talking about!
ROLL ROLL ROLL

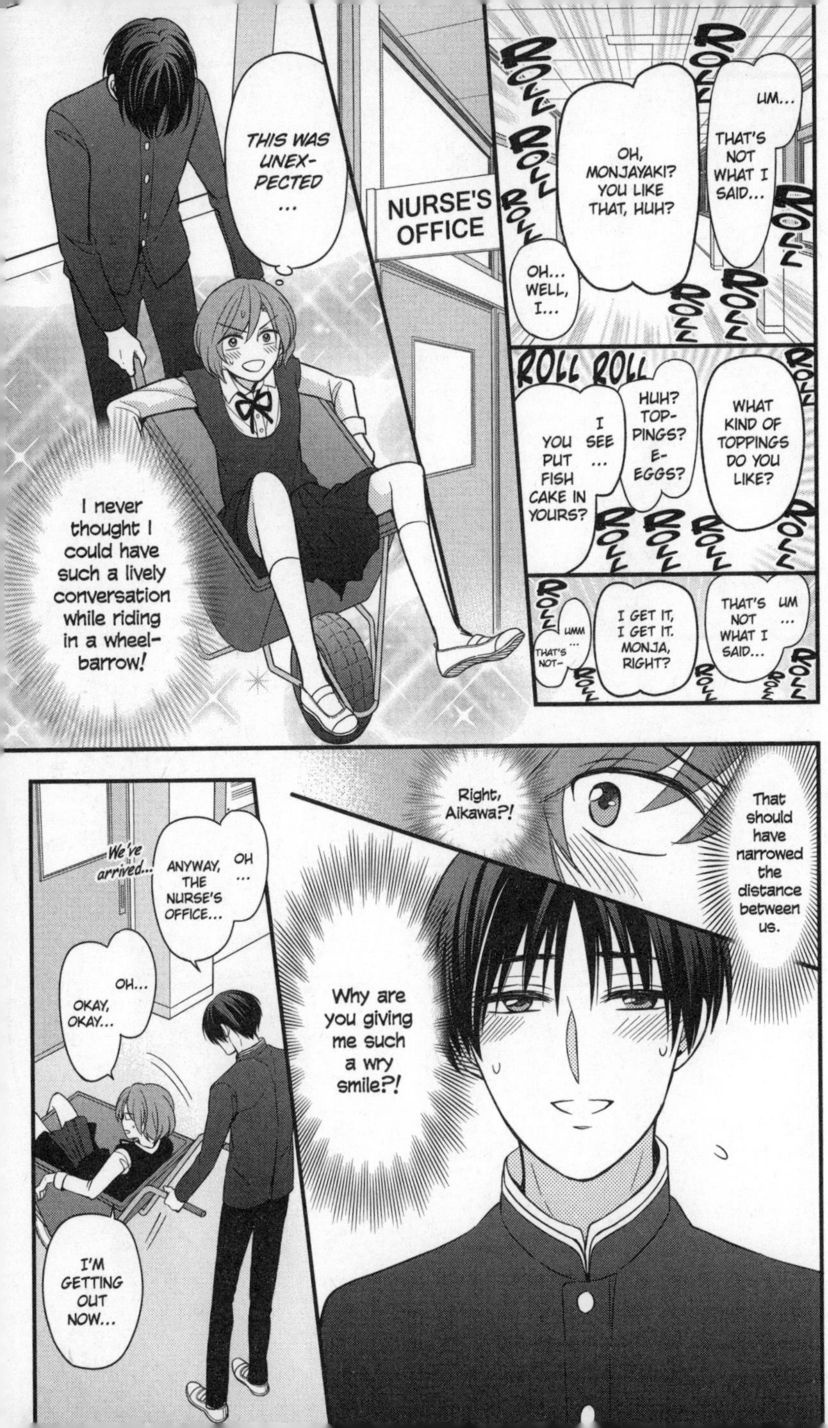
ROLL ROLL ROLL ROLL
UM... THAT'S NOT WHAT I SAID...
OH, MONJAYAKI? YOU LIKE THAT, HUH?
OH... WELL, I...
ROLL ROLL ROLL ROLL
ROLL ROLL
WHAT KIND OF TOPPINGS DO YOU LIKE?
HUH? TOPPINGS? E-EGGS?
I SEE... YOU PUT FISH CAKE IN YOURS?
ROLL ROLL ROLL ROLL
ROLL ROLL
UM... THAT'S NOT WHAT I SAID...
I GET IT, I GET IT. MONJA, RIGHT?
UMM... THAT'S NOT-
ROLL ROLL ROLL
THIS WAS UNEXPECTED...
NURSE'S OFFICE
I never thought I could have such a lively conversation while riding in a wheelbarrow!
That should have narrowed the distance between us.
Right, Aikawa?!
Why are you giving me such a wry smile?!
OH... ANYWAY, THE NURSE'S OFFICE...
We've arrived...
OH... OKAY, OKAY...
I'M GETTING OUT NOW...

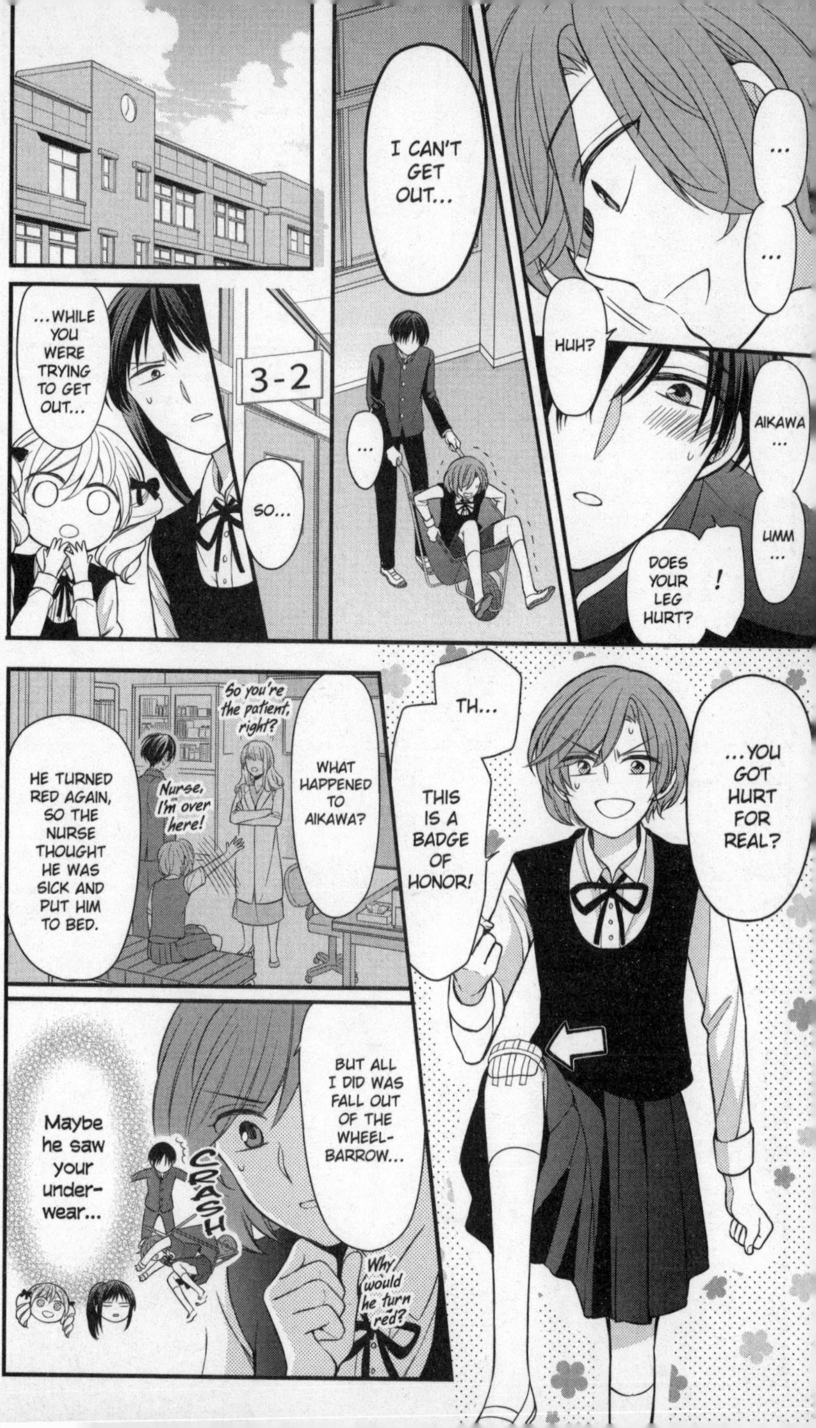
...
...
HUH?
AIKAWA...
UMM...
!
DOES YOUR LEG HURT?
I CAN'T GET OUT...
...
...WHILE YOU WERE TRYING TO GET OUT...
3-2
SO...
...YOU GOT HURT FOR REAL?
TH...
THIS IS A BADGE OF HONOR!
So you're the patient, right?
WHAT HAPPENED TO AIKAWA?
Nurse, I'm over here!
HE TURNED RED AGAIN, SO THE NURSE THOUGHT HE WAS SICK AND PUT HIM TO BED.
BUT ALL I DID WAS FALL OUT OF THE WHEEL-BARROW...
Why would he turn red?
CRASH
Maybe he saw your under-wear...

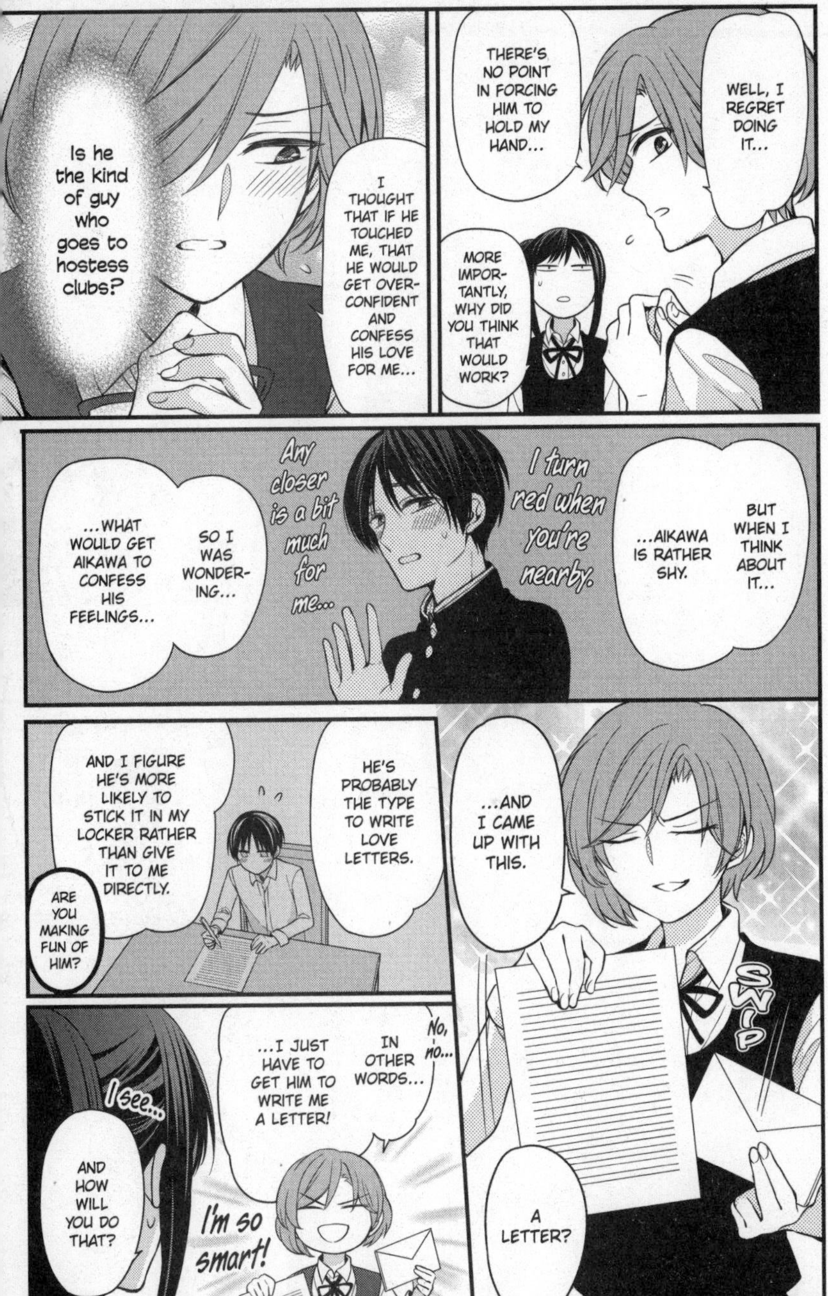
WELL, I REGRET DOING IT...
THERE'S NO POINT IN FORCING HIM TO HOLD MY HAND...
MORE IMPORTANTLY, WHY DID YOU THINK THAT WOULD WORK?
I THOUGHT THAT IF HE TOUCHED ME, THAT HE WOULD GET OVER-CONFIDENT AND CONFESS HIS LOVE FOR ME...
Is he the kind of guy who goes to hostess clubs?
BUT WHEN I THINK ABOUT IT...
...AIKAWA IS RATHER SHY.
I turn red when you're nearby.
Any closer is a bit much for me...
SO I WAS WONDERING...
...WHAT WOULD GET AIKAWA TO CONFESS HIS FEELINGS...
...AND I CAME UP WITH THIS.
SWIP
A LETTER?
HE'S PROBABLY THE TYPE TO WRITE LOVE LETTERS.
AND I FIGURE HE'S MORE LIKELY TO STICK IT IN MY LOCKER RATHER THAN GIVE IT TO ME DIRECTLY.
ARE YOU MAKING FUN OF HIM?
No, no...
IN OTHER WORDS...
...I JUST HAVE TO GET HIM TO WRITE ME A LETTER!
I'm so smart!
I see...
AND HOW WILL YOU DO THAT?

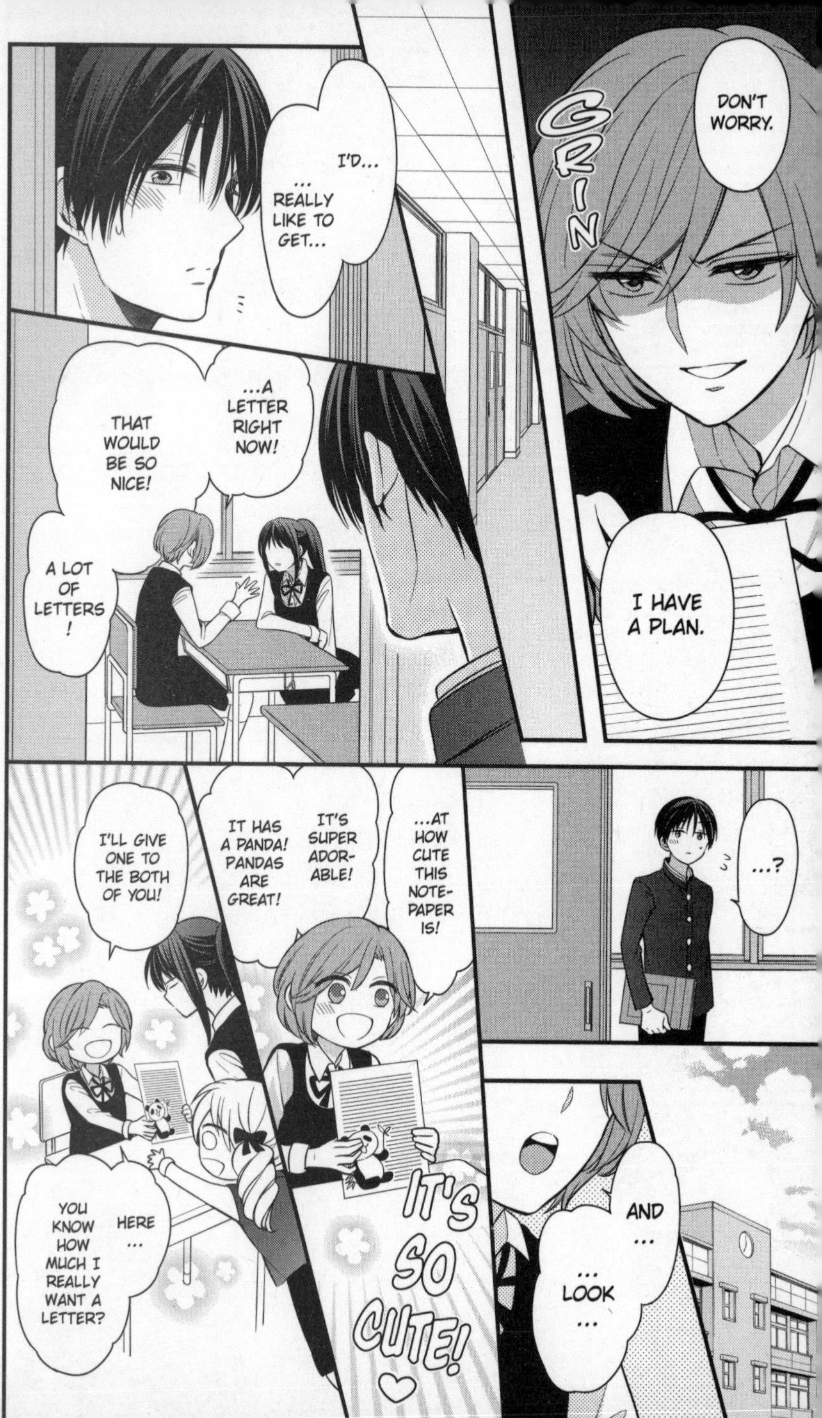
DON'T WORRY.
GRIN
I HAVE A PLAN.
I'D...
... REALLY LIKE TO GET...
...A LETTER RIGHT NOW!
THAT WOULD BE SO NICE!
A LOT OF LETTERS!
...?
AND...
... LOOK ...
...AT HOW CUTE THIS NOTE-PAPER IS!
IT'S SUPER ADOR-ABLE!
IT HAS A PANDA! PANDAS ARE GREAT!
I'LL GIVE ONE TO THE BOTH OF YOU!
IT'S SO CUTE!
HERE...
YOU KNOW HOW MUCH I REALLY WANT A LETTER?

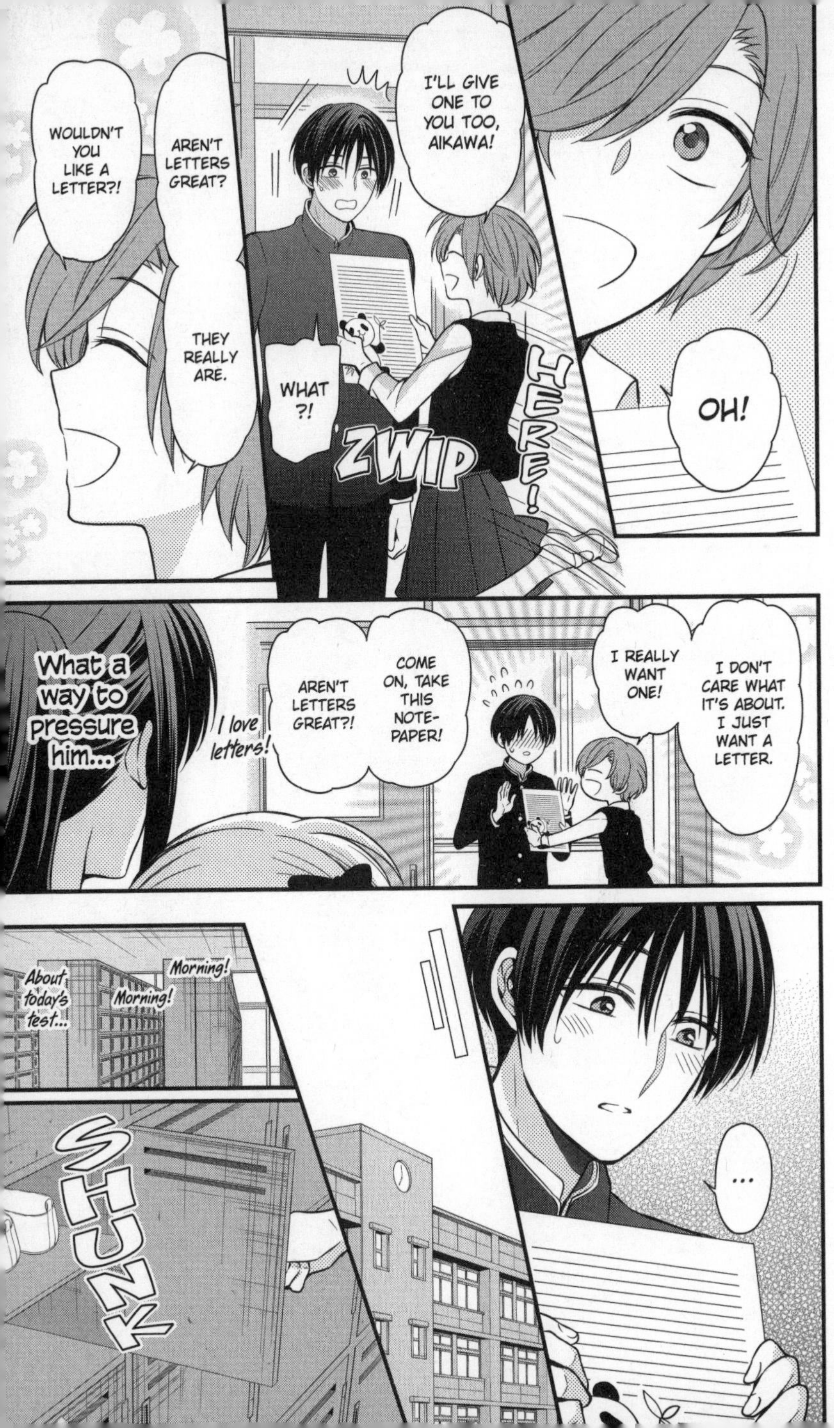
OH!
I'LL GIVE ONE TO YOU TOO, AIKAWA!
WHAT?!
HERE!
ZWIP
AREN'T LETTERS GREAT?
WOULDN'T YOU LIKE A LETTER?!
THEY REALLY ARE.
I DON'T CARE WHAT IT'S ABOUT. I JUST WANT A LETTER.
I REALLY WANT ONE!
COME ON, TAKE THIS NOTE-PAPER!
AREN'T LETTERS GREAT?!
I love letters!
What a way to pressure him...
...
Morning!
Morning!
About today's test...
SHUNK

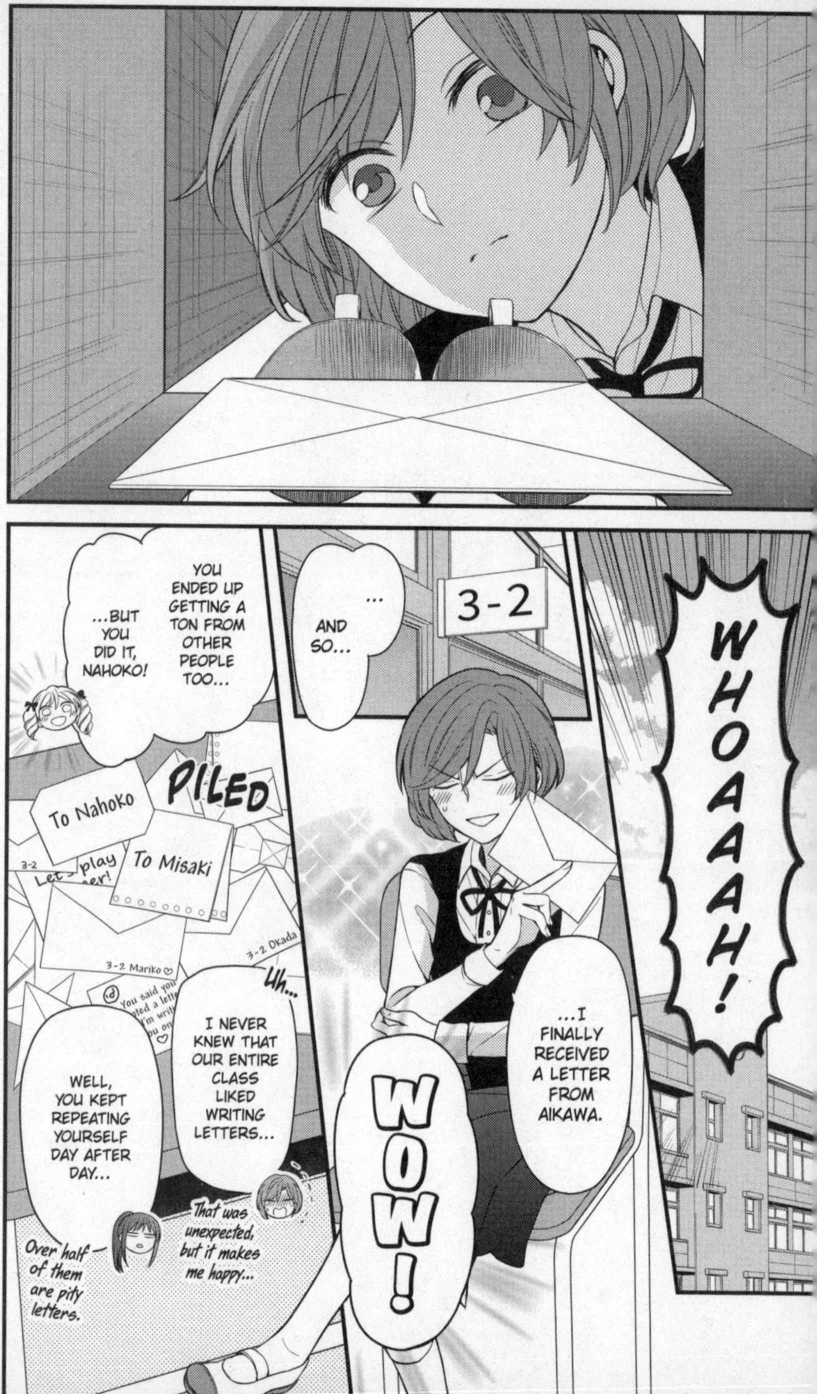
WHOAAAH!
... AND SO...
...I FINALLY RECEIVED A LETTER FROM AIKAWA.
WOW!
YOU ENDED UP GETTING A TON FROM OTHER PEOPLE TOO...
...BUT YOU DID IT, NAHOKO!
PILED
To Nahoko
To Misaki
3-2
3-2 Okada
3-2 Mariko ♡
Uh...
I NEVER KNEW THAT OUR ENTIRE CLASS LIKED WRITING LETTERS...
WELL, YOU KEPT REPEATING YOURSELF DAY AFTER DAY...
That was unexpected, but it makes me happy...
Over half of them are pity letters.

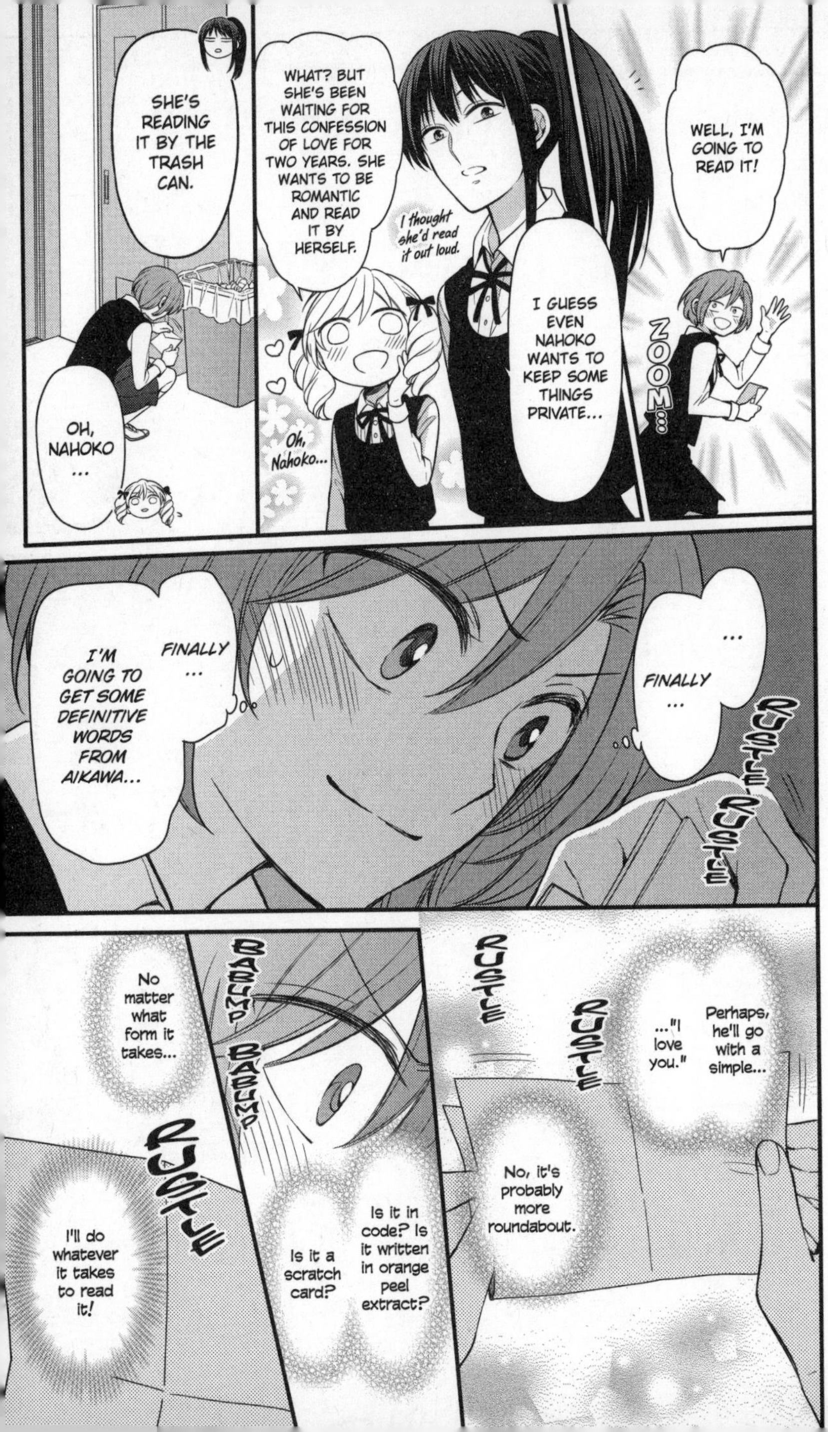
WELL, I'M GOING TO READ IT!
ZOOM...
WHAT? BUT SHE'S BEEN WAITING FOR THIS CONFESSION OF LOVE FOR TWO YEARS. SHE WANTS TO BE ROMANTIC AND READ IT BY HERSELF.
I thought she'd read it out loud.
I GUESS EVEN NAHOKO WANTS TO KEEP SOME THINGS PRIVATE...
Oh, Nahoko...
SHE'S READING IT BY THE TRASH CAN.
OH, NAHOKO...
... FINALLY ...
FINALLY ...
I'M GOING TO GET SOME DEFINITIVE WORDS FROM AIKAWA...
RUSTLE RUSTLE
RUSTLE
RUSTLE
Perhaps, he'll go with a simple...
..."I love you."
No, it's probably more roundabout.
Is it in code? Is it written in orange peel extract?
Is it a scratch card?
BABUMP BABUMP
No matter what form it takes...
RUSTLE
I'll do whatever it takes to read it!

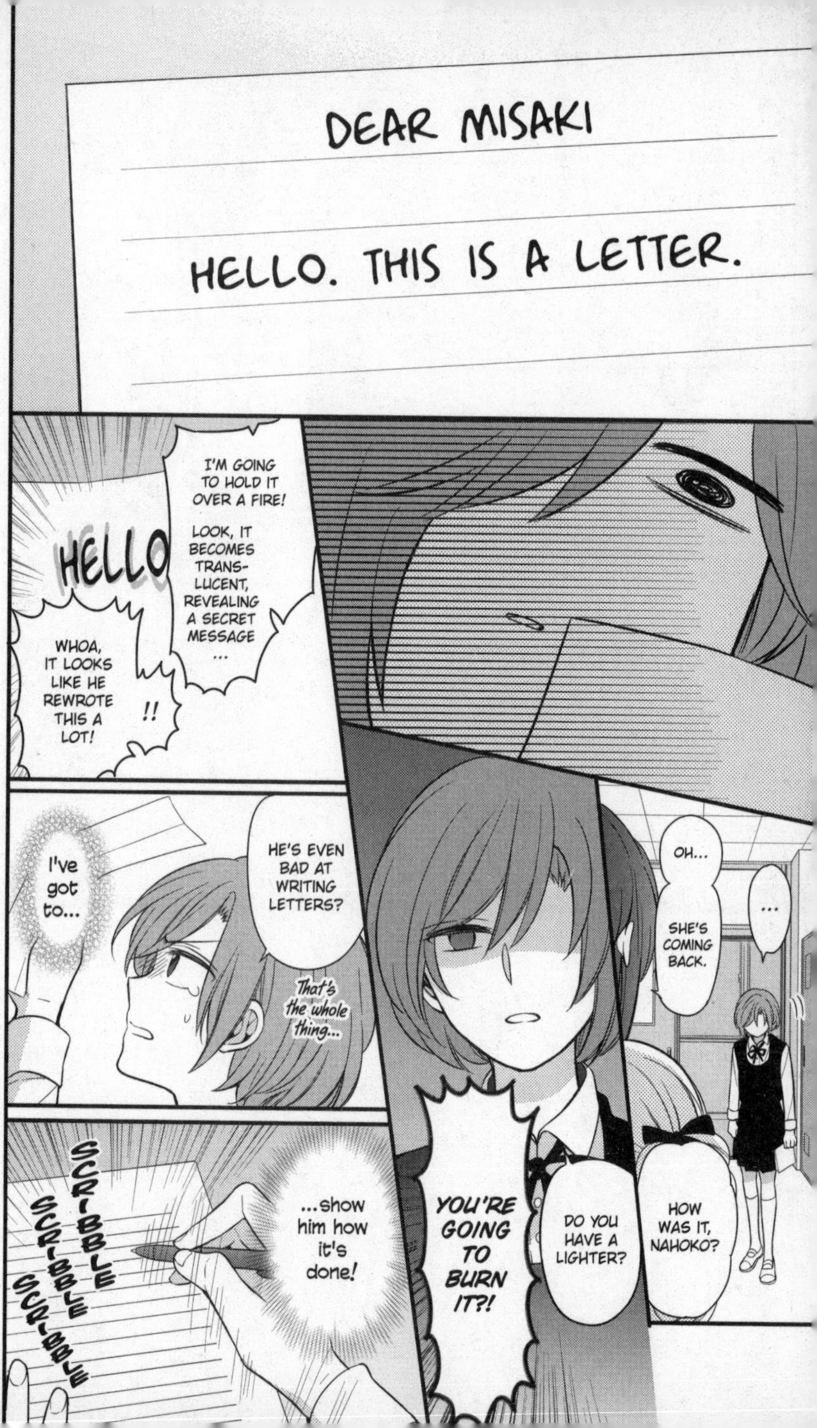
DEAR MISAKI
HELLO. THIS IS A LETTER.
I'M GOING TO HOLD IT OVER A FIRE!
LOOK, IT BECOMES TRANS-LUCENT, REVEALING A SECRET MESSAGE ...
HELLO
!!
WHOA, IT LOOKS LIKE HE REWROTE THIS A LOT!
OH...
SHE'S COMING BACK.
...
HOW WAS IT, NAHOKO?
DO YOU HAVE A LIGHTER?
YOU'RE GOING TO BURN IT?!
HE'S EVEN BAD AT WRITING LETTERS?
That's the whole thing...
I've got to...
...show him how it's done!
SCRIBBLE
SCRIBBLE
SCRIBBLE

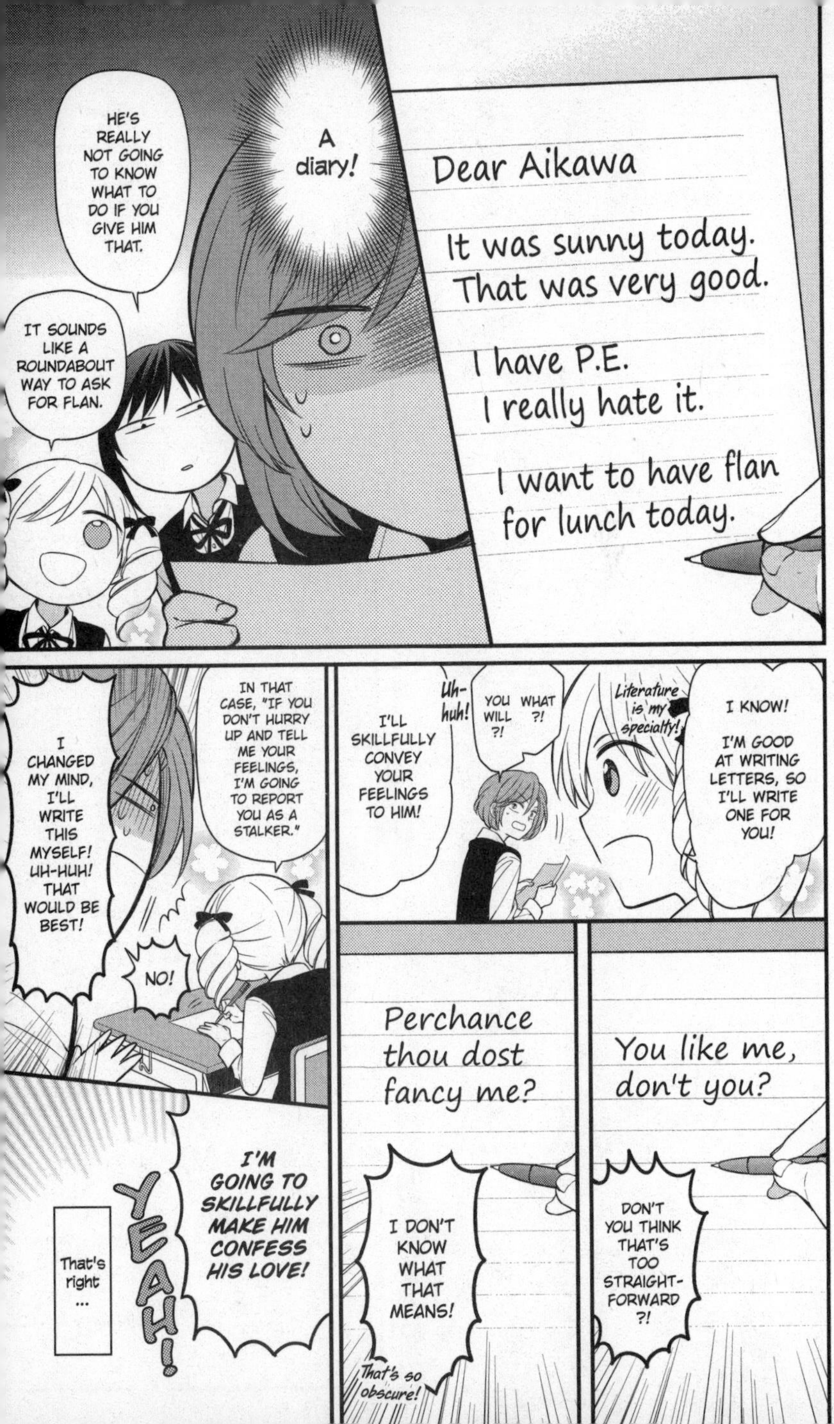
Dear Aikawa
It was sunny today. That was very good.
I have P.E. I really hate it.
I want to have flan for lunch today.
A diary!
HE'S REALLY NOT GOING TO KNOW WHAT TO DO IF YOU GIVE HIM THAT.
IT SOUNDS LIKE A ROUNDABOUT WAY TO ASK FOR FLAN.
I KNOW! I'M GOOD AT WRITING LETTERS, SO I'LL WRITE ONE FOR YOU!
Literature is my specialty!
WHAT ?!
YOU WILL ?!
Uh-huh!
I'LL SKILLFULLY CONVEY YOUR FEELINGS TO HIM!
You like me, don't you?
DON'T YOU THINK THAT'S TOO STRAIGHT-FORWARD ?!
Perchance thou dost fancy me?
I DON'T KNOW WHAT THAT MEANS!
That's so obscure!
IN THAT CASE, "IF YOU DON'T HURRY UP AND TELL ME YOUR FEELINGS, I'M GOING TO REPORT YOU AS A STALKER."
I CHANGED MY MIND, I'LL WRITE THIS MYSELF! UH-HUH! THAT WOULD BE BEST!
NO!
I'M GOING TO SKILLFULLY MAKE HIM CONFESS HIS LOVE!
YEAH!
That's right ...

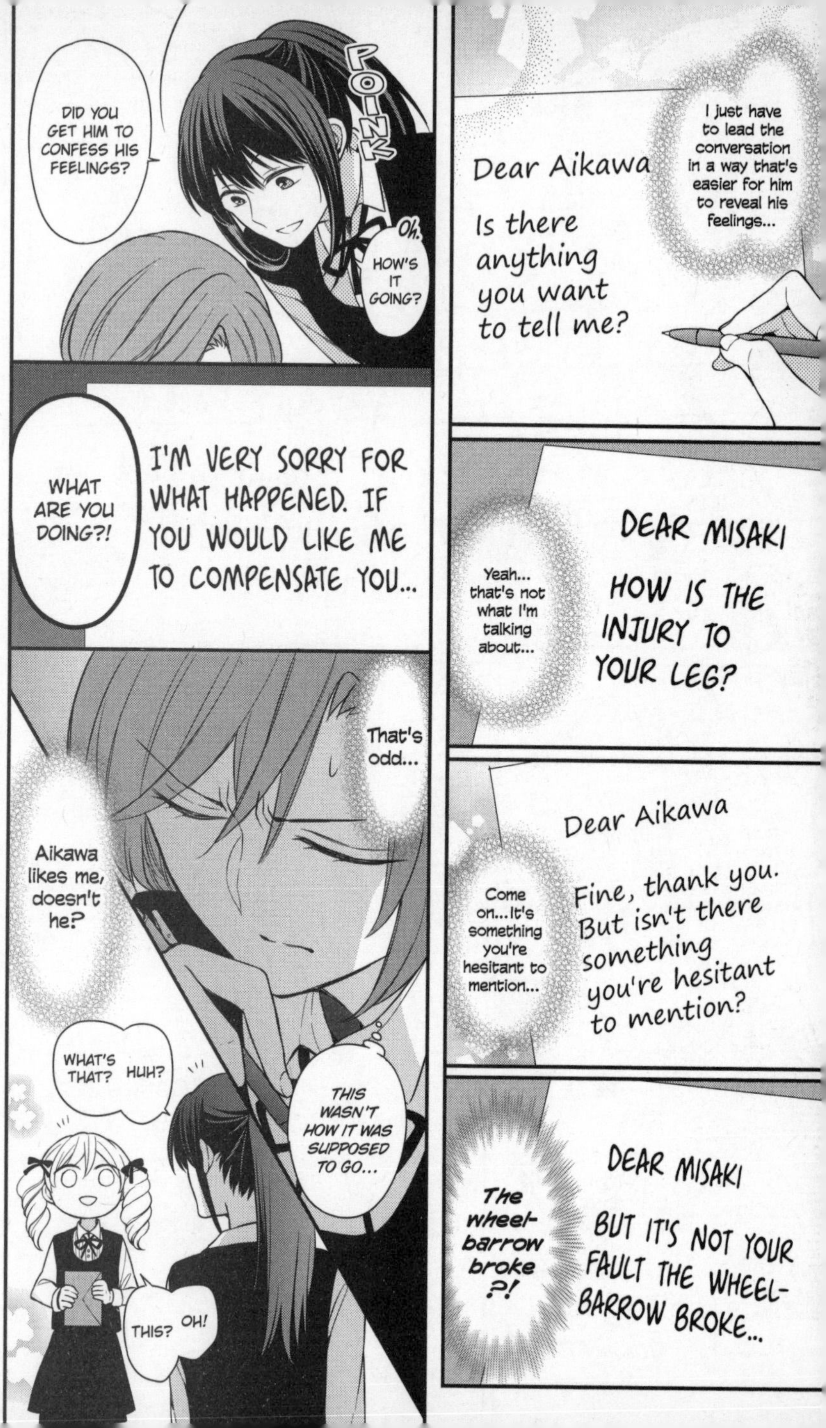
I just have to lead the conversation in a way that's easier for him to reveal his feelings...
Dear Aikawa
Is there anything you want to tell me?
DEAR MISAKI
HOW IS THE INJURY TO YOUR LEG?
Yeah... that's not what I'm talking about...
Dear Aikawa
Fine, thank you. But isn't there something you're hesitant to mention?
Come on...It's something you're hesitant to mention...
DEAR MISAKI
BUT IT'S NOT YOUR FAULT THE WHEEL-BARROW BROKE...
The wheel-barrow broke?!
POINK
Oh.
HOW'S IT GOING?
DID YOU GET HIM TO CONFESS HIS FEELINGS?
I'M VERY SORRY FOR WHAT HAPPENED. IF YOU WOULD LIKE ME TO COMPENSATE YOU...
WHAT ARE YOU DOING?!
That's odd...
Aikawa likes me, doesn't he?
THIS WASN'T HOW IT WAS SUPPOSED TO GO...
HUH?
WHAT'S THAT?
OH!
THIS?

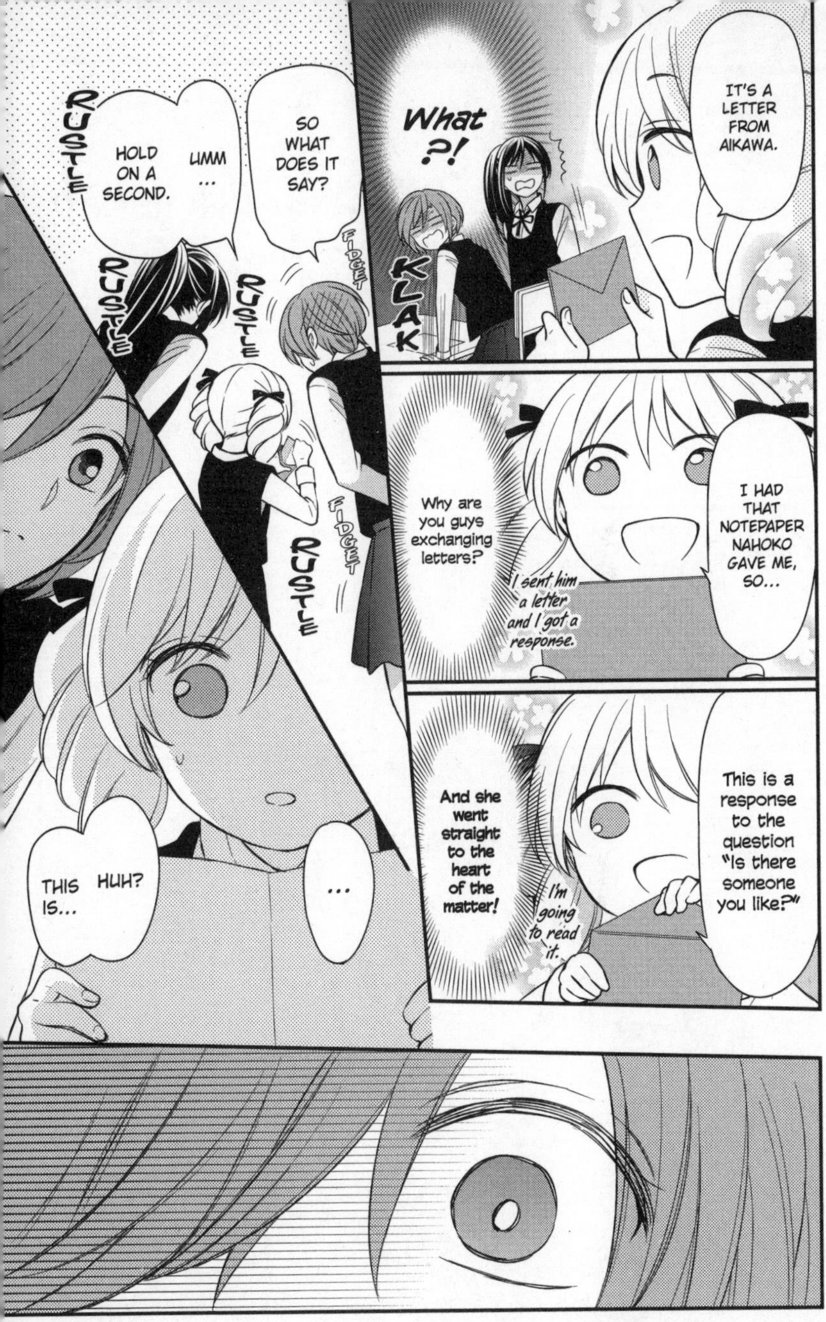
IT'S A LETTER FROM AIKAWA.
What?!
KLAK
I HAD THAT NOTEPAPER NAHOKO GAVE ME, SO...
I sent him a letter and I got a response.
Why are you guys exchanging letters?
This is a response to the question "Is there someone you like?"
I'm going to read it.
And she went straight to the heart of the matter!
SO WHAT DOES IT SAY?
FIDGET
UMM ...
HOLD ON A SECOND.
RUSTLE
RUSTLE
RUSTLE
FIDGET
RUSTLE
...
HUH?
THIS IS...

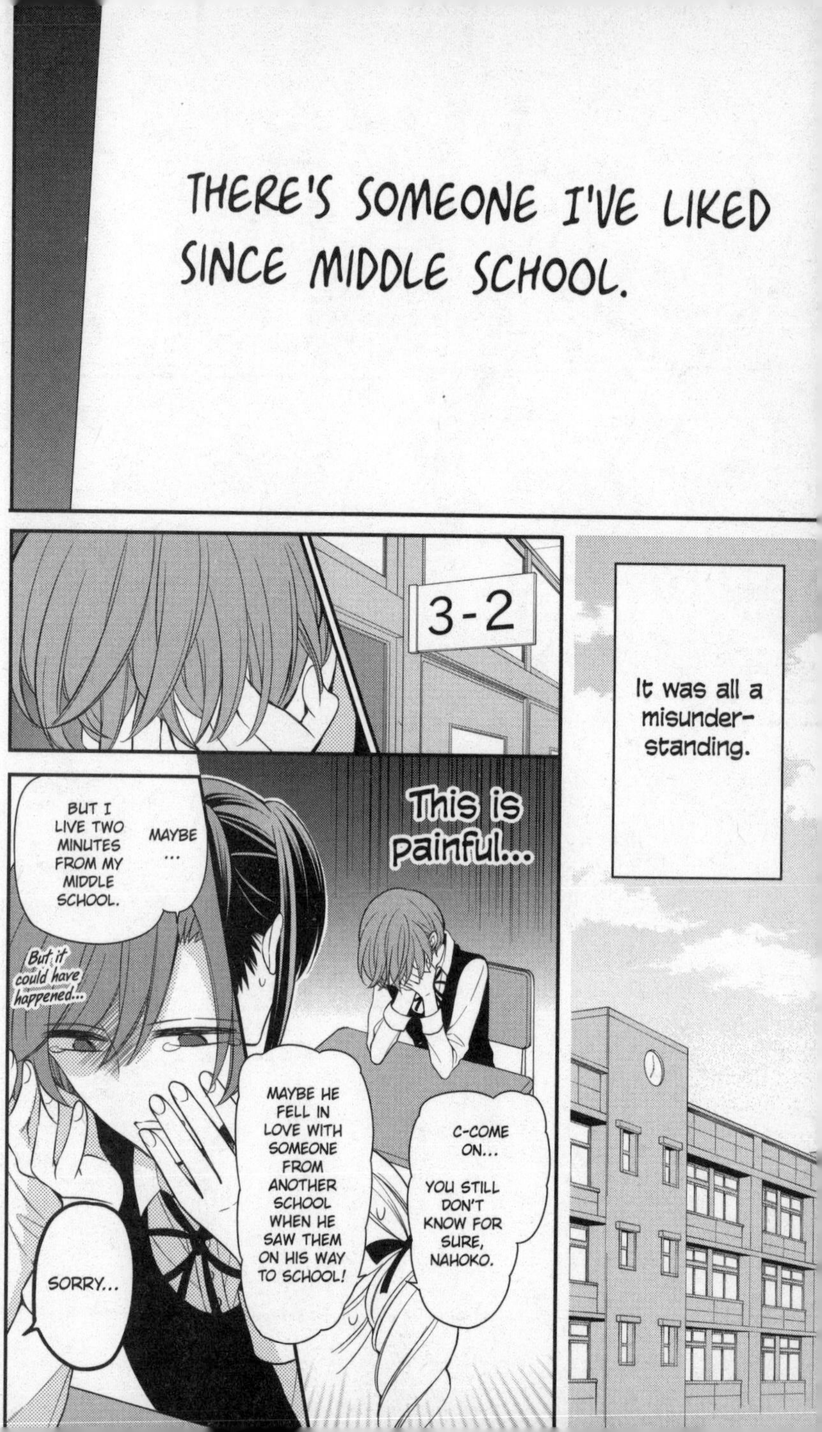
THERE'S SOMEONE I'VE LIKED SINCE MIDDLE SCHOOL.
It was all a misunder-standing.
3-2
This is painful...
MAYBE ...
BUT I LIVE TWO MINUTES FROM MY MIDDLE SCHOOL.
But it could have happened...
C-COME ON... YOU STILL DON'T KNOW FOR SURE, NAHOKO.
MAYBE HE FELL IN LOVE WITH SOMEONE FROM ANOTHER SCHOOL WHEN HE SAW THEM ON HIS WAY TO SCHOOL!
SORRY...

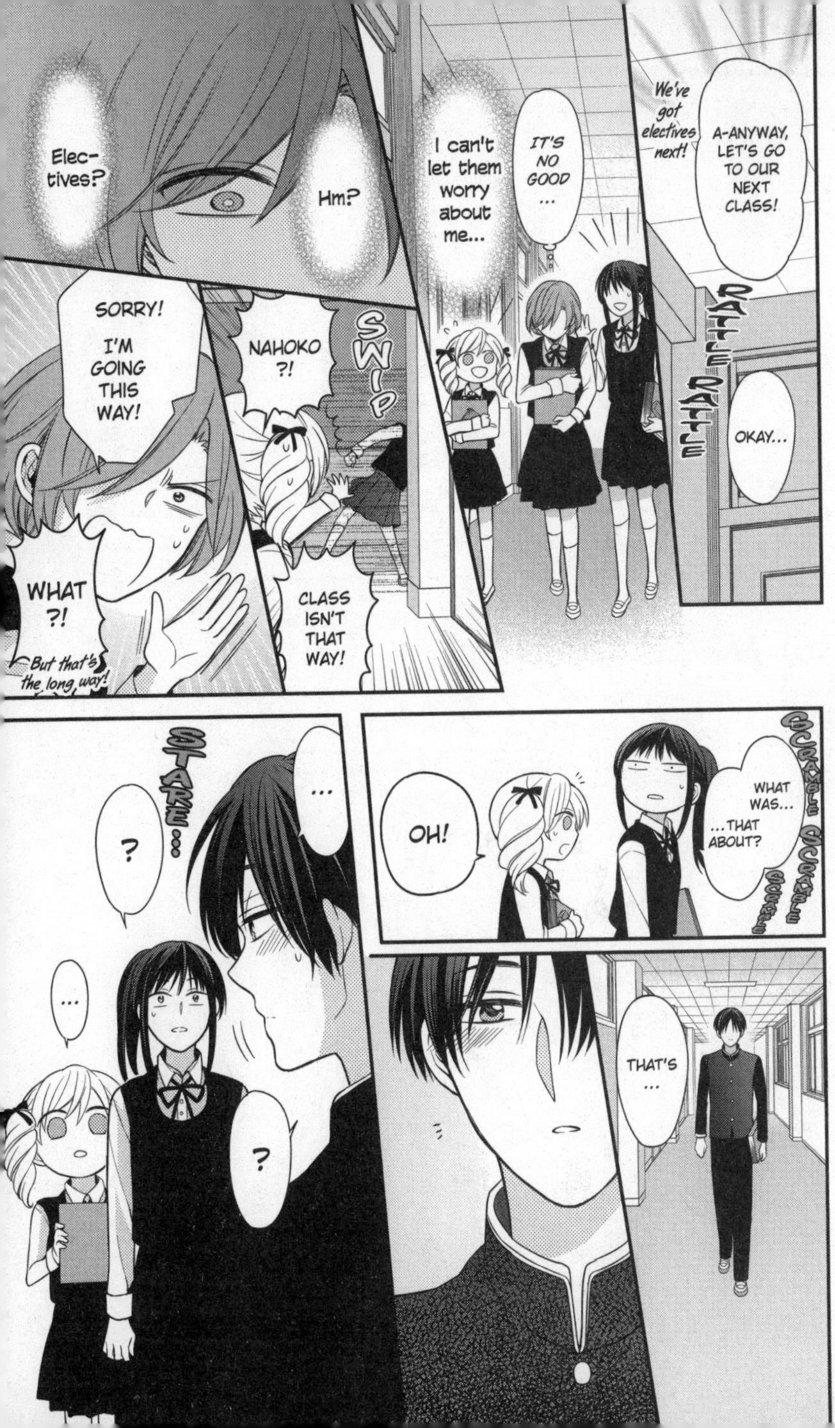
A-ANYWAY, LET'S GO TO OUR NEXT CLASS!
We've got electives next!
RATTLE RATTLE
OKAY...
IT'S NO GOOD...
I can't let them worry about me...
Hm?
Elec-tives?
SWIP
NAHOKO?!
CLASS ISN'T THAT WAY!
SORRY! I'M GOING THIS WAY!
WHAT?!
But that's the long way!
SCRAMBLE SCRAMBLE SCRAMBLE
WHAT WAS... ...THAT ABOUT?
OH!
THAT'S...
...
STARE...
?
...
?

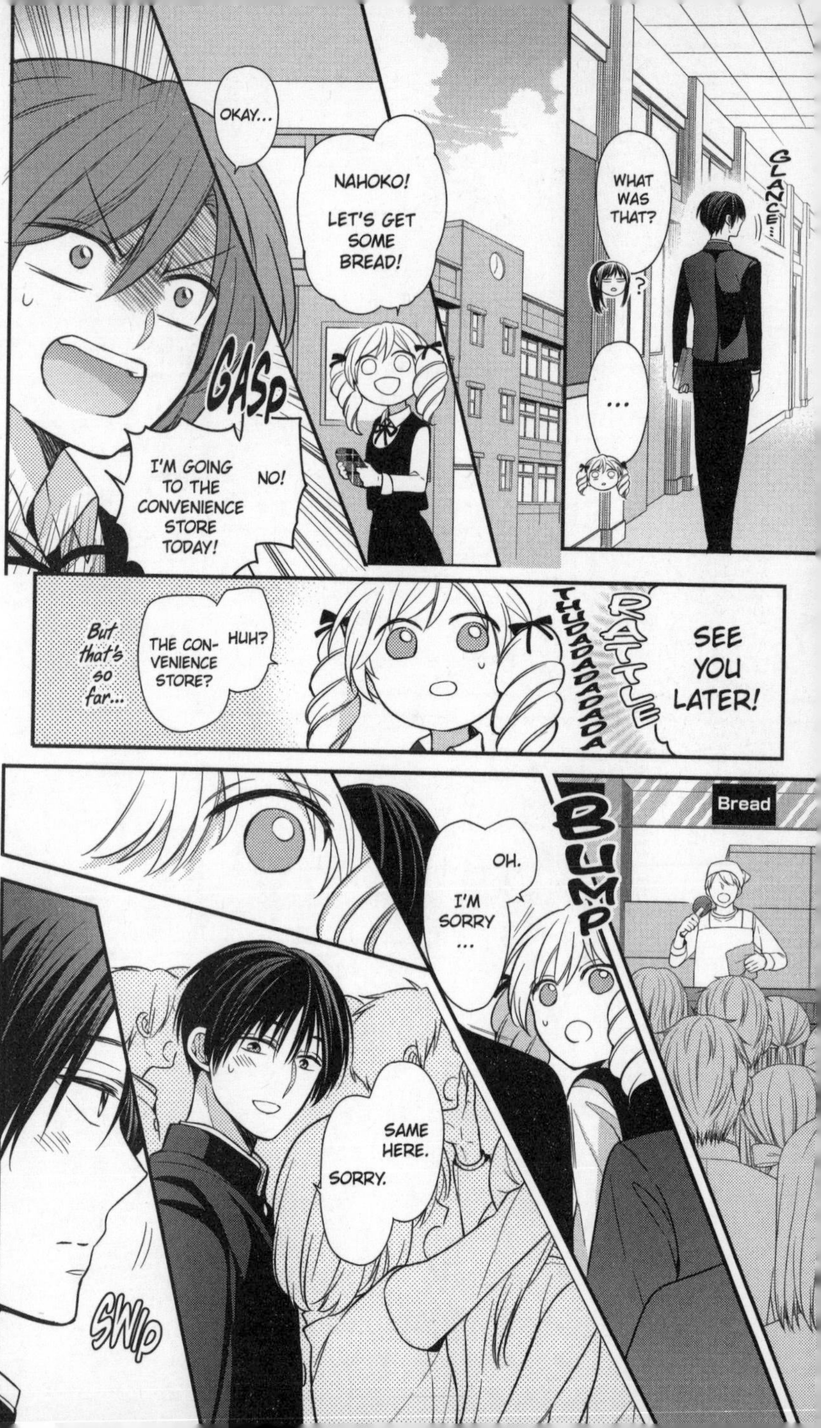
GLANCE...
WHAT WAS THAT?
?
...
NAHOKO! LET'S GET SOME BREAD!
OKAY...
GASP
NO!
I'M GOING TO THE CONVENIENCE STORE TODAY!
SEE YOU LATER!
RATTLE
THUDADADADADA
HUH?
THE CON-VENIENCE STORE?
But that's so far...
Bread
BUMP
OH. I'M SORRY...
SAME HERE. SORRY.
--
SWIP

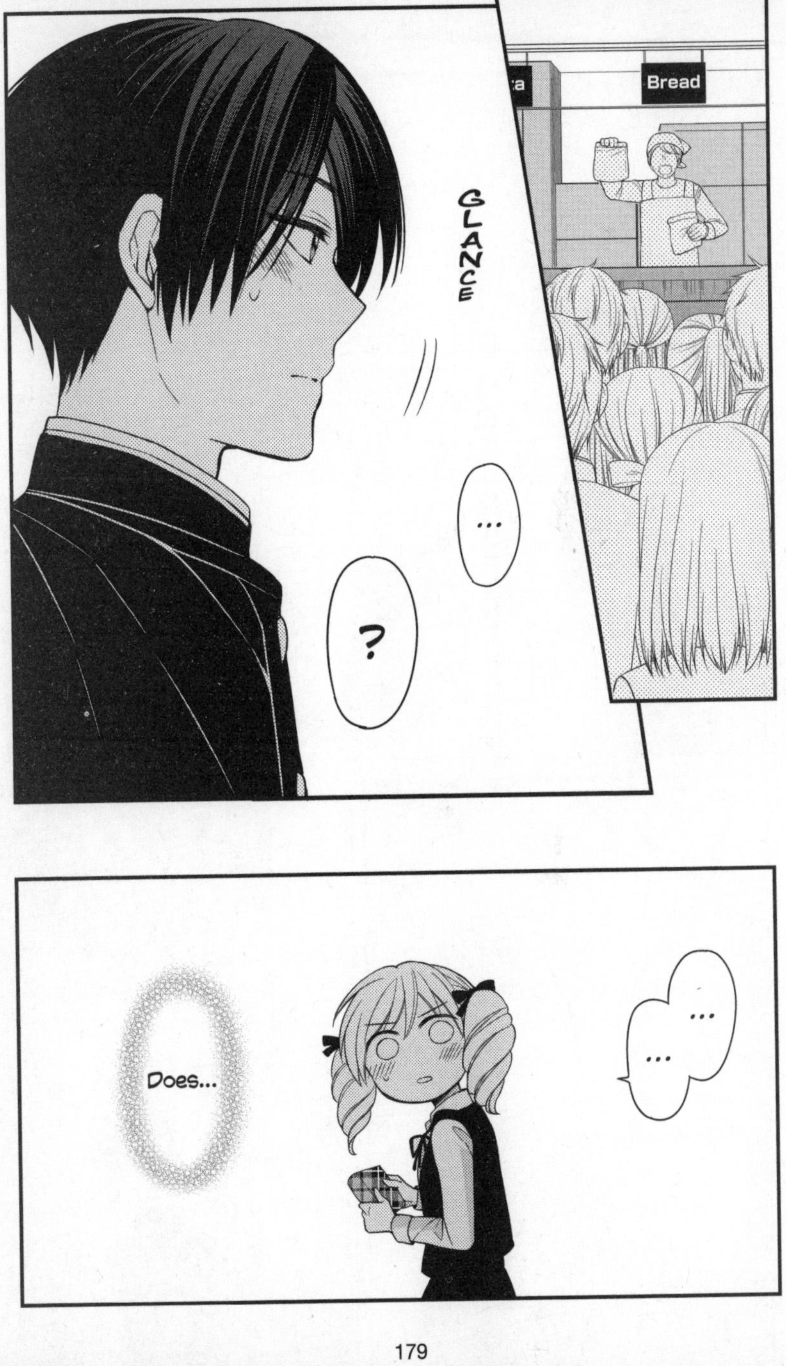
Bread
GLANCE
...
?
... ...
Does...

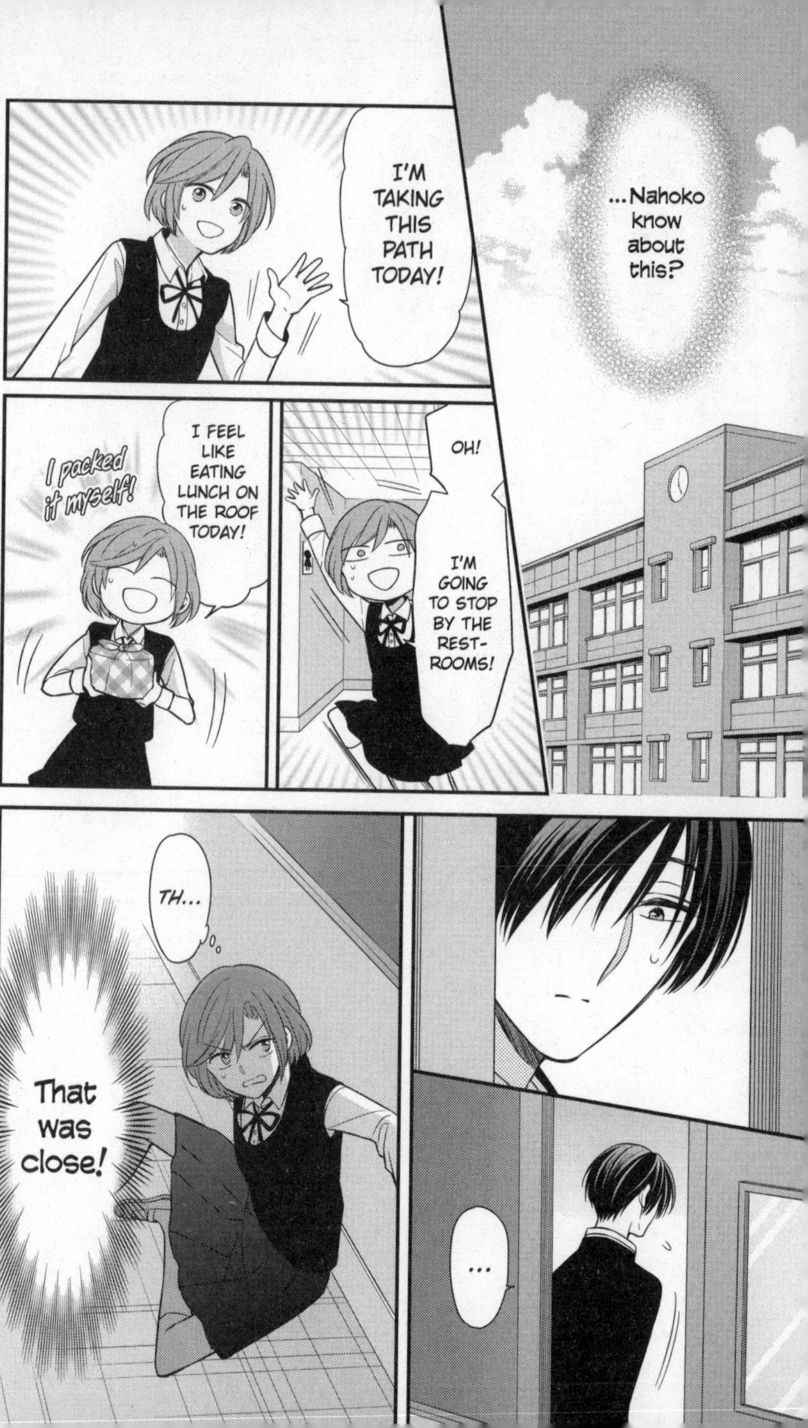
...Nahoko know about this?
I'M TAKING THIS PATH TODAY!
OH!
I'M GOING TO STOP BY THE REST-ROOMS!
I FEEL LIKE EATING LUNCH ON THE ROOF TODAY!
I packed it myself!
...
TH...
That was close!

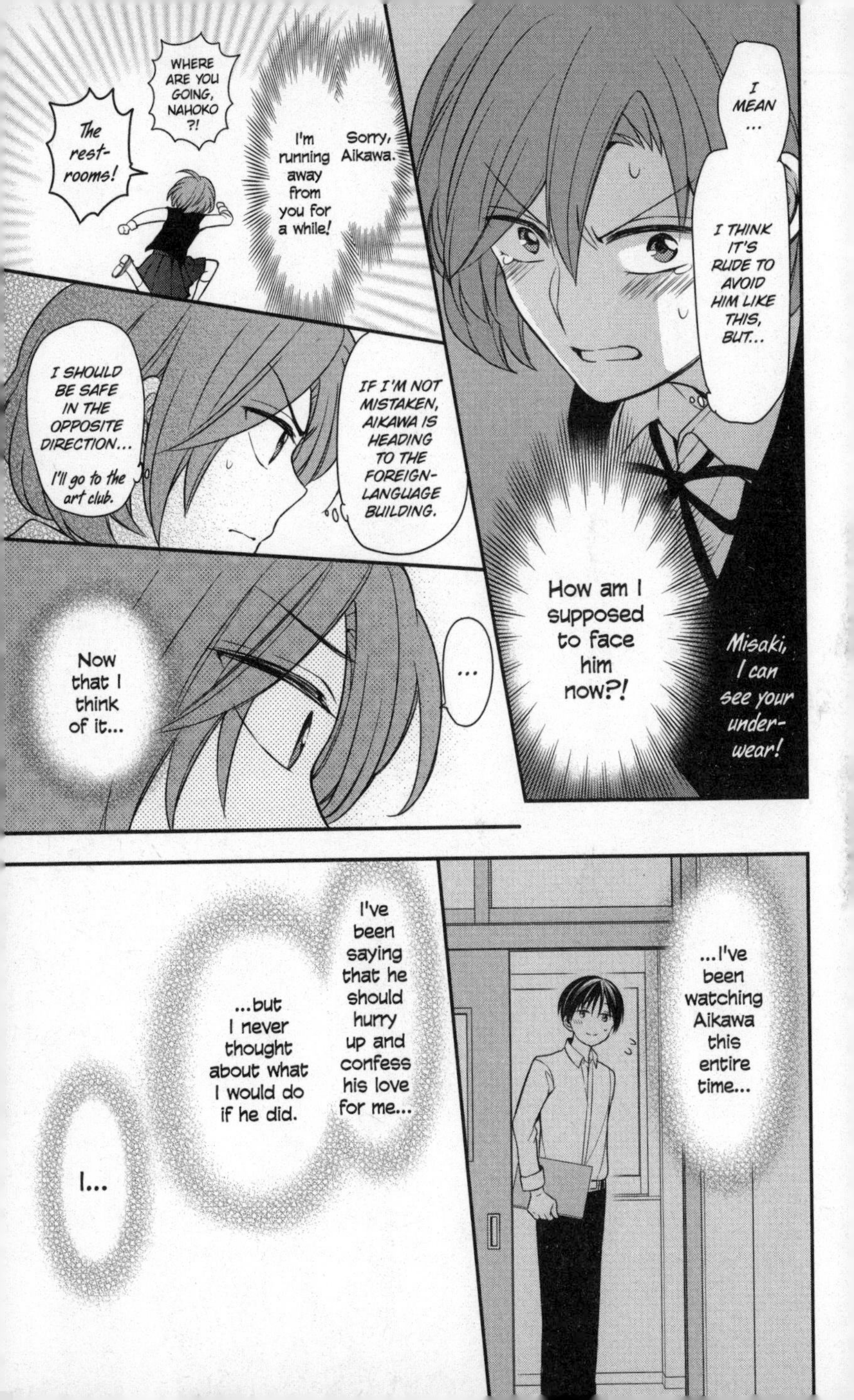
I MEAN...
I THINK IT'S RUDE TO AVOID HIM LIKE THIS, BUT...
Misaki, I can see your underwear!
How am I supposed to face him now?!
Sorry, Aikawa.
I'm running away from you for a while!
WHERE ARE YOU GOING, NAHOKO?!
The restrooms!
IF I'M NOT MISTAKEN, AIKAWA IS HEADING TO THE FOREIGN-LANGUAGE BUILDING.
I SHOULD BE SAFE IN THE OPPOSITE DIRECTION...
I'll go to the art club.
...
Now that I think of it...
...I've been watching Aikawa this entire time...
I've been saying that he should hurry up and confess his love for me...
...but I never thought about what I would do if he did.
I...

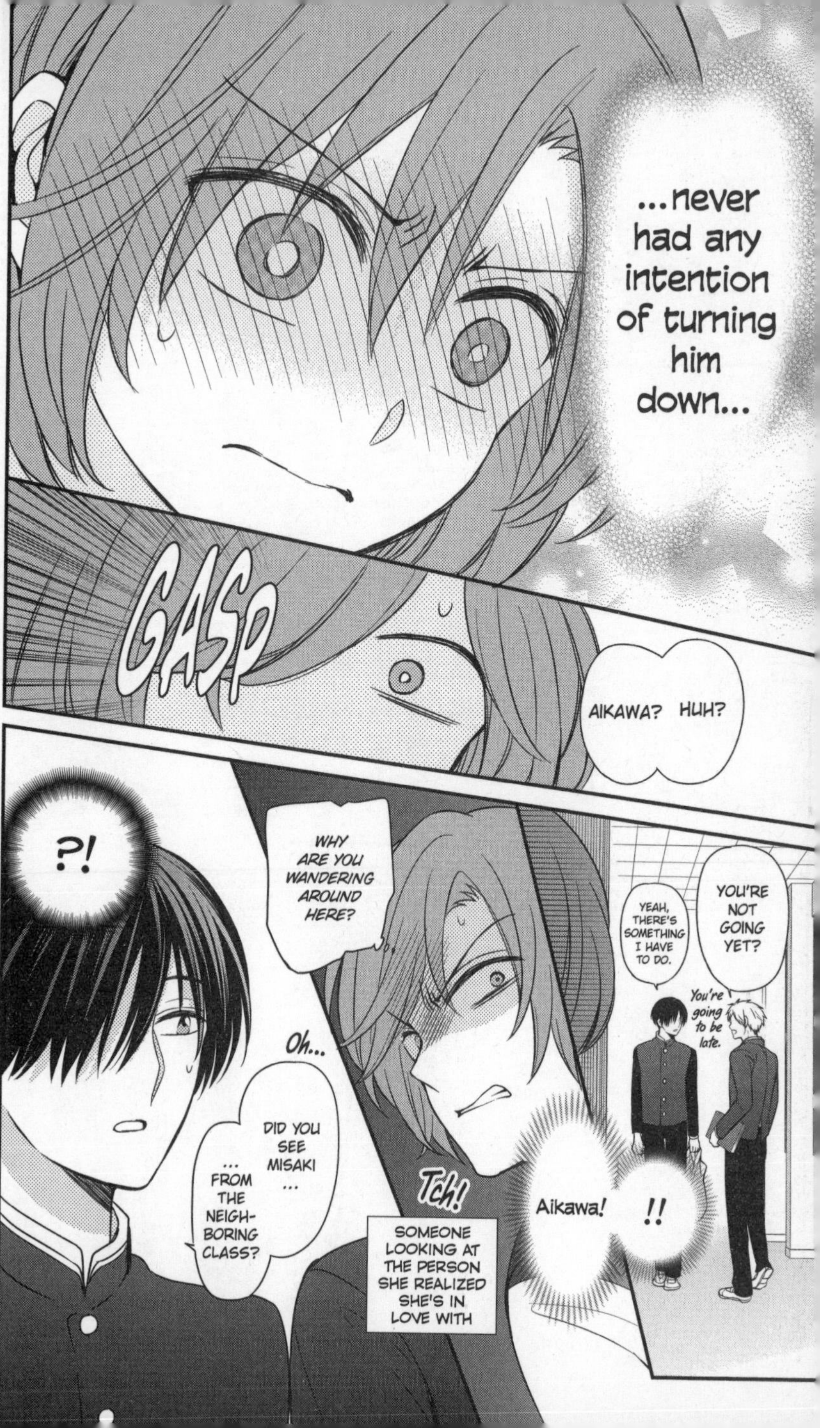
...never had any intention of turning him down...
GASP
AIKAWA? HUH?
YOU'RE NOT GOING YET?
You're going to be late.
YEAH, THERE'S SOMETHING I HAVE TO DO.
Aikawa!
!!
WHY ARE YOU WANDERING AROUND HERE?
Tch!
SOMEONE LOOKING AT THE PERSON SHE REALIZED SHE'S IN LOVE WITH
?!
Oh...
DID YOU SEE MISAKI ... FROM THE NEIGHBORING CLASS?

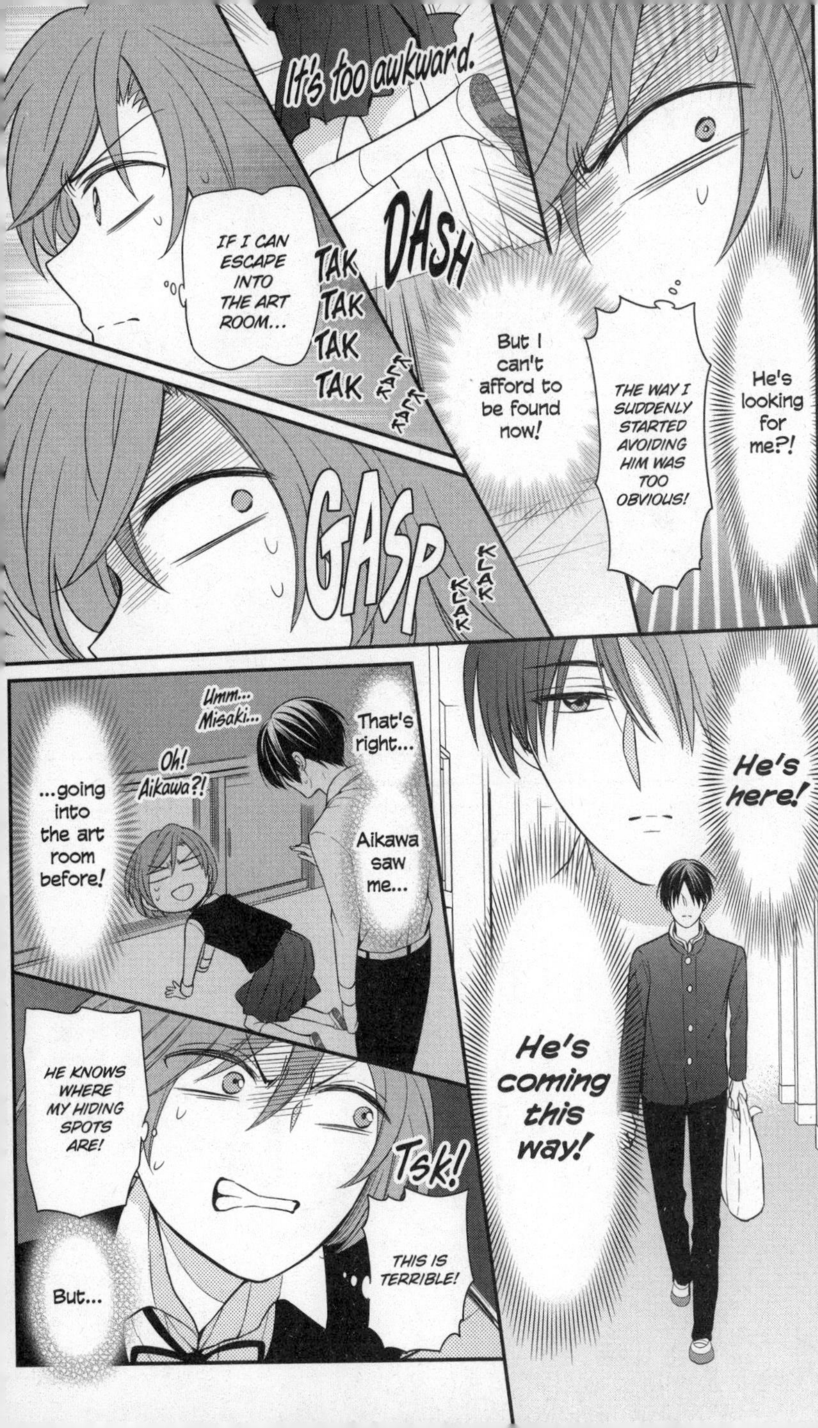
He's looking for me?!
THE WAY I SUDDENLY STARTED AVOIDING HIM WAS TOO OBVIOUS!
But I can't afford to be found now!
It's too awkward.
DASH
IF I CAN ESCAPE INTO THE ART ROOM...
TAK TAK TAK TAK
TAKK TAKK
GASP
KLAK KLAK
He's here!
He's coming this way!
That's right...
Aikawa saw me...
...going into the art room before!
Umm... Misaki...
Oh! Aikawa?!
HE KNOWS WHERE MY HIDING SPOTS ARE!
Tsk!
THIS IS TERRIBLE!
But...

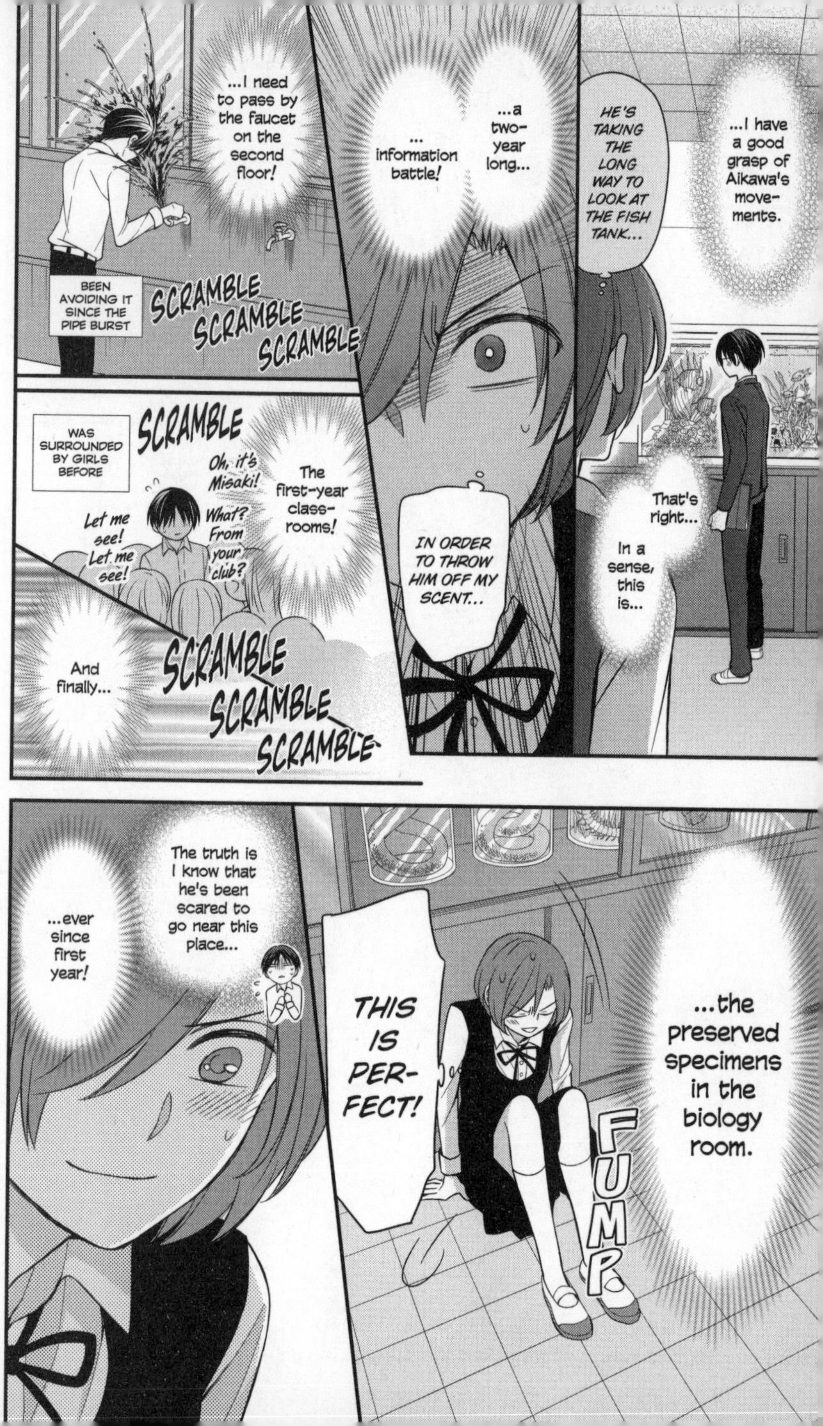

...I have a good grasp of Aikawa's move-ments.
HE'S TAKING THE LONG WAY TO LOOK AT THE FISH TANK...
That's right...
In a sense, this is...
...a two-year long...
...information battle!
IN ORDER TO THROW HIM OFF MY SCENT...
...I need to pass by the faucet on the second floor!
BEEN AVOIDING IT SINCE THE PIPE BURST
SCRAMBLE SCRAMBLE SCRAMBLE
The first-year class-rooms!
Oh, it's Misaki!
What? From your club?
Let me see! Let me see!
WAS SURROUNDED BY GIRLS BEFORE
SCRAMBLE
SCRAMBLE SCRAMBLE SCRAMBLE
And finally...
...the preserved specimens in the biology room.
FUMP
THIS IS PER-FECT!
The truth is I know that he's been scared to go near this place...
...ever since first year!

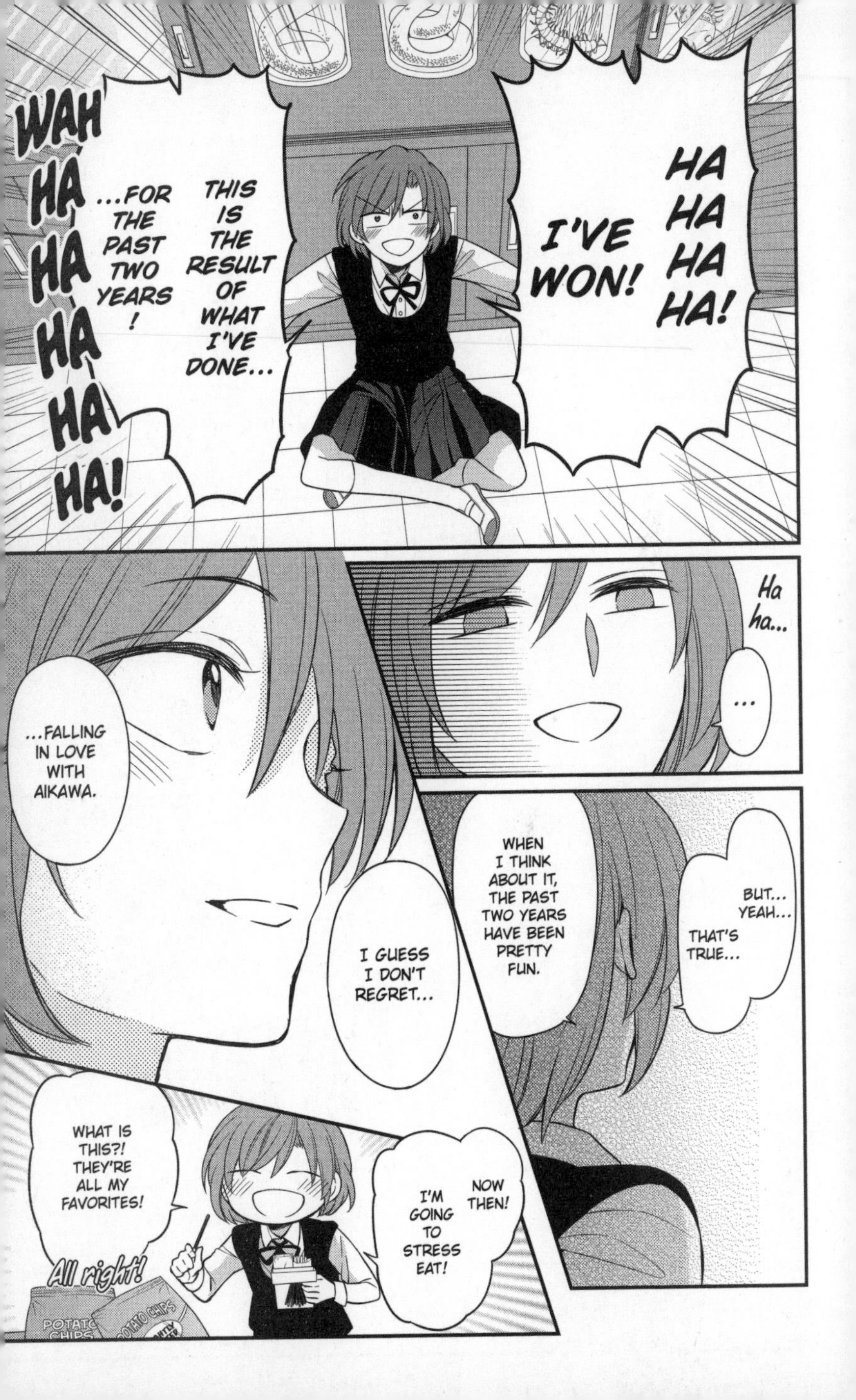
HA HA HA HA!
I'VE WON!
THIS IS THE RESULT OF WHAT I'VE DONE...
...FOR THE PAST TWO YEARS!
WAH HA HA HA HA HA HA!
Ha ha...
...
BUT... YEAH... THAT'S TRUE...
WHEN I THINK ABOUT IT, THE PAST TWO YEARS HAVE BEEN PRETTY FUN.
I GUESS I DON'T REGRET...
...FALLING IN LOVE WITH AIKAWA.
NOW THEN! I'M GOING TO STRESS EAT!
WHAT IS THIS?! THEY'RE ALL MY FAVORITES!
All right!
POTATO CHIPS
POTATO CHIPS

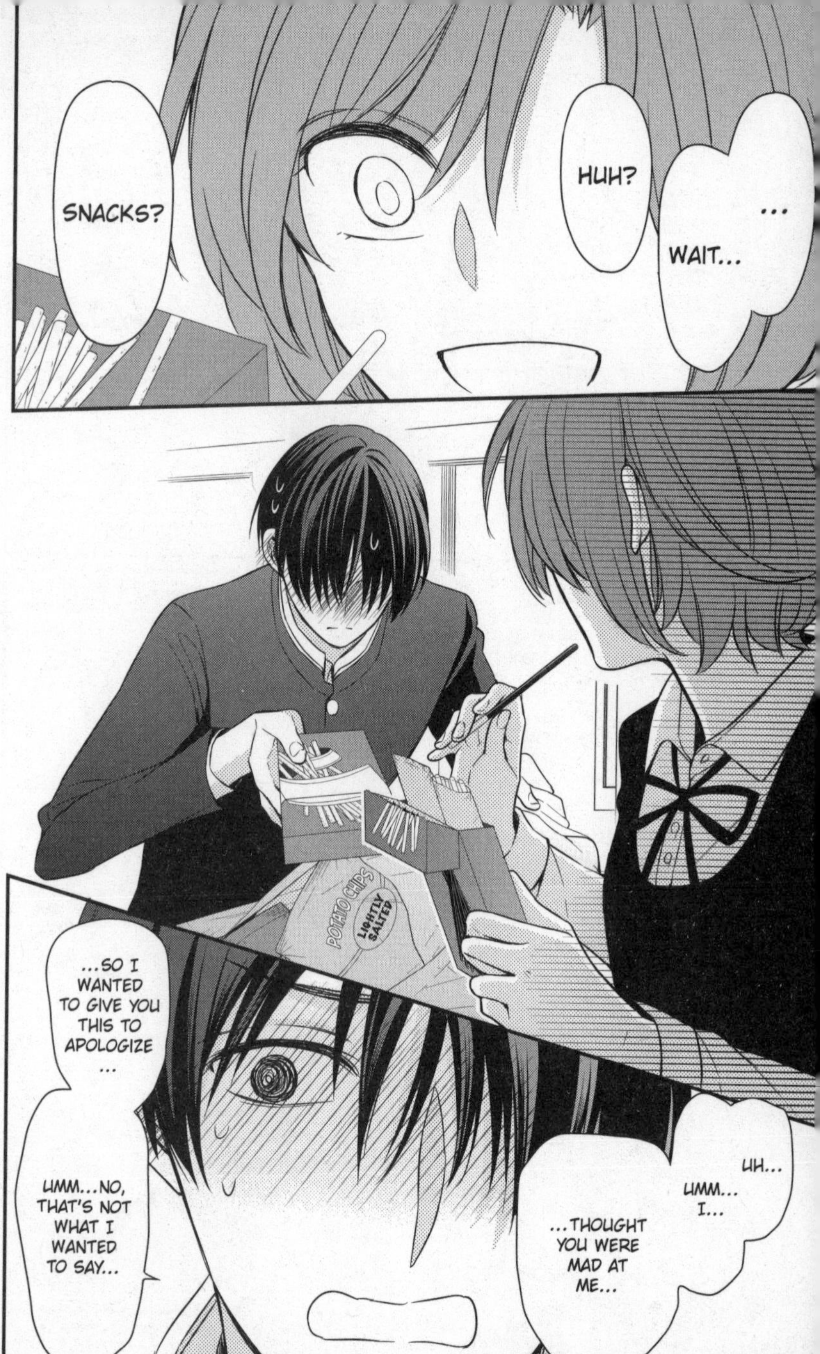
... WAIT...
HUH?
SNACKS?
POTATO CHIPS
LIGHTLY SALTED
UH... UMM... I...
...THOUGHT YOU WERE MAD AT ME...
...SO I WANTED TO GIVE YOU THIS TO APOLOGIZE ...
UMM...NO, THAT'S NOT WHAT I WANTED TO SAY...

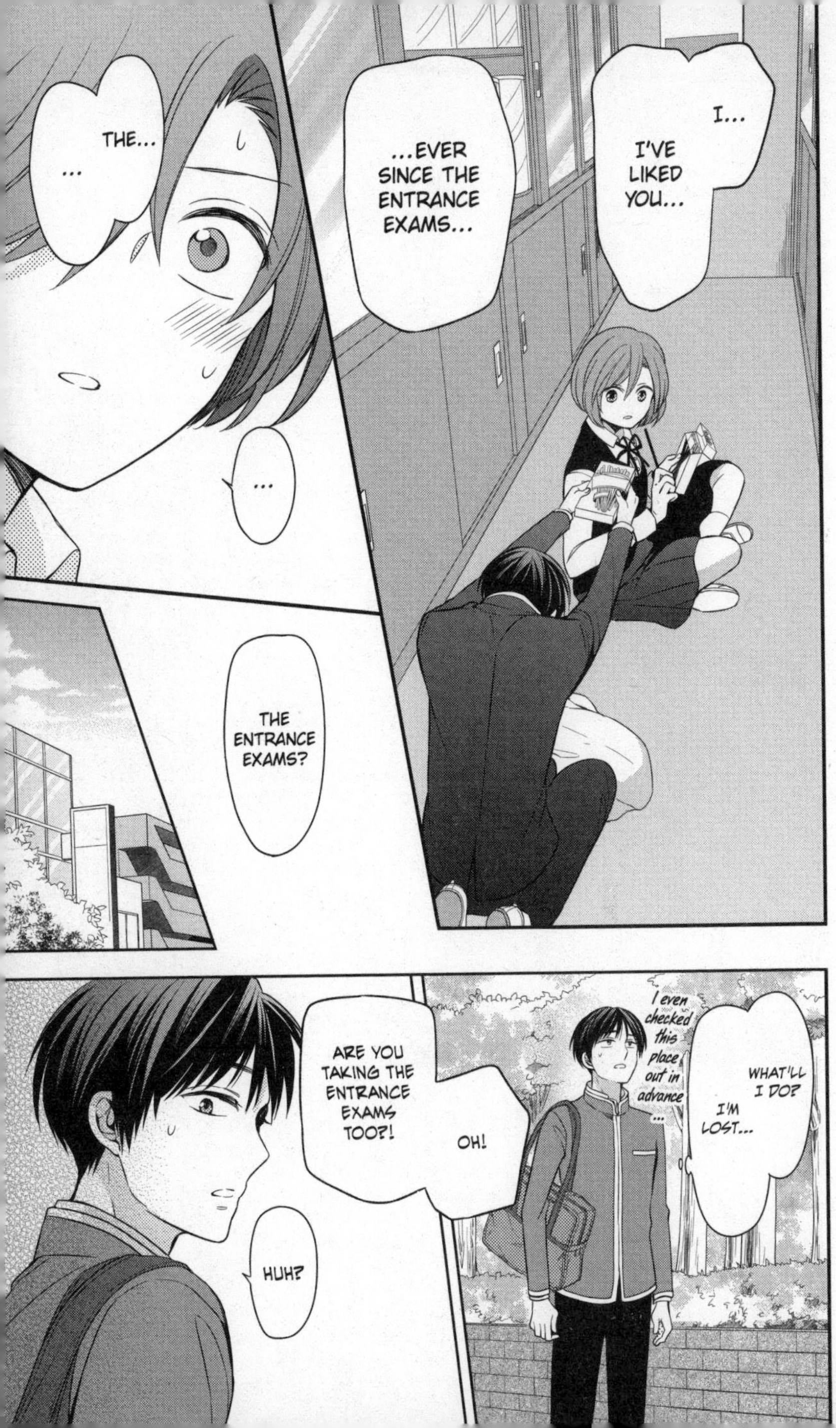
I...
I'VE LIKED YOU...
...EVER SINCE THE ENTRANCE EXAMS...
THE... ...
...
THE ENTRANCE EXAMS?
WHAT'LL I DO? I'M LOST...
I even checked this place out in advance...
OH!
ARE YOU TAKING THE ENTRANCE EXAMS TOO?!
HUH?

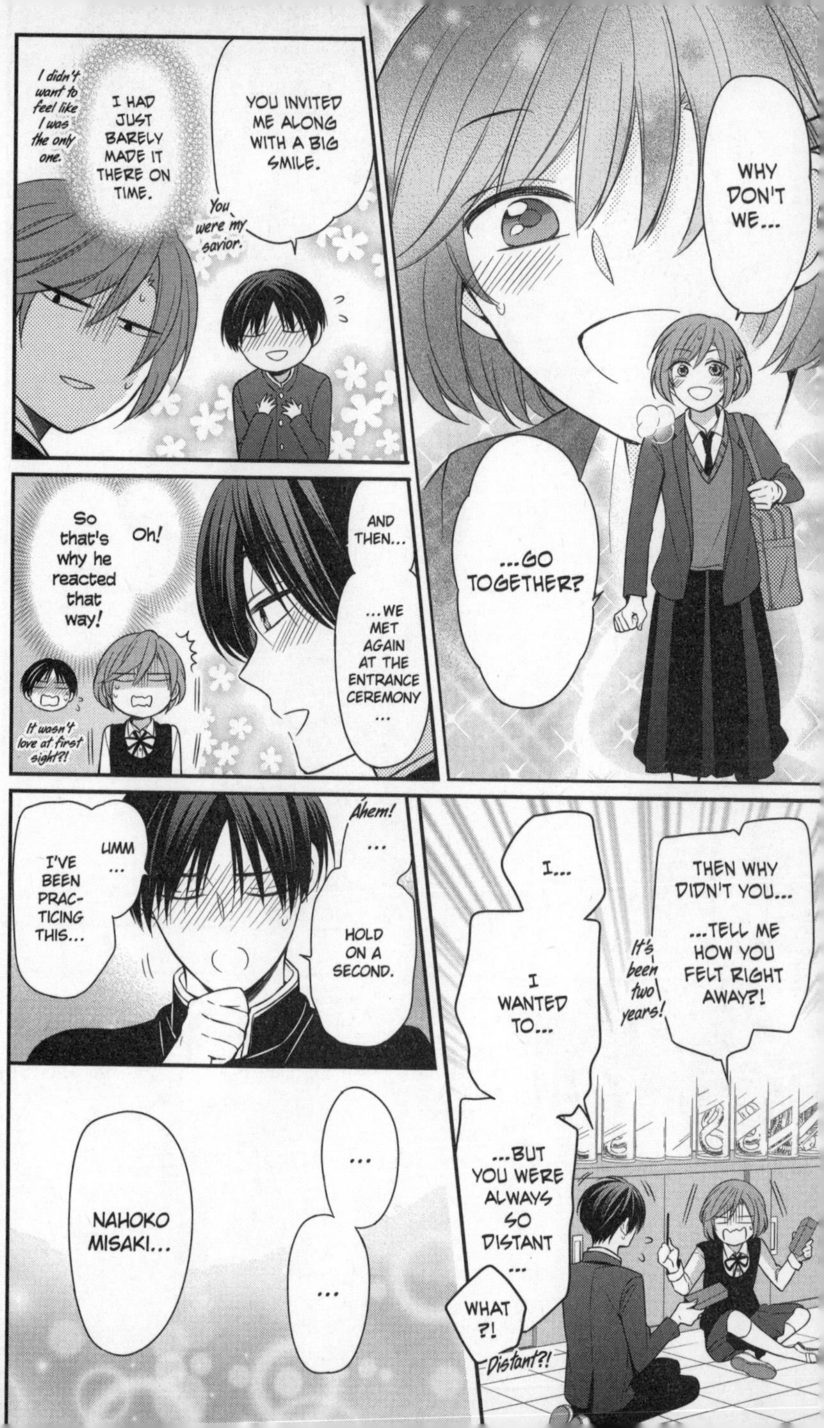
WHY DON'T WE...
...GO TOGETHER?
YOU INVITED ME ALONG WITH A BIG SMILE.
You were my savior.
I HAD JUST BARELY MADE IT THERE ON TIME.
I didn't want to feel like I was the only one.
AND THEN...
...WE MET AGAIN AT THE ENTRANCE CEREMONY...
Oh!
So that's why he reacted that way!
It wasn't love at first sight?!
THEN WHY DIDN'T YOU...
...TELL ME HOW YOU FELT RIGHT AWAY?!
It's been two years!
I...
I WANTED TO...
...BUT YOU WERE ALWAYS SO DISTANT...
WHAT?!
Distant?!
Ahem! ...
HOLD ON A SECOND.
UMM...
I'VE BEEN PRACTICING THIS...
...
...
NAHOKO MISAKI...

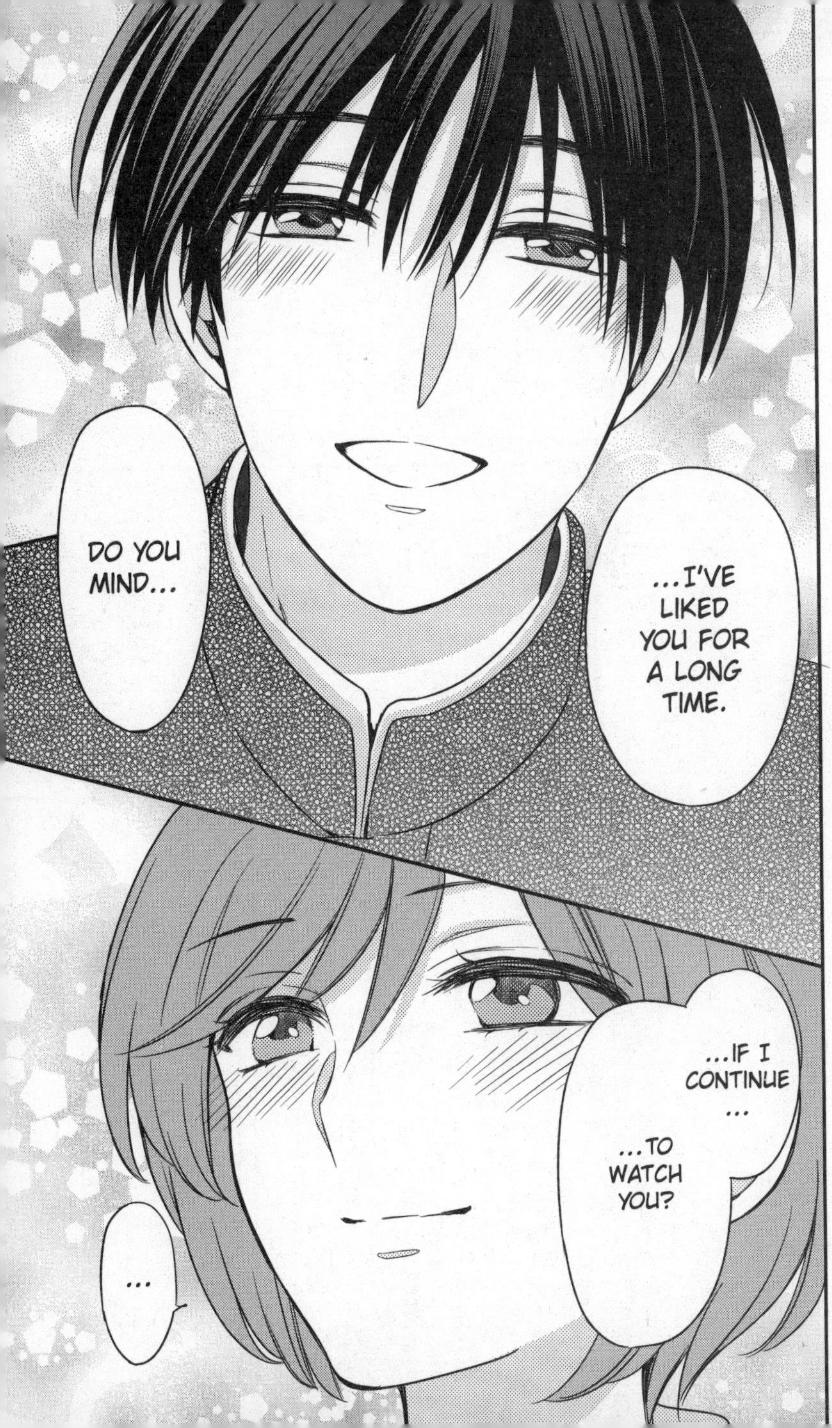
...I'VE LIKED YOU FOR A LONG TIME.
DO YOU MIND...
...IF I CONTINUE ... ...TO WATCH YOU?
...

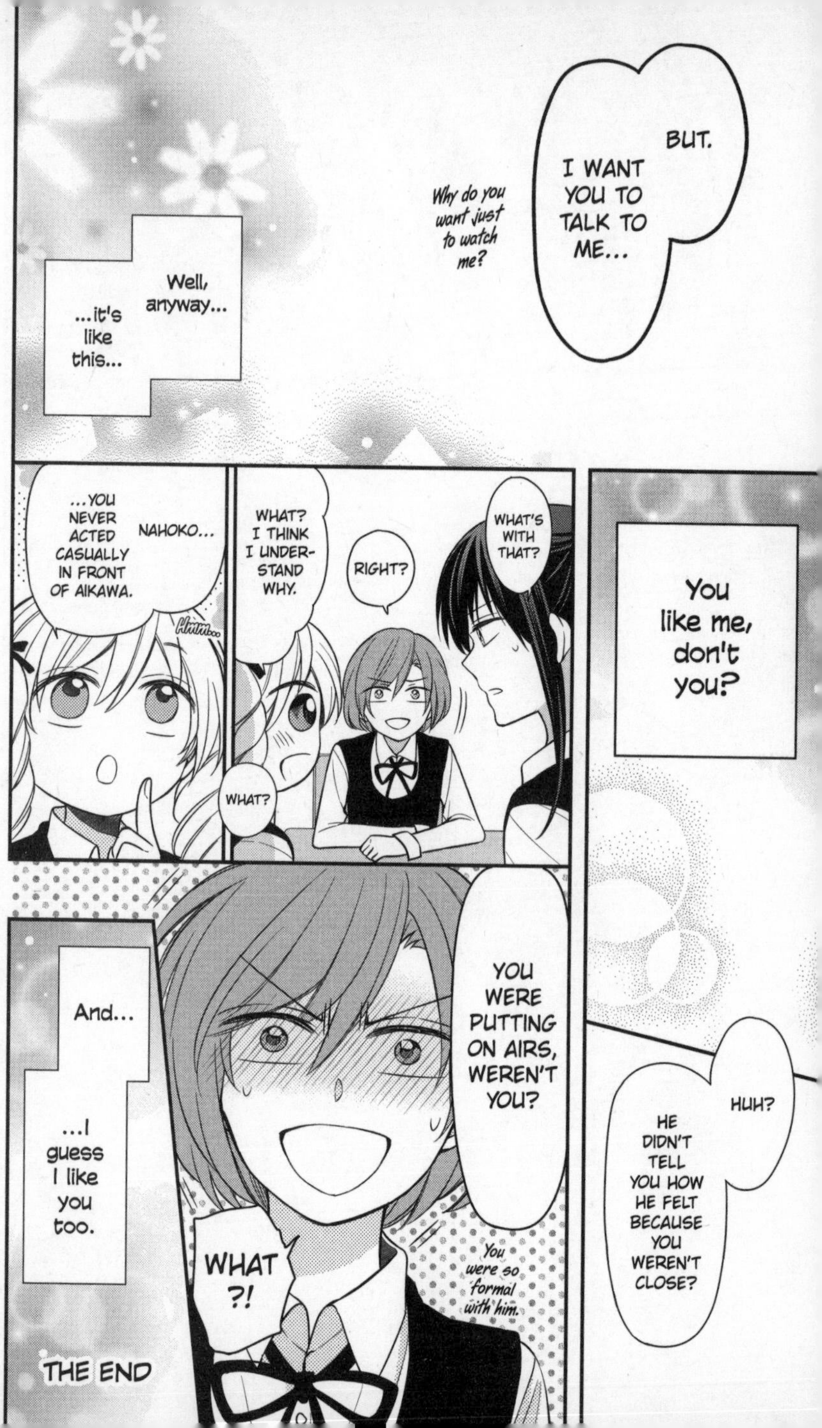

BUT. I WANT YOU TO TALK TO ME...
Why do you want just to watch me?
Well, anyway...
...it's like this...
You like me, don't you?
WHAT'S WITH THAT?
RIGHT?
WHAT? I THINK I UNDERSTAND WHY.
WHAT?
NAHOKO...
...YOU NEVER ACTED CASUALLY IN FRONT OF AIKAWA.
Hmm...
HUH?
HE DIDN'T TELL YOU HOW HE FELT BECAUSE YOU WEREN'T CLOSE?
YOU WERE PUTTING ON AIRS, WEREN'T YOU?
You were so formal with him.
WHAT ?!
And...
...I guess I like you too.
THE END

Thank you for sticking
with me until the end!

Izumi
Tsubaki

If you listen to the drama CD,
you'll find out what happens
afterward, and the epilogue! ♡
I hope you listen to it! ♡

ORESAMA
TEACHER

End Notes

Page 112, panel 5: Uniform buttons
On middle school or high school graduation day in Japan, males students give the second button of their uniform jacket to the girls they like. Other buttons are also given out, but the second button is special because it is closest to the heart. In *Oresama Teacher* volume 22, Mafuyu and Hayasaka introduce their own version of the tradition.

Page 165, panel 1: Monjayaki
Monjayaki is a type of pan-fried batter served with savory additions, much like *okonomiyaki*, although *monja* batter tends to be runnier.

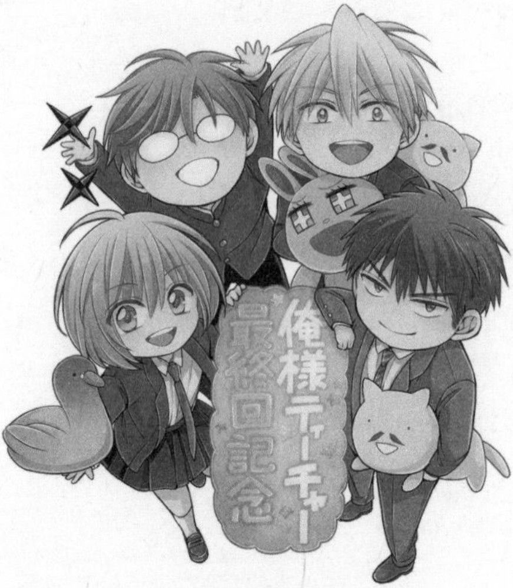
俺様ティーチャー
最終回記念

In commemoration of the final chapter of Oresama Teacher!

Thank you for 13 years of support!

Izumi Tsubaki began drawing manga in her first year of high school. She was soon selected to be in the top ten of *Hana to Yume's* HMC (*Hana to Yume* Mangaka Course), and subsequently won *Hana to Yume's* Big Challenge contest. Her debut title, *Chijimete Distance* (Shrink the Distance), ran in 2002 in *Hana to Yume* magazine, issue 17. Her other works include *The Magic Touch* (*Oyayubi kara Romance*) and *Oresama Teacher*.

ORESAMA TEACHER
Vol. 29
Shojo Beat Edition

STORY AND ART BY
Izumi Tsubaki

English Translation & Adaptation/JN Productions
Touch-up Art & Lettering/Eric Erbes
Design/Yukiko Whitley
Editor/Pancha Diaz

Printed in the U.S.A.

Published by VIZ Media, LLC
P.O. Box 77010
San Francisco, CA 94107

10 9 8 7 6 5 4 3 2 1
First printing, July 2021

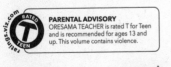

viz.com   shojobeat.com

Takane & Hana

STORY AND ART BY
Yuki Shiwasu

After her older sister refuses to go to an arranged marriage meeting with Takane Saibara, the heir to a vast business fortune, high schooler Hana Nonomura agrees to be her stand-in to save face for the family. But when Takane and Hana pair up, get ready for some sparks to fly between these two utter opposites!

Beat

shojobeat.com

IDOL dreams

STORY & ART BY
ARINA TANEMURA

At age 31, office worker Chikage Deguchi feels she missed her chances at love and success. When word gets out that she's a virgin, Chikage is humiliated and wishes she could turn back time to when she was still young and popular. She takes an experimental drug that changes her appearance back to when she was 15. Now Chikage is determined to pursue everything she missed out on all those years ago—including becoming a star!

Behind the Scenes!!

STORY AND ART BY BISCO HATORI

From the creator of Ouran High School Host Club

Ranmaru Kurisu comes from a family of hardy, rough-and-tumble fisherfolk and he sticks out at home like a delicate, artistic sore thumb. It's given him a raging inferiority complex and a permanently pessimistic outlook. Now that he's in college, he's hoping to find a sense of belonging. But after a whole life of being left out, does he even know how to fit in?!

Surprise!

You may be reading the wrong way!

It's true: In keeping with the original Japanese comic format, this book reads from right to left—so action, sound effects, and word balloons are completely reversed. This preserves the orientation of the original artwork—plus, it's fun! Check out the diagram shown here to get the hang of things, and then turn to the other side of the book to get started!